T0220922

Medical Imaging
and Health Informatics

Scrivener Publishing
100 Cummings Center, Suite 541J
Beverly, MA 01915-6106

Next-Generation Computing and Communication Engineering

Series Editors: Dr. G. R. Kanagachidambaresan and Dr. Kolla Bhanu Prakash

Developments in articial intelligence are made more challenging because the involvement of multi-domain technology creates new problems for researchers. Therefore, in order to help meet the challenge, this book series concentrates on next generation computing and communication methodologies involving smart and ambient environment design. It is an effective publishing platform for monographs, handbooks, and edited volumes on Industry 4.0, agriculture, smart city development, new computing and communication paradigms. Although the series mainly focuses on design, it also addresses analytics and investigation of industry-related real-time problems.

Publishers at Scrivener
Martin Scrivener (martin@scrivenerpublishing.com)
Phillip Carmical (pcarmical@scrivenerpublishing.com)

Medical Imaging and Health Informatics

Edited by

Tushar H. Jaware
K. Sarat Kumar
Ravindra D. Badgujar
and
Svetlin Antonov

Scrivener
Publishing

WILEY

This edition first published 2022 by John Wiley & Sons, Inc., 111 River Street, Hoboken, NJ 07030, USA and Scrivener Publishing LLC, 100 Cummings Center, Suite 541J, Beverly, MA 01915, USA
© 2022 Scrivener Publishing LLC
For more information about Scrivener publications please visit www.scrivenerpublishing.com.

Wiley Global Headquarters
111 River Street, Hoboken, NJ 07030, USA

For details of our global editorial offices, customer services, and more information about Wiley products visit us at www. wiley.com.

Limit of Liability/Disclaimer of Warranty

Library of Congress Cataloging-in-Publication Data

ISBN 978-1-119-81913-4

Cover image: Pixabay.Com
Cover design by Russell Richardson

Set in size of 11pt and Minion Pro by Manila Typesetting Company, Makati, Philippines

Printed in the USA

10 9 8 7 6 5 4 3 2 1

Contents

Preface

There are many aspects to medical imaging and health informatics, including how they can be applied to real-world biomedical and healthcare challenges. Therefore, a collection of cutting-edge artificial intelligence (AI) and other allied approaches for healthcare and biomedical applications are provided in this book. Moreover, a diverse collection of state-of-the-art techniques and recent advancements in AI approaches are given, which are geared toward the challenges that healthcare institutions and hospitals face in terms of early detection of diseases, data processing, healthcare monitoring and prognosis of diseases.

Medical imaging and health informatics is a subfield of science and engineering which applies informatics to medicine and includes the study of design, development, and application of computational innovations to improve healthcare. The health domain has a wide range of challenges that can be addressed using computational approaches; therefore, the use of AI and associated technologies is becoming more common in society and healthcare. Currently, deep learning algorithms are a promising option for automated disease detection with high accuracy. Clinical data analysis employing these deep learning algorithms allows physicians to detect diseases earlier and treat patients more efficiently. Since these technologies have the potential to transform many aspects of patient care, disease detection, disease progression and pharmaceutical organization, approaches such as deep learning algorithms, convolutional neural networks, and image processing techniques are explored in this book.

This book also delves into a wide range of image segmentation, classification, registration, computer-aided analysis applications, methodologies, algorithms, platforms, and tools; and gives a holistic approach to the application of AI in healthcare through case studies and innovative applications. It also shows how image processing, machine learning and deep learning techniques can be applied for medical diagnostics in several specific health scenarios such as COVID-19, lung cancer, cardiovascular diseases, breast cancer, liver tumor, bone fractures, etc. Also highlighted are the significant issues and concerns regarding the use of AI in healthcare together with other allied areas, such as the internet of things (IoT) and medical informatics, to construct a global multidisciplinary forum.

Since elements resulting from the growing profusion and complexity of data in the healthcare sector are emphasized in this book, it will assist scholars in focusing on future research problems and objectives. Our principal goal is to leverage AI, biomedical and health informatics for effective analysis and application to provide a tangible contribution to innovative breakthroughs in healthcare.

Dr. Tushar H. Jaware
Dr. K. Sarat Kumar
Dr. Ravindra D. Badgujar
Dr. Svetlin Antonov
April 2022

Machine Learning Approach for Medical Diagnosis Based on Prediction Model

Hemant Kasturiwale[1]*, Rajesh Karhe[2] and Sujata N. Kale[3]

[1]Thakur College of Engineering and Technology, Kandivali (East), Mumbai, MS, India
[2]Shri Gulabrao Deokar College of Engineering, Jalgaon, MS, India
[3]Department of Applied Electronics, Sant Gadge Baba University, Amravati, MS, India

Abstract

The electrocardiography is the most crucial biosignals for critical analysis of the heart. The heart is the human body's most vital and variety of control mechanisms that regulate the heart's activities. The heart rate is an essential measure of cardiac function. The heart rate is represented as a time interval equal between two corresponding electrocardiogram (ECG) "R" peaks. The heart rate varies with the heart's state. A machine learning technique is used to categorize the statistical parameters mentioned above to predict the individual's physical state, including sleep, examination, and exercise, based on a physiologically important factor known as HRV. The chapter is focused on uses of manual classified data. Each hospital, clinic, and diagnostic center produces massive quantities of information such as patient records and test results to predict the presence of heart disease and provide care for the early stages. The results are validated and compared with predictions obtained from different algorithms. Classification and prediction are a mining technique that uses training data to construct a model, and then, that model is applied to test data to predict outcomes. Different algorithms are employed to disease datasets to diagnose chronic disease, and the findings have been positive. There is a need to establish an appropriate technique for the diagnosis of chronic diseases. This chapter discusses with insight various kinds of classification schemes for chronic disease prediction. Here, readers will come to choice know machine learning and classifiers made to get knowledge out of datasets.

Keywords: ECG, biosignals, machine learning, HRV, classification, prediction, cardiac diseases

*Corresponding author: hemantkasturiwale@gmail.com

Tushar H. Jaware, K. Sarat Kumar, Ravindra D. Badgujar and Svetlin Antonov (eds.) Medical Imaging and Health Informatics, (1–22) © 2022 Scrivener Publishing LLC

1.1   Introduction

Biosignals are being used in various medical data, such as the electroencephalography (EEG), capturing electric fields created by brain cell activity, and magnetoencephalography (MEG) capturing magnet fields produced by electrical brain cell activity. The electrical stimulation comes from biological activity in various parts of the body. The most popular types of methods currently used to record biosignals in clinical research are described below, along with a brief overview of their functionality and related clinical application signals [1].

1.1.1   Heart System and Major Cardiac Diseases

The electrical activity generates the following types of signals:

- Magnetoencephalography (MEG) signals
- Electromyography (EMG) signals
- Electrooculography (EOG)signals
- Phonocardiography (PCG) signals
- Electrocorticography (ECoG) signals
- Electrocardiography (ECG or EKG) signals

Intervals between the waves are used as indicators of irregular cardiac operation, e.g., a prolonged PR interval from atrial activation to the start of ventricular activation may indicate cardiac failure [2, 3]. In addition, ECGs are used to study arrhythmias [4], coronary artery disease [5], and other heart failure disorders. In biosignals, the sampling frequency (or sampling rate) and the recording period are directly proportional to the data size and the data acquisition process speed. The ECG will be essential for the heart rhythm and disease research. The different heart conditions are as follows:

a) Arrhythmias
b) Coronary heart disease
c) Various types of heart blocks
d) Fibrillations
e) Congestive heart failure (CHF)
f) Myocardial infarction (MI)
g) Premature ventricular contraction (PVC)

1.1.2   ECG for Heart Rate Variability Analysis

Electrocardiogram (ECG) is a waveform pattern that describes the state of cardiac activity and cardiac safety. The ECG signal is non-stationary and non-linear. The ECG has a spectrum of frequencies between 0.05 and 100 Hz [6]. ECG analysis methods, including the heart rate variability (HRV), QRS identification, and ECG post-processing, have advanced considerably since device implementation. The word HRV reflects the interval difference between successive heartbeats.

1.1.3 HRV for Cardiac Analysis

The biomedical signal is an important health assessment parameter. For example, it has been used to detect and predict human stress [1], stroke, hypertension, sleep disorder, age, gender, and many more. The popular techniques to analyze the HRV fall into three categories as time domain, spectral or frequency domain based on fast Fourier transform (FFT) [7], and nonlinear methods consisting of Markov modeling, entropy-based metrics [8], and probabilistic modeling [9]. There are seven commonly used statistical time domain parameters [10] calculated from HRV segmentation during 5-min recording, comprising of RMSSD, SDNN, SDANN, SDANNi, SDSD, PNN50, and autocorrelation, which are considered for implementation. The HRV is also calculated by a device called PPA (peripheral pulse analyzer); it works based on pulses measured, which is different from HRV measurement using ECG. However, the focus would be on ECG-based HRV measurement, but the validation PPA-based method is considered [11]. Nonlinear measurement approaches aim to calculate the structure and complexity of the time series of RR intervals. HRV signals are non-stationary and nonlinear in nature. Analysis of HRV dynamics by methods based on chaos theory and nonlinear system theory is based on findings indicating that the processes involved in cardiovascular control are likely to interact with each other in a nonlinear manner. The more on indices (features/parameters) are discussed in Section 1.3.2.

1.2 Machine Learning Approach and Prediction

Learning is closely connected to (and sometimes overlaps with) quantitative statistics, which often concentrate on forecasting computers' use. It has close connections with mathematical optimization, which provides the fields of methodology, theory, and implementation. The second sub-area focuses more on the study of exploratory data and is also known as non-monitored learning [2]. Unsupervised machine learning (ML) is also possible [11] and can be used to learn and construct baseline conduct profiles for different entities [12]. To gain knowledge of the past and to detect useful trends from massive, unstructured, and complex databases, machine learning algorithms use a range of statistical, probabilistic, and optimization methods [12]. These algorithms include automatic categorization of texts, network intrusion detection, junk e-mail filtering, credit-card fraud detection, consumer buying behavior, manufacturing optimization, and disease modeling. Most of these applications are performed using managed variants of the algorithms of ML rather than unattended [13].

The heart disease detail includes several features that predict heart disease. This large amount of medical data allowed data mining techniques to discover trends and diagnose patients. The historical medical data is very high, so it requires computational methods to process it. Data mining is a technique that removes the hidden pattern and uses as an analytical tool to analyze historical data. There are several different classification schemes for disease datasets. ML techniques are applied for classifying the statistical parameters above in a cardiological signal analysis to predict the RR interval estimate cannot be overemphasized. A precise method of calculation therefore needs to be developed. It is clear from the existing research theory that the conventional systems for chronic disease prediction are unable to establish reliable diagnostic systems as workers make it difficult to get correct responses and can minimize response time. Adaptive systems, by comparison, can increase the chances of success and can advise clinicians on care decisions. Current healthcare programmers can be enhanced by the efficient use of parallel classification systems, as they promote parallel implementation on multiple systems. Parallel classification systems also have a great potential to increase the predictive performance of diagnostic systems for chronic diseases [13, 14]. Here, classifiers are discussed out of the available are K-Nearest Neighbor (KNN), Support Vector Machine (SVM), Ensemble AdaBoost (EAB), and Random Forest (RF).

1.3   Material and Experimentation

The proposed method comprises of two phases:

    a. processing the enrolment database (PEP) and
    b. Prediction (P).

    Figure 1.1 shows that the research purpose types of database are created based on acquisition units. The standard database has varying sampling frequency which comprises of different age groups of male and female.

    A total number of subjects and corresponding signal were acquired with different set conditions. This may comprises of female and male with varying age group with sampling frequency of 256 and 500 Hz [6, 15]. The model will be testing for cardiac HRV-based analysis with both the ECG and non-ECG (PPA). For the research purpose, the congestive heart failure, arrhythmia, sudden cardiac death, ventricular arrhythmia, CHF database data being considered along with externally obtained ECG and non-ECG.

1.3.1   Data and HRV

The research uses the normal and cardiac subject's standard data [16] and externally acquired ECG or non-ECG data. Hence, the proposed techniques for the classification of cardiac diseases use data with varying characteristics. The DAQ cards help in

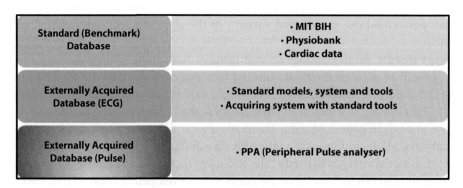

Figure 1.1 Acquisition system and sources [source: 14].

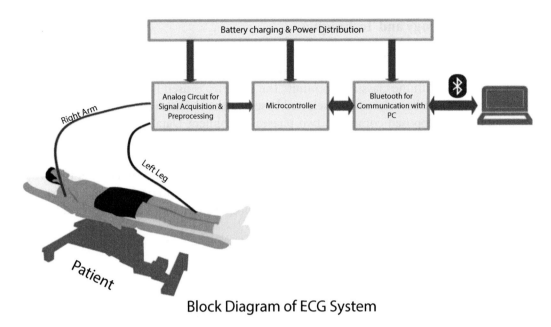

Block Diagram of ECG System

Figure 1.2 ECG acquisition system with connection (low cost).

creating a database of ECG or non-ECG signals. Figure 1.2 shows the HRV data and categorization, ensuring the data obtained is free from significant artifacts or noise. The sources of data and systems related to signal acquiring are a part of system. For more insight, the following methods/techniques are used for data acquisition in support of standard tools.

1.3.1.1   HRV Data Analysis via ECG Data Acquisition System

The analog circuit for ECG acquisition is possible with one or three channels. The analog devices as a signal conditioning circuit are used for data collection electronically.

The three-channel data acquiring system is attached to the body of the subject for recording purpose. These probes collect the ECG signal and give it as input to the ECG kit. The ECG kit comprises low-pass filters and an ECG chip. The electronic assembly is customized to acquired signal and processed further till detection. The myDAQ software, which works with NI DAQ, records the ECG wave, processes it, and provides analysis regarding the subject's heart condition. Three probes are connected to the ECG kit to test the signal and CRO to verify the signal. The extracted ECG signal from the subject is filtered as first step of process. The NIDAQ card processes a pure electrical signal. The front panel of the analog circuit with MCP6004 and instrumentation amplifier with other passive components is preferred as low cost and effective option. The circuit removes the baseline noise, line interference, and extracting data even for a few more seconds. It is effective for short duration records and has low storage capacity. The mechanism to reduce noise or artifact is effective to some extent for this circuit. The wireless connectivity is also major advantage of chapter system.

1.3.2   Methodology and Techniques

The proposed method breaks down HRV signals with the collection of features and checks consistency. Features are derived from the HRV signals components. Eventually, the classification is done with the classification unit. The classifier is used here for inspection and checking earlier. The best classifier is selected based on the classification parameters.

The approach proposed comprises two phases: Enrolment Database Processing (PEP) and Prediction and Identification (PI). All available data samples and ECG signals obtained by the units are fed for analysis as shown in Figure 1.3. However, the proposed model is compatible with age, gender, and feature (static) as other input conditions [17]. The proposed model design, heart disease dataset, data pre-processing, and performance measurement are critical and have been taken care of. The proposed methods are developed based on the following essential parameters:

- Short-term and long-term analysis
- Feature's indices and their sequencing
- Mathematical indices
- The technique for a standard database and classifiers

- The noise and impact study on ECG-HRV
- Noise impact on non–ECG-HRV

- The technique for an acquired database (ECG and non-ECG HRV) and classifiers
- Performance evaluation criteria and validation

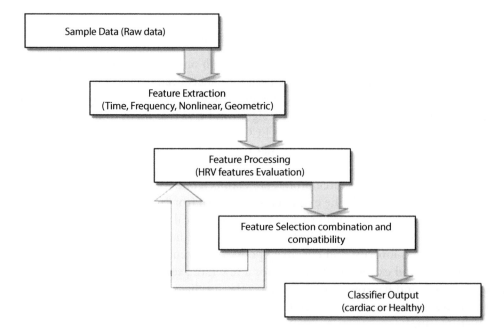

Figure 1.3 Cardiac diseases identification model for cardiac diseases [source: 24].

1.3.2.1 *Classifiers and Performance Evaluation*

The parameters used for evaluating the algorithm's performance are accuracy, precision, F-measures, recall, and execution time [18, 19]. These parameters are defined using four measures: True Positive (TP), True Negative (TN), False Positive (FP), and False Negative (FN) [20, 21].

1.3.2.1.1   Performance Metrics

Performance metrics calculate how well a given algorithm performs with accuracy, precision, sensitivity, specificity, and other parameters. The different performance metrics are as below.

1.3.2.1.1.1   Confusion Matrix

The confusion matrix shows the performance of the algorithm. It depicts how the classifier is confused while predicting. The rows indicate the class label's actual instance, while the columns indicate the predicted class instances. Table 1.1 shows a confusion matrix for binary classification. TP value means the positive value is correctly predicted, FP means positive value is falsely classified, FN means the negative value is falsely predicted, while the TN means negative value is correctly classified. A confusion matrix table used to calculate different performance metrics.

1.3.2.1.2   Major Features Contributors With Analysis

The details added mathematical features are an essential part of the total of 24 features in Tables 1.2A and B. The formulation of Table 1.2 is a restructured table looking into the needs of research to analyze short term and long-term duration data size. The mathematical features Dalton DSD index, Dalton MABB index, and De Hann LTV index are added and have significant in view of analysis.

The HRV indices are known as HRV parameters or HRV features. The feature acronym and feature name reflected in Table 1.2. The time domain and frequency domain, and linear and some of the nonlinear indices are part of the research [22]. The indices are divided into four groups. The proposed model works on the development of a new set of indices group [23, 24]. The mathematical indices, namely, Dalton and De Hann, are being figured as part of the feature group (Group 4), as shown in Table 1.2B. The feature group's novelty is that they are created as per their essential characteristics to improve the model's performance. The mathematical equation explains the dependency of variables with features [25].

Table 1.1 Confusion matrix.

Actual label	Predicted label	
	+(1)	−(0)
+(1)	True Positive	False Negative
−(0)	False Positive	True Negative

Table 1.2 (A) New proposed HRV indices with groups.

Sr. no.	Feature acronym	Feature name
Time domain (Group 1)		
1	meanRR	Mean value RR period
2	SDNN	Standard deviation of intervals (NN)
3	Mean	Mean value of the heart rate (HR)
4	sdHR	Standard heart rate
5	NNx	Total number of interval successive NN intervals greater than "x" ms
6	HRVTi	Integral of the density of the RR interval histogram divided by its height
7	TINN	Baseline width of the RR interval histogram
8	pNNx	Percentage of successive RR intervals differ by more than "x" ms
9	RMSSD	Root mean square of successive RR interval differences
Frequency domain (Group 2)		
10	aHF	Areas within a higher frequency band (0.15–0.4 Hz)
11	aLF	Areas within a lower frequency band (0.04–0.15 Hz)
12	Raio (aLF/aHF)	The ration of LF to HF
Nonlinear (Group 3)		
13	Ent	Sample entropy
14	Hval	Hurst component
15	avgpsdf	Average power spectral density
16	hfdf	Higuchi fractal dimension
17	D	The factor of the dimension of time series
18	Alpha	Scaling exponent for alignment of series points
Other features (parameters/indices) (Group 4)		
19	SD1	The standard deviation of the distance of each point from the y-axis
20	SD2	The standard deviation of the distance of each point from the x-axis

1.3.3 Proposed Model With Layer Representation

The HRV analysis for cardiac diseases is complicated, so the step-by-step processes are defined as a part of HRV analysis. The research work has come up with the development of a robust model via the layer model. The features contribution and impact is a significant

Table 1.2 (B) New proposed HRV indices with groups.

21	CD	Correlation dimension
22	Dalton DSD index	The standard deviation of RR of length HR signal (long-term variability index)
23	Dalton MABB index	Absolute of one-half of arithmetic mean value of differences of subsequent RR intervals (short-term variability index)
24	De Hann LTV index	As an interquartile range of radius location of particular RR intervals (long-term variability index)

contribution of research that helps in the classification of cardiac diseases. The model development has a three-part fixed set feature model (FSM), flexi intra group selection model, and qualitative analysis, as shown in Figure 1.4. The long-term and short-term analyses are unique with the development of the model. The model performs under all conditions, and so the results obtained are encouraging for future growth. Figures 1.4 and 1.5 show a novel approach to identify and predict cardiac diseases with many features like feature extraction, feature concatenation, and combination. The responsiveness of the algorithm is on HRV parameters (linear, nonlinear, time, and frequency). Here, research work has included mathematical parameters like Dalton and Higuchi to enhance the method's efficiency.

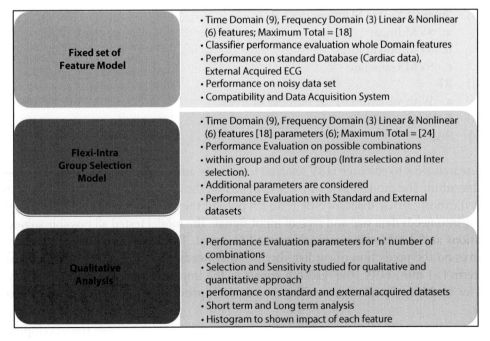

Figure 1.4 Robust model layers.

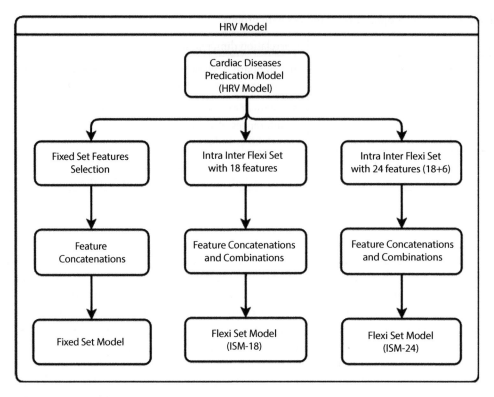

Figure 1.5 HRV model for cardiac prediction.

   i)   Support Vector Machine (SVM)
      a. SVM linear
      b. SVM polynomial
      c. SVM Gaussian
  ii)   RF
      a. With variation in the number of trees
 iii)   KNN
 iv)   EAB

The research aims to enhance HRV analysis to identify and predict cardiac diseases using a ML algorithm. The model's performance depends on the quality of input data and features for predication cardiac diseases. The research present the model which can be customized looking into needs data size and type of input signal. The model tested all possible subjects' conditions and database like raw and non-ECG signal. The research reviews current perspectives on the prediction of cardiac diseases that needs 24 h, short-term (~1 min), and long term (>1 min) HRV. The research enhances the importance of HRV and its implications for health and performance. The investigation provides an insight into widely used

HRV time domain, frequency domain, and nonlinear metrics, along with mathematical indices for better understanding; the information is shared here using graphs. The research goal is to show the classifiers' effectiveness and ease of use in predicting heart diseases. The research provides HRV assessment strategies for clinical and optimal performance interventions nervous system. The extraction and selection of the change (variation) of heart rate during short term (5 min) is analyzed using the time domain and frequency domain to provide the degree of balance and activity of the autonomic. The proposed research work on an algorithm meets the standards of measurement and physiological interpretation and biosignal processing algorithms. The development flow works with feature concatenations and the model's outcome with 18 features with fixed set and grouped as time domain, frequency, and linear-nonlinear domain. The other side of the flow is more adaptable with feature concatenations and combinations with 18 features extending it to 24 features. The ML model has been successful in overcoming the challenges to large extents mentioned by researchers.

1.3.4   The Model Using Fixed Set of Features and Standard Dataset

The HRV model using a fixed set of features is the first HRV model developed for prediction. The fixed function is time domain (nine functions), frequency domain (three features), and linear-nonlinear (fix features). The model needs to work on a specific domain or combination of a group such as time-frequency, time-nonlinear, and time-nonlinear. After applying a ML algorithm, to each domain and combinations (group), the 18 sets of features [Time-Frequency Linear-Nonlinear (TFLN)] have the best amongst this analysis. The comparison of results is with other groups. Although all the four types of data, the external dataset, have been tested, the following section presents the model's analysis with standard datasets and classifiers. The performance of the model evaluates with specific metrics using a set of features. The model identifies the input signal and predicts cardiac diseases using ML. The prediction model uses 18 features, and the model worked well based on performance evaluation parameters.

1.3.4.1   *Performance of Classifiers With Feature Selection*

Table 1.3 shows the performance of classifiers for a given input, i.e., standard data. The table shows accuracy, sensitivity, and specificity, which are the most crucial performance evaluation measures. The same has been shown graphically in Figure 1.6. The proposed model distinguishes the CHF accurately from normal ones with accuracy, sensitivity, and specificity. The accuracy, sensitivity, and specificity are 99.78%, 100%, and 100%, respectively. The accuracy of the classifier KNN and RF is comparable and close to 100%. RF classifiers' accuracy for datasets is essential, which is high SDDB, ARRTHY, and VENT-ARRTHY. The performance of KNN, EAB, and SVM is but lower than RF classifier. The FNR is 20% for EAB against 0% for other classifiers, which is one of the indications of performance classifier along with TPR (TP Rate), TNR (TN Rate), and FPR (FP Rate).

Table 1.3 Performance measurement on a standard dataset.

Classifier performance	Database (Standard)	Accuracy	Sensitivity	Specificity
RF	CHF (A)	99.78	100	100
	ARRTHY (B)	99.88	100	100
	SDDB (C)	99.77	100	100
	VENT_ARRTHY (D)	95	97.01	97.74
EAB	CHF (A)	92.31	80	100
	ARRTHY (B)	97.48	100	100
	SDDB (C)	95.24	100	87.5
	VENT_ARRTHY (D)	97	97.67	98.18
SVM	CHF (A)	92.31	100	87.5
	ARRTHY (B)	95.65	100	75
	SDDB (C)	95.24	100	87.5
	VENT_ARRTHY (D)	86	88.02	91.52
KNN	CHF (A)	99.79	100	100
	ARRTHY (B)	97.83	100	87.5
	SDDB (C)	66.67	46.15	100
	VENT_ARRTHY (D)	56	66.41	77.07

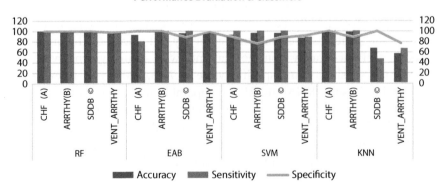

Figure 1.6 Performance evaluation of model on standard database.

1.4   Performance Metrics and Evaluation of Classifiers

The F-score, also known as the F-measure, is a measure of a test's accuracy. The precise calculation is shown in Figure 1.6 and Table 1.4 and the F-score recall together.

The exactness is the number of positive results correctly identified divided by the number of all positive results, including those not correctly identified. The reminder is the number of positive findings correctly detected, divided by the number of positive samples. For TFNL functions, the F1 scoring is high compared to time features only. The statistics for Kappa from Cohen are an excellent metric that can deal with the problems of both classes and classes. A 100% score against other groups has been registered by KNN. Cohen's Kappa offers a prediction in which precision cannot be expected. The Matthews correlation code (MCC) or phi coefficient is used to calculate binary (two-class) grade quality in ML. Intradialytic hypotension is predicted by the region under the recipient operating characteristic (AUROC). For KNN, it is 100% and for EAB it is 84.3%. The higher the value, the better the model efficiency. The Threat Score (TS) is also called Critical Success Index (CSI), the categorical output prediction verification metric is equivalent to the total number of accurate predictions for events. At 80%, CSI with EAB is the lowest. The outcome of the model using evaluation measures has shown that the model is responsive to input signal changes and is thus used for short- and long-term analysis. The rising availability of personal computers and computing power has led significantly to increased HRV analyses.

1.4.1   Cardiac Disease Prediction Through Flexi Intra Group Selection Model

The HRV feature–based technique is a novel way of having a high degree of precision and accuracy. As the barriers between domains no longer exist for combinations purpose, so the model is named Flexi Inter-Intra Group Selection Model (ISM). Sometimes, here,

Table 1.4 HRV model and classifier performance.

Database (Standard)	HRV model with fixed set features			
Classifier	RF	EAB	SVM	KNN
ERROR rate	1	6.77	5.69	1
Precision	83.3	100	83.3	100
Negative Predictive value	100	88.9	100	100
Recall	100	80	100	100
F-score	86.2	95.2	86.2	100
Critical success index	83.3	80	83.3	100
MCC	85.4	84.3	85.4	100
Cohen's kappa	84.3	83.1	84.3	100

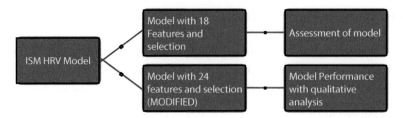

Figure 1.7 ISM HRV model.

it will be called as Flexi Group Selection Model or Flexi Group Model. The qualitative and quantitative assessment is possible due to feature concatenations and combination stages. The model with intra and inter indices set selection of feature, compatibility with classifiers, and extraction is the main highlight of the above-modified HRV model. After de-noising, feature extraction, and dimensionality reduction, the raw data parameters will process the input signal based on the carrying information. The evaluation is done on classifier output and parameters and validated with input pre-processed signals. The evaluation parameters are essential to the analysis set for knowing exactly redundancies and conversion factor. The ISM model works very well with ECG HRV analysis or non-ECG HRV analysis for cardiac diseases identification and prediction. The HRV model is developed for ECG or non-ECG input conditions followed by feature selection and feature concatenation within 24 features. The ML approach ensures the system is adequately trained for specified samples and tested. Figure 1.7 shows the ISM structure with 18 features and 24 features. The 24-feature model is a modified and improved model to boost classifier performance. From the testing, it is clear that a model with RF and SVM have better-performing characteristics. ML is important because of its remarkable ability to adapt and provide solutions to complex problems effectively and quickly.

1.4.2 HRV Model With Flexi Set of Features

The model is developed for 18 features with selection and extraction within 18 as a group now. Here, the flexi feature set model (ISM) works well for data combinations of ECG and non-ECG signals. This model works with 18 features like FSM, but combination and concatenations are possible with the model. The data size is an important consideration along with short train or long train data. The FSM accuracy decreases on external data input and works well for fixed sampling frequency data. Table 1.5 shows the performance of the Flexi Set Feature model with 18 features. It is important to have results and assessment of each to take the analysis to a model compatible with input conditions, making the model Robust. Figure 1.8 shows all important classifiers considered for study and experimentation.

- The qualitative analysis of 18 feature flexi set of feature model is as follows:
- Classifier outcome of 18 features flexi approach is as
  a. EAB and KNN accuracy is almost the same as that of the FSM.
  b. SVM performance is at 85.90% and RF accuracy increases to 94.89%.
- The performance on expanded dataset and for a varied length of samples.

Table 1.5 Accuracy comparison with fixed set feature model.

Accuracy							
EAB		**KNN**		**SVM**		**RF**	
FSM	ISM (18)	FSM	ISM (18)	FSM	ISM (18)	FSM	ISM (18)
61.54	61.54	85.55	85.41	84.77	85.90	89.89	**94.87**

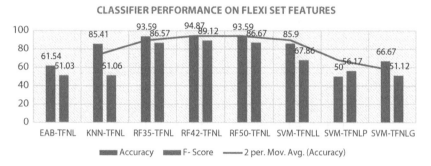

Figure 1.8 Classifier performances on flexi set features (ISM-18).

- Sensitivity rates of RF-42 and F1-score are 91.27% and 89.12%, respectively.
- Accuracy rates of RF-35, RF-42, and RF-50 are 93.59%, 94.87%, and 93.59%, respectively.

Figure 1.8 shows that 2 per mov. average (accuracy) suggests scope for a smooth transition from one point to another, especially in RF. The ISM with 18 has shown a lot of promises with its outcome, which has led to improve version of ISM (18). The model describes feature concatenation and combinations with limited success.

1.4.3   Performance of the Proposed Modified With ISM-24

The aim is to assess the impact of ML methods in developing a model that classifies normal and cardiac failure in long-term ECG time series. The robust HRV model comprises a combination generator model, parameter array, feature selection and computation, and feature segregation at the top and bottom unit. The qualitative assessment is possible using the HRV ISM model. The RF algorithm is one of the best classification algorithms. RF can identify extensive data with precision. Figure 1.6 shows a learning method; a number of decision trees based on the time of training and the performance of the modal. RF acts as a random vector for all systems. Table 1.6 compares the traditional methods and ML model with the proposed ISM-24.

Whenever there are a more significant number of training samples available, building an ML model is advisable. From Table 1.7, the proposed ISM outperforms the other traditional and ML techniques. As compared to the conventional classification algorithms, ISM-24 captures deeper features and produces a nearly accurate classification using RF-45.

Table 1.6 Comparison of proposed methods with traditional methods with RF.

Long term and short term

Techniques	Author	Database	Features	Results ACC, SEN, and SPE (%)	Duration	Outcome
Existing Methods	Mahajan et al. [2017]	69 NSR (NSR1 and NSR2), 38 CHF (CHF1) and (CHF2)	Probabilistic symbolic, pattern recognition (eight features), long scale AVNN, and SDNN	98.1 | 94.7 | 100.0	Short term	CHF and with standard dataset only
	A. Jovic, K. Brkic and G. Krstacic [2019]	NSR1 (49), NSR2 (17), CHF1 (27), and CHF2 (15)	Linear, nonlinear (111 total)	90.7 | 78.6 | 98.6	Long term	CHF and with standard dataset only
	Turky N. Alotaiby et al. [2019]	NSR, cardiac, and other health ailments (total 290)	11 statistical features, and DWT	99.37 | 99.6 | 98.6	Short term	CHF and to specific standard dataset, wide health ailment

(Continued)

Table 1.6 Comparison of proposed methods with traditional methods with RF. (*Continued*)

Long term and short term

Techniques	Author	Database	Features	Results ACC, SEN, and SPE (%)	Duration	Outcome
Proposed Methods	Fixed set features model	NSR and cardiac ailments (standard)	18 features	**99.78** | 100 | 100	Long term	major dataset (CHF, SDDB, ARRTHY, and VENT-ARRTHY) but tested individual
		NSR, cardiac ailments (standard) with external acquired data)	18 features	**89.89** | 90 | 85	Long term	Major dataset (CHF, SDDB, ARRTHY, and VENT-ARRTHY) but tested individual with variation in accuracy
	Flexi set features model (ISM)	NSR, cardiac ailments (standard), and combined	18 features, combination, and concatenations	**94.55** | 91.15 | 99	Short term and long term	Major dataset (CHF, SDDB, ARRTHY, and VENT-ARRTHY) combined data and performance evaluation
		NSR, cardiac ailments (standard), and combined	24 features, combination, and concatenations	**96.79** | 92.40 | 99.38	Short term and long term	Major dataset (CHF, SDDB, ARRTHY, and VENT-ARRTHY) combined data and with improved performance

Table 1.7 Training and testing set combinations vs. evaluation parameters.

Training-testing split	Accuracy	Precision	Recall	F-score
30%–70%	83.24	92.12	82.02	87.16
50%–50%	92.30	92.66	84.80	88.41
70%–30%	**96.79**	**93.45**	**96.15**	**90.5**

The ISM-18 performs well on the combined database; the classification accuracy increases significantly compared to the existing traditional algorithm. The highest accuracy on the online dataset by the proposed method is 96.79% showing an improvement of around 2% over the ISM-18 model. The more the features have high accuracy in RF-45 but not always guarantee the results unless each feature's impact is known. The traditionally features like RMSSD, SDNN, and LF; HF has used DWT for HRV-based analysis for cardiac diseases. It is extremely important to see the impact of time parameters within the domain, particularly for biosignals. The proposed methods and their qualitative analysis explain the mechanism for the identification of each dominating feature.

1.5   Discussion and Conclusion

Training of the system with a good dataset is key to achieving a high classification efficiency. Therefore, in this analysis, after training, the classifier was fed with all the combination of features in the absolute test process. The ANOVA was used once only to test input and correlation factors for suitability. Under time domain, frequency domain, and nonlinear domain, the proposed classification approach is tested by fixed set and accuracy was found to be much less than intra group selection methods. For the best feature selection process, extraction was evaluated before and run for multiple times to test robustness, based on computational time and the highest precision metrics. The model's versatility intra community selection and adaptability for such varied and complex data is one of the unique features and is shown here using evaluation parameters. These results show that if a good dataset trains a classifier system, it gives higher performance. One of the major advantages of the proposed approach is that the use of combination set with standard ML will obtain a high classification efficiency. The limitation of the proposed method is that due to the number of complex data inputs, the training takes time. While the ML technology has many advantages, it is not flawless. In some ways, the following variables hinder their capacity.

- ML algorithms are proven to be effective in predicting all scenarios.
- Another problem is the right interpretation of the tests of ML algorithms.
- The high sensitivity to errors is another drawback of ML algorithm.
- A particular dataset will determine good results show most of the time.
- This is also a big problem for the field of choosing successful or sorting algorithms.
- In order to collect datasets, ML algorithms typically need large datasets.
- Many service and system are needed in the algorithms.

The main contributions of the proposed research work are as follows:

(a) All the efficiency of the classifiers has been tested for maximum features in terms of classification accuracy and time of execution.
(b) The device is intelligent in the sense that the transition step is reported at the highest or lowest accuracy
(c) Compared with three classifiers and previous studies, the proposed diagnostic system achieved excellent classification results
(d) This study suggests that the best classifier is suitable for the selection of features and robustness studies being carried out for the best classifier.

1.5.1   Conclusion and Future Scope

This research has successfully addressed cardiac diseases prediction and classification from the ECG acquiring system with the proposed model. There is a scope for further research work on the following points:

a) **Robust Physical Dataset:** To develop the model as a prototype, result validation is essential with varying data condition, subject conditions. A more advanced study would have to be done with human subject testing procedures. The number of electronic sensors and their compatibility for extraction of the signal will solve real-time processing of data and analysis.

b) **Broader Physical Activity Dataset:** Abnormal rhythms with several features need to consider for experimentation. The physical activities depicted in the physical activity dataset only include a limited range of activities and are performed on a small number of individuals. In the future, these subjects and contextual attributes can be combined with more individuals to create a larger dataset. Handling large combinations in quick time is to resolve ML techniques to be wisely used to reduce computation time.

c) **Cardiac Diseases datasets:** The geographical conditions will impact HRV features, so research needs to have benching marking by a clinical expert for accurate prediction of diseases. Researchers HRV should be clubbed for the future development of a model. ML requires large data. As a result, the availability of authentic data will assist the researcher in making better predictions. Having a greater number of subjects and collecting continuous data, which involves long-term continuous observations of the subject, will improve the statistical significance and precision accuracy.

d) **Raw Healthcare Data:** Identifying the processing of raw healthcare data of heart information will help in the long-term saving of human lives and early detection of abnormalities in heart conditions. Lowering mortality rates can be done by detecting the disease early and taking preventative steps as soon as possible. The medical expert's approval agencies can help in validation and will encourage the researcher to come up with a model for real-time prediction.

e) **Clinical ECG Machine and Benchmarking:** Another challenge in this analysis is the difference between the types of ECGs used in clinical research and those available. This made automating clinical research discovery incredibly difficult. As previously observed, the findings of previous research could not be repeated for the same topic due to differences in the form of ECGs. Hence, it is extremely important to have standardization for the same.

f) **Lack of database of Non-ECG HRV:** There are very few methods, and devices are used for HRV analysis. Hence, future research needs to focus on non-ECG–based HRV analysis for real-time and correct prediction.

References

1. St. Louis, E., *et al.*, *Electroencephalography (EEG): An Introductory Text and Atlas of Normal and Abnormal Findings in Adults, Children, and Infants*, American Epilepsy Society, 2, 2016.
2. Karwiky, G., Ahmad, C., Caesarendra, W., Ismail, R., Kurniawan, D., Suddent cardiac death predictor based on spatial QRS-T angle feature and support vector machine case study for cardiac disease detection in Indonesia,. *IECBES 2016 - IEEE-EMBS Conf. Biomed. Eng. Sci.*, pp. 186–192, 2016.
3. Inamdar, A. and Inamdar, A., Heart Failure: Diagnosis, Management and Utilization. *J. Clin. Med.*, 5, 7, 62, 2016.
4. Germán-Salló, Z. and Germán-Salló, M., Non-linear Methods in HRV Analysis. *Proc. Technol.*, 22, 645–651, Jan. 2016.
5. Avanzato, R. and Beritelli, F., Automatic ecg diagnosis using convolutional neural network. *Electronics*, 9, 6, 1–14, 2020.
6. Acharya, U.R. *et al.*, Automated characterization and classification of coronary artery disease and myocardial infarction by decomposition of ECG signals: A comparative study. *Inf. Sci.*, 377, October, 17–29, Jan. 2017.
7. Dua, S., Du, X., Vinitha Sree, S., Thajudin Ahamed, V., II, Novel classification of coronary artery disease using heart rate variability analysis. *J. Mech. Med. Biol.*, 12, 4, 3, 2012.
8. Ashkenazy, Y. *et al.*, Discrimination between healthy and sick cardiac autonomic nervous system by detrended heart rate variability analysis. *Fractals*, 7, 1, 85–91, 1999.
9. Pan, W., He, A., Feng, K., Li, Y., Wu, D., Liu, G., Multi-Frequency Components Entropy as Novel Heart Rate Variability Indices in Congestive Heart Failure Assessment. *IEEE Access*, 7, 37708–37717, 2019.
10. Deshmukh, M., Kumar Jain, R., Parashar, D., Jaiswal, S., Derivative-Based Peak Detection Algorithm for PPA Waveforms. *2018 IEEE Int. Conf. Comput. Intell. Comput. Res. ICCIC*, 2018, pp. 1–5, 2018.
11. Anwar, S.M., Gul, M., Majid, M., Alnowami, M., Arrhythmia Classification of ECG Signals Using Hybrid Features. *Comput. Math. Methods Med.*, 2018, 3, 2018.
12. Uma, K. and Hanumanthappa, M., Data Collection Methods and Data Preprocessing Techniques for Healthcare Data Using Data Mining. *International Journal of Scientific & Engineering Research*, 8, 6, 1131–1136, 2017.
13. Uddin, S., Khan, A., Hossain, M.E., Moni, M.A., Comparing different supervised machine learning algorithms for disease prediction. *BMC Med. Inform. Decis. Mak.*, 19, 1, 1–16, 2019.
14. Kasturiwale, H. and Kale, Dr. S. N., Qualitative analysis of Heart Rate Variability based Biosignal Model for Classification of Cardiac Diseases. *Int. J. Adv. Sci. Technol.*, 29, 7, 296–305, 2020.
15. Pandit, D., Zhang, L., Liu, C., Chattopadhyay, S., Aslam, N., Lim, C.P., A lightweight QRS detector for single lead ECG signals using a max-min difference algorithm. *Comput. Methods Programs Biomed.*, 144, 61–75, 2017.

16. https://physionet.org/about/database/

17. Beckers, F., Verheyden, B., Aubert, A.E., Aging and nonlinear heart rate control in a healthy population. *Am. J. Physiol. Heart Circ. Physiol.*, 290, 6, 2006.

18. Čukić, M., Pokrajac, D., Stokić, M., Simić, S., Radivojević, V., Ljubisavljević, M., EEG machine learning with Higuchi's fractal dimension and sample entropy as features for successful detection of depression, *Computer Science, Mathematics, Biology,* arXiv. 1–34, 2018.

19. Šimundić, A.-M., Measures of Diagnostic Accuracy: Basic Definitions. *EJIFCC*, 19, 4, 203–211, 2009. [Online]. Available:http://www.ncbi.nlm.nih.gov/pubmed/27683318%0Ahttp://www.pubmedcentral.nih.gov/articlerender.fcgi?artid=PMC4975285.

20. Jelinek, H.F., Cornforth, D.J., Tarvainen, M.P., Khalaf, K., Investigation of linear and nonlinear properties of a heartbeat time series using multiscale Rényi entropy. *Entropy*, 21, 8, 7, 2019.

21. Zhang, Y., Li, J., Wang, J., Exploring stability of entropy analysis for signal with different trends. *Phys. A Stat. Mech. Appl.*, 470, 60–67, 2017.

22. Bolea, J., Pueyo, E., Orini, M., Bailón, R., Influence of heart rate in non-linear HRV indices as a sampling rate effect evaluated on supine and standing. *Front. Physiol.*, 7, Nov. 2016.

23. Sharma, M., Tan, R.S., Acharya, U.R., Automated heartbeat classification and detection of arrhythmia using optimal orthogonal wavelet filters. *Inform. Med. Unlocked*, 16, May, 100221, 2019.

24. Kasturiwale, H.P. and Kale, S.N., BioSignal Modelling for Prediction of Cardiac Diseases Using Intra Group Selection Method. *Intell. Decis. Technol.*, 15, 1, 151–160, 2021. 10.3233/IDT-200058.

25. Moczko, J.A., Advanced Methods of Heart Rate Signals Processing and Their Usefulness in Diagnosis Support. I. Mathematical Heart Rate Descriptors and Virtual Instrumentation. *Comput. Methods Sci. Technol.*, 8, 2, 65–76, 2002.

2

Applications of Machine Learning Techniques in Disease Detection

M.S. Roobini*, Sowmiya M., S. Jancy and L. Suji Helen

Sathyabama Institute of Science and Technology, Chennai, Tamil Nadu, India

Abstract

Machine learning (ML) is utilized to fabricate predictive models by separating designs from enormous datasets. In predictive information, these models are useful. It is utilized in examination applications like value forecast, hazard appraisal, anticipating client conduct, and report order. With nonstop information flooding in, the ML models guarantee that the arrangement is continually refreshed. With proper and continually changing information sources with regard to the Machine Learning Methods. ML is the structure of procedures and their use in the right scope. It is based on the knowledge of improvement of computer platforms that can access the information, examine it, and study from it. It is a portion of Artificial Intelligence (AI) and must be able to adapt through knowledge. It must identify errors and correct them without being explicitly automated. The concepts of ML are used for getting the better predictive models. ML is required for tasks that are too difficult for humans to program openly. Certain tasks are so difficult that it is impossible, if not difficult, for humans to work out all of the nuances and program for them openly. So instead, we deliver a huge volume of information to a ML algorithm and let the algorithm effort it out by exploring that information and examining for a model that will complete what the programmers have agreed it out to attain. How well the model implements are determined by a cost function providing by the programmer and the task of the process is to discover a model that reduces the cost function. AI is the extensive learning of representing human capabilities; ML is an exact subclass of AI that trains ML. ML permits the customer to feed a computer algorithm a huge volume of information and have the computer evaluate and create data-driven approvals and decisions based on only the given input data. If any modifications are identified, then the algorithm can integrate that evidence to develop its future decision making. To better realize the usages of ML, consider various models where ML is applied. For example, the self-driving Google car, cyber fraud finding, and online recommendation engines such as Amazon and Netflix. Machines can allow all of these belongings by filtering suitable portions of information and restoring them together based on patterns to get accurate results. In this chapter, ML along with deep learning algorithms is explained. Nowadays, ML plays a vital role in prediction and analysis of various kinds of diseases. It is helpful in keeping track of the patient details and helps in identifying the most efficient algorithms in analysis of the patient data. In this chapter, we will discuss about the various algorithms and its applications in disease prediction. This chapter also analyzes how ML is applicable in medical field and challenges.

---

*Corresponding author: roobinims@gmail.com

Tushar H. Jaware, K. Sarat Kumar, Ravindra D. Badgujar and Svetlin Antonov (eds.) *Medical Imaging and Health Informatics*, (23–46) © 2022 Scrivener Publishing LLC

Keywords: Machine learning, classification, supervised learning, unsupervised learning, predictive model, reinforcement learning, regression

2.1   Introduction

Machine learning (ML) is to fabricate predictive models by separating designs from enormous datasets by applying some artificial intelligence (AI) algorithms. The ML techniques are classified into various types.

- Supervised learning
- Unsupervised learning
- Semi-supervised learning
- Reinforcement learning

2.1.1   Overview of Machine Learning Types

This section discusses about the overview of the different types of ML techniques.

Unsupervised Learning: The AI calculation follows up on data without direction. It bunches unsorted data as per similitude, examples, and contrasts with no earlier preparing or management. Since there is no preparation given to the machine, the machine itself finds the shrouded structure in unlabeled information and deciphers it.

Supervised Learning: This type has marked highlights that characterize the importance of information. For example, the AI application can be made that recognizes a large number of creatures, in respect to pictures and composed depictions. The general classification of the supervised learning method is illustrated in Figure 2.1.

Semi-Supervised Learning: This type of learning was a combination of directed and solo learning. It utilizes modest marked information, which gives the advantages of both

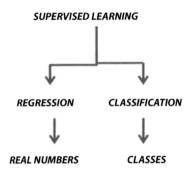

Figure 2.1 Supervised learning.

unaided and regulated learning while at the same time evading the difficulties of finding a lot of named information.

Reinforcement Learning: Reinforcement learning is an exceptionally intriguing sort of learning. There is no answer key which can determine what is correct. Be that as it may, the fortification learning specialist despite everything concludes acceptable behaviour to play out its undertaking.

2.1.2   Motivation

The ML algorithm is used in more applications such as healthcare diagnosis such as stroke prediction and tumor prediction. The main motivation of this ML algorithm is to predict it with high accuracy, less error rate, true positive, true negative, less communication head, and less communication cost [16, 17].

2.1.3   Organization the Chapter

This chapter organizes as Section 2.1 as introduction, overview of ML types, and motivation. Sections 2.2 discusses the types of ML and the different types of ML algorithms. Section 2.3 describes about the few future research challenges.

2.2   Types of Machine Learning Techniques

2.2.1   Supervised Learning

This type has marked highlights that characterize the importance of information. For example, the AI application can be made that recognizes a large number of creatures, in respect to pictures and composed depictions. The objective of a supervised learning calculation is to utilize the dataset to create a model that takes an element vector x as information and yields data that permits deriving the name for this component vector. Supervised learning as the name recommends getting administered by somebody. It is a learning wherein the machine utilizes information, which now labeled with the correct answer. The machine is furnished with another arrangement of information. With the assistance of supervised learning, the calculation breaks down the preparation informational collection (of preparing models) and creates a right result from marked information. Here, the machine has just taken in the things from past information [17]. Along these lines, this is the ideal opportunity it utilizes the adapting astutely. Diagram representing the supervised learning model is given below in Figure 2.2.

2.2.2   Classification Algorithm

- KNN Algorithm
- Decision Trees
- Random Forest Algorithm

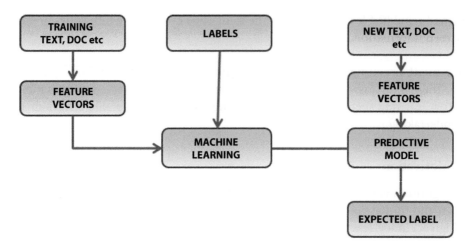

Figure 2.2 Supervised learning model.

- Naive Bayes Algorithm
- Logistic Regression
- Support Vector Machine (SVM)

2.2.3   Regression Analysis

Regression analysis consists of many ML techniques, which allows us to expect a consistent result variable (y) considering the evaluating x [18]. Example: Suppose there is a promoting organization A, who does different commercial consistently and get deals on that. The below list shows the advertisement made by the organization over 5 years and the relating deals. Regression analysis deal with forecast issues in ML. Regression is helpful in finding the connection among factors and empowers us to foresee the constant yield variable dependent on the at least one indicator factors [19]. "Regression shows a line or bend that goes through all the data points on track indicator diagram so that the vertical separation between the data points and the regression line is least [20]." The separation among data points indicates that a methodology was caught a solid association [11].

Example:
Identifying the downpour utilizing temperature and different elements

- To find the market patterns
- Determining the street mishaps because of rash driving.

Terminologies:

Outliers: Outliers is an observation that contains either low worth or high incentive in contrast with other watched values. An anomaly may obstruct the outcome, so it ought to be maintained a strategic distance from.

Multicollinearity: If the independent variables are profoundly connected with one another than different variables, at that point, such condition is called multicollinearity. It ought not be available in the dataset, on the grounds that it makes issue while positioning the most influencing variable.

Underfitting and Overfitting: If our calculation functions admirably with the preparation dataset yet not well with test dataset, at that point, such issue is called overfitting. In addition, in the event that our calculation does not perform well even with preparing dataset, at that point such, issue is called underfitting.

2.2.4 Linear Regression

1. Linear regression is a measurable regression strategy, which is utilized for predictive investigation.
2. It is one of the exceptionally straightforward and simple calculations, which takes a shot at regression and shows the connection between the continuous variables.
3. It is utilized for taking care of the regression issue in AI.
4. Linear regression shows the linear connection henceforth called linear regression.
5. The connection between variables in the linear regression model can be clarified utilizing the underneath picture. Here, we are anticipating the compensation of a representative based on the time of understanding. Predicting students drop out by considering educational details of their parents, family problem, and finance. We exploit ML techniques such as decision tree [9].

2.2.4.1 *Applications of Linear Regression*

2.2.4.1.1 Forecasting

A top preferred position of utilizing a linear regression model in ML is the capacity to conjecture patterns and make expectations that are doable. Information researchers can utilize these forecasts and make further conclusions dependent on ML. It is fast, effective, and precise. This is transcendently since machines process enormous volumes of information and there is least human mediation. When the calculation is set up, the way toward learning gets rearranged [10].

2.2.4.1.2 Beneficial to Small Businesses

By modifying a couple of factors, machines can comprehend the effect on deals. Since conveying linear regression is financially savvy, it is significantly invaluable to private companies since short- and long-haul figures can be made with regard to deals. This implies independent companies can design their assets well and make a development direction for themselves. They will likewise be to comprehend the market and its inclinations and find out about flexibly and request [21].

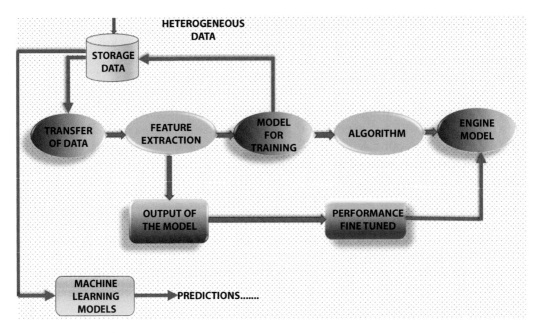

Figure 2.3 Process flow.

2.2.4.1.3 Preparing Strategies

Since ML empowers forecast, perhaps, the greatest preferred position of a linear regression model in it is the capacity to set up a system for a given circumstance, well ahead of time, and break down different results. Important data can be gotten from the regression model of forecasting accordingly helping organizations plan deliberately and settle on chief choices [22]. Figure 2.3 shows the complete flow of the process.

2.2.5 KNN Algorithm

1. It is an upfront algorithm dependent on labeled learning method.
2. K-nearest Neighbor (KNN) calculation accepts the closeness among the new data.
3. KNN calculation supplies all the accessible data.
4. KNN calculation is used for classification regression generally.

2.2.5.1 Working of KNN

Step-1: Select the K no of closest element.
Step-2: Euclidean separation of K.
Step-3: Consider the K nearest neighbors as per the decided separation.
Step-4: From these k neighbors, check amount of informations.
Step-5: The model is prepared.

The Euclidean separation is the separation between two centers, which is quite recently packed in math. It might be resolved as follows:

2.2.5.2 Drawbacks of KNN Algorithm

Continuously needs in choose assessment of K which may be awesome some time [23].

2.2.6 Decision Tree Classification Algorithm

It just poses an inquiry, and dependent on the appropriate response (Yes/No), it further divided the tree into subtrees [24].

2.2.6.1 Attribute Selection Measures

It is in any case called separating rules since it makes us choose breakpoints. Best trait with good score will be picked as a splitting quality (source). Because of an interminable regarded quality, part centers for branches moreover need to portray [14].

2.2.6.2 Information Gain

It implies the contaminating impact in a social occasion of models. It is the reducing in entropy. Information gain calculates the qualification between entropy subject to given property regards.

Where,

- Info (D) is the typical proportion of information expected to perceive the class sign of a tuple in D.
- $|Dj|/|D|$ goes about as the weight of the jth package.
- InfoA(D) is the ordinary information needed to amass a tuple from D subject to the distributing A.

2.2.6.3 Gain Ratio

For instance, think about a characteristic with a novel identifier, for instance, customer_ID has zero info(D) considering unadulterated package. This enhances the information addition and makes silly allocating.

2.2.7 Random Forest Algorithm

Arbitrary backwoods are such a regulated AI count subject to bunch learning. Gathering learning is a sort of acknowledging where you join different kinds of counts or same figuring on various events to outline an even more significant forecast model. The arbitrary forest count combines various figuring of a comparable sort for instance different decision trees, achieving a timberland of trees, from this time forward the "Random Forest" [25].

2.2.7.1 How the Random Forest Algorithm Works

Below are the fundamental advances associated with playing out the random forest calculation:

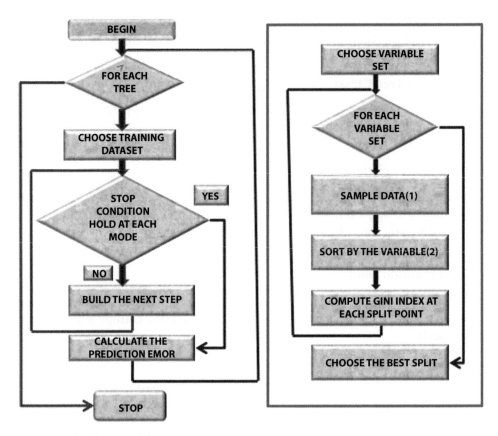

Figure 2.4 Random forest model.

1. Choose the N random records from the dataset.
2. Assemble a choice tree subjectto these N records.
3. Pick the quantity of trees you need in the calculation along with stages 1 and 2.
4. If there should arise an occurrence of a relapse issue, for another record, every tree in the forest finds an incentive of Y (yield). The last value is determined by considerable number of qualities anticipated by all the trees in forest. At last, the new value is relegated to the class that successes the greater part vote. Diagram representing the random forest model is given in Figure 2.4.

2.2.7.2   Advantage of Using Random Forest

In the same way, with any calculation, there are some preferences and inconveniences to utilizing it.

1. This estimation is not uneven; each tree is set up on a subset of data. Basically, the irregular forest count relies upon the force of "the gathering"; thusly, the general prejudice of the thinking is reduced.
2. This count is really consistent. Whether or not another data point is introduced in the dataset the overall count is not impacted.
3. The random forest calculation purposes numerical information.

2.2.7.3   *Disadvantage of Using the Random Forest*

The significant disservice of the random forests lies in their multifaceted nature. It needs considerably more computational assets, attributable to enormous trees combined.

2.2.7.3.1   Using Random Forest for Regression

In this segment, we will concentrate how Random forest can be utilized to take care of relapse issues utilizing scikit-learn. In the following area, we will take care of order issue by means of random forests.

Steps Involved:

1. Import libraries
2. Bringing in dataset
3. Getting ready data for training
4. Highlight scaling
5. Preparing the algorithm
6. Assessing the algorithm

2.2.8   Naive Bayes Classifier Algorithm

It relies upon Bayes as well as utilized for taking care of collection issues.
   Most part utilized for gathering incorporates getting ready dataset.

2.2.8.1   *For What Reason is it Called Naive Bayes?*

It is considered as naive in light of the fact that it recognizes the event of a specific section that is freed from the event of different highlights.
   Bayes: It is called Bayes since it depends on the norm of Bayes' Theorem.

2.2.8.2   *Disservices of Naive Bayes Classifier*

It expects highlights, self-administering, and immaterial, which cannot get to know the relationship between highlights. It will in general be used continuously desires in light of the fact that Naive Bayes Classifier is a vivacious understudy. It is utilized in text portrayal, for instance, Spam isolating and Sentiment examination.

2.2.9   Logistic Regression

2.2.9.1   *Logistic Regression for Machine Learning*

In this post, you will find the calculated decline calculation for AI. We can consider a Logistic Regression a Linear Regression model yet the Logistic Regression use a more unstable cost work, this cost capacity can be characterized as the "Sigmoid capacity" or otherwise called the "calculated capacity" rather than a straight capacity.

KNN is presumably the least perplexing computation utilized in backslide as well as order issue. This calculation uses orchestrate new data center subordinate around comparability measures (for instance, separation work). The content is distributed with neighbors.

2.2.10   Support Vector Machine

It is an achieved AI model, which utilizes characterization calculations for two-bunch arrangement issues. The architectural diagram for SVM is given in Figure 2.5.

Therefore, you are chipping away at a book order issue. You are refining your preparation information, and perhaps, you have even given stuff a shot utilizing Naive Bayes. However, presently you are feeling certain about your dataset and need to make it one stride further.

Points to be considered are as follows:

- Understand the hyperplane.
- Distinguish the privileged one.

2.2.11   Unsupervised Learning

The AI calculation follows up on data without direction. It bunches unsorted data as per similitude, examples, and contrasts with no earlier preparing or management. Since there is no preparation given to the machine, the machine itself finds the shrouded structure in unlabeled information and deciphers it. In this way, assume if the machine is furnished with the picture of a pen and pencil and its data is not accessible, then it tends to be arranged by the likenesses, examples, and contrasts. It is fundamentally separated based on pre-characterized ideas [29, 30]. The machine can gauge what sort of gatherings it can shape to separate.

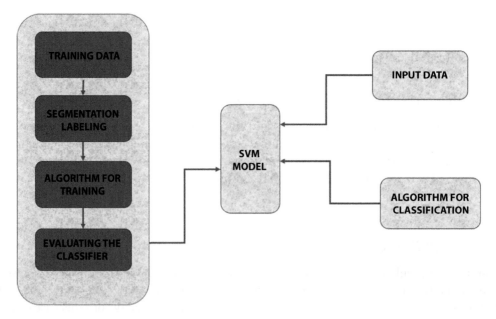

Figure 2.5 Diagram for support vector machine.

Unsupervised learning is used when the problem needs more amount of unlabeled information. For instance, internet-based life applications, for example, Twitter and Instagram, all have a lot of unlabeled information. Understanding the importance behind this information requires calculations that order the information dependent on the examples or groups it finds. This type of learning conducts an iterative procedure, breaking down information without human mediation. AI, in view of bunching and affiliation, is applied to distinguish undesirable email. The objective of an unsupervised learning calculation is to make a model that takes an element vector x as information and either changes it into another vector or into a worth that can be utilized to tackle a pragmatic issue.

Types of Unsupervised Algorithm:

- k-means clustering
- PCA (Principal Component Analysis)

2.2.11.1 Clustering

AI issues manage an assortment of new information on the off chance that it is extended to a more extensive setting. For instance, think about the instance of picture acknowledgment for lions and felines. The information some of the time traverses' pictures of these creatures, yet in addition may have creatures with comparative similarity. This will introduce issues in preparing calculations. They may perceive the creatures wrongly and the learning exactness goes down altogether. At the point when you are attempting to find out about something, state music, one methodology may be to search for important gatherings or assortments. You may sort out music by class, while your companion may compose music by decade. How you decide to aggregate things causes you to see more about them as individual bits of music. You may find that you have a profound liking for underground rock and further separate the class into various methodologies or music from various areas. Then again, your companion may take a gander at music from the 1980s and have the option to see how the music across types around then was affected by the socio-political atmosphere. In the two cases, you and your companion have gotten the hang of something intriguing about music, despite the fact that you adopted various strategies. In AI as well, we frequently bunch models as an initial step to comprehend a subject (informational collection) in an AI framework. Gathering unlabeled models is called grouping. As the models are unlabeled, grouping depends on unaided AI. In the event that the models are marked, at that point clustering becomes arrangement.

Before you can amass comparable models, you first need to discover comparative models. You can quantify similitude between models by consolidating the models' element information into a measurement, called a closeness measure. At the point when every model is characterized by a couple of highlights, it is anything but difficult to quantify comparability. For instance, you can discover comparable books by their writers. As the quantity of highlights increments, making a comparability measure turns out to be more mind boggling. We will later perceive how to make a comparability measure in various situations.

2.2.11.1.1   Clustering Algorithms

It includes consequently finding regular gathering in information. In contrast to regulated learning (like prescient demonstrating), clustering calculations just decipher the info information and discover regular gatherings or groups in highlight space. While picking a clustering calculation, you ought to consider whether the calculation scales to your dataset. Datasets in AI can have a large number of models, however not all grouping calculations scale productively. Many clustering calculations work by figuring the similitude between all sets of models. This implies their runtime increments as the square of the quantity of models n, signified as O(n2) in unpredictability documentation. O(n2) calculations are not down to earth when the quantity of models is in millions. This course centers around the k-implies calculation, which has a multifaceted nature of O(n), implying that the calculation scales straight with near class of calculations called unaided learning calculations are utilized. These calculations work with information that are moderately new and obscure information so as to find out additional. This class is again partitioned into two classifications, grouping, and affiliation (additionally called Apriori). This article talks about clustering calculations and its sorts much of the time utilized in unaided AI. A group is frequently a territory of thickness in the component space where models from the area (perceptions or lines of information) are nearer to the bunch than different groups. The bunch may have a middle (the centroid) that is an example or a point highlight space and may have a limit or degree. Clustering is the way toward sorting out items (information) into bunches dependent on comparative highlights inside the individuals (information purposes) of the gathering. To get this, consider the model referenced before. The lions can be isolated into bunches dependent on the species (Indian lion, Barbary lion, Congo lion, etc.). The properties (species, in the above case) learn the lion type. In addition, this is relevant to other ML issues which show similitude in information. This is the objective of unaided learning. Gathering a lot of new information dependent on likenesses among them relies upon the prerequisites indicated by the client for ML.

2.2.11.1.2   Types of Clustering
Clustering Algorithms

There are numerous kinds of clustering calculations. Numerous calculations use similitude or separation measures between models in the element space with an end goal to find thick locales of perceptions. Thusly, it is regularly acceptable practice to scale information before utilizing grouping calculations.

2.2.11.1.2.1   HIERARCHICAL CLUSTERING ALGORITHMS

These calculations have bunches arranged in a request dependent on the progressive system in information likeness perceptions. Various leveled grouping is arranged into two kinds: divisive (top-down) clustering and agglomerative (base up) grouping. The previous kind gatherings all information focuses/perceptions in a solitary bunch and partitions it into two groups on least likeness between them, while the last sort doles out each datum point as a bunch itself and totals the most comparable groups. This essentially implies uniting the correct information.

2.2.11.1.3   Uses of Clustering

Grouping has a huge number of utilizations spread across different spaces. Probably, the most mainstream uses of clustering are as follows:

- Recommendation motors
- Market division
- Social organize examination
- Search result gathering
- Medical imaging
- Image division
- Anomaly identification

2.2.11.2   PCA in Machine Learning

PCA is a broadly utilized procedure for dimensionality decrease of the enormous informational collection. Lessening the quantity of parts or highlights costs some precision and then again, it makes the enormous informational index more straightforward, simple to investigate and imagine. In addition, it diminishes the computational multifaceted nature of the model which makes AI calculations run quicker. It is consistently an inquiry and far from being obviously true how much precision it is relinquishing to get less perplexing and decreased measurements informational collection. We do not have a fixed response for this anyway we attempt to keep the vast majority of the fluctuation while picking the last arrangement of segments. It is a solo learning calculation as the headings of these segments is determined simply from the informative list of capabilities with no reference to reaction factors. The quantity of highlight mixes is equivalent to the quantity of measurements of the dataset and as a rule set the greatest number of PCAs which can be developed. PCA is a broadly utilized procedure for dimensionality decrease of the huge informational index. Diminishing the quantity of segments or highlights costs some precision and then again, it makes the huge informational collection more straightforward, simple to investigate and picture. In addition, it lessens the computational intricacy of the model which makes AI calculations run quicker. It is consistently an inquiry and easy to refute how much precision it is giving up to get less unpredictable and decreased measurements informational collection. We do not have a fixed response for this anyway we attempt to keep the vast majority of the change intuitively.

- Dimensionality: It is the quantity of irregular factors in a dataset or just the quantity of highlights, or rather more essentially, the quantity of sections presents in your dataset.
- Correlation: It indicates how unequivocally two factors are identified with one another. Positive demonstrates that when one variable expands, different increments too, while negative shows different declines on expanding the previous. In addition, the modulus estimation of shows the quality of connection.
- Orthogonal: Uncorrelated to one another, i.e., relationship between any pair of factors is 0.

- Eigenvectors: Eigenvectors and eigenvalues are in itself a major area, how about we confine ourselves to the information on a similar which we would require here. In this way, consider a non-zero vector v. It is an eigenvector of a square grid An, if Av is a scalar various of v. Or, on the other hand, essentially

$$Av = \lambda v$$

High dimensionality implies that the dataset has an enormous number of highlights. The essential issue related with high-dimensionality in the AI field is model overfitting, which lessens the capacity to sum up past the models in the preparation set. The capacity to sum up accurately turns out to be exponentially harder as the dimensionality of the preparation dataset develops, as the preparation set covers a lessening part of the info space. Models likewise become more productive as the decreased list of capabilities supports learning rates and lessens calculation costs by evacuating repetitive highlights. PCA can likewise be utilized to channel uproarious datasets, for example, picture pressure. The primary head part communicates the most measure of change. Each extra part communicates not so much difference but rather more commotion, so speaking to the information with a littler subset of head segments protects the sign and disposes of the clamor. PCA is a solo learning calculation as the bearings of these parts is determined absolutely from the informative list of capabilities with no reference to reaction factors. The quantity of highlight blends is equivalent to the quantity of measurements of the dataset and as a rule set the most extreme number of PCAs which can be built.

Covariance Matrix: This system involves the covariances between the arrangements of elements.

2.2.11.2.1 Properties of Principal Component

All things considered, a chief section can be portrayed as a straight blend of undeniably weighted watched factors. The yields of PCA are these basic sections, the amount of which is not actually or comparable to the number of remarkable variables.

The PCs have some significant properties which are recorded underneath:

1. The PCs are essentially the immediate mixes of the main factors, the heaps vector in this blend is actually the eigenvector found which subsequently satisfies the standard of least squares.
2. The PCs are even, starting at now discussed.
3. The assortment present in the PCs decay as we move from the principal PC to the last one, hereafter the centrality.

2.2.11.2.2 Steps Involved in PCA

Head part investigation (PCA) is a quantifiable framework that uses a balanced change, which changes over a great deal of related elements to a ton of uncorrelated variables. PCA is a most by and large used gadget in exploratory data examination and in AI for perceptive models. Likewise, PCA is an independent authentic strategy used to investigate the inter-relations among a great deal of variables. It is generally called a general factor examination where backslide chooses a line of best fit.

PCA make us understand the associations between the parameters and good in gathering image related data. It does the implementation more efficiently and also shows the associated parameters. ML is helpful in working with image related data efficiently [2].

These are fundamentally performed on square symmetric grid method [3]. It tends to be an unadulterated entry of squares and cross items network or covariance grid or correlation framework. A connection grid is utilized if the individual difference varies a lot.

Destinations of PCA

- It is a technique which diminishes space from a greater number of factors to a smaller number of components.
- PCA is actually measurement decrease process however there is no assurance that the measurement is interpretable.
- Main task in this PCA is to do noteworthy connection with the chief sum.

2.2.11.2.3   Steps in PCA

Stage 1: Standardization

The purpose of movement is to extent of the unending starting elements with the objective that each and every assessment.

Even unequivocally, inspiration driving is essential extremely. Thusly, changing the data to essentially indistinguishable factors can solve this problem.

At the point, when the standardization is done, all the elements will be changed to a comparable scale.

Stage 2: Calculation of Covariance Matrix

The purpose is to perceive the components by fluctuating to check whether there is any association between them. Since to a great extent, factors are significantly associated.

Three-dimensional Data

It is really an indication of the covariance that issues:
- If it is positive, then the two factors increment or lessening together (associated).
- If it is negative, then one increments when different reductions (inversely corresponded).

Presently, we realize that the covariance lattice is not in excess of a table that rundowns the relationships between all the potential sets of factors, how about we move to the following stage.

Stage 3: Eigenvectors and Eigenvalues

Eigenvectors plus eigenvalues are straight variables-based math ideas that we have to register from the covariance lattice so as to decide the chief parts of the information. Before getting to the clarification of these ideas, we should initially comprehend what we mean by head parts.

Head segments are new factors that are developed as direct mixes or blends of the underlying factors. These mixes are done so the factors (i.e., head parts) are not connected and massive data inside the underlying factors is pressed or packed into the primary segments.

Sorting out data, therefore, will permit you to lessen dimensionality without losing a lot of data, and this by disposing of the segments with uninformed and thinking about the rest of the segments as your new factors.

2.2.12   Semi-Supervised Learning

This type of learning was a combination of directed and solo learning. It utilizes modest marked information, which gives the advantages of both unaided and regulated learning while at the same time evading the difficulties of finding a lot of named information. That implies you can prepare a model to name information without utilizing as much named preparing information.

2.2.12.1   What is Semi-Supervised Clustering?

Bunch investigation is a strategy that looks to parcel a dataset into homogenous subgroups, which means gathering comparable information with the information in each gathering being not the same as different gatherings. Clustering is customarily done utilizing unsupervised techniques. Since the objective is to distinguish likenesses and contrasts between information focuses, it does not require any given data about the connections inside the information.

Be that as it may, there are circumstances where a portion of the bunch marks, result factors, or data about connections inside the information are the place where clustering comes in. This clustering utilizes some known group data so as to order other unlabeled information, which means it utilizes both named and unlabeled information simply like semi-supervised AI.

2.2.12.2   How Semi-Supervised Learning Functions?

The way that semi-supervised learning figures out how to prepare the model with less named preparing information than supervised learning is by utilizing pseudo marking. This can consolidate numerous neural system models and preparing techniques. Here is the means by which it works:

- Train the model with the limited quantity of marked preparing information simply like you would in supervised learning, until it gives you great outcomes.

- At that point use it with the unlabeled preparing dataset to anticipate the yields, which are pseudo marks since they may not be very precise.
- Connection the marks from the named preparing information with the pseudo names made in the past advance.
- Connection the information contributions to the marked preparing information with the contributions to the unlabeled information.
- At that point, train the model a similar route as you did with the named set before all else so as to diminish the blunder and improve the model's precision [12].

2.2.13   Reinforcement Learning

- Reinforcement learning is an exceptionally intriguing sort of learning. There is no answer key which can determine what is correct. Be that as it may, the fortification learning specialist despite everything concludes acceptable behaviour to play out its undertaking. This AI procedure is tied in with taking activities that are reasonable and expand the prize in a specific circumstance. It is the point at which the student gets prizes and disciplines for their activities.
- This describes about the procedure being implemented, on the grounds that it best in tackling the issue at hand. The machine can execute activities in each state. Various activities bring various rewards and could likewise move the machine to another condition of nature. The objective of reinforcement learning calculation is to become familiar with an approach. Reinforcement learning takes care of a specific sort of issue where dynamic is successive, and the objective is long haul, for example, game playing, mechanical autonomy, asset the executives, or coordination. The overview architecture of ML is given in Figure 2.6.

2.2.13.1   Artificial Intelligence

AI is firmly identified with numerical insights; however, it contrasts from measurements in a few significant manners. That measurable model is thought to be utilized by one way or another to take care of the down to earth issue. Not at all like insights, AI will, in general, be in arrangement with huge, complex datasets (for example, a dataset of a huge number of pictures, each comprising of a huge number of pixels). Thus, AI and particularly profound learning, shows relatively minimal numerical hypothesis. It is a hands-on discipline where thoughts are demonstrated exactly more regularly than hypothetically AI is firmly identified with numerical insights; however, it varies from measurements in a few significant manners.

AI is simply any code or technique or algorithm that can able to change the mimic, develop and demonstrate human behaviour. Machines can do all the things which humans do. AI enables the machine to think.

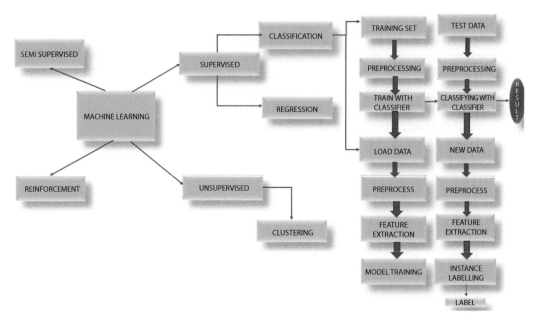

Figure 2.6 Machine learning architecture.

2.2.13.2   Deep Learning

Deep learning is very useful if you are handling with designs as well as any kind of unstructured information. Deep learning complex neural systems describes how the how the human mind works, so PCs can be prepared to manage ineffectively characterized reflections and issues. Neural network systems are utilized in many image related applications. AI necessitates that the correct arrangement of information be applied to a learning procedure. An association does not have huge information to utilize AI methods; in any case, enormous amount of data can help improve exactness of models [26]. What people think can they make the machine to learn like human that was the main idea behind deep learning. In deep

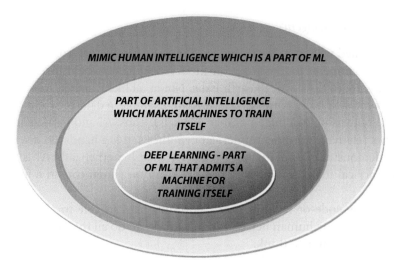

Figure 2.7 Deep learning vs. artificial intelligence vs. machine learning.

learning, to create an architecture which is called as multi-neural network architecture, so at the end of the day, we are using multi-neural network architecture and we are creating deep learning. The main aim using this application of ML and deep learning is to derive artificial application. Many classification algorithms use CNN for efficiently classifying the data [13, 15]. The comparison diagram of deep learning, AI, and ML is given in Figure 2.7.

2.2.13.3 Points of Interest of Machine Learning

1. **Useful in understanding patterns as well as examples**
   AI can work with large amount of data or information and helpful in identifying the explicit patterns which is evident to people. For example: Amazon.
2. **Less human interaction**
   It is an enabling machine and it takes less expectations and also improves the calculations done. It knows how to handle the new problems when faced.
3. **Constant Improving changes**
   As ML after good understanding, they keep of increasing the efficiency and also work on good productivity. If you want to do any continuous improvement in finding out the climatic changes, you keep on doing the predictions again and again, which gives the better results.
4. **Taking care of information**
   AI calculations can deal with data which can solve any complex kinds of problems. This is used to face unique and complex scenarios.

2.2.13.4 Why Machine Learning is Popular

The cutting-edge difficulties are "high-dimensional" in nature. With rich information sources, it is critical to fabricate models that tackle issues in high-dimensional space. Through it, the models can be incorporated into working programming. It bolsters the sorts of items that are being requested by the business. A ton of data is accessible today due to IoT. Long-range interpersonal communication, online journals, digital recordings, or some other hotspot so far as that is concerned. Likewise, to keep that data in an organized way, it is additionally important to stay aware of the pattern and increase a serious edge. In the event that bungles like missing valuable substance happens, at that point, a business may lose a fortune. Nobody knows where the thought can emerge out of and strike you [27, 28]. With the bounty of information, individuals enjoying and hating were totally remembered before the chief idea of making a show. There is a bounty of information at the present time and information that is being gathered and put away. "Data overburden" is occurring and quality is the thing which everybody is searching for. So much data are spamming us every day, beginning from email, long-range informal communication, websites, and digital recordings (and the ceaseless rundown). It is difficult to keep up through and through, however, not any longer. Presently, there will be no more worries about missing valuable substance and the pressure of finding and following the best substance there is. With ML techniques, the instruments to find and suggest the most important substance are available. So now, you can beat the data overburden, take a secondary lounge since everything is arranged. ML helps in identifying the diseases, which is a very important part in agriculture [1]. ML algorithms is helpful in diagnosis of plant diseases [1].

2.2.13.5   Test Utilizations of ML

Web search: positioning page dependent on what you are destined to tap on.

1. **Detecting Patterns**
   Web crawlers are utilizing AI for design identifications that help to copy content. They basic characteristics of inferior quality substance are identified.
2. **Picture Search to Understand Photos**
   This assignment is ideal for AI since it can dissect shading and shape examples and pair that with any current blueprint. This is the means by which Google cannot just list pictures for Google Image list items, yet in addition controls its component that permits clients search by a photograph record (rather than a book inquiry).
3. **Recognizing Similarities Between Words in a Search Query**
   Not exclusively does inquiry information get utilized by AI to distinguish and customize a client's later questions, it likewise makes designs in information that shapes the list items different clients are getting. For instance, a learning-based web index that utilizes supervised AI strategies like determination based and survey-based calculations to develop a positioning model. Data recovery methods are utilized to recover the applicable URLs by creeping the Web in a Breadth-First way, which are then utilized as preparing information for the directed and survey-based AI strategies to prepare the crawler. The Gradient Descent Algorithm to think about the two methods and for result investigation [8].

- **Finance:** conclude who to send what charge card offers to; assessment of hazard using a loan offer; step-by-step instructions to choose where to put away cash. AI has had productive applications in fund a long time before the appearance of portable banking applications, capable chat bots, or web search tools. Given the high volume, precise authentic records, and quantitative nature of the money world, barely any ventures are more qualified for man-made brainpower. There are more uses instances of AI in account than any time in recent memory, a pattern propagated by more available registering force and more open AI devices (for example, Google's TensorFlow). AI in money may do something amazing, despite the fact that there is no enchantment behind it [2].
- **E-trade:** Predicting client beat. Regardless of whether an exchange is deceitful. Appropriate from the maker, entire merchant, retailer, and purchaser to the shoppers, each individual knows the best he needs and how promote he can get in this aggressive world. Both E-business and M-commerce stages are very mindful of the market structure, showcase practices, and advertise patterns, the deviations, and assorted varieties. This can be ascribed just to the help of AI. The required information and calculations are in their range to assume the parts of a vender or a purchaser [7].
- **Robotics:** how to deal with vulnerability in new situations; self-ruling; self-driving vehicle. By joining Robotics Process Automation with psychological advancements, for example, AI, discourse acknowledgment, and common language handling, organizations can mechanize higher-request

undertakings with AI help that in the past required the perceptual and judgment abilities of humans. Companies enough comprehend that expanding business effectiveness and representative efficiency is of incomparable significance to flourish in a profoundly serious computerized condition. Any procedure can be computerized as long as there is a reasonable working method available. Companies are starting to comprehend that expanding business proficiency and representative efficiency is of incomparable significance to flourish in a profoundly serious advanced condition [4].

- **Information extraction:** Ask inquiries over databases over the web. Data extraction is worried about applying normal language preparing to naturally separate the fundamental subtleties from text records. An incredible burden of recent methodologies and inherent reliance area [5].
- **Space investigation:** space tests and radio stargazing. The eager present moment and somewhere near engineering territories, structure of smart operators in space absolutely being one of them. In any case, in the present status of the workmanship, a few open issues and gems can be recognized [6]. Through incremental frequent mining, human activity patterns are detected; it is intensively used in healthcare applications [4].

2.3   Future Research Directions

The future research direction in healthcare has numerous challenges and research is still ongoing. The research direction for privacy and communication between medical personnel is discussed in this section.

2.3.1   Privacy

The medical data which is recorded is having meaningful information. More medical data is stored in dataset. Each data should be more secure. The data should be more confidential, not sharable, authentic data. If the data is modified by unknown user, then it will lead to more issues. The important research in healthcare is securing the data from unwanted users.

2.3.2   Accuracy

The prediction of disease is a complicated task. The disease is predicted with the help of existing data. If the data is fake data, then the prediction accuracy is less. The data for the healthcare application should be checked clearly.

References

1. Rajesh, B., Sai Vardhan, M.V., Sujihelen, L., Leaf Disease Detection and Classification by Decision Tree. *2020 4th International Conference on Trends in Electronics and Informatics (ICOEI) (48184)*, Tirunelveli, India, pp. 705–708, 2020.

2. Asrith, M. J. N. V. S. K., Reddy, K.P., Sujihelen, Face Recognition and Weapon Detection from Very Low-Resolution Image. *2018 International Conference on Emerging Trends and Innovations In Engineering And Technological Research (ICETIETR)*, Ernakulam, pp. 1–5, 2018.

3. Zhou, Y., Liu, D., Huang, T., Survey of face detection on low-quality images. In *2018 13th IEEE international conference on automatic face & gesture recognition (FG 2018)*, IEEE, pp. 769–773, May 2018.

4. Sai, G.V.K., Kumar, P.S., Mary, Dr. A. V. A., Incremental Frequent Mining Human Activity Patterns for Healthcare Applications. *IOP Conf. Series: Materials Science and Engineering*, vol. 590, p. 012050, 2019.

5. Mohanaprasad, K. and Cubert, A.C., Fuzzy Means Clusterisation Of Land Based On User Priority. *Int. J. Appl. Eng. Res.*, 10, 9, 8166–8170, 2015.

6. Prasad, Dr. K. M., Efficient Dynamic Clustering Mechanism through Unfathomed Clustering Techniques. *J. Adv. Res. Dyn. Control Syst.*, 10, 06-Special Issue, 934–939, 2018.

7. Prasad, K.M. and Sabitha, Dr. R., Formulation of Clusters with Minimum Limitations Using AKM and LIC Techniques. *J. Pharm. Sci. Res.*, 9, 1, 70–73, 2017.

8. Prasad, K.M. and Manalina, Effective Clusters Culled Out Through Algorithmic Implementations. *ARPN J. Eng. Appl. Sci., 9*, 11, 5574–5579, 2016.

9. Selvan, M.P., Navadurga, N., Prasanna, N.L., An Efficient Model for Predicting Student Dropout using Data Mining and Machine Learning Techniques. *IJITEE*, 8, 9S2, 750–752, July 2019.

10. Roobini, M.S. and Lakshmi, M., Application of Big Data for Medical Data Analysis Using Hadoop Environment., in: *International Conference on Intelligent Data Communication Technologies and Internet of Things*, Springer, Cham, pp. 1128–1135, 2018.

11. Roobini, M.S. and Lakshmi, Dr. M., Classification of Diabetes Mellitus using Soft Computing and Machine Learning Techniques. *IJITEE*, 8, 6S4, 1541–1545, 2019.

12. Roobini, M.S. and Lakshmi, M., Exploration of Magnetic Resonance Imaging for Prognosis of Alzheimer's Disease Using Convolutional Neural Network, in: *Artificial Intelligence Techniques for Advanced Computing Applications*, pp. 153–165, Springer, Singapore, 2021.

13. Christy, A., Jesudoss, A., Roobini, M.S., Driver Helper: A Mobile Based Application to Predict Driver Behaviour Using Classification Techniques. *Int. J. Adv. Sci. Technol.*, 29, 7s, 4429–4438, 2020. Retrieved from http://sersc.org/journals/index.php/IJAST/article/view/25672.

14. Vignesh, R., Deepa, D., Anitha, P., Divya, S., Roobini, S., Dynamic Enforcement of Causal Consistency for a Geo-Replicated Cloud Storage System. *Int. J. Electr. Eng. Technol.*, 11, 3, 181–185, 2020. Available at SSRN: https://ssrn.com/abstract=3636026.

15. Vignesh, R., Deepa, D., Samhitha, B.K., Mana, S.C., Jose, J., Roobini, M.S., Movie success prediction using recommendation techniques. *J. Electr. Eng. Technol.*, 11, 4, 422–426, Article ID: IJEET_11_04_047, June 2020.

16. El Abbadi, N.K. and Al Saadi, E.H., Blood Vessels Extraction using Mathematical Morphology. *J. Comput. Sci.*, 9, 10, 1389–1395, 2013.

17. Adarsh, P. and Jeyakumari, D., Multiclass SVM-Based Automated Diagnosis of Diabetic Retinopathy. *Proceedings of the IEEE International conference on Communication and Signal Processing*, India, pp. 206–210, 2013.

18. Agrawal, A. and McKibbin, M., Purtscher's retinopathy: epidemiology, clinical features and outcome. *Br. J. Ophthalmol.*, 91, 11, 1456–1459, 2007.

19. Agurto, C., Murray, V., Yu, H., Wigdahl, J., Pattichis, M., Nemeth, S., Barriga, E.S., Soliz, P., A Multiscale Optimization Approach to Detect Exudates in the Macula. *IEEE J. Biomed. Health Inform.*, 18, 4, 1328–1336, 2014.

20. Sopharak, A., Dailey, M.N., Uyyanonvara, B., Barman, S., Williamson, T., Nwe, K.T., Moe, Y.A., Machine learning approach to automatic exudate detection in retinal images from diabetic patients. *J. Mod. Opt.*, 57, 2, 124–135, 2010.

21. Akita, K. and Kuga, H., A computer method of understanding ocular fundus images. *Pattern Recognit.*, 15, 431–443, 1982.

22. Alghamdi, H.S., Tang, L., Jin, Y., Ensemble Learning Optimization for Diabetic Retinopathy Image Analysis. *Proceedings of the tenth international conference on computer vision theory and applications*, pp. 471–477, 2015.

23. Antal, B., Lazar, I., Hajdu, A., An adaptive weighting approach for ensemble-based detection of microaneurysms in color fundus images. *Proceedings of 34th IEEE International Conference of the IEEE EMBS*, San Diego, pp. 5955–5958, 2012.

24. Ayyachamy, S. and Manivannan, V.S., Distance Measures for image Retrieval. *Int. J. Imaging Syst. Technol.*, 23, 1, 9–21, 2013.

25. BahadarKhan, K., Khaliq, A.A., Shahid, M., A Morphological Hessian Based Approach for Retinal Blood Vessels Segmentation and Denoising Using Region Based Otsu Thresholding. *PloS One*, 11, 7, 1–19, 2016.

26. McDonald, C., Machine Learning: A Survey of current Techniques 1989. *Artif. Intell. Rev.*, 3, 243–280, 1989.

27. Bonarini, A., Lazaric, A., Montrone, F., Restelli, M., Reinforcement distribution in fuzzy Q-learning. *Fuzzy Sets Syst. Spec. Issue Fuzzy Sets Interdiscip. Percept. Intell.*, 160, 10, 1420–1443, 2009.

28. Ge, L., Zhang, H., Xu, G., Yu, W., Chen, C., Blasch, E.P., Towards map reduce based machine learning techniques for processing massive network threat monitoring data, in: *Networking for Big Data*, CRC Press & Francis Group, USA, 2015.

29. Nguyen, G., Dlugolinsky, S., Bobák, M., Tran, V., Machine learning and deep learning frameworks and libraries for large-scale data mining: a survey. *Artif. Intell. Rev.*, 52, 77–124, 2019.

30. Qiu, J., Wu, Q., Ding, G., Xu, Y., Feng, S., A survey of machine learning for big data processing. *EURASIP J. Adv. Signal Process.*, 2016, 67, 1–16, 2016.

3

Dengue Incidence Rate Prediction Using Nonlinear Autoregressive Neural Network Time Series Model

S. Dhamodharavadhani* and R. Rathipriya†

Department of Computer Science, Periyar University, Salem, India

Abstract

Dengue fever is a vector-borne disease spread by female mosquitoes in tropical and sub-tropical regions worldwide. The leading cause of severe illness and death in children and adults predicts dengue. Therefore, this chapter aims to develop a model for dengue incidence rate (DIR) prediction using Nonlinear Autoregressive (NAR)–Neural Network Time Series (NNTS) and to study the performance of this proposed model by adjusting configuration parameters of neural networks such as the different types of training algorithms with different parameter setup. This model avoids the problem of overfitting and enhances prediction accuracy. The results have shown that the NAR-NNTS model using Bayesian Regularization (BR) outperformed other training algorithms for the same.

Keywords: Neural network, nonlinear autoregressive, neural network time series, Levenberg-Marquardt, Bayesian regularization, scaled conjugate gradient, dengue prediction, time series model

3.1 Introduction

Dengue is an insect viral infection. It is one of the leading conditions of severe illness and deaths in some states of India, particularly in Tamil Nadu [1]. The dengue virus (DENV) causes dengue disease in children and adults. Four closely related viruses cause dengue, i.e., DEN1, DEN2, DEN3, and DEN4. For the past decade, the global incidence of dengue has overgrown, and about 50% of the population in the world is now at risk. World Health Organization's report said that there is no specific treatment for dengue [2]. However, early detection of dengue possibility and access to proper medical assistance lowers fatality rates below 1%.

The reports were given by the (National Vector Borne Disease Control Programme), which highlights that majority of dengue cases found Tamil Nadu, India, in recent years [1, 2]. The Government of Tamil Nadu has planned to make efficient and necessary measures to control dengue outbreaks in the state. However, currently, there is no systematic

---

Corresponding author: vadhanimca2011@gmail.com

†*Corresponding author*: rathipriyar@gmail.com

Tushar H. Jaware, K. Sarat Kumar, Ravindra D. Badgujar and Svetlin Antonov (eds.) Medical Imaging and Health Informatics, (47–68) © 2022 Scrivener Publishing LLC

process to assess the dengue outbreak seasons or conditions in advance. Therefore, this work aims to develop a DIR Prediction System using historical time series data.

Nonlinear Autoregressive (NAR)–Neural Network Time Series (NNTS) model [3] is used to implement the proposed DIR prediction system. It also reduces the morbidity and mortality associated with this. This model can identify patterns in nonlinear past variables and forecast future variables. In this work, the accuracy this model has tested with the different parameter setup under specific heuristics to construct an optimal NAR-NNTS model for achieving a highly accurate number of dengue cases.

The rest of this paper is arranged as follows: Section 3.2 expounds on the related work. Section 3.3, presents the methods needed for the proposed work. Section 3.4 illustrates the working of the DIR prediction model and discusses and analyzes the experimental results. The proposed work is summarized in Section 3.5.

3.2   Related Literature Study

This section mainly discussed to emphasize and summarize without making any further inputs to the claims and ideas of existing works relating to the proposed project. These are as follows:

In [4], the authors proposed a nonlinear autoregressive recurrent neural network with exogenous input (NARX) to forecast solar radiation (SR) in Mutah city. Hourly, weather data of three variables (temperature, wind speed, and humidity) were collected for the year 2015 was used. Mean squared error (MSE) and regression (R) values measures were used to evaluate the model. It has developed an SR prediction model based on the NARX with exogenous inputs T, W, and H, which had very efficient and accurate. The result had shown that the estimated SR had a very close correlation to the exposed SR.

In [5], the Zika epidemic outbreak was predicted for America at weekly temporal and spatial resolution data. The features like population, epidemiological data, travel details, vector habitat, and socioeconomic information were used to develop the prediction model. The authors suggested that the proposed outbreak prediction model was more accurate for short term prediction.

In [6], the authors proposed NAR and NARX model with different network parameter values. They used wind dataset which was collected from different meteorological stations. To evaluate the different network setup, the error measures (like MAE, MAPE, and RMSE) and R2 were used. NARNN and NARXNN both models had low error value [7–12]. However, when associated with logsig (NAR) and tansig (NAR), it has a smaller error value. In addition, the average value of logsig-NARXNN has provided a lower value than tansig NARXNN.

The authors [1] forecast the dengue cases using NN model. They analyzed dengue cases' trend using physical characteristics such as temperatures, humidity, and rainfall from the Singaporean National Environment Agency (NEA). To measure the performance of the model, root mean square (RMS) errors, and correlation value used. The result of this model proved to be a very effective prediction model.

In [13], fuzzy association rule mining method is used for malaria prediction in Korea. They used four types of datasets such as epidemiological, meteorological, climatic, and socio-economic. The results were measured by sensitivity, positive predictive value (PPV), and F-score. The fuzzy association rule mining method was significantly better than other classical methods like Holt-Winters methods and decision Trees, for the high-class and medium-class categories.

In [14], the authors used NAR and NARX to predict energy dataset. They used past energy consumption database for this work. Both models were efficient for energy consumption prediction. They also to improve the accuracy of the prediction model using exogenous data.

Authors in [15] predicted the SR using various nonlinear prediction models using wavelet and fuzzy models, ANFIS, RF, kNN, and ANN. A daily direct SR dataset is taken. NARX model was better than other nonlinear models because it gives better results.

In [2], the author to predict the dengue cases used ensemble models with different models such as statistical models, NN models, and naive models. They used clinical and meteorological data from 2000 to 2016. Dengue dataset was taken from São Paulo State Department of Health. Meteorological data are taken from the National Institute of Meteorology. This result illustrated one month ahead of predictions.

In another work, a set of recursive neural networks [16] proposed to predict the hospital bed status. The findings of this prediction models suggested that automated monitoring and decision-making be used in hospitals. In [3], the authors hybridized NAR with a discrete wavelet transform to forecast the transformer oil dissolved gas applications. The data were collected from the transformer equipment. The proposed model predicted multiple future values.

In [17], the NARX-ANN model was implemented and compared with the five different ANN training algorithms. The perfect fit optimization technique for predicting the soil temperature was discovered using this model. In [18], the authors proposed a hybrid model associated with ARIMA and NAR model which was used for both linearity and nonlinearity data sets. Three dengue endemic locations, namely, Philippines, San Juan, and the Iquitos, gathered the dengue cases dataset. Authors have claimed that the proposed hybrid models ensure high accuracy value.

They investigate the NARX associated with multi-objective genetic algorithm optimization to damp modes of oscillation in the local and inter-area. This analysis is used to fine-tune a Power System Stabilizer (PSS) in a four-machine network with two zones [19]. In [20], they suggested framework is to develop the Smart Prognosis Dengue (SPD) AI Technology System Program for Predicting Constant Dengue Disease. The impact of climate on the risk of dengue fever was investigated in this study (DHF) [21].

In the current research [22], the most essential climate elements which donate to dengue epidemics have been identified. In [23], they developed four models using generalized linear model analysis of the negative binomials. Rainfall, temperature, and humidity are considered as independent factors, with the dengue cases reported monthly as the dependent variable [24]. They developed a web-based simulation tool for dengue illness [25].

Authors [26] proposed an Event Orient Scheduling Algorithm (EOSA) based on developing a no memory continuous time model to obtain a timely response. Within this article [27], it discussed the use of intelligent technology in system failure diagnosis, and it motivated the use of fuzzy neural network technology in system failure detection. It also revealed the principles of fuzzy and neural network technology. In this paper [28], to increase robustness and generality, to suggested neural network training methods based on multiple training samples variability.

3.2.1   Limitations of Existing Works

The identified limitations from the existing works are as follows:

- Statistic-based time series analysis methods are applied frequently for dengue disease prediction. However, it has lower predictive accuracy.
- In a very few existing works, ANN was used, but it also has lower predictive accuracy.
- These methods are not able to handle the nonlinear dynamics in the dataset.

3.2.2   Contributions of Proposed Methodology

Therefore, in this present study, NAR-NNTS model is used to predict the dengue incidence rate (DIR). This DIR will be categorized into two classes: low and high. NAR-NNTS is the combination of the neural network and time series analysis method. This model helps to detect patterns in nonlinear dataset and forecast the values based on previous data. To investigate the performance of this proposed model by adjusting configuration parameters of neural networks such as the different types of training algorithms and different network parameters. It avoids the chances of data over-fitting and enhances forecast reliability. The main purpose of this study is that trained and evaluated the performance of NAR-NNTS with different sets of neural network configuration parameters and training algorithms. The following shows the advantages of this work:

- In the dengue dataset where non-linearity occurs, the NAR-NNTS model is able to capture the model in a nonlinear dataset.
- NAR-NNTS model is one of the varieties of neural networks that mainly depend on non-linearity.
- It handles the nonlinear time series data very effectively.
- The experimental result helps the health sector to know dengue case dynamics and improve surveillance by developing early warning systems.
- NAR-NNTS with BR becomes more accurate when trained with more data points, and overfitting problem occurs. So, it is suitable for modeling the small data.
- The proposed scheme has the possible to deliver an analytical tool for evaluating the existing level of cases and intensity, as well as assist government and healthcare professionals in making smart decisions to reduce DIRs.

3.3   Methods and Materials

3.3.1   NAR-NNTS

NAR-NNTS is a time series model for forecasting the future series based on the input series [6]. It is effective for nonlinear data and uses a re-feeding method to forecast the future values. The expected value could be used as a starting point for further projections at more distant time intervals [2, 3]. This model is developed and implemented through an open-loop network using true target values as input and approving significant improvement in training. After training, the open loop network was converted to a closed-loop model and the feedback the network is given a new predicted value as input. Figure 3.1 is displaying the NAR neural network architecture. In this chapter, NAR-NNTS model used to predict the dengue cases as follows: There is one input in the network structure (dengue cases at x1) and one output (y1 to be predicted dengue cases) [10, 29]. DIR prediction workflow is discussed in Figure 3.2, and algorithm steps are discussed in Figure 3.3.

Figure 3.4 illustrates the structure of the NAR-NN open loop and closed loop, respectively. In general, a training network's effectiveness is dependent on the back-propagation mechanism and applies a descent time-step process. Even during forecast, it has a low error and good accuracy.

$$(ts) = f(y\,(ts - 1), ..., y(ts - d)) \tag{3.1}$$

Equation (3.1) denotes as the mathematical form of NAR, the new predicted values are represented as y(ts), and past values are denoted as y(ts − 1), y(ts − 2), ..., y(ts − d), NAR-NNTS model developing an overfitting value as time series x(ts − 1), x(ts − 2), ..., x(ts − d), where d is the time delay parameter.

This chapter primarily aims at evaluating the model performance (NAR-NNTS) with the different network parameters and training algorithms for prediction of DIR in Tamil Nadu, India, at the highest level accuracy. The NAR model is represented in Table 3.1. Table 3.2 describes the basic parameters setup of the NAR model, such as training algorithms, activation function, error measure, and epoch.

3.3.2 Fit/Train the Model

The effectiveness of the proposed NAR-NNTS model tested on the dengue case time series dataset. The configuration parameters for the NAR-NNTS model are shown in Table 3.3. Each neural network creates different initial weights for neurons, whose size ranges from 10, 15, to 20 neurons. In this study, random initial weight size set as 2, 3, and 4, and the maximum neuron size is 20. This configuration applied to the NAR-NNTS model with

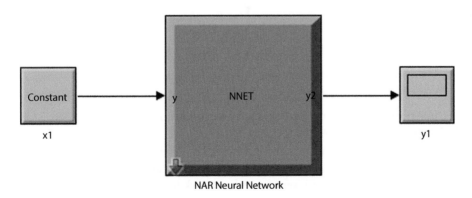

Figure 3.1 Architecture of NAR neural network.

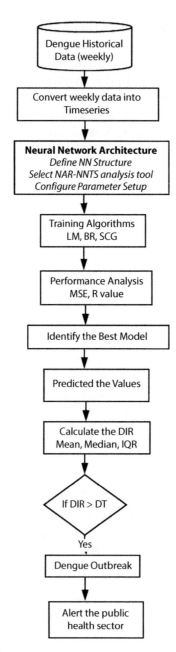

Figure 3.2 Flow chart for DIR prediction system.

different three training functions, and the data division ratio is 70/15/15 (i.e., 70% for training, 15% for validating, and 15% for testing).

The performance study comprises two phases, namely, development phase and analyze phase. In the development stage, the NAR-NNTS model is developed with the three different training algorithms and different neural network topology parameters of delay (i.e., number of hidden layers). In the analyzing stage, the developed NAR-NNTS model is based

Algorithm: NAR-NNTS Model using DIR Prediction

Input: Dengue weekly Data (1990-2009)

   Step: 1 Convert weekly data into timeseries data
   Step: 2 Data divided into three set of target (training, validation, testing)
   Step: 3 Bulit Network Architecture
        Define number of hidden neurons and delays
   Step: 4 Choose the training algorithm (LM, BR, SCG) and train the
        network model
   Step: 5 Evaluate the Network model (MSE, R value)
   Step: 6 Identify the best network model
   Step: 7 Predicted the future value (best model)
   Step: 8 Calculate DIR (mean, median, IQR)
   Step: 9 If DIR > DT = Dengue outbreak

Output: Dengue outbreak (Alert the public sector)

Figure 3.3 Algorithm for NAR-NTTS using DIR prediction.

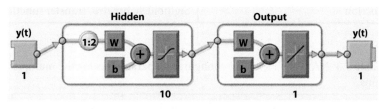

Open loop of NAR network

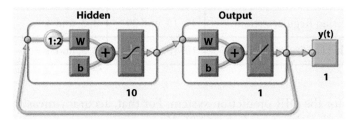

Closed loop of NAR network

Figure 3.4 Architecture of open and closed loop of NAR network.

Table 3.1 NAR-NNTS model.

Model	Network model	Equations	Description
NAR	y(t)	$y(t) = f(y(t - 1), \ldots, y(t - d))$	Predict values y(t) given d previous values of y(t).

Table 3.2 Parameters setup for NAR model structure.

Parameters	Setup value
Training Algorithms	Levenberg-Marquardt (LM) Bayesian Regularization (BR) Scaled Conjugate Gradient (SCG)
Number of input, hidden, and output layers	1, 1, 1
Normalization interval	0.05–0.95
Error measure	MSE
Learning rate	0.1
Error goal	$0.001(110^{-3})$
Epoch	1,000
Momentum	0.95
Activation function	Sigmoid symmetric transfer function

Table 3.3 NAR-NNTS model configuration parameters for the multiple runs.

Training algorithms	Neuron size	Initial weight
Levenberg-Marquardt	10, 15, and 20	2, 3, and 4
Bayesian Regularization	10, 15, and 20	2, 3, and 4
Scaled Conjugate Gradient	10, 15, and 20	2, 3, and 4

on the measures for the DIR prediction system. For that, accuracy measures such as MSE and R value are used in the second phase [30–35].

3.3.3   Training Algorithms

3.3.3.1   Levenberg-Marquardt (LM) Algorithm

For nonlinear data and optimization issues, the LM algorithm is widely implemented [1–4]. It delivers a nonlinear least-squares minimization as a result, representing the minimization function specified in Equation (3.2). The supervised LM is best for nonlinear datasets.

$$f(x) = \frac{1}{2} \sum_{j=1}^{m} r_j^2(x)$$

$$(3.2)$$

Here, x is represented as a vector, r_j referred to as model residuals, and it is supposed that $m \geq n$.

3.3.3.2 Bayesian Regularization (BR) Algorithm

The BR algorithm consumes two parameters denoted as α and β, named Bayesian hyper-parameters; the function of this is to show the extent to which the training algorithm must desire: one of the minimum weights or one of the minimum errors [1–4]. In Equation (3.3) defined as the process of the BR algorithm. Here, S_e is represented as the amount of squared error, and S_w is represented amount of squared weight.

$$C(i) = \alpha \cdot S_w + \beta \cdot S_e \tag{3.3}$$

3.3.3.3 Scaled Conjugate Gradient (SCG) Algorithm

This algorithm is a fully automated system that excludes critical app-dependent factors. To minimize a time-consuming path scan that is used by CGL and BFGS in each execution to decide a suitable phase size [1–4]. The conjugate gradient approaches include a training procedure for feed-forward neural networks. The SCG algorithm searches in the route that permits the unbiased value to reduce as quickly as feasible during the first epoch but instead conducts a route search to gather the intervals for use as a phase in the approach focusing. In Equation (3.4), x, α, and g are variables to optimize.

$$x_{i+1} = x_i + \alpha_i g_i \tag{3.4}$$

3.3.4 DIR Prediction

In [8, 12], "the Disease Incidence Rate (DIR)" was used to categorize the infectious period into either the HIGH incidence group or the LOW incidence group. The dengue data is normalized by using Equation (3.5):

$$DIR = \frac{alpha * (new\ dengue\ reported\ case\ counts)}{Population} \tag{3.5}$$

where alpha is some constant scaling factor. The IQR-based threshold (T) is used to determine the high and low classes.

The interquartile range (IQR): Generally, when a dataset has outliers or extreme values, one can summarize a typical value using the median as different to the mean. Similarly, when a dataset has outliers, variability is often summarized by a statistical measure called the IQR, which is the difference between the first and third quartiles.

The first quartile Q_1 is the value in the dataset that holds 25% of the values below it. The third quartile Q_3 is the value in the dataset that holds 25% of the values above it. The

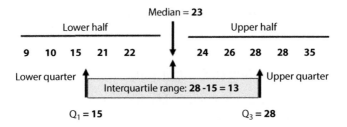

Figure 3.5 An example of IQR calculation.

quartiles can be determined using the median. The IQR is defined as Equation (3.6) and an example for IQR in Figure 3.5.

$$Interquartile\ range\ (IQR) = Q3 - Q1 \qquad (3.6)$$

3.4   Result Discussions

3.4.1   Dataset Description

In this research, based on dengue historical dataset for Tamil Nadu, India, is taken for analyses to predict the DIR using Equation (3.4). The dataset contains weekly dengue case data for the periods 1990–2009 of Tamil Nadu, India. A sample dataset is shown in Table 3.4. Figure 3.6 shows the historical time series pattern of the dengue dataset that is graphically represented.

Table 3.4 Sample dataset.

week_start_date	total_cases
4/30/1990	4
5/7/1990	5
5/14/1990	4
5/21/1990	3
5/28/1990	6
6/4/1990	2
6/11/1990	4
6/18/1990	5
6/25/1990	10
7/2/1990	6

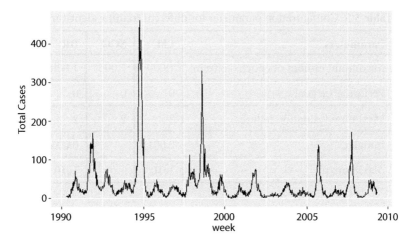

Figure 3.6 Historical time series pattern of dengue dataset.

3.4.2   Evaluation Measure for NAR-NNTS Models

The measures like R value and MSE taken for study to evaluate the performance of the models. The results of these NAR-NNTS models tabulated in the following section.

MSE is the average squared difference between the observed value and the predicted value. Equation (3.7) represents n is the number of data points, Yi is the observed value, and Y is the predicted value [23–25, 35–38].

$$\mathrm{MSE} = \frac{1}{n}\sum_{i=1}^{n}(Yi - \bar{Y}i)^2 \tag{3.7}$$

R value is a correlation coefficient, which is used to measure the strength of a linear association between the observed value and predicted value. In Equation (3.8), R = 1 indicates a perfect positive correlation, and the R= −1 means a perfect negative correlation. The R closer to 1 indicates a strong relationship between the observed and predicted value [23, 24, 35–38].

$$R = \frac{n\left(\sum PA\right) - \left(\sum P\right)\left(\sum A\right)}{\sqrt{\left(n\sum P^2 - \left(\sum P\right)^2\right)\left[n\sum A^2 - \left(\sum A\right)^2\right]}} \tag{3.8}$$

3.4.3   Analysis of Results

Dengue cases data are available from the year 1990 to 2009. For the training process, the 19-year data divided into three categories: training data, validation data, and testing data

Table 3.5 Configuration parameter for different training algorithms.

Parameters	LM	SCG	BR
Maximum number of epochs to train	1,000	1,000	1,000
Performance goal	0	0	0
Maximum validation failures	2	2	2
Initial μ	0.001	-	0.005
Maximum μ	1e10	-	1e10

with ratio 70:15:15 (13/3/3) years of data. Table 3.5 represented the configuration parameters with values for LM, SCG, and BR training algorithms.

The results of performance measures in train, validation, and test dengue dataset reported in the following features.

- NAR-NNTS model used MSE for forecasting error.
- The complexity of the model for number of neuron in the hidden layer (H).
- Training time and convergence speed (epoch) of the model.
- Performance measure and R value used to find the accuracy of the model.

Here, the prediction model with lower MSE value is the better model. If MSE is zero, then there is no error between output and target values. The higher value in R (i.e., R=1) indicates a close relationship between output and target values.

Tables 3.6 to 3.8 show the parameters of the NAR-NNTS model, namely, epoch, time, performance, gradient, Mu, and validation checks with three types of training algorithms. Each algorithm is implemented by different hidden layer and initial weight.

Tables 3.9 to 3.11 illustrate the MSE error performance assessment of NAR-NNTS with the three training algorithms, hidden neuron count and initial weight such that (10:2, 15:3, and 20:4). The MSE error metric was evaluated to identify the best prediction model for DIR prediction in this study. The best prediction model has been found to be the NAR-NNTS model with BR (H = 20, IW = 4). Since it has a smaller MSE than the other two algorithms under consideration. From these results, it has observed that the best configuration parameter setup for the NAR-NNTS model is hidden neuron count 20, and the initial weight is 4 while predicting DIR.

Tables 3.12 to 3.14 illustrate the R value to validate the NAR-NNTS model performance with three algorithms, hidden neuron count and initial weight such that (10:2, 15:3, and 20:4). The R value accuracy metric is utilized in this study to choose the best DIR prediction model. The NAR-NNTS model with BR (H = 20, IW = 4) proved that the best prediction model. Since its R value is greater (i.e. much closer to 1) than the other two training algorithms in this study. From these results, it has observed that the best configuration parameter setup for the NAR-NNTS model is hidden neuron count 20, and the initial weight is 4 while predicting DIR.

Figure 3.7 shows the validation performance of BR (H = 20, IW = 4). It signifies that there is the minimal error between validation and the training and testing phases. Hence,

Table 3.6 Performance of Levenberg-Marquardt (LM) training algorithm.

	LM	LM	LM
	(H = 10, IW = 2)	(H = 15, IW = 3)	(H = 20, IW = 4)
EPOCH	11	12	10
Time (in s)	.01	0.0	.01
Performance (e^{+05})	129	89.0	72.7
Gradient (e^{+06})	445	88.6	644
Mu	1.00	1.00	0.10
Validation checks	6	6	6

Table 3.7 Performance of Bayesian regularization (BR) training algorithm.

	BR	BR	BR
	(H = 10, IW = 2)	(H = 15, IW = 3)	(H = 20, IW = 4)
EPOCH	827	1,000	1,000
Time (in s)	0.05	0.06	0.08
Performance (e^{+05})	85.1	80.3	62.9
Gradient (e^{+06})	0.355	0.689	5.45
Mu	5.00	0.500	0.500
Effective # param	34.5	48.2	80.5
Sum squared param	426	244	568

Table 3.8 Performance of scaled conjugate gradient (SCG) training algorithm.

	SCG	SCG	SCG
	(H = 10, IW = 2)	(H = 15, IW = 3)	(H = 20, IW = 4)
EPOCH	18	20	18
Time (in s)	.00	.00	.00
Performance (e^{+05})	357	631	678
Gradient (e^{+06})	1.55	3.03	7.54
Validation checks	6	6	6

Table 3.9 NAR-NNTS model performance error for training algorithms (H = 10, IW = 2).

Algorithms	Training MSE	Validation MSE	Testing MSE
LM	134.54122e−0	323.66689e−0	309.57222e−0
BR	8.29E+01	0.00E+00	1.22E+03
SCG	3.42E+02	1.22E+02	2.71E+02

Table 3.10 NAR-NNTS model performance error for training algorithms (H = 15, IW = 3).

Algorithms	Training MSE	Validation MSE	Testing MSE
LM	130.04505e−0	473.70605e−0	496.01571e−0
BR	77.11606e−0	0.00000e−0	784.89183e−0
SCG	265.89106e−0	232.55524e−0	393.20655e−0

Table 3.11 NAR-NNTS model performance error for training algorithms (H = 20, IW = 4).

Algorithms	Training MSE	Validation MSE	Testing MSE
LM	130.04505e−0	473.70605e−0	496.01571e−0
BR	48.95888e−0	0.00000e−0	5404.62756e−0
SCG	296.39444e−0	214.15394e−0	315.23157e−0

Table 3.12 Validation of the NAR-NNTS model's performance using three training algorithms (H = 10, IW = 2).

Algorithms	Training R value	Validation R value	Testing R value
LM	9.65462e−1	9.37618e−1	9.49567e−1
BR	9.82221e−1	0.00000e−0	8.45763e−1
SCG	9.48709e−1	9.53431e−1	8.50648e−1

Table 3.13 Validation of the NAR-NNTS model's performance using three training algorithms (H = 15, IW = 3).

Algorithms	Training R value	Validation R value	Testing R value
LM	9.72489e−1	9.43792e−1	9.59286e−1
BR	9.85128e−1	0.00000e−0	8.49553e−1
SCG	9.45084e−1	8.94334e−1	9.70598e−1

Table 3.14 Validation of the NAR-NNTS model's performance using three Training Algorithms (H = 20, IW = 4).

Algorithms	Training R value	Validation R value	Testing R value
LM	9.81053e−1	8.98602e−1	9.48386e−1
BR	9.87581e−1	0.00000e−0	9.57680e−1
SCG	9.40291e−1	9.54368e−1	9.57295e−1

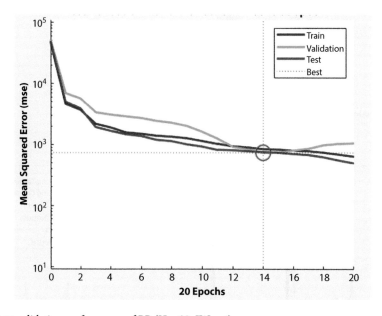

Figure 3.7 Best validation performance of BR (H = 20, IW = 4).

the result shows that the validation curve and test curve are almost the same. They are also reduces training and validation errors until the highlighted epoch.

Autocorrelations error for the BR algorithm is shown in Figure 3.6. This explains how time-related errors in forecasting. For a good prediction model, the autocorrelation function should only have a non-zero value and should occur at zero.

Figure 3.8 shows the regression plot for BR (H = 20, IW = 4). It represents the relationship between the output of the network model and the target. Hence, the black color rounds represent dengue case observation; the red line represents the model best fit and dotted line as the predicted target value.

In Figure 3.9, x-axis represented the time, and the y-axis represented output, targets, and errors. It also displays the training, testing, and validation time points that were chosen.

Figure 3.10 plot demonstrates the autocorrelation function of the error. This explains how the errors of prediction are linked in time. There should be the minimal non-zero value of the autocorrelation function for a perfect prediction model, and it should occur at zero delays.

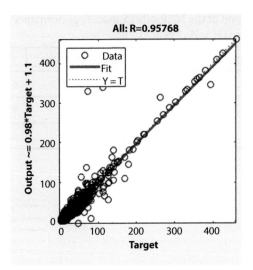

Figure 3.8 Regression plot.

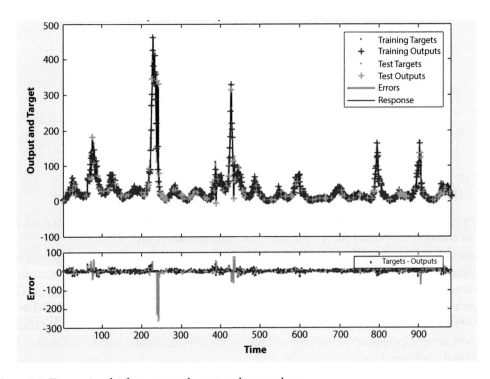

Figure 3.9 Time series plot for output and target, and error values.

The cross-correlation input-error method shows in Figure 3.11 how the input series x(t) compares the errors. All correlations should be zero for a perfect prediction model. If the feedback is consistent with the error, then the prediction should be improved, perhaps by increasing the number of delays in the delay lines that have been tapped. All correlations

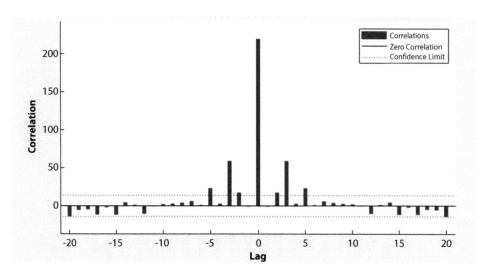

Figure 3.10 Autocorrelation of error 1.

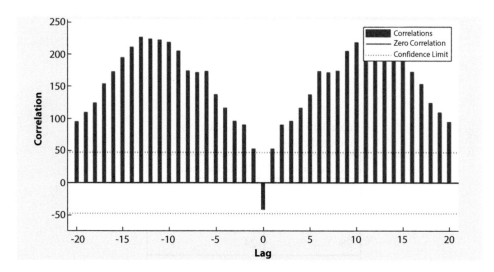

Figure 3.11 Correlation between input 1 and error 1 = target 1 − output 1.

fall within the boundaries of confidence around zero in this case. The error histogram plot displays in Figure 3.12.

The best results (0.00048 for MSE and 9.8 for R value) are obtained for a dataset of weekly, a NAR-NNTS model consisting of 20 H and 3 IW on the input and the hidden layers, function, which included the sigmoid activation function, and tansig activation function and random IW for the output layer. Table 3.15 represents as the dengue actual cases vs dengue predicted cases.

To categorize the DIR into a low and high class, three different decision thresholds (DTs) (or classification thresholds) such as mean, median, and IQR used. Its performance was given in Table 3.16. The following are observed from the results:

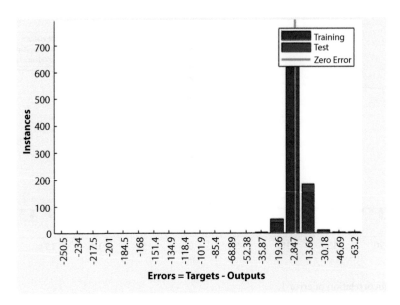

Figure 3.12 Error histogram with 20 bins.

Table 3.15 Dengue actual cases vs.
predicted cases.

Actual cases	Predicted cases
35	36
28	25
28	24
22	18
26	22
24	28
9	12
21	18
10	9
15	18

Table 3.16 Performance
of different DIR decision
threshold.

DIR classification		
Mean	**Median**	**IQR**
High	High	High
Low	High	Low
Low	High	Low
Low	Low	Low
Low	High	Low
Low	High	High
Low	Low	Low
Low	Low	Low
Low	Low	Low
Low	Low	Low

- Mean used as DT, 90% of values fell into a low class.
- IQR used as DT, 80% of values fell into a low class.
- Median used as DT, 50% of values fell into a low class.

Thus, the median-based DT has a significant role in discriminating the class than the other two. Because all almost of the predicted values are low, then there is no use of developing the prediction. Therefore, the median-based DT is better for early warning of dengue outbreak.

3.5   Conclusion and Future Work

This chapter proposed a NAR-NNTS model for the DIR prediction using dengue cases time series data for Tamil Nadu, India. The main purpose of this study NAR-NNTS model with three different training algorithms (LM, BR, and SCG) based on different initial weights for 10, 15, and 20 neurons, and random initial weight size set as 2, 3, and 4 weights. They evaluated the performance of NAR-NNTS with different sets of neural network configuration parameters and training algorithms by using MSE and R value. The MSE values of these models were compared, and it was noticed that the NAR-NNTS with Bayesian Regularization (BR) performed better for the DIR prediction. The DIR has categorized into two classes, namely, low and high using mean, median, and IQR of the dataset.

The finding of this study is that the NAR-NNTS model is suitable for a nonlinear dataset. In this study, NAR-NNTS model performance for dengue datasets found that almost no single neural network model can be declared the best, since it is totally dependent on the network parameters and the data features. The proposed scheme can serve as a prediction tool for determining the present level of infection and harshness and also assist government and healthcare personnel in actionable insights to prevent DIR in India.

Deep learning forecasting models will be implemented in the future to improve dengue DIR prediction accuracy. In addition, for developing the high precision prediction model for the dengue infection data, this analysis will be strengthened by incorporating many aspects or parameters such as demographic and economic parameters, environmental features, and weather factors (temperature, humidity, wind speed, and rainfall).

Acknowledgment

The first author acknowledges the UGC-Special Assistance Programme (SAP) for the financial support to her research under the UGC-SAP at the level of DRS-II [Ref. No. F.5-6/2018/DRS-II (SAP-II)], 26 July 2018, in the Department of Computer Science, Periyar University.

Data Availability: https://dengueforecasting.noaa.gov/

Conflict of Interest: Authors have no conflict of interest.

References

1. Aburas, H.M., Cetiner, B.G., Sari, M., Erratum to 'Dengue confirmed-cases prediction: A neural network model' [Expert Systems with Applications 37 (2010) 4256–4260]. *Expert Syst. Appl.*, 38, 10, 13495–13496, 2011.
2. Baquero, O.S., Santana, L.M.R., Chiaravalloti-Neto, F., Dengue forecasting in São Paulo city with generalized additive models, artificial neural networks and seasonal autoregressive integrated moving average models. *PloS One*, 13, 4, 1–12, 2018.
3. Pereira, F., Bezerra, F., Junior, S., Santos, J., Chabu, I., Souza, G., Micerino, F., Nabeta, S., Nonlinear Autoregressive Neural Network Models for Prediction of Transformer Oil-Dissolved Gas Concentrations. *Energies*, 11, 7, 1691, 2018.
4. Al-Sbou, Y.A. and Alawasa, K.M., Nonlinear Autoregressive Recurrent Neural Network Model For Solar Radiation Prediction. *Int. J. Appl. Eng. Res.*, 12, 4518–4527, 2017.
5. Akhtar, M., Kraemer, M.U.G., Gardner, L.M., A dynamic neural network model for predicting the risk of Zika in real-time. *BMC Med.*, 17, 1, 1–16, 2019.
6. Dhamodharavadhani, S. and Rathipriya, R., A pilot study on climate data analysis tools and softwar. *2016 Online International Conference on Green Engineering and Technologies (IC-GET)*, 2016.
7. Dhamodharavadhani, S. and Rathipriya, R., Forecasting Dengue Incidence Rate in Tamil Nadu Using ARIMA Time Series Model. *Mach. Learn. Healthc.*, 750, 187–202, 2020.
8. Dhamodharavadhani, S. and Rathipriya, R., Region-Wise Rainfall Prediction Using MapReduce-Based Exponential Smoothing Techniques. *Adv. Intell. Syst. Comput.*, 750, 229–239, 2018.

9. Sivabalan, S., Dhamodharavadhani, S., Rathipriya, R., Arbitrary walk with minimum length based route identification scheme in graph structure for opportunistic wireless sensor network, in: *Swarm Intelligence for Resource Management in Internet of Things*, pp. 47–63, 2020.

10. Sivabalan, S., Dhamodharavadhani, S., Rathipriya, R., Opportunistic Forward Routing Using Bee Colony Optimization. *Int. J. Comput. Sci. Eng.*, 7, 5, 1820–1827, 2019.

11. Kaleeswaran, V., Dhamodharavadhani, S., Rathipriya, R., A Comparative Study of Activation Functions and Training Algorithm of NAR Neural Network for Crop Prediction. *2020 4th International Conference on Electronics, Communication and Aerospace Technology (ICECA)*, 2020.

12. Kaleeswaran, V., Dhamodharavadhani, S., Rathipriya, R., Multi-crop Selection Model Using Binary Particle Swarm Optimization, in: *Innovative Data Communication Technologies and Application*, pp. 57–68, 2021.

13. Sarkar, R., Julai, S., Hossain, S., Chong, W.T., Rahman, M., A Comparative Study of Activation Functions of NAR and NARX Neural Network for Long-Term Wind Speed Forecasting in Malaysia. *Math. Probl. Eng.*, 2019, 1–14, 2019.

14. Buczak, A.L., Baugher, B., Guven, E., Ramac-Thomas, L.C., Elbert, Y., , S. M. Babin, and "Fuzzy association rule mining and classification for the prediction of malaria in South Korea. *BMC Med. Inform. Decis. Mak.*, 15, 1, 1–17, 2015.

15. Ruiz, L., Cuéllar, M., Calvo-Flores, M., Jiménez, M., An Application of Non-Linear Autoregressive Neural Networks to Predict Energy Consumption in Public Buildings. *Energies*, 9, 9, 684, 2016.

16. Boussaada, Z., Curea, O., Remaci, A., Camblong, H., Bellaaj, N.M., A Nonlinear Autoregressive Exogenous (NARX) Neural Network Model for the Prediction of the Daily Direct Solar Radiation. *Energies*, 11, 3, 620, 2018.

17. Kutafina, E., Bechtold, I., Jonas, S.M., Recursive neural networks in hospital bed occupancy forecasting. *BMC Med. Inf. Decision Making*, 19, 1, 1–10, 2019.

18. Al-Allaf, O.N.A. and Abdalkader, S.A., Nonlinear Autoregressive Neural Network For Estimation Soil Temperature: A Comparison Of Different Optimization Neural Network Algorithms. *Ubicc J.*, 42–51, 2011.

19. Chakraborty, T., Chattopadhyay, S., Ghosh, I., Forecasting dengue epidemics using a hybrid methodology. *Phys. A: Stat. Mech. Appl.*, 527, 121266, 2019.

20. Carbonera, L.F.B., Bernardon, D.P., Karnikowski, D.D.C., Farret, F.A., The nonlinear autoregressive network with exogenous inputs (NARX) neural network to damp power system oscillations. *Int. Trans. Electr. Energy Syst.*, 11, 620, 2020.

21. Divya, A. and Lavanya, S., Real-Time Dengue Prediction Using Machine Learning. *Indian J. Public Health Res. Dev.*, 11, 2, 406, 2020.

22. Siregar, F.A. and Makmur, T., Time Series Analysis of Dengue Hemorrhagic Fever Cases and Climate: a Model for Dengue Prediction. *Journal of Physics: Conference Series*, vol. 1235, p. 012072, 2019.

23. Nejad, F.Y. and Varathan, K.D., Identification of Significant Climatic Risk Factors and Machine Learning Models in Dengue Outbreak Prediction. *preprint*, 21, 141, 2020.

24. Nigam, R., Climatic Factors influencing Dengue cases in Bhopal city: A model for Dengue prediction. *Int. J. Infect. Dis.*, 73, 197, 2018.

25. Nigam, R.K., Role of Climatic factors influencing Dengue incidence in central India: A model for Dengue prediction. *Access Microbiol.*, 2, 2, 852–860, 2020.

26. Shah, Z.M., Dengue Influx Management and Analysis Tools (Dimat) For Prediction Modelling And Simulation. *ICMR 2019 8th International Conference on Multidisciplinary Research*, 2020.

27. Zhilenkov, A. and Chernyi, S., Models and algorithms of the positioning and trajectory stabilization system with elements of structural analysis for robotic applications, in: *International Journal of Embedded Systems*, vol. 11, p. 806, 2019.

28. Xu, X., Cao, D., Zhou, Y., Gao, J., Application of neural network algorithm in fault diagnosis of mechanical intelligence. *Mech. Syst. Signal Process.*, 141, 106625, 2020.

29. Seibold, C., Samek, W., Hilsmann, A., Eisert, P., Accurate and robust neural networks for face morphing attack detection. *J. Inf. Secur. Appl.*, 53, 102526, 2020.

30. Dhamodharavadhani, S. and Rathipriya, R., Variable Selection Method for Regression Models Using Computational Intelligence Techniques, in: *Handbook of Research on Machine and Deep Learning Applications for Cyber Security Advances in Information Security, Privacy, and Ethics*, pp. 416–436, 2020.

31. Dhamodharavadhani, S. and Rathipriya, R., Enhanced Logistic Regression (ELR) Model for Big Data, in: *Handbook of Research on Big Data Clustering and Machine Learning Advances in Data Mining and Database Management*, pp. 152–176, 2020.

32. Dhamodharavadhani, S. and Rathipriya, R., Region-Wise Rainfall Prediction Using MapReduce-Based Exponential Smoothing Techniques, in: *Advances in Intelligent Systems and Computing Advances in Big Data and Cloud Computing*, pp. 229–239, 2019.

33. Devipriya, R., Dhamodharavadhani, S., Selvi, S., SEIR model FOR COVID-19 Epidemic using DELAY differential equation. *Journal of Physics: Conference Series*, 1767, 012005, 2021.

34. Dhamodharavadhani, S. and Rathipriya, R., Novel COVID-19 Mortality Rate Prediction (MRP) Model for India Using Regression Model With Optimized Hyperparameter. *J. Cases Inf. Technol.*, 23, 4, 1–12, 2021.

35. Dhamodharavadhani, S., A survey on clustering based routing protocols in Mobile ad hoc networks. *2015 International Conference on Soft-Computing and Networks Security (ICSNS)*, 2015.

36. Namasudra, S. and Rathipriya, R., Nonlinear Neural Network Based Forecasting Model for Predicting COVID-19 Cases. *Neural Process Lett.*, 1–21, 2021, https://doi.org/10.1007/s11063-021-10495-w.

37. Dhamodharavadhani, S., Rathipriya, R., Chatterjee, J.M., COVID-19 Mortality Rate Prediction for India Using Statistical Neural Network Models, in: *Frontiers in Public Health*, vol. 8, 2020.

38. Dhamodharavadhani, S. and Rathipriya, R., COVID-19 mortality rate prediction for India using statistical neural networks and gaussian process regression model, in: *African Health Sciences*, vol. 21, 2021.

4

Early Detection of Breast Cancer Using Machine Learning

G. Lavanya* and G. Thilagavathi

¹Sri Ramakrishna Engineering College, Coimbatore, India
²Coimbatore Institute of Technology, Coimbatore, India

Abstract

According to cancer statistics, breast cancer is the major causes of cancer death, and it is more common in women than men. A total of 50% to 80% of breast cancer usually occur over the age of 50. However, nowadays, due to lack of proper nutrition, it arises earlier. It is very difficult to diagnose for the doctors. If it is identified earlier, then we have better treatment and cure earlier. Usually, two different abnormalities present in the breast cancer micro calcification and masses. Out of which, first condition, i.e., micro calcification, is considered as benign so there is less severity. We can treat the problem and cannot spread to different parts of the body. However, masses present in breast adipose tissue make it difficulty to identify, and it can be spread to other regions of the human body [1, 2]. To overcome this problem, computer-aided diagnosis was developed, which is very helpful for the doctors and act as a second reader to the radiologist who is helpful for identifying the breast cancer which makes the right decisions at a correct time. Here, modality chosen to detect breast cancer is mammography.

Current breast cancer identification methods are experimental so it is difficult to diagnose it earlier. Hence, the use of probability algorithm is to identify and diagnose the breast cancer. It is divided into three categories: feature extraction, segmentation, and classification [11–13]. Features are extracted with the help of human expert knowledge. Various features were extracted from the image. Extracted features are segmented with the help of segmentation algorithm. Here, we have chosen region growing segmentation algorithm, and after segmentation, it goes to final step classifier. Probability classifier such as naive bayes was selected as a classifier that helps to identify the breast cancer mass [5–10].

The radial basis function neural network (RBFNN) is an artificial neural network, which helps to classify the abnormal region, and it has good knowledge and estimate capabilities. Probabilistic classifier such as naive Bayes algorithm was selected, and it is based on the Bayes theorem. With the help of probability based theorem, we can predict the feature and also does not affect the other. Based on probabilistic model, it can able to solve the problem. It works well and also better for complex situations. The proposed method provides an accuracy of 92% with naive Bayes classifier and 93% with RBFNN classifier.

Keywords: Breast cancer, CAD, RBFN, neural network, naive Bayes classifier, mammogram, region growing

Corresponding author: lavanyagangadharan@gmail.com

Tushar H. Jaware, K. Sarat Kumar, Ravindra D. Badgujar and Svetlin Antonov (eds.) Medical Imaging and Health Informatics, (69–82) © 2022 Scrivener Publishing LLC

4.1   Introduction

Machine learning approach was used to identify the masses in the breast cancer. computer-aided diagnosis (CAD) system was developed, which helps to doctors and radiologist to reduce their time for identifying the cancer. Based on the system, doctors can identify early stage of cancer and treatment option was taken based on that. Use of digitized images can detect the cancer without required painful procedures like biopsy. With the help of our system, the chances of recovery are too high.

4.1.1   Objective

In breast cancer, cells present in the breast started to grow abnormally in that region. Thus, here, mammography imaging modality was chosen to identify the cancer present in the region. Most commonly, breast cancer started in milk-producing ducts, but cancer occurs in the lobule region or in the tissue.

With the help of machine learning techniques, it identifies the problem earlier and gives solutions for it. It also saves time.

4.1.2   Anatomy of Breast

It consist of various parts such as lobes, glandular tissue, milk ducts, nipple, areolae, blood vessel, lymph vessel, and nerves. Breast is made up of 20 lobes; it is present like wheel. There is a smaller part of tissue found inside lobes, which contains glands that produce milk with the help of nipples. The areola is surrounding region of nipple. Blood vessels supply blood to all the regions in around the breasts and human body. Lymph vessels are a fluid that helps the body's immune system to fight against the infection as shown in Figure 4.1.

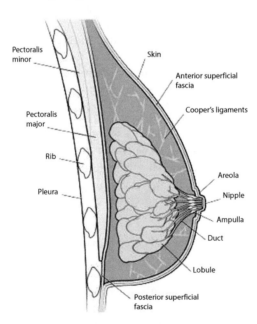

Figure 4.1 Anatomy of breast.

4.1.3   Breast Imaging Modalities

Digital mammography is considered as screening tool to detect the cancer stages. However, there are various techniques to identify the breast cancer such as magnetic resonance image and ultrasound imaging. However, here, mammography was selected due to their advantages such as efficiency; CAD system was employed and easily diagnostic.

The mammography projection of the breast can be done at two projections: mediolateral view, i.e., we can able to view side view clearly, and cranio-caudal, which helps to view from top to bottom.

In cranial view, cassette is placed under the bottom of the breast. Sometimes, it does not show correctly related to chest wall but medio-lateral view can be taken at side view. It is possible to view the pectoral muscles also. Hence, here, we have chosen medio-lateral oblique images that are taken to analyze the breast cancer. Signs of breast cancer include lump in the breast, nipple discharge, and changes in the shape of the nipple or breast.

4.2   Methodology

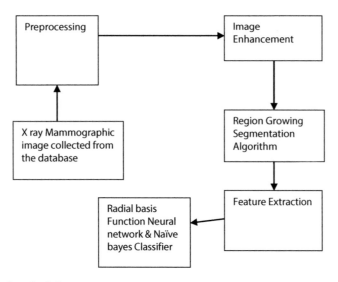

Figure 4.2 Proposed methodology.

4.2.1   Database

Images were collected from the database and the proposed methodology as shown in Figure 4.2.

4.2.2   Image Pre-Processing

An artifact removing is a histogram-based approach that is applied to the region of interest that helps to remove the artifacts appeared in the segmented area as bright spots.

Contrast enhancement can also be done mapping the pixel intensity due to that improves the contrast of the image.

4.3   Segmentation

Next step is segmentation, which partitioning the images further into classification of breast cancer. CAD is another important segmentation system. Segmentation helps to portioning of images in to subsets. Complete automation of the CAD system provides better facilities to identify earlier. Accuracy of segmentation is also considered very due to that more number of features can be extracted which will be useful for discriminating the images, based on that, decision was made whether benign or malignant lesions [3, 4, 14–16, 20, 21, 23–25].

Algorithms to be followed in region growing
Step 1: Initially, choose the seed pixel based on some criteria.
Step 2: Identify neighbouring pixels and if it is similar, add them to the region.
Step 3: Steps were repeated untill all the regions are allocated.

4.4   Feature Extraction

- Once segmentation is completed, various features were identified such as mean, median, and standard deviation, which help to identify the masses present in the breast cancer. We have taken various features related to geometry and texture, whch were identified [19].
- The mammographic features of breast masses are quite complex and difficult to extract. Here, we have consider 11 geometric features and analyzed 12 textural features.
- Textural features are fundamental property, which helps to extract the various features to correctly classify tumoral masses.

4.5   Classification

4.5.1   Naive Bayes Neural Network Classifier

Dataset was collected from breast cancer Wisconsin dataset, which contains various image datasets that can be selected for training and testing phase. Naive Bayes classifier is based on the Bayes' theorem; it assumes the independence between each and every pair of features from the dataset [17, 18, 22, 26–31].

$$C = \frac{\text{argmax}}{C} P(C_i|X) \frac{P(X|C_i) \cdot P(C_i)}{P(X)}$$

$$P(X|C_i)=\prod_{k=1}^{d} P(X_k|C_i)$$

The accuracy and performance of the classifier was 91.3%.

4.5.2   Radial Basis Function Neural Network

Radial basis function neural network (RBFNN) is an artificial neural network with use of Gaussian activation function. It consists of three layers input layer, hidden layer, and output layer as shown in Figure 4.3.

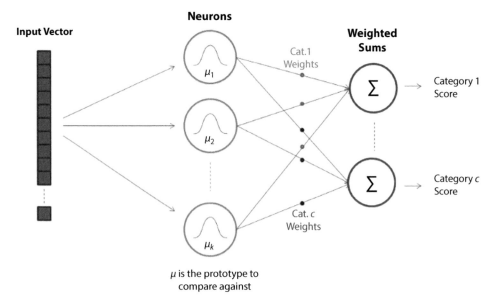

Figure 4.3 Radial basis function neural network.

4.5.2.1   Input

Input vector is usually n dimensional vector. Here, 23 features were extracted from the image that is considered to be an input.

4.5.2.2   Hidden Layer

> ➢ In the hidden layer, it uses radial basis functions as activation function; output depends upon the distance of input vector and centre. Distance measure is calculated by using the following equation:

$$\|r_j\|=\sqrt{\sum_{i=1}^{n}(x_i-w_{ij})^2}$$

The shape of radial basis function artificial neural network is bell-shaped; it is shown in figure.

4.5.2.3   Output Nodes

The neural network in the output layer consists of a set of nodes, which we are trying to classify the image as benign or malignant.

4.6   Performance Evaluation Methods

These evaluation methods help to identify the classifier performance as shown in Figure 4.4.

Sensitivity: Sensitivity has able to identify the patient with breast cancer correctly

$$SE = TP \backslash TP+FN \tag{4.2}$$

Specificity: Specificity has able to identify the healthy women correctly

$$SP = TN \backslash FP+TN \tag{4.3}$$

Accuracy: It has able to classify healthy and unhealthy women

$$ACCURACY = (TP+TN) \backslash (TP+TN+FP+FN) \tag{4.4}$$

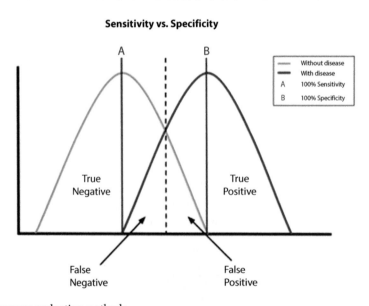

Figure 4.4 Performance evaluation methods.

4.7   Output

4.7.1   Dataset

Datasets were collected from Breast Cancer Dataset (Wisconsin). Initially, regions of interest were extracted, which help to remove unwanted area.

4.7.2   Pre-Processing

In next step, luminance helps to varying the shades. Next, histogram was plotted for the image, which determines intensity value of that region. Contrast enhancement helps to improve the quality of image.

4.7.3   Segmentation

Region growing segmentation algorithm was employed to segment the abnormal regions present in mammogram images. Outputs are shown in the Figures 4.5 to 4.5.6.

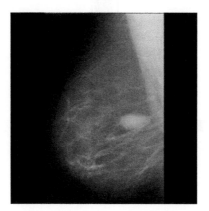

Figure 4.5 Database.

Figure 4.5.1 Region of interest.

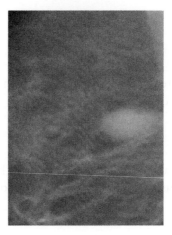

Figure 4.5.2 Luminance.

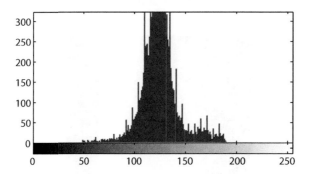

Figure 4.5.3 Histogram.

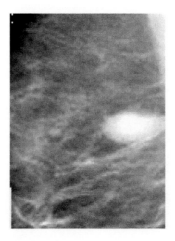

Figure 4.5.4 Contrast Enhancement.

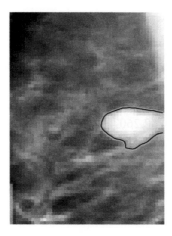

Figure 4.5.5 Segmented boundary ROI.

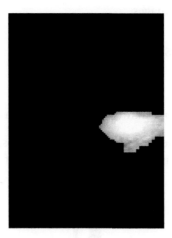

Figure 4.5.6 Segmentation result.

4.7.4   Geometric Feature Extraction

Features taken
Area, f1 = 0.0564
Perimeter, f2 = 96
Mean, f3 = 12.3978
Standard deviation, f4 = 38.0685
Skew, f5 = 3.5075
Kurtosis, f6 = 26.1385
Circularity, f7 = 1.2998e+004
Eccentricity, f8 = 0.1388
Rectangularity, f9 = 152.8423
Boundary roughness, f10 = 0.1983
Zero crossing, f11 = 76.6417

Texture features

Entropy, f12 = 0.3131

Angular second moment, f13 = 12.3978

Sum of squares, f14 = 38079174

Correlation, f15 = 0.1460

Contrast, f16 = 0.0564

Inverse difference moment, f17 = 12.2607

Sum average, f18 = 1.2522e+003

Sum variance, f19 = 2.3955e+005

Sum entropy, f20 = 21.3770

Entropy of the cooccurrence matrix, f21 = 0.3373

Difference variance, f22 = 2.0662e+004

Difference entropy, f23 = 0.1813

Features were extracted from mammography images which gives information about geometry and texture features. After feature extraction, it is passed in to classifier to identify the abnormality present in the images.

4.8   Results and Discussion

4.8.1   Database

Here, both the normal and abnormal images are compared as shown in the Figure 4.6.

- Out of different classifiers, we find naive Bayes classifier and RBFNN classifier showing the promising results with accuracy of 92% and 93% as shown in the Table 4.1.

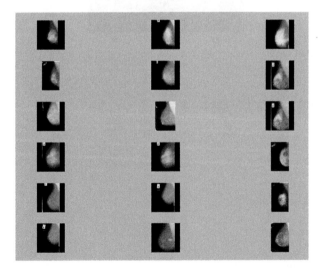

Figure 4.6 Database.

Table 4.1 Comparison table for Naive bayes and RBFN classifiers.

Classifier algorithm	Sensitivity	Specificity	Accuracy
Naive Bayes probabilistic classifier algorithm	0.86	1.2	92%
Radial basis function ANN	0.89	1.5	93%

- RBFN has advantages capable to eliminate input noise, and also, network training is faster so it is assumed to be better with other methods. Naive Bayes classifier is simplest probabilistic algorithm that can make quick predictions of cancer cells.

Here, all the three conditions are compared as shown in the Figures 4.6.1–4.6.3.

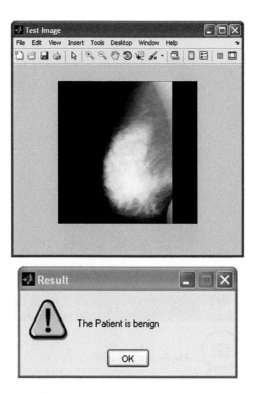

Figure 4.6.1 Database (benign condition).

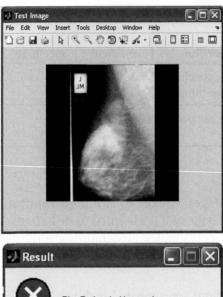

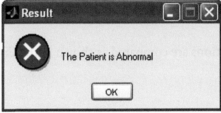

Figure 4.6.2 Malignant condition.

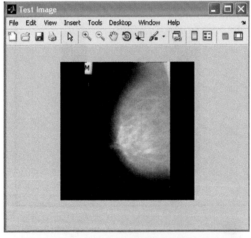

Figure 4.6.3 Normal breast.

4.9   Conclusion and Future Scope

Breast cancer mass is a serious problem associated to women worldwide. If we cannot find earlier, then it leads to critical conditions. So with the help of machine learning techniques it is possible to identify the mass cells from malignant cancer cells. Due to the usage of advanced techniques, we can take appropriate treatment to the cancer and also avoid severity.

In future incorporating various deep learning algorithms to classify the benign and malignant cancer cells. Deep learning algorithm has various advantages, which can extract the features automatically with the help of the algorithm so it can reduce the human error. Many dataset images can be taken to classify the images. Use of deep learning algorithms, we can able to detect the cancer earlier and improve the diagnosis.

References

1. Islam, M.J., An Efficient Automatic Mass Classification Method in Digitized Mammograms using Artificial Neural Network. *Int. J. Artif. Intell. Appl. (IJAIA)*, 1, 3, 1–13, 2010.
2. Rabottino, G. *et al.*, Mass Contour Extraction in Mammographic Images for Breast Cancer Identification. *16th IMEKO TC4 Symposium Exploring New Frontiers of Instrumentation and Methods for Electrical and Electronic Measurements*, pp. 22–24, 2008.
3. Kekre, Dr. H.B. *et al.*, Image Segmentation of Mammographic Images Using Kekre's Proportionate Error Technique on Probability Images. *Int. J. Comput. Electr. Eng.*, 2, 6, 1048–1052, 2010.
4. Mencattini, A. *et al.*, Assessment of a Breast Mass Identification Procedure Using an Iris Detector. *IEEE Trans. Instrum. Meas.*, 95, 10, 2505–2512, October 2010.
5. Gorgel, P. *et al.*, Mammographic mass classification using wavelet based support vector machine. *J. Electr. Electron. Eng.*, 9, 1, 867–875, 2009.
6. Kekre, Dr. H.B., Tumor Detection in Mammography Images using Vector Quantization Technique. *Int. J. Intell. Inf. Technol. Appl.*, 2, 5, 237–242, 2009.
7. Dehghani, S. *et al.*, Breast Cancer Diagnosis System Based on Contourlet Analysis and Support Vector Machine. *World Appl. Sci. J.*, 13, 5, 1067–1076, 2011.
8. Mohammed, S.A., Darrab, S., Noaman, S.A., Saake, G., Analysis of Breast Cancer Detection Using Different Machine Learning Techniques. *International Conference on Data Mining and Big Data DMBD 2020: Data Mining and Big Data*, pp. 108–117.
9. Giri, P. and Kumar, K.S., Breast Cancer Detection using Image Processing Technique. *Oriental J. Comput. Sci. Technol.*, 10, 2, 391–398, 2017.
10. Viswanath, V.H., Guachi-Guachi, L., Thirumuruganandham, S.P., *Breast Cancer Detection Using Image Processing Techniques and Classification Algorithms*, EasyChair preprints, Dec 2019.
11. Sahni, P. and Mittal, N., Breast cancer detection using image processing. *Adv. Interdiscip. Eng.*, Springer, Singapore, 813–823, 2019.
12. Cahoon, T.C., Sutton, M.A., Bezdek, J.C., Breast Cancer Detection Using Image Processing Techniques. *IEEE International Conference on Fuzzy Systems*, 2, pp. 973–976, 2000.
13. Bushra, M., Nazeer, M., Muhammad, S., Tanzila, S., Amjad, R., Extraction of breast border and removal of pectoral muscle in wavelet domain. *Biomed. Res.*, 28, 1–3, 2017.
14. Wei, K., Guangzhi, W., Hui, D., Segmentation of the breast region in mammograms using watershed transformation. Annual International Conference of the IEEE Engineering in Medicine

and Biology Society. IEEE Engineering in Medicine and Biology Society. Conference 6:6500-3. *Eng. Med. Biol. Soc.*, 2005.

15. Rahmati, P., Hamarneh, G., Nussbaum, D., Adler, A., A new preprocessing filter for digital mammograms. *Image Sig. Proc.*, pp. 585–592, 2010.

16. Singh, A.K. and Gupta, B., A novel approach for breast cancer detection and segmentation in a mammogram, *Eleventh International Multi-Conference on Information Processing-2015 (IMCIP2015), Procedia Computer Science*, 54, pp. 676–682, 2015.

17. Oliver, A., Marti, J., Marti, R., Bosch, A., Freixenet, J., A new Approach to the classification of mammographic masses and normal breast tissue. *The 18th International Conference on Pattern Recognition (ICPR'06)*, p. 1 4.

18. Král, P. and Lenc, L., (2016, September). LBP features for breast cancer detection. *IEEE International Conference on In Image Processing (ICIP)*, pp. 2643–2647, 2016.

19. Yadav, P. and Jethani, V., Breast Thermograms Analysis for Cancer Detection Using Feature Extraction and Data Mining Technique, in: *Proceedings of the ACM International Conference on Advances in Information Communication Technology & Computing*, p. 87, 2016, August.

20. Rangayyan, R.M., Ayres, F.J., Desautels, J.E.L., A review of computer-aided diagnosis of breast cancer: Toward the detection of subtle signs. *J. Franklin Inst.*, 344, 3, 312–348, 2007.

21. Gubern-Merida, A., Kallenberg, M., Mann, R.M., Marti, R., Karssemeijer, N., Breast segmentation and density estimation in breast MRI: a fully automatic framework. *IEEE J. Biomed. Health Inform*, 19, 1, 349, 2015.

22. Kaymaka, S., Helwan, A., Uzuna, D., Breast cancer image classification using artificial neural networks, in: *9th international conference on theory and application of soft computing, computing with*, 201724–25 August 2017.

23. Singh, A.K. and Gupta, B., A novel approach for breast cancer detection and segmentation in a mammogram, in: *Eleventh international multi-conference on information processing-2015*, 2015Imcip-2015.

24. Tobias, C. C. A M. A. and Suttorf, J.E.B., Breast Cancer Detection Using Image Processing Techniques. *Int. J. Comput. Appl.*, 87, 14, 391–399, February 2014.

25. Gubern -M´erida, A., Kallenberg, M., Mann, R.M., Mart ´ý, R., Karssemeijer, N., Breast Segmentation and Density Estimation in Breast MRI. *IEEE J. Biomed. Health Informat.*, 19, 1, 349–357, January 2015.

26. Lavanya, G. and sree Padmini, R., Classificatio n Of Breast Tumor Mass Using Probabilistic Neural Network And Radial Basis Function Neural Network Algorithm. *Int. J. Adv. Sci. Tech. Res.*, 2, 4, 685–694, March-April 2014.

27. Nahid, A.-A., Mikaelian, A., Kong, Y., Histopathological breast-image classification with restricted Boltzmann machine along with backpropagation. *Biomed. Res.*, 29, 10, 2068–2077, 2018.

28. Yap, M.H. *et al.*, Automated Breast Ultrasound Lesions Detection Using Convolutional Neural Networks. *IEEE J. Biomed. Health Informat.*, 22, 4, 1218–1226, July 2018.

29. Araújo, T., Aresta, G., Castro, E., Rouco, J., Aguiar, P., Eloy, C. *et al.*, Classification of breast cancer histology images using Convolutional Neural Networks. *PloS One*, 12, 6, e0177544, 2017. [online] Available: https://doi.org/10.1371/journal.pone.0177544.

30. Islam, M.M., Iqbal, H., Haque, M.R., Hasan, M.K., Prediction of breast cancer using support vector machine and K-Nearest neighbors. *2017 IEEE Region 10 Humanitarian Technology Conference (R10-HTC)*, pp. 226–229, 2017.

31. Ghongade, R.D. and Wakde, D.G., Detection and classification of breast cancer from digital mammograms using RF and RF-ELM algorithm. *2017 1st International Conference on Electronics Materials Engineering and Nano-Technology (IEMENTech)*, pp. 1–6, 2017.

5

Machine Learning Approach for Prediction of Lung Cancer

Hemant Kasturiwale[1]*, Swati Bhisikar[2] and Sandhya Save[1]

[1]Thakur College of Engineering and Technology, Kandivali (East), Mumbai, MS, India
[2]Rajarshi Shahu College of Engineering, Tathawade, Pune, MS, India

Abstract

In the current era of the introduction of artificial intelligence, there have been advances in the use of this field in image enhancement. The use of the histogram [local energy shape histogram (LESH)] approach based on local energy has previously helped diagnose breast cancer. The current support vector machine (SVM) algorithm is further advanced to AdaBoost algorithm for image extraction. The boosting algorithm of AdaBoost on the accuracy of the results will provide a much better result. For lung cancer diagnosis utilizing CT images, the LESH feature extraction algorithm is presented for lung cancer diagnoses using CT images [1]. This research builds on previous work by using the LESH with AdaBoost feature extraction methodology to detect lung cancer. The main objective of this research is to compare the LESH and HTF feature extraction approaches of SVM and AdaBoost. It is difficult to detect the specific symptoms of lung cancer since most cancer tissues are formed, and enormous tissue structures are crossed. Images will be evaluated using the LESA algorithm's basic operation in this method. In this study, the GLCM technique is used to prepare snap photos and to evaluate the level of a patient's condition at an early stage so that it may be established regularly or extraordinarily. The cancer stage is determined by the results. The survival rate of cancer patients can be determined using the dataset and results. The outcome is totally determined by the correct or erroneous arrangement of tissue patterning. Hence, a method must be such that it will remove the noise, extract vital information, and, at the same time, make it easy for a person to understand what is the problem with the given lung signal. In addition, the algorithm must have the ability to track the important changes and our approach should provide accurate, non-invasive assessment in clinical practice. After analyzing the signal, the method used provides vital information of linear methods, i.e., time domain and frequency domain parameters, and also provides the details of the indices of a cardiac patient and normal person which will be helpful to initiate treatment for a cardiac patient as soon as possible.

Keywords: Artificial intelligence, LESH, SVM, AdaBoost, lung cancer, algorithm

*Corresponding author: hemantkasturiwale@gmail.com

Tushar H. Jaware, K. Sarat Kumar, Ravindra D. Badgujar and Svetlin Antonov (eds.) Medical Imaging and Health Informatics, (83–102) © 2022 Scrivener Publishing LLC

5.1   Introduction

In a country like India, cancer of the lung is a modern disease and one of the most common causes of death. It is the deadliest cancer of all the known forms of cancer and kills more people than those suffering from any other form of cancer. The most common explanation is Tabaco chewing. According to the World Health Organization's Global Burden of Disease analysis, there will be 1,766,000 lung cancer deaths worldwide in 2014. It is predicted that the death toll would continue to grow, reaching a staggering 2 lac deaths by 2030. In 2008, the rank order of cancers among Indians revealed that 356 cases of lung cancer accounted for 7.7% of all newly diagnosed cancer cases in both males and females. The second most frequent cause of death among males and the 10th most common cause of death among females is lung cancer [2].

5.1.1   Disorders in Lungs

When it comes to lung disorders, they are classified into three types: airway illnesses, lung tissue diseases, and lung circulation illnesses. The airway disease affects the tubes that transfer gases such as oxygen and other gases into and out of the lungs, causing a blockage in the airway. Airway diseases include asthma, COPD, and bronchiectasis, to name a few. The structure of the lung tissue is affected by lung tissue disorders. Scarring or inflammation of the tissue prevents the lungs from properly expanding (restrictive lung disease). This makes it difficult for the lungs to absorb oxygen and expel carbon dioxide. Cancer is one of the most prevalent tissue-related disorders. Lung circulation illnesses are conditions that affect the blood arteries of the lungs. They are caused by clotting of blood vessels, scarring, or inflammation. They reduce the ability of the lungs to absorb oxygen and expel carbon dioxide. These conditions have the potential to impair heart function. A lung circulation disease is a form of pulmonary hypertension [3].

5.1.2   Background

This study aims to provide a new automated diagnostic system for lung cancer based on Haralick texture characteristics retrieved from the image slices in Digital Imaging and Communications in Medicine (DICOM) lung CT. This approach has four steps: preparing data, segmenting the lungs, removing features, and classifying. In order to examine various characteristics and determine which factors are the most important in classifying patients and in distinguishing between lung cancer, ordered edema patients, and healthy controls, statistical analysis is performed. Next, read these sections, which go into greater detail on these steps. The image analysis was completed with no knowledge of the patient's clinical characteristics or status.

Computer tomography is a computerized approach for taking images of the x-ray that projects a narrow beam of x-ray to the patient and rotates swiftly around him to obtain images of the X-rays. The computer processes these photos to produce cross-sectional body pictures. These cross-sectional images are known as tomographic images, and they contain more detail than standard X-Ray images. The cross-sectional images are stacked together and form a three-dimensional (3D) image.

A circular opening called a portal is the rotational x-ray tube. The patient is lying on the bed and moving across the portico slowly. A narrow x-ray beam is thrown into the patient's body by a revolving x-ray tube. The images are taken using digital x-ray detectors that are opposite the x-ray source. Once the x-rays are picked up by the detector, they are transmitted to the computer. Once the x-ray source completed one full rotation, a 2D cross-sectional image or slice is generated with the help of mathematical calculations by the computer. Once the scan is completed the bed is moved forward. This scanning process is repeated, and this process continues till the desired number of slices are received. The usual thickness of the tissue obtained from CT images is in the range of 1–10 mm. The stacking of individual slices and generating a 3D image helps in the proper formation of organs, skeleton, and tissues in the image, and this helps the physician to catch the abnormalities if there are present in the image.

CT scan images are highly used for lung cancer detection because the normal x-ray detection is not capable to show defects indicating lung cancer presence. CT scan pictures for the lungs are useful when acute and chronic lung parenchyma alterations are detected. A CT scan reveals small lesions in the lungs. A low-dose computed tomography is recommended for screening tests for lung cancer detection for just 30 seconds. As per the recent study, a low-dose CT scan can help in detecting lung cancer in people at higher risk of getting lung cancer. LDCT scan uses lower amounts of radiations compared to standard chest CT scan and does not require the use of intravenous contrast dye [4].

5.1.3   Material, Datasets, and Techniques

➢ Dataset
  Patients with either a pulmonary or lung cancer tumor have been included in this study. The first dataset was the Department of Radiology of New Elkasr ElAiny Hospital of the University of Cairo. The Cancer Imaging Archive (TCIA), sponsored by SPIE, NCI/NIH, AAPM, and the University of Chicago, also supported this additional dataset [5]. The two datasets included a total of more than 500 CT scans from over 30 different patients. The images are captured with 512 × 512 pixels in DICOM format. The left lung is automatically split from the right lung on each pulmonary CT image, and the dataset information [6] classifies each distinct lung as normal or edema/cancer.

➢ Preprocessing
  The purpose of the initial processing stage is to increase the image quality while making it suitable for other methods of processing, such as hand or computer processing [7]. This proposed improvement, based on the integration of filters and noise reduction techniques, uses histogram equalization (HE) [8, 9], followed by Wiener filters [10, 11]. Figure 5.1 shows the lung contrast improvement achieved using histogram balance. However, the resulting gray picture integrates noises like white noise and noise of salt and pepper. This removes these sounds from the enlarged pulmonary image with the Wiener filter.

➢ Lung Segmentation
  Lung segmentation is a term used to describe the process of segmenting the lungs.

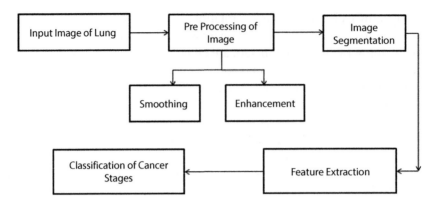

Figure 5.1 Pointcare plot for the image of the lung for feature extraction.

The lung separation process is intended to derive voxels from surrounding lung architecture that match the cavity of the lung in the axial CT scans. The segmentation method provided in [12] is used. The preprocessed CT picture is turned into a binary picture in the first stage; a threshold of 128 was used. The outcome is that masks are formed both rights and left. These masks are multiplied by the corresponding original picture areas and projected on the original two lung images by the lung masks. Finally, update every black pixel to its original value in the pictures collected; all other pixels are set to 255.

5.2 Feature Extraction and Lung Cancer Analysis

In 1973, the Gray Level Cooccurrence Matrix (GLCM) and texture features are introduced [13]. In the field of image analysis, this method is widely used, especially in the biomedical sector. For feature extraction, it is separated into two pieces.

GLCM illustrates how often each gray level happens to a pixel located in the position of a given geometric pixel compared to each other [13] as a function of the gray level. The horizontal direction 00 was employed for this work, covering the range 1 (nearest neighbor). The nine texture descriptions used in (4) to (13) are revealed to be the normalized GLCM symmetric dimensional and the normalized GLCM element [13], where the gray levels are counted. Since the coefficient of attenuation of the air is essentially negligible, a change in the attenuation coefficient of water of one Hounsfield unit (HU) is 0.1%. It is the phrase used to describe CT scanners calibrated to water.

> ➤ Extraction Feature
> The plots of change can be displayed as values spread across four quadrant specified areas. If heart rate changes happen randomly and independently, then all four quadrants will have the same number of points. It went up quicker than it went down.

5.3   Methodology

5.3.1   Proposed Algorithm Steps

As per the proposed diagram in Figure 5.2 of the block system, we have five major stages which are input image of the lung, pre-image enhancement, LESH feature extraction, feature selection and classification with support vector machine (SVM), AdaBoost, and final output result. The standard format of medical photographs is DICOM. The format most commonly used for medical data storage/transmission is different from other formats such as the Portable Graphics Network (PGN) (jpeg). DICOM separates from the rest of the format by the feature of forming groups of all the information into datasets. The pictures that will be used are axial CT images of the lungs. The Gabor filter will be used for image pre-processing. The Gabor filter is used for picture enhancement and thresholding. It is used to find any certain frequency content in an image in certain directions in a localized region around the analysis pointer.

A bank of 2D log Gabor filters with variable orientations o and scales s is used to convolute the image. LESH-based feature extraction is a technique that involves determining the histogram of the image's local energy pattern. The phase congruency (PC) method is used to compute this energy along various orientations. The aforementioned Gabor filter computes this PC technique. The algorithm for LESH feature extraction is given as follows:

Begin:

1. Convolute the image I with 2D-Log Gabor filter with different orientations o and scales s.
2. Calculate the amplitude of the response.
3. Calculate sensitive phase deviation.
4. Calculate local energy.
5. Calculate 2D PC.
6. Calculate the LESH feature vector

End;

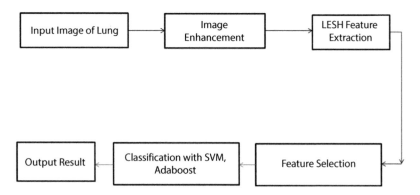

Figure 5.2 Proposed system block diagram.

5.3.2 Classifiers in Concurrence With Datasets

Chest radiographs have low contrast for which we can apply CLAHE (Contrast Limited Adaptive Histogram Equalization), which enhances the image. First, the image is divided into contextual blocks. Using a specific number of bins for the grey value, we can calculate a histogram for each block. SVM is trained on training the dataset to generate a model which specifies the class of feature vector among the test dataset. In case high-dimensional spaces in the case of the SVM are non-linear, they can be mapped with the kernel. Adaptive Boost or AdaBoost is an algorithm for machine learning. The output of other study algorithms ("weak learners"), which are the final output of the enhanced classification, is integrated into a weighted amount. AdaBoost is adaptive in the sense of tinkering successively with weak learners to reward examples misclassified by previous classification systems. AdaBoost is susceptible to noise and outliers in data. Boosting is a type of linear regression in which the characteristics of each sample are the results of some weak learner h applied to xi. AdaBoost corresponds to a single iteration of the back fitting algorithm in the scenario where all weak learners are known a priori. The methodology of this research involves going through

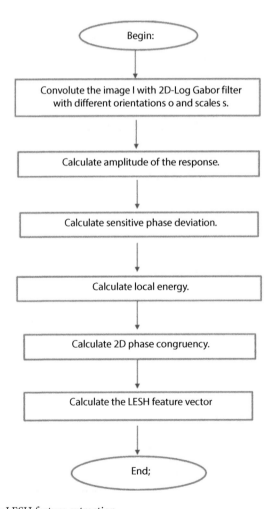

Figure 5.3 Algorithm for LESH feature extraction.

certain steps in the preprocessing, decomposition of the LUNG LESH signals, and Artificial Neural Network (ANN) creation, training, testing, and validation.

This chapter deals with the overall methodology of the research work and the various pre-processing done in the research work and also deals with the signal decomposition as shown in Figure 5.3. It is essential in this context to remember that the main aim of this research is to evolve a system:

a. To find whether the person is suffering from a health disorder.
b. To measure the percentage of deviation of the person from the normal LUNG LESH signals, with the help of which the doctor will be able to give priority to the seriously affected persons and speed up the treatment.

5.4   Proposed System and Implementation

5.4.1   Interpretation via Artificial Intelligence

The above diagnosis is achieved based on LUNG LESH signal analysis, first by applying the pre-processing steps involving denoising, feature extraction, and classification and secondly applying Discrete Wavelet Transform (DWT) for the decomposition of the LUNG LESH signals into different frequency domains, together with ANN training [14, 15].

Figure 5.4 depicts the two stages of classification using a ML.

➤ Training phase: We will train a machine algorithm on a dataset of pictures and their labels during this phase [16].

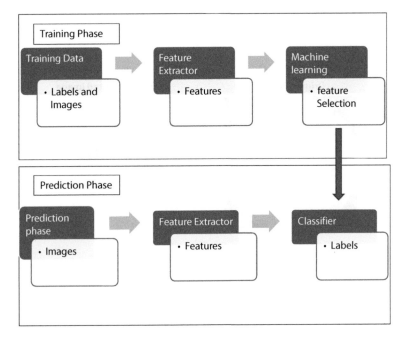

Figure 5.4 Machine learning phases.

➤ Prediction phase: The trained model is used to forecast unviewed image labels in this stage.

5.4.2   Training of Model

The training phase of an image classification issue consists of two major steps:

1. Feature Extraction: In this phase, we leverage domain knowledge to extract new features that the machine learning algorithm will use. Image categorization features such as HoG and SIFT are examples [17].
2. Model Training: We utilize a clean dataset consisting of image characteristics and labels to train the learning model of the machine in this step.

In the predictive stage, on the fresh photographs, we repeat the extraction technique and pass the features to the taught machine study algorithm, which predicts the label.

5.4.3   Implementation and Results

We first filter the image and we calculated the HU using the DICOM metadata. We created a binary image with a large pixel less than −500 set as 1 as they represent lungs. Then, the boundaries and other holes with nodules were cleared out to focus only on lungs and nodules present within it as shown in Figures 5.5 and 5.6. Figure 5.7 classified figure out of the sample.

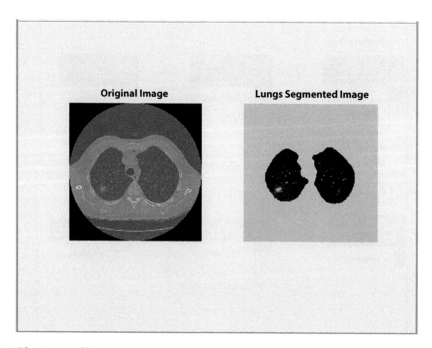

Figure 5.5 Filter image of lung segments.

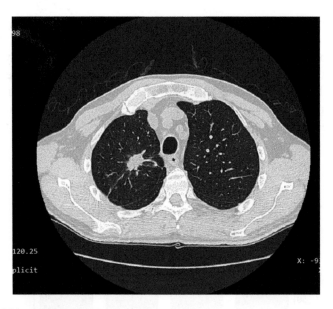

Figure 5.6 House field unit using DICOM metadata.

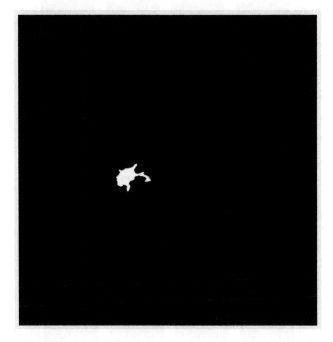

Figure 5.7 Tumor classified.

With LESH with AdaBoost, we can attain better outcomes than with the present SVM HTF or SVM LESH. The sensitivity, specificity, and precision charts are also visible. The confusion plot provides 89.2% of correct findings, demonstrating the success of malignant cells and 10.8% of the incorrect ones. The ROC AdaBoost plus LESH track indicates that it is near to 1. However, it is more important because the ROC track covers a larger area under the curve.

The classification accuracy, sensitivity, and specificity were used to analyze the results.

MATLAB was used to run the experiments. For ESN, we utilized the version developed by [18], while for ELM, we used the original model developed by G-B. Huang. After training the classifier on the training dataset using 10-fold cross-validation, testing is carried out, and the results are evaluated using the performance measures provided in the next section.

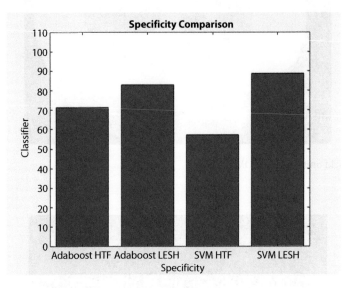

Figure 5.8 Specificity comparison for AdaBoost and SVM.

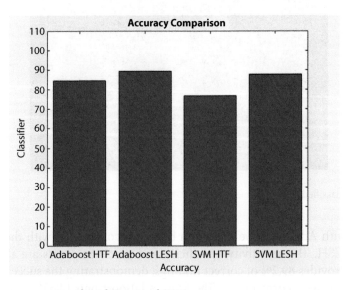

Figure 5.9 Accuracy comparison for AdaBoost and SVM.

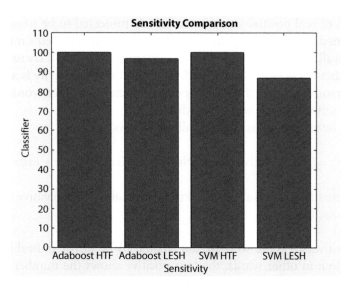

Figure 5.10 Sensitivity comparison for AdaBoost and SVM.

We have drawn the plot of characteristics that yielded more than 80%. Specificity is defined as the percent of real negatives predicted to be negative (or true negative). This indicates that a portion of true negatives, as it may be called false positives, are predicted to be positive. The faulty positive rate of this fraction is also known. There is always one thing that sums the specificity and false positives. Let us try to explain it using the model to predict if a person is living with the condition. Specificity is a measure of the share of persons who have not been precisely anticipated to suffer from the condition. In other words, the healthy person was correctly projected to be healthy, as illustrated in Figures 5.8 to 5.10.

Specificity can be calculated mathematically as follows:

Specificity = (True Negative + False Positive) / (True Negative + False Positive)

The following are the specifics about True Negative and False Positive in the aforementioned equation.

- True Negative = Persons anticipated to be disease-free (or healthy) are found to be disease-free (or healthy); in other words, the true negative represents the number of people who are healthy and are projected to be healthy.
- False Positive = People who were anticipated to be sick (or ill) are found to be healthy (healthy). In other words, the false positive shows the number of people who are healthy but were incorrectly forecasted to be unwell. A greater specificity score would imply a higher true negative rate and a lower false-positive rate. A lower specificity rating would imply a lower value of true negative and a higher value of false positive.

***Accuracy* can be as follows:**
Sensitivity is a measure of the percentage of positive real cases that are rightly expected to be positive (or true positive). The reminder is another sensitivity synonym. This shows that

a further fraction of real positive cases is incorrectly projected to be negative (and, thus, could also be termed as the false negative). This can also be considered a misleading rate of negation. The overall sensitivity and false adverse rates are one. Let us try to explain it using the model to predict if a person is living with the condition. Sensitivity is a measure of the proportion of persons with the disease properly predicted. In other words, it was rightly expected that the unwell person was unhealthy [19].

Sensitivity can be calculated mathematically as follows:

- Sensitivity = (True Positive + False Negative)/(True Positive + False Negative)

The following are the specifics about the True Positive and False Negative terms employed in the aforementioned equation.

➢ True Positive = People who are anticipated to be ill (or unhealthy) are ill (unhealthy); in other words, the true positive shows the number of people who are ill and are projected to be ill.
➢ False Negative = People who are truly suffering from the sickness (or are unwell) are predicted not to be suffering from the condition (healthy). To put it another way, the false negative shows the number of people who are unwell but were anticipated to be healthy. We would prefer the model to have a low false negative rate because it could be life-threatening or business-threatening.

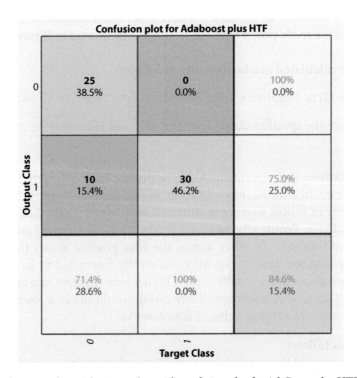

Figure 5.11 Plot for target class with output class with confusion plot for AdaBoost plus HTF.

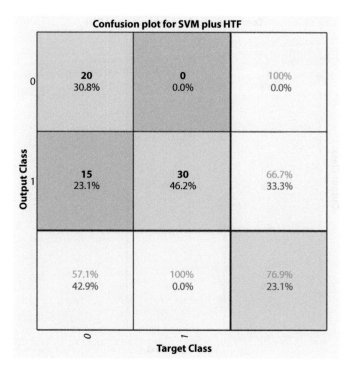

Figure 5.12 Plot for confusion plot for SVM plus HTF.

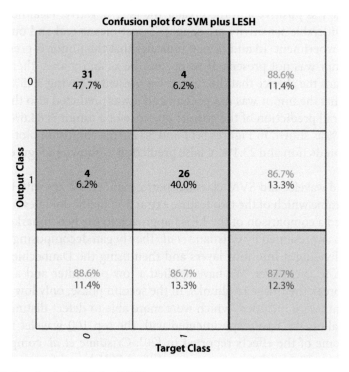

Figure 5.13 Confusion plot for SVM plus LESH.

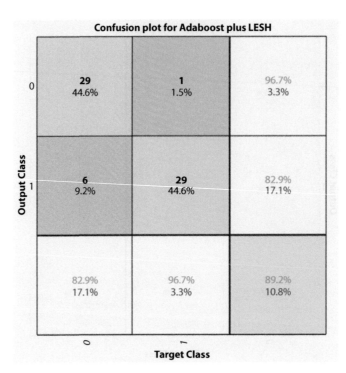

Figure 5.14 Confusion plot for AdaBoost plus LESH.

The greater the sensitivity, the more positive the real and the less negative the false. The less sensitivity, the less positive and the greater the false negative. Healthcare and finance models with considerable sensitivity are sought. Target means real and output means our output from our experiment. In addition, 0 indicates that the tumor is present and 1 indicates that the tumor was not present. If we see on the x- and y-axes, then the 0-0 plot is 38.5%, which means the chance that the tumor was present is having 38.5% correct chance and the chances that the tumor was not present and it was predicted also that it is not present is 46.2%. Overall prediction of the correct presence of a tumor is 84.6% and the wrong prediction is 15.4% as shown in Figures 5.11 and 5.12. This confusion plot gives a result of 76.9% of correct prediction and 23.1% of false prediction as shown in Figures 5.13 and 5.14.

> LESH and wavelet and SVM classifier performance analyzes with t-test
> To determine which of the two feature extraction methodologies is better, we conducted a comparison of the LESH approach to the benchmarked wavelet approach as presented by Cristiane *et al.* They began decomposing the image by first dividing it into four layers and then using the Daubechies wavelets approach to each layer. We have applied a low-pass filter and a high-pass filter to break the image in chunks. In the second phase, only low frequency coefficients were included, which were more able to detect distinct patterns of anomalies. We have experimented with the top 100 wavelet features to mimic some of the effects reported in [20]. Cristiane *et al.* compared with wavelet-based t-test the performance of the LESH-based feature extraction technique. The difference of the resulting accuracy in the classification

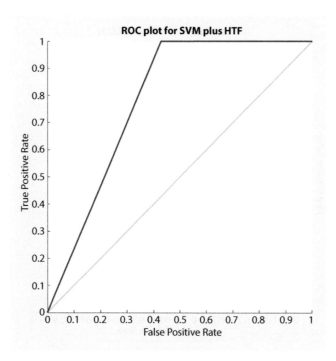

Figure 5.15 ROC plot for SVM plus HTF.

obtained by the LESH extraction technique is at a significance threshold of 0.05 (100 features selected) and the wavelet feature extraction methodology (100 features picked) was compared. In our situation, the correct prediction rate is 89.2%, while the incorrect prediction rate is only 10.8%. This is our strategy, and it explains all of the plots above as well as every step of 0-0, 0-1, and 1-0-1-1. As demonstrated in Figure 5.15, the ROC curve has been able to predict the stability and sensitivity concerning prediction.

The methods of lung cancer detection are subjected to several problems because of the inhomogeneous lung areas and the resemblance of the nodules, including the cavities and the glass nodules, not to arteries, ribs, bronchi, veins, and bronchial forms in a pulmonary region. This all makes segmentation, extraction, and classification of lungs and nodules challenging. Nodules can predict malignancy by form, size, texture, and other features. The capture of images and reconstructed parameters, nodule location, dataset size, and systems optimization via cross-validation are further variables that can increase system performance in the recognition of lung malformations.

A. A multi-approach segmentation

The literature provides several segmentation strategies. When it comes to these tactics, the problem is that important information is lost. Every segmentation image is created using a different process. By using this method, new discoveries can be made about knowledge that would not have been found using any other approach.

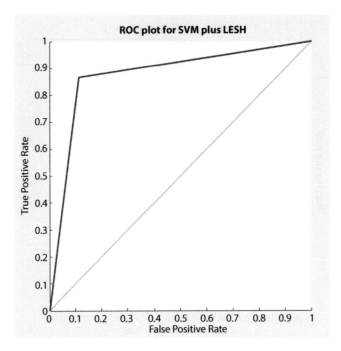

Figure 5.16 ROC plot for SVM plus LESH.

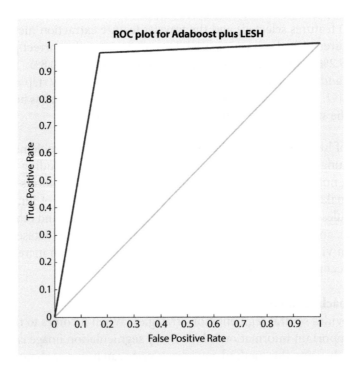

Figure 5.17 ROC plot for AdaBoost plus LESH.

B. Feature selection

Feature selection is vital to the classification process, while, at the same time, it prevents the curse of dimensionality. Figure 5.16 shows ROC plot for SVM LESH. Figure 5.17 shows ROC plot for AdaBoost LESH. This indicates about the plot that our plot is near to one which means our result is more toward a true positive rate as shown in Figure 5.17. In addition, this gives a much area under the curve, which indicates a good use of adabost plus lesh methodology.

5.5   Conclusion

The CDSS reported in this work can best be described as having 100% accuracy because it uses the polynomial SVM kernel for classification. The preliminary findings presented in this research should be interpreted with caution because they illustrate the feasibility of leveraging LESH features for lung cancer detection utilizing tiny datasets. To further evaluate the performance of the suggested strategy, additional comparative examination with large-scale clinical datasets is required. On trailing SVM technique with HTF and LESH and AdaBoost with HTF and LESH, it is observed that the AdaBoost algorithm, when masked with LESH gives a better result. In the below figures we can see the Sensitivity, Accuracy, specificity, and better true positivity rate. The greater area under the curve indicates that the more accurate rate at which correct cancer nodules were detected. The confusion plot for LESH and HTF techniques. The 0 indicated non-tumorous nodules and 1 indicated tumorous nodules. The confusion plot of AdaBoost plus LESH indicates that the probability of calculating non-tumorous nodules is 96.7% and that of calculating tumorous nodules is 82.9%. The overall probability is 89.2% which is highest for AdaBoost with LESH compared to SVM with HTF, AdaBoost with HTF, and SVM with LESH. The authors have come up with an algorithm that runs feature selection and classification systems like the arbitrary norm SVM and sparsely connected SVM by Huang *et al.* and multi-layered echo state machine by Malik *et al.* in the future. Magnetic resonance imaging (MRI) is one of the most commonly used 3D imaging modalities for detecting cancer in clinical settings (MRI). In addition, for enhancing classification performance, it may be studied whether a hybrid strategy that utilizes many state-of-the-art feature extraction techniques, such as LESH features, is employed alongside picking out essential features. The authors decided to utilize a form of sensitivity analysis, known as SA, to discover LESH attributes that have little impact on classification outcomes [21]. SA allows you to rank these features based on how they affect the model output. This will aid in decreasing imperfections caused by dimensionality reduction.

5.5.1   Future Scope

To complete this chapter, consider the following points, which may lead to better and more interesting outcomes. The research could be expanded in the future in the following directions:

- The system may be applied to the patients currently suffering from the diseases taken up for the research, and the data regarding the time and the lives saved could be collected. This may give insights to the medical professionals and computer technologists into the utilitarian value of such systems.

- In the preprocessing, at the denoising stage, the results produced by median filters can be compared with other filters like adaptive filters and non-local filters.
- Real-time tracking and diagnostics are to be explored with lung.

References

1. Ferchichi, A., Boulila, W., Farah, I.R., Using Evidence Theory in Land Cover Change Prediction to Model Imperfection Propagation with Correlated Inputs Parameters. *IJCCI (FCTA)*, pp. 47–56, 2015.
2. Tong, J., Da-Zhe, Z., Ying, W., Xin-Hua, Z., Xu, W., Computer-Aided Lung Nodule Detection Based On CT Images. *IEEE/ICME International Conference on Complex Medical Engineering*, 2007.
3. Bhuvaneswari, P. and Therese, A.B., Detection of Cancer in Lung with K-NN Classification Using Genetic Algorithm. *Proc. Mater. Sci.*, 10, 433–440, 2015.
4. Bhuvaneswari, C., Aruna, P., Loganathan, D., A new fusion model for classification of the lung diseases using genetic algorithm. *Egypt. Inform. J.*, 15, 2, 69–77, July 2014.
5. Huang, K., Zheng, D., King, I., Lyu, M.R., Arbitrary Norm Support Vector Machines. *Neural Comput.*, 21, 2, 560–582, 2009.
6. Jaffar, M.A., Hussain, A., Jabeen, F., Nazir, M., Mirza, A.M., GA- SVM Based Lungs Nodule Detection and Classification, in: *Signal Processing, Image Processing, and Pattern Recognition*, pp. 133–140, Springer, Berlin Heidelberg, 2009.
7. Wajid, S.K. and Hussain, A., Local Energy-based Shape Histogram (LESH) Based Clinical Decision Support System for Breast Cancer Detection using Magnetic Resonance Imaging (MRI). *Expert Syst. Appl.*, 4, 101–115(13).
8. Malik, Z.K., Hussain, A., Wu, J., Multi-Layered Echo State Machine: A novel Architecture and Algorithm for Big Data applications. *IEEE Trans. Cybern.*, 32, 101–121, 2016 (in press).
9. Farah, I.R., Boulila, W., Ettabaâ, K.S., Ahmed, M.B., Multi approach System Based on Fusion of Multispectral Images for Land-Cover Classification. *IEEE Trans. Geosci. Remote Sens.*, 46, 12, 4153–4161, 2008.
10. Quan, Y. *et al.*, A Novel Image Fusion Method of Multi-Spectral and SAR Images for Land Cover Classification. *Remote Sens.*, 12, 3801, 2020.
11. Boulila, W., Bouatay, A., Farah, I.R., A Probabilistic Collocation Method for the Imperfection Propagation: Application to Land Cover Change Prediction. *J. Mater. Process. Tech.*, 5, 1, 12–32, 2014.
12. Jaeger, H., The "echo state" approach to analyzing and training recurrent neural networks. GMD Report 148, German National Research Center for Information Technology, p. 43, 86, 2001.
13. Huang, G.B., What is Extreme Learning Machines? Filling the Gap between Frank Rosenblatt's Dream and John von Neumann's Puzzle. *Cognit. Comput.*, 7, 263–278, 2015.
14. Karhe, R.R. and Kale, S.N., Digitization of Documented ECG Signals using Image processing. *Int. J. Eng. Adv. Technol.*, 9, 1, 1286–1289, October 2019.
15. Karhe, R.R. and Kale, S.N., Classification of Cardiac Arrhythmias using Feedforward Neural Network. *Helix*, volume 10, 5, 15–20, 2020.
16. Kasturiwale, H. and Dr., S.N., Kale, Qualitative analysis of Heart Rate Variability based Biosignal Model for Classification of Cardiac Diseases. *Int. J. Adv. Sci. Technol.*, 29, 7, 296–305, 2020.

17. Kasturiwale, H.P. and Kale, S.N., BioSignal Modelling for Prediction of Cardiac Diseases Using Intra Group Selection Method. *Intell. Decis. Technol.,* 15, 1, 151–160, 2021.

18. Malik, Z.K., Hussain, A., Wu, J., Novel biologically inspired approaches to extracting online information from temporal data. *Cognitive Computation,* 6, 3, 595–607, 2014.

19. Farah, I.R., Boulila, W., Ettabaâ, K.S., Solaiman, B., Ahmed, M.B., Interpretation of Multisensor Remote Sensing Images: Multi approach Fusion of Uncertain Information. *IEEE Trans. Geosci. Remote Sens.,* 46, 4142–4152, 12, 2008.

20. Farah, I.R., Boulila, W., Ettabaâ, K.S., Ahmed, M.B., Multi approach System Based on Fusion of Multispectral Images for Land-Cover Classification. *IEEE Trans. Geosci. Remote Sens.,* 46, 12, 4153–4161, 2008.

21. Sarvani, B. and Kasturiwale, H., Detection of Lung Cancer using Local Energy Based Shape Histogram (LESH) Feature and Adaboost Machine Learning Technique. *IJITEE,* 9, 3, 99, January 2019.

6

Segmentation of Liver Tumor Using ANN

Hema L. K.[1]* and R. Indumathi[2]†

[1]Department of Electronics and Communication Engineering, Aarupadai Veedu Institute of Technology, Vinayaka Mission's Research Foundation, Paiyanoor, Tamil Nadu, India
[2]Department of Biomedical Engineering, Bharath Institute of Higher Education & Research, Chennai, Tamil Nadu, India

Abstract

Liver is a vital organ to detoxify the blood and break down the fat molecules from the food that we consume. Most of the liver diseases are inherited from their parents. Liver can get damaged due to various factors, the liver can be damaged due to many reasons. Among this, cancer is one cause of liver damage. Considering the Indian population, the rate of mortality due to liver cancer is 6.8 per one lakh in men and 5.1 per one lakh in women. The computed tomography is the common method to screen, diagnose, staging, and prognosis assessment; thereby, the liver cancer patient can be given proper treatment. While using image processing techniques for liver tumor segmentation, we adopted a binary segmentation task where a network has been designed to segment liver and liver tumor segments. The proposed system focuses on medical image sequences of the liver tumor segmentation based on region. The abnormality structure of the liver has been altered based on the position and by setting a threshold for segmenting. A deep neural network was used to compare the dataset images, and the input dataset has been trained and verified. Finally, the status of liver tumor would be inferred whether it is malignant or benign.

Keywords: Liver tumor, computed tomography, artificial neural network, malignant, hemangiomas, deep learning, embolization, segmentation

6.1 Introduction

The liver is a vital organ located in vertebrates, and it detoxifies various metabolites, and proteins are synthesized. It produces a biochemical that is needed to digest the food and growth. The liver in human being is located in the right hand upper side of the abdomen cavity. The liver does the glycogen regulation and storage. The liver helps to decomposition of red blood cells and also hormones production. The liver is affected or get damaged by various causes, namely, infections by difference kinds of parasites and viruses causing the

---

*Corresponding author: hemjith2005@gmail.com
†Corresponding author: indhu.maheshradha@gmail.com

Tushar H. Jaware, K. Sarat Kumar, Ravindra D. Badgujar and Svetlin Antonov (eds.) *Medical Imaging and Health Informatics*, (103–120) © 2022 Scrivener Publishing LLC

inflammatory reaction over the liver surfaces, for example, hepatitis B and C and some genetically inherited features leading to Wilson's disease, in turn, leads to hepatocellular carcinoma (HCC)—liver cancer. It is reported by American Cancer society that the liver and intrahepatic bile duct cancer for 2021 would be around 42,230 new cases will be diagnosed.

6.2   Liver Tumor

The liver cells mutate unusually and this abnormality happening in the Liver is called as liver tumor [7]. A unique kind of tumors that is formed in the liver comprises different cell types. The basic classifications of the liver tumors are i) benign and ii) malignant as in other kind of tumors. Using the imaging techniques, the presence of liver tumor can be diagnosed, but the final conclusion can be arrived at after conducting the biopsy of the liver tissues. Asymptomatic patients with a stomach mass, hepatomegaly, stomach agony, jaundice, or some other liver brokenness have different signs and manifestations of liver masses. Once it is confirmed as malignant, i.e., harmful, and based on the severity (type and stage), the treatment will differ.

Figure 6.1 shows the structure of liver cancer cells.

6.2.1   Overview of Liver Tumor

Estimates for intrahepatic and primary liver cancer in the United States for 2021 are as follows: Approximately, 42,230 new cases will be diagnosed (29,890 in males and 12,340 in females). Approximately, 30.230 people will die from this cancer (20.300 men and 9.930 women). Since 1980, the incidence of liver cancer has more than tripled, while during this time, death rates have more than doubled. The number of patients suffering from liver cancer is more in some of the Southeast Asian countries as compared to the United States. It is the most common type of cancer in many of these countries. This cancer is diagnosed annually by over 800,000 people worldwide. Liver cancer is also the world's leading cause of deaths, with more than 700,000 deaths annually. Advances in clinical science have led to new treatment options for patients with liver malignancy. Blood supply to the tumor is hindered and chemistry is directly controlled by the tumor called trans-blood vessel chemotherapy; radiation therapies by means of blood supply radiotherapy to the tumor are

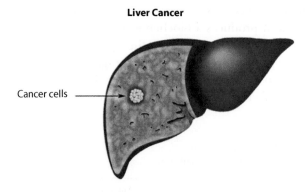

Figure 6.1 Structure of liver tumor.

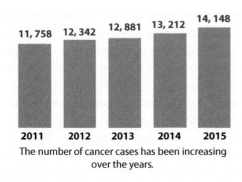

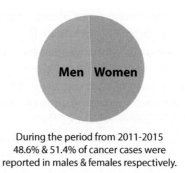

2011   2012   2013   2014   2015
The number of cancer cases has been increasing
over the years.

During the period from 2011-2015
48.6% & 51.4% of cancer cases were
reported in males & females respectively.

Figure 6.2 Overview of liver cancer cases.

valuable for life removal and for the disguise of numerous patients from inoperative liver malignancy. It can be amazingly helpful to tumor through the vein that provides blood to the liver. Nonetheless, the high cost of treatment is a major impediment, particularly in developing countries. There can be 6–9 lakh ropes for one part of the treatment. The lack of competence, and the lack of admission to state-of-the-art medical services, is a major factor in our lack of attention.

Many specialists are not aware that liver disease is being dealt with, in particular broad professionals. Just recently, 10 to 15 years ago, for example, before a hepatic disease, liver medical procedure was considered untreatable and high mortality. Any persistent liver tumor has been advised that no hope exists. Enhancing physician services and progressing late with medicines and medications at this point, the liver medical procedure is not outrageous. Unfortunately, many specialists have accepted that liver tumors are incurable. Numerous diseases go untreated as a result of patients' trust in their own PCPs and a lack of mindfulness. In fact, some benign liver tumors are also treatable. Auxiliary malignancy is a type of cancer that has spread to the liver from other organs. Because of a lack of awareness, many patients are unaware of clinical assistance from specialists. Figure 6.2 depicts the overview of cancer cases among men and women over years.

6.2.2   Classification

6.2.2.1   Benign

There are different categories of harmless liver tumors are diagnosed. The main causes of these kinds of benign tumors are due to following reasons: i) by abnormal neoplastic cell growth and ii) by regenerative nodules or liver damage. The classification of benign hepatocellular, bile, or stromal tumors is by its anatomic source.

6.2.2.1.1   Hemangiomas

The most widely recognized kind of liver tumor found in 3% to 10% of the people is enormous hemangioma, which is also called as hepatic hemangioma. It consists of blood bunches enclosed by endothelial cells. These hepatic hemangiomas are obtained from the hepatic pipes and branches of their blood. Generally, in women, these tumors are essential.

Wherever there is a major innate or hereditary sector, the reason for the liver hemangioma remains obscure. It is not known that they depend on existing literature. They are dangerous, and these hepatic hemangiomas in the liver usually cause symptoms for the tumor growth. Usually, the size of the hemangioma is very tiny and is of 10 cm in size. Normally, this size remains consistent over a period of time. If the hemangioma's growth is large, then it will lead to stomach torment, feeling of fullness, cardiac problems, and coagulatory dysfunction in the right upper region of the stomach. Cavernous hemangiomas have clinical imaging determined. In view of their kindness and often asymptomatic nature, huge hemangiomas are usually unexpectedly analyzed (for example, at the point when clinical imaging is gotten for another reason). As far as the board is concerned, the individual's pregnancy is normally checked with occasional imagery just as carefully. If the hemangioma grows rapidly and also the patient is indicative, then, for sure, the clinical mediation is needed through open or laparoscopic, careful resection, embolization, or ablation of the blood vessel. It is rare for a hepatic hemangioma to break down or drain. As far as entanglements of hepatic hemangiomas are concerned, the drain of breakdown of hepatic hemangioma is atypical.

6.2.2.1.2   Liver Cell Adenomatiosis

The liver cell adenomatiosis is the conclusion arrived from hepatocellular adenoma also known as hepatic adenomatosis. They are equivalent to hepatic adenomas in clinical imagery and histopathological biopsy results. Liver adenomatiosis varies from hepatic adenomatosis, which differs from increase of 10 hepatic adenomas that are found in both liver flaps in a person and they would not take exogenous hormones, as a result of which, glycogen storage disease is not present and does not occur. The association of use of steroids and liver cell adenomatosis is that the size is not affected while taking the oral contraceptives that contains estrogens. Liver cell adenomatosis is fairly related to hepatic fracture and higher filament rates than hepatic adenomas alone. Draining on an average of 63% patients with liver cell adenomatosis is recommended in available evidence. In addition, HCC has been linked to liver cell adenomatosis. Like hepatic adenomas, images and biopsies depend on the situation. They are determined. Adenomatose is troubling because of various wide-ranging injuries in the liver cell. Liver imagery should be examined to see if tumors can be removed precisely. For some patients, liver transplant is a treatment option.

6.2.2.1.3   Liver Cyst

The buildings inside the liver are filled with liquid. In women and children, basic liver blisters are mostly seen. They are framed by formation opportunities and due to injury and inflammation, with regard to pathophysiology. What is more, polycystic kidney disease and echinocococcal contamination may cause liver sores (hydatid disease).

6.2.2.1.4   Pseudo Tumor

The major difference between the liver tumor and pseudo tumor is not merely a mutation of strange cells. It is noticed that the pseudo-liver tumors may be mistaken for liver tumor when an early picture test shows that a liver mass is agitated. Pseudo-tumor examples include unmistakable locations of hepatical fibrosis, incendiary pseudotumors, and pockets of changes in grey liver.

6.2.2.2   Malignant

In most cases the metastases of various tumors, GI parcels (e.g., colon, malignant growth and carcinoid supplementation tumors) are nonetheless not only bosomal, ovarian malignant growth, lung cell breakdown, renal malignancy, and HCC but also as an inherently threatening and essential liver malignancy. Cholangiocarcinoma, blended tumors, sarcoma, and hepatoblastoma are various essential types of liver malignant growth.

6.2.2.2.1   Hepatocellular Carcinoma

The most famous kind of essential liver disease of grown-ups, the HCC, has become the prime cause of mortality among people having cirrhosis since then. It is most strongly related to persistent viral contamination of liver or openness to drinks such as liquors, pyrrolizidine alkaloids, or aflatoxins in the environment of constant liver irritation. The danger of HCC has been increased by the diseases, namely, hemochromatosis and alpha 1-antitrypsin failure. In addition, nonalcoholic steatohepatitis (NASH) and metabolism are also seen as risk factors for HCC. Similarly to malignancy, the therapy and the visualization of HCC change depends on the tumor histology, size, extent, and overall well-being of the disease. It is found that the majority of HCC has been diagnosed in Southeast Asia and few parts of Africa in countries with endemic hepatitis B infection and many with birth defects. HCC frequency is quite increasing in the United States and, in other agricultural countries, as hepatitis C diseases are increasing. For obscure reasons, it is more normal in men than women.

6.2.2.2.2   Cholangiocarcinoma

Cholangiocarcinoma is a rapid and regularly deadly type of liver disease or bile pipe malignancy. A tumor that develops in the bile ducts of the hepatic is generally uncommon but strong. Cholangiocarcinoma has only approximately 5,000 new incidences a year, and it is a difficult condition to resolve. Treatment options for cholangiocarcinoma: Careful resection of liver or liver transplant is the favored cholangiocarcinoma therapy. Alternatives to cholangiocarcinoma treatment depend on how best the disease is in class.

6.2.2.2.3   Hepatoblastoma

The most known kind of liver malignance growth in children is the hepatoblastoma. It influences children younger than three most and is more prevalent among children who have been prematurely conceived. It is not clear why hepatoblastoma. The majority of young people with hepatoblastoma show no evidence and the disease progresses in 40% of patients. The malignant growth metastasized (spreads) to the lungs in 20% of patients when it is complete. However, late analysis and therapy advances in young people with hepatoblastoma have led to incredibly better forecasts.

Main causes of liver tumor:

❖ HCC is occurring due to defects at the time of birth, consumption of alcohol, and chronic hepatitis B and hepatitis C.
❖ Hemochromatosis will be caused due to more iron formation in liver, hereditary, and cirrhosis.

Table 6.1 Different modalities of diagnosing liver cancer.

Diagnosis methods	Methodology
Radio frequency ablation (RFA)	Radio frequency removal (RFA) is negligibly obtrusive treatment that includes utilizing imaging (ultrasound, CT, or MRI) to manage a needle cathode into a tumor.
Embolization	Little particles called microspheres are infused into the hepatic course to stop the progression of blood to the tumor. Embolization "starves" the tumor and captures its development.
Ultrasound	Ultrasonography of liver tumors includes two phases: recognition and characterization.
Computed Tomography	A CT scan of the abdomen helps to find different types of liver tumors. It gives specific information about the size, shape, and location of any tumors in the liver or elsewhere in the abdomen and in nearby blood vessels.
MRI	It provides detailed images of soft tissues in the body. However, MRI scans use radio waves and strong magnets and helpful in identifying the tumor that is benign or malignant.

❖ Hemochromatosis and chronic hepatitis B lead to liver failure.
❖ Due to fatty liver and obesity.

Table 6.1 describes the different modalities in diagnosing the liver cancer [12–14].

6.3   Benefits of CT to Diagnose Liver Cancer

A CT output of the liver and biliary plot might be performed to evaluate the liver as well as gallbladder and their connected constructions for tumors and different sores, wounds, dying, diseases, abscesses, unexplained stomach agony, checks, or different conditions, especially when another kind of assessment, for example, X-beams, actual assessment, and ultrasound; it is not definitive [25]. A CT sweep of the liver might be utilized to recognize obstructive and non-obstructive jaundice. Another utilization of CT outputs of the liver and biliary plot is to give direction to biopsies or potentially goal of tissue from the liver or gallbladder. There might be different purposes behind your PCP to suggest a CT output of the liver and biliary plot [18–20].

6.4   Literature Review

In the work of AtrayeeDutta and AdityaDubey (2019) *et al.*, the system used a liver MRI image to detect liver tumor. For pre-processing, the system uses Anotsu method, and for segmentation, the watershed method has been used. In this paper, tumor is segmented by the foreground and background objects location [1]. The morphological operation is used to detect the liver cancer from liver CT image. This method achieves a less computational power and minimum number of calculations. The accuracy is achieved is 96%. The limitation of the system is that it can detect only the single mass of tumor [2]. This paper proposed a method to detect tumor from CT liver image. The system used a CLAHE method and median filter for pre-processing. After pre-processing to segment the tumor from the liver the FCN algorithm is employed. This paper provides a good accuracy [3]. The MRF embedded level set method is used in this research to remove noise and artifacts. After pre-processing, the sparse field method is applied for tumor segmentation from liver CT image [9–11]. This paper provides a 3D visualization and the accuracy also good [4]. The lesions are separated from the liver CT image. The given input image is contrast enhanced. Then, each pixel in the image is labeled as either lesion or normal tissue that depends on the pixel intensity. However, this method provides the accuracy of 77% [5]. Abhay Krishan *et al.* used a CLAHE and CVHE methods used for enhancement of CT liver image. The SVM classifier is applied to the segmented image for classification of CT liver image [5]. Priyanka Kumar *et al.* proposed an automatic detection of liver tumor using fuzzy logic technique. The neural network and windowing method used with fuzzy method to detect the liver tumor effectively [6]. V. Kannan *et al.* proposed a system to detect liver cancer. Otsu's and k-means clustering methods adopted to segment the cancer from liver CT image. The performance of the system is assessed by the PSNE, MSE, and SNR. This paper shows better results for segmentation [8]. Dr. Alyaa *et al.* described a 2D liver segmentation for the purpose of liver tumor treatment. To achieve a good accuracy, the modified K-means clustering is employed and this provides a good output [27]. The features of liver such as perimeter, area, and diameter were calculated to know the regularity of the tumor.

6.5 Interactive Liver Tumor Segmentation by Deep Learning

In this system, the liver part is segmented from the whole abdominal CT scan; if it consists of any type of lesion in the liver, then it segments and filters the image and, later on, after completion of all processes, the result is displayed in the system explaining about the type of liver tumor with the texture of tumor; it explains whether it is an benign or malignant one [15–17].

6.6 Existing System

In earlier systems, a multi-scale candidate generation and fractal residual network has been adopted, and they came up with a training model that cascades to segment liver tumors, suing the abdomen CT image volumes [21–23]. The challenge involved in this model was that two networks have to be designed one for liver and the other one is for liver tumor. Here, the liver tumor division techniques on CT image volumes have been carried out by MCG, 3D FRN, and ACM techniques [27, 28].

6.7 Proposed System

In this chapter, we proposed an image processing technique to detect the liver tumor. The liver CT images have been collected from the hospital and online data database. The proposed system focuses on tumor segmentation of medical image sequences using active contour segmentation. The proposed system comprises three modules, namely, pre-processing module, segmentation module, and classification. Figure 6.3 shows the block diagram of the proposed method.

6.7.1 Pre-Processing

The input CT images are given to the pre-processing stage. In this pre-processing stage, if the input images are colour images, then it converts into grayscale image before segmenting it.

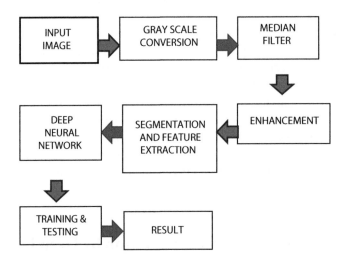

Figure 6.3 Block diagram of the proposed system.

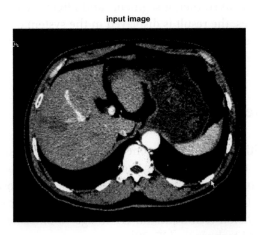

Figure 6.4 Input image.

Grayscale image

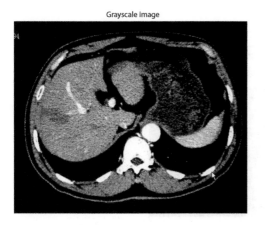

Filter image

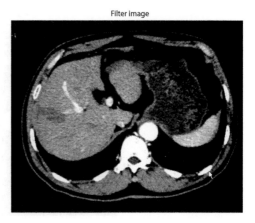

Figure 6.5 Grayscale image and filter image.

Enhancement Image

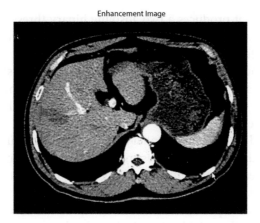

Figure 6.6 Enhancement image.

After the grayscale conversion, the image is undergoing for normalization process. Usually, the image normalization is used for preparing the input datasets for further process. Here, the various images are put into the uniform statistical distribution. Then, the normalized images are filtered by using the median filter. The median filter is used to remove the noise or any other distortion from the image. The filtered image is enhanced by the histogram equalization. This equalization method is used to adjust the image intensities, and hence, the contrast is enhanced. Figures 6.4 to 6.6 shows the input, grayscale, filter, and enhancement images, respectively.

6.7.2   Segmentation

Segmentation plays an important part in medical image analysis. Segmentation is a method to divide medical images into multiple parts. It helps doctor to study the images for further analysis. Before going to do segmentation, first, the image is threshold. In thresholding, the image is converted into binary image. The proposed system uses an absolute threshold

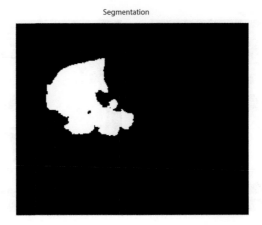

Figure 6.7 Active contoured segmented image.

value binarization, where it produces a two absolute binary threshold images. In this, the image having threshold value greater than the initial threshold is considered as one image and the threshold value less than the initial threshold is considered as another image.

After thresholding, the boundary has been detected more precisely for further analysis of image. The proposed system uses a boundary detection algorithm to identify the exact boundary regions in the CT liver image. This boundary detection helps us to segment the exact working area in the image.

From the thresholded image, the boundary has detected. The unwanted region in the image has been removed for further processing of image. Furthermore, by using the area property of the connected components of region grow operators, the tumor is segmented from the CT liver image. The neighboring pixels of each and every pixel in an image are compared with the reference pixel. The resultant compared value is equal or less than the threshold value, and then, the neighboring pixel is added to current selected pixel. In this, the tumor exact location and area affected by the tumor also identified. Finally, the tumor and their properties like area, location, and time of execution were determined. Figure 6.7 shows the segmented image.

6.7.3   Feature Extraction

Feature extraction is the process of decreasing the dimensionality. Here, the given raw data is divided into meaningful groups. The feature extraction method is useful when the large dataset is used. The feature extraction helps to reduce the no of features from the given dataset and creates the new one. With the help of new dataset, it is able to define the information contained in the original information.

6.7.4   GLCM

The GLCM algorithm is used to extract texture features from the mage. The texture features are calculated from the statistical distribution of pixels in a specified area. The GLCM consist of matrix where the number of rows and columns is equal to the number of gray

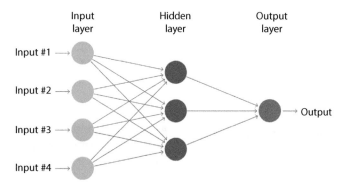

Figure 6.8 Structure of ANN.

levels in an image. This statistical approach calculates how often a gray level occurs horizontally, vertically, or diagonally to adjacent pixels value. The GLCM identifies the nearby pixels position, and this can expose the spatial distribution property. By using the GLCM, the characteristics of texture statistics of a liver CT image are extracted. In this paper, the important features, energy, entropy, and correlation homogeneity are measured.

6.7.5   Backpropagation Network

The artificial neural network is the structure of connected input and out units. Figure 6.8 shows the structure of ANN. Between this input and output layer, the hidden layer is present. This network is used to predict models from large database. With the help of neural network, it is helpful to analyze image. Backpropagation network fine tune the weights of a neural network based on the error rate which is obtained from previous iteration. While doing proper weight adjustment, the error rate is reduced, and the system becomes a more reliable. For a given set of input patterns, the backpropagation algorithm trains a feedforward network with known classification. When the input enters into the network, it will calculate the output response. This output response is compared with the desired response and examines the error rate. Depends on the error, the weight is adjusted. The weight adjust process continues until the error rate is minimized. In BPN, the weight adjustment is done through the mean square error of the output. The algorithm has the important steps of feedforward computation, backpropagation to output and hidden layer, and weight updates. Figure 6.8 depicts the structure of ANN [24, 26].

6.8   Result and Discussion

This software system segments the only liver part from whole abdominal CT scan image and provides the location of tumor along with its stage information whether it is benign or malignant by comparing it with datasets stored in the system. The threshold is required for adjusting itself according to segmented area and position. Deep learning method is used while comparing the data information fed into the system [29].

This system helps to get a result in less processing time, which is also reliable and accurate through which it displays that the tumors' location, size, and the stage that is it is a cancerous lesion or non-cancerous one by applying different process mentioned above.

6.8.1   Processed Images

Figure 6.9 shows the output of the various process applied to the input liver image. Figure 6.10 shows that the the proposed algorithm gives the result that the given input liver image is normal. Figure 6.11 shows the segmentation of tumor from the liver image.

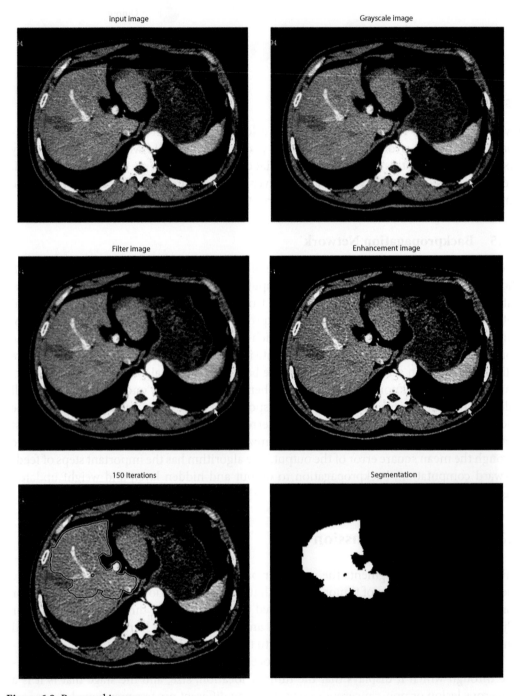

Figure 6.9 Processed images.

normal

OK

Figure 6.10 Result.

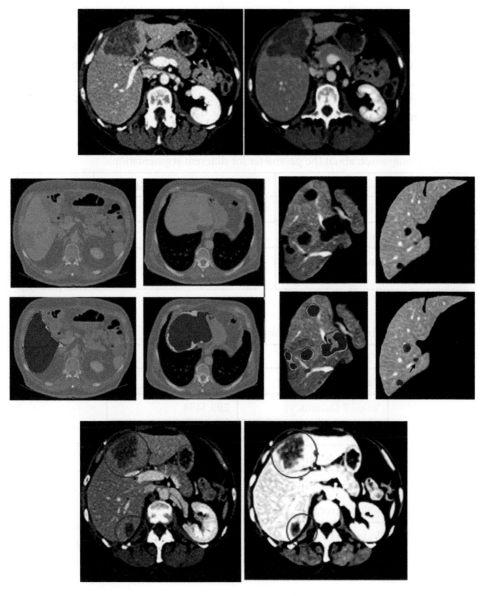

Figure 6.11 Segmented images.

Figure 6.12 shows that various plots which is result of gradient values, performance, error histogram, regression and fit.

6.8.2   Segmentation

Table 6.2 shows the comparison results of the parameters for different segmentation methods, and the system parameters are depicted in Table 6.3.

The datasets are trained by using the artificial neural network [30] and tested by the backpropagation method, which is used to find the gradient values of the error function by varying weights applied in it. The dataset is divided into training set of 70%, validation set of 15%, and testing set of 15%; through this, the graph is plotted by calculating the gradient and validation values. The system generates the output on the basis of values, which is summed together and the conditions are as follows:

If (area > 5,000 and area < 9,000), then it is normal; if area is greater than 9,000, then it is abnormal, and if the area is lesser than 5,000, then it is non-tumor condition.

Here, in this system, we gave 22 input datasets, and around 85 images are saved for comparing purpose in the system, which processes the input and provides the result that whether it is tumor or non-tumor or normal.

Table 6.2 Comparison about the parameter for different segmentations.

Segmentation	Average dice	Sensitivity	Accuracy
FCN with manual segmentation	0.68	0.80	86%
Graph cuts and watershed	1.5	0.75	88%
Region-based segmentation with active contour	–	1	94%

Table 6.3 System parameters.

Values	Readings
Value 1 (image size)	235 × 290 logical
Value 2 (accuracy)	290.3484
Value 3 (sensitivity)	1
Value 4 (specificity)	0.4676
Value 5 (precision)	0.1085
Value 6 (recall)	1
Value 7 (F1 score)	0.1957

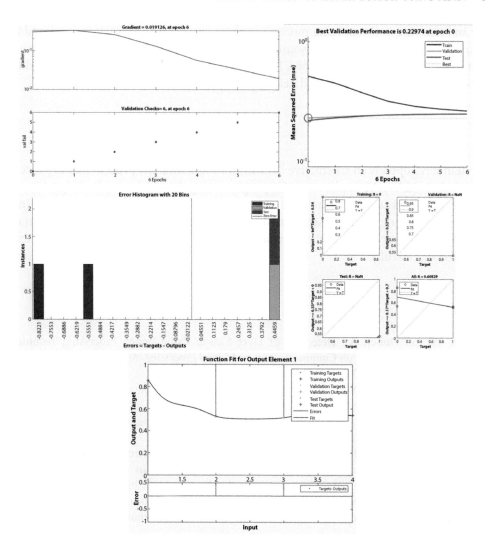

Figure 6.12 Plots showing the gradient values, performance, error histogram, regression, and fit.

6.9   Future Enhancements

In the future application, we expect more accuracy and explaining the name of cancer with stages by applying some more methods and classifying it in the report that is provided with the patients name and the data information will also be stored for future references. This also safeguards the information of a particular patient history by maintaining and comparing this data report with another patients report for studying about the particular tumor and studying it. By applying more algorithms, we can get accuracy and reduced time consumption, and we can also add some other specifications like providing the numerous patients database for research purpose. It will be also useful in identifying the mortality or tumors' infectious nature, which will help doctors or researchers to know about it.

6.10   Conclusion

The system developed is an interactive liver tumor segmentation process that is processed with the help of MATLAB applications for programming the system; various algorithms are used here for processing the segmented data into a form of output. Segments of the image are enhanced resulting in a clear segmented image. This system also has classifiers that classify the stage of tumor and produce the result. Thus, the system processes are implemented and verified successfully.

References

1. Dutta, A. and Dubey, A., Detection of Liver Cancer using Image Processing Techniques. *International Conference on Communication and Signal Processing*, April 4-6, 2019, India, IEEE, ©2019, 978-1-5386-7595-3/19/$31.00.
2. Aarthi, R., Nivetha, S., Vikashini, P., Balamurugan, V.T., Liver cancer detection using image processing. *Int. Res. J. Eng. Technol. (IRJET)*, 07, 03, 1425, Mar 2020.
3. Saranya, S. and Pushpa, M., Liver tumor detection for CT images using image processing technques. *Int. J. Curr. Res.*, 8, 06, 32426–32429, June, 2016.
4. Raj, A. and Jayasree, M., Automated Liver Tumor Detection Using Markov Random Field Segmentation, International Conference on Emerging Trends in Engineering, Science and Technology, (ICETEST - 2015). *Procedia Technol.*, 24, 1305–1310, 2016.
5. Militzer, A. *et al.*, Automatic detection and segmentation of focal liver lesions in contrast enhanced CT images. *Pattern Recognition (ICPR), 2010 20th International Conference on IEEE*, 2010.
6. Krishan, A. and Mittal, D., Detection and Classification of Liver Cancer using CT Images. *Int. J. Recent Technol. Mech. Electr. Eng. (IJRMEE)*, 2, 5, 093–098, May 2015,
7. Kumar, P. and Bhalerao, S., Detection of Tumor in Liver Using Image Segmentation and Registration Technique. *IOSR J. Electron. Commun. Eng. (IOSR-JECE)*, 9, 2, Ver. VIII , 110–115, Mar - Apr. 2014.
8. Kannan, V. and Jagan Naveen, V., Detection of Liver Cancer Using Image Segmentation. *Int. J. Adv. Sci. Technol.*, 29, 3, 7067–7078, 2020, Retrieved from http://sersc.org/journals/index.php/IJAST/article/view/7565.
9. Ali, A.H. and Hadi, E.M., Diagnosis of Liver Tumor from CT Images using Digital Image Processing. *Int. J. Sci. Eng. Res.*, 6, 1, 685, January-2015.
10. Masuda, Y., Tateyama, T., Xiong, W., Zhou, J., Wakamiya, M., Kanasaki, S. *et al.*, Liver tumor detection in CT images by adaptive contrast enhancement and the EM/MPM algorithm. *Proc. 18th IEEE Int. Conf. Image Process*, 1421–1424, Feb. 2012.

11. Jiang, H., Shi, T., Bai, Z., Huang, L., AHCNet: An application of attention mechanism and hybrid connection for liver tumor segmentation in CT volumes. *IEEE Access*, 7, 24898–24909, 2019.

12. Bellver, M., Maninis, K.-K., Pont-Tuset, J., Giro-I-Nieto, X., Torres, J., Van Gool, L., Detection-aided liver lesion segmentation using deep learning. arXiv:1711.11069, 2017.

13. Vorontsov, E., Abi-Jaoudeh, N., Kadoury, S., Metastatic liver tumor segmentation using texture-based omni-directional deformable surface models, in: *Abdominal Imaging. Computational and Clinical Applications*, pp. 74–83, Springer, Cham, Switzerland, 2014.

14. Kumar, S.S., Moni, R.S., Rajeesh, J., Contourlet Transform Based Computer-Aided Diagnosis System for Liver Tumor on Computed Tomography Images. *International Conference on Signal Processing, Communication, Computing and Networking Technologies*, 2011.

15. Gibson, E., Robu, M.R., Thompson, S., Deep residual networks for automatic segmentation of laparoscopic videos of the liver. *Medical Imaging*, 2017, spiedigitallibrary.org.

16. Vorontsov, E., Cerny, M., Régnier, P., Di Jorio, L., Deep learning for automated segmentation of liver lesions at CT in patients with colorectal cancer liver metastases. *Radiology: Artificial*, 2019.

17. Krizhevsky, A., Sutskever, I., Hinton, G., Image Net Classification with Deep Convolutional Neural Networks. *Adv. Neural Inf. Process. Syst.*, 1097–1105, 2012.

18. Moghbel, M., Mashohor, S., Mahmud, R., Saripan, M.I.B., Automatic liver tumor segmentation on computed tomography for patient treatment planning and monitoring. *EXCLI J.*, 15, 406–23.4. 2016.

19. Almotairi, S., Kareem, G., Aouf, M., Almutairi, B., Liver tumor segmentation in CT scans using modified segnet. *Sensors*, 2020.

20. Ben-Dan, I. and Shenhav, E., Liver Tumor segmentation in CT images using probabilistic methods. *MICCAI Workshop*, 2008.

21. Kuo, C.L., Cheng, S.C., Lin, C.L., Hsiao, K.F., Texture-based treatment prediction by automatic liver tumor segmentation on computed tomography. *Systems (CITS)*, 2017.

22. Todoroki, Y., Han, X.H., Iwamoto, Y., Lin, L., Hu, H., Detection of liver tumor candidates from CT images using deep convolutional neural networks. *on Innovation in*, 2017.

23. Abdel-Massieh, N.H. and Hadhoud, M.M., Automatic liver tumor segmentation from CT scans with knowledge-based constraints. *2010 5th Cairo*, 2010.

24. Montagnon, E., Cerny, M., Cadrin-Chênevert, A., Deep learning workflow in radiology: A primer. *Insights into Imaging*, 2020.

25. Joshi, D. and Londhe, N.D., Automatic liver tumor detection in abdominal CT images. *Int. J. Comput. Technol.*, 2013.

26. Gregory, J., Burgio, M.D., Corrias, G., Vilgrain, V., Ronot, M., Evaluation of liver tumor response by imaging. *JHEP Rep.*, 2020.

27. Randhawa, S., Alsadoon, A., Prasad, P.W.C., Deep learning for liver tumor classification: Enhanced loss function. *Multimed. Tools Appl.*, 2021.

28. Brunetti, A., Carnimeo, L., Trotta, G.F., Bevilacqua, V., Computer-assisted frameworks for classification of liver, breast and blood neoplasias via neural networks: A survey based on medical images. *Neurocomputing*, 2019.

29. Prakash, T., Medical image processing methodology for liver tumor diagnosis. *Int. J. Soft Comput. (IJSC)*, 2017.

30. Mohana Priya, R., Hema, L.K., Vanitha, V., Karthikeyan, R., Classification and Detection of Malarial Parasite in Blood Samples Using K-Means Clustering Algorithm and Support Vector Machine Classifier, in: *Micro electronics and Telecommunication Engineering*, pp. 423–428.

7

DMSAN: Deep Multi-Scale Attention Network for Automatic Liver Segmentation From Abdomen CT Images

Devidas T. Kushnure[1,2]* and Sanjay N. Talbar[1]

[1]Department of Electronics and Telecommunication Engineering, Shri Guru Gobind Singhji Institute of Engineering & Technology, Vishnupuri, Nanded, Maharashtra, India
[2]Department of Electronics and Telecommunication Engineering, Vidya Pratishthan's Kamalnayan Bajaj Institute of Engineering and Technology, Baramati, Pune, Maharashtra, India

Abstract

Automatic liver segmentation plays a decisive role in the medical realm for a clinical interpretation of hepatic diseases. In clinical routine, the manual procedure utilized to delineate the liver. However, manual delineation is a time-intensive and laborious task that could introduce error and variation in the estimation. The amount of error in the segmentation results reliant on the skills and expertise of the operator. Recently, many researchers exploiting the deep convolutional neural network (CNN) for medical image segmentation. In this chapter, the authors proposed a CNN-based deep multi-scale feature representation model that empowers CNN to characterize granular details by amalgamating various features with diverse scales, resulting in an enhancement of the receptive field of CNN. In addition, the learning capability of the network layers boosted by fusing high- and low-level features.

Furthermore, segmentation performance refined by recalibrating the skip-connection features using the attention layer. The network trained end-to-end for liver segmentation on the LiTS and CHAOS challenge dataset. The authors demonstrated the efficacy of a deep multi-scale attention network (DMSAN) on publicly available 3DIRCADb and CHAOS CT test datasets. The proposed network achieved the dice score (DSC) of 0.973 and 0.964 on 3DIRCADb and CHAOS datasets, respectively. The comparative result analysis signifies that DMSAN outperforms the state-of-the-art methods.

Keywords: CNN, attention network, multi-scale features, feature recalibration, feature fusion, liver segmentation, CT images

7.1 Introduction

Radio imaging is the non-invasive procedure of analyzing internal body parts and structures. It plays a vital position in the clinical procedure and treatment planning of diseases.

---

*Corresponding author: devidas.kushnure@gmail.com

Tushar H. Jaware, K. Sarat Kumar, Ravindra D. Badgujar and Svetlin Antonov (eds.) Medical Imaging and Health Informatics, (121–140) © 2022 Scrivener Publishing LLC

Medical imaging modalities like ultrasound, CT, and magnetic resonance imaging (MRI) preferred for analysis and diagnosis purposes. The CT images become medical experts' choice for hepatic complications due to their immense availability, less scanning period, robustness, and higher resolution [1]. The liver segmentation from radio imaging is essential for many medical applications, including liver transplantation, liver resection planning, radiation dose determination in radioembolization for liver tumors, treatment planning, post-treatment assessment, liver volume measurement, and computer-assisted diagnosis (CAD). Currently, the radiologist manually delineates the liver, which is tedious, labor-exhaustive, and susceptible to error, making segmentation become operator reliant [2]; because of these grounds, automatic segmentation of the liver has been of interest for many researchers.

In the last decade, many researchers proposed liver segmentation methods to foster the medical domain requirements. Several frameworks proposed for automatic liver segmentation without human intervention could be the second opinion for the medical experts to make the correct decision in less time. Despite that, automatic liver segmentation remains challenging because of its shape variability, fewer intensity variations between the liver and adjacent organs, overlap with nearby organs, and confusing liver boundaries. The liver is squashy because the liver shape is dependent on surrounding organs. Furthermore, the CT images are acquired by injecting a contrast agent for enhancement; the quantity of contrast decides the noise in CT images, which is already noisy without contrast. Due to these difficulties, the automatic liver segmentation from CT images remains a challenging task [3].

In this chapter, the following contributions are incorporated by the authors:

- The conventional encoder path in UNet architecture is replaced with a Res2Net (R2N) module that has the competence to extract the multi-scale features with more granular details and expand the receptive field of CNN. Because of many features with diverse scales that better represent the liver region from input CT images.
- In addition, the high-resolution features are fused with multi-scale low-resolution features to further enhance the liver region more prominently in the feature map that boosts the learning of the successive encoding stages.
- Furthermore, added an attention layer that recalibrates the skip-connection features by focusing more on the liver region. As a result, it refines the network's segmentation performance in the decoding path.
- Designed and trained the end-to-end network and demonstrated segmentation performance on two publicly available datasets (3DIRCADb and CHAOS). The statistical performance is compared with state-of-the-art methods, and submitted the segmentation results on the CHAOS challenge leaderboard and validated the model's liver segmentation performance.

7.2   Related Work

Segmentation of the liver from abdominal images is a process of extracting the liver region from the images. For separation of the liver parenchyma in CT slices, the conventional image segmentation methods based on the distribution of HU values in CT images used to extract the features, shape information, and texture of liver region such as gray level, structure-based, and texture-based methods [4, 23]. However, the drawback of these models is that the model's parameters need to be decided by the expert's prior knowledge, which is significantly affected by expert to expert.

Recently, deep learning has become widespread in the medical imaging field. Deep learning algorithms, in specific convolutional neural networks (CNNs), have become a technique for examining medical images for various applications that are summarized [5, 6]. CNN becomes prevalent in computer vision applications due to its adequate nonlinear feature abstraction latent using numerous filters at various network layers and processing a massive data volume [7]. Moreover, the architectures based on CNN outdid in the many visual recognition applications like image classification, object recognition, and action recognition. In particular, AlexNet, VGGNet, and GoogleNet proved their calibre in ImageNet Large Scale Visual Recognition Challenge (ILSVRC) for visual recognition applications [8]. Later, researchers expanded the classification network's backbone for semantic segmentation by modifying the last fully dense layers with convolutional layers. These networks referred to the fully convolutional neural network (FCN) [9] architecture utilized explicitly for semantic segmentation.

For segmentation, the FCN decoder network became the most effective because the segmentation maps are the same as that of input image size. Therefore, the FCN encoder-decoder architecture proposed [10] for the biomedical image segmentation becomes the decision for the medical image segmentation. The encoding path shrinks the feature maps because of consecutive convolution layer and max-pooling layers, which extracts high-level information and pass it to the next layer, encoding the feature maps downsampled by convolution and pooling layers to acquire the low-resolution feature maps. The feature maps rebuild to the identical size of the input image by upsampling the encoded feature maps using a decoding path. The skip connection is utilized to bring high-level feature maps in the encoder to the decoder at the respective stages to construct the segmentation map [11].

In UNet architecture, the segmentation performance is limited due to the following reasons: at the encoder, the input features resolution reduced noticeably due to consecutive downsampling and convolution operations that lead to a loss in spatial details of the object. As the number of layers increased, the context information about the object cannot be propagated to the deeper layers. This context detail is critical in examining medical images for precise segmentation of the region of interest.

This chapter proposed the deep learning framework based on the encoder-decoder architecture called deep multi-scale attention network (DMSAN) for automatic segmentation of the liver in CT images. The proposed approach utilized the multi-scale feature depiction and combined high-level features from the preceding layer with the next layer's multi-scale features. The attention mechanism recalibrates the features of the skip connection to enhances the liver segmentation performance.

7.3   Methodology

7.3.1   Proposed Architecture

This chapter proposed the deep learning framework called DMSAN for the automatic segmentation of the liver in CT images. The proposed method is inspired by the architecture proposed in the paper [12]. Figure 7.1 shows the proposed network, which has an encoder path different from UNet architecture to achieve better segmentation performance, whereas the decoder path is kept intact. The encoder path utilized the R2N bottleneck module that enhances the feature extraction capability of the CNNs. In addition, the R2N block can characterize the more detailed granular features layer-wise by improving the receptive field.

In FCN, during the encoding process, due to consecutive pooling and convolution operations, the feature map size becomes downsampled at each stage, which results in spatial resolution loss of input image that degrades the model performance. The multi-scale feature representation approach extracts the more detailed features because of the number of small convolution layers employed in the architecture of the R2N, which advances the CNN's cumulative receptive field [13]. The proposed architecture also employed a high-resolution feature fusion mechanism from the previous encoding stage to the next stage, improving the network's potential to represent the more prominent liver region features. A more explicit portrayal of the multi-scale features could lead to better liver segmentation. Moreover, the multi-scale fused feature maps merged into an attention strategy based on feature recalibration achieved using 1×1 convolution with sigmoid activation, uplifting the deep networks' feature representation ability. The recalibrated features concatenated with the corresponding upsampling stage employing skip connection while decoding segmentation map.

The entire training and testing pipeline of the DMSAN is demonstrated in Figure 7.2. First, the input CT dataset is prepared in preprocessing steps for training network and trained model tested on the test dataset, and then, network segmentation outcome is evaluated.

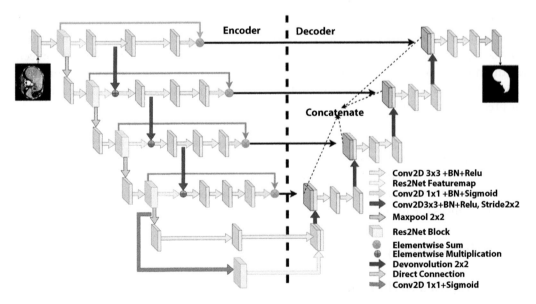

Figure 7.1 The proposed DMSAN architecture.

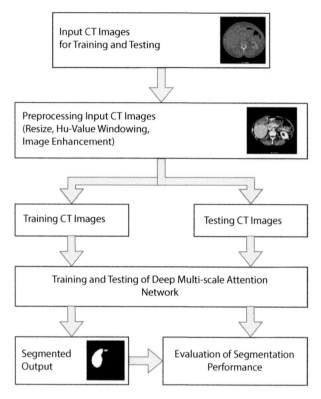

Figure 7.2 Illustration of training and testing pipeline of the DMSAN.

7.3.2 Multi-Scale Feature Characterization Using Res2Net Module

In numerous vision recognition tasks such as object detection, face detection, semantic segmentation, salient object detection, face detection, and skeleton detection [13], multi-scale feature representation has immense significance. It is essential to abstract the relative information of objects CNN models required to exercise features at various scales for effective semantic segmentation. For competent CNN models, it is essential to represent the region of interest at different scales in an image.

Figure 7.3 shows the R2N module employed in the network to advance the proficiency of CNN by characterizing granular details layer-wise that leads to improvement in the receptive field. The R2N module exhibits a new aspect, and the number of features is divided into a small group in the R2N block, the term, namely, scale. The multi-scale features extraction achieved by employing a cluster of small size convolution filters with size 3×3 with n channels that decide the scaling factor(s). In addition, the computational burden of the network reduced, and feature learning enhanced. The small set of filters attached in a residual hierarchical approach ensures a different scale and improves the output feature representation. Lastly, all features from the subsets representing distinct features of different resolutions and varying mixtures of the receptive field are fused to represent complete information [13, 32].

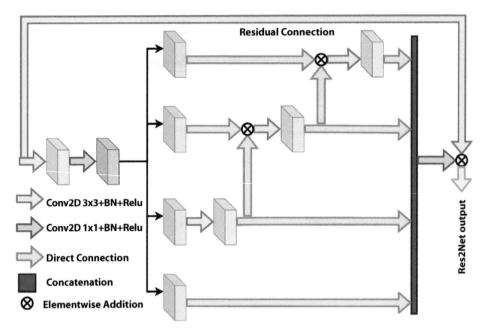

Figure 7.3 Res2Net (R2N) module.

The R2N module extracts the global and local multi-scale features by splitting the features, and the concatenation operation fuses the features of various scales to represent the information. Through the split and concatenation operation, it allows the transformation of the features more proficiently. The multiple identical information passed through 3×3 convolutions increases the receptive field due to aggregation effects.

7.4   Experimental Analysis

7.4.1   Dataset Description

The experimentation performed on the Liver Tumor Segmentation (LiTS) Challenge [14, 15] dataset is provided by the hospital worldwide. It comprises 201 contrast-enhanced CT volumes, out of which 131 cases are provided with ground truth for liver and tumor region. Each axial slice has a 512×512 spatial resolution.

The publicly available 3DIRCADb dataset [16] is a part of the LiTS Challenge dataset. 3DIRCADb database comprises anonymous CT volumes of various patients and various structures of interest manually annotated by expert radiologists. A dataset containing the 20 CT volumes was acquired in an enhanced venous phase from various European hospitals with various CT scanners with spatial resolution is 512×512 of each axial slice.

The proposed network is trained on the LiTS dataset and Combined Healthy Abdominal Organ Segmentation challenge (CHAOS) dataset. Training data comprise 60 CT volumes from the LiTS dataset and 20 CT volumes from the CHAOS training dataset. The CHAOS dataset [17, 18] provides 40 CT volumes (20 train + 20 test) acquired at the portal venous

Table 7.1 LiTS, 3DIRCADb, and CHAOS dataset statistics.

Dataset parameters	LiTS	3DIRCADb	CHAOS
Total 3D CT volumes	201 (131 train + 70 test)	20	40 (20 train + 20 test)
Spatial resolution	512×512	512×512	512×512
Total slices in all the volumes [minimum–maximum]	[42–1026]	[74–260]	[78–294]
Voxel spacing in X axis (mm) [minimum–maximum]	[0.60–0.98]	[0.56–0.87]	[0.54–0.79]
Voxel spacing in Y axis (mm) [minimum–maximum]	[0.60–0.98]	[0.56–0.87]	[0.54–0.79]
Voxel spacing in Z axis (mm) (CT slice thickness) [minimum–maximum]	[0.45–0.5]	[1.60–4.00]	[2.00–3.20]

phase after injecting contrast agents of different patients who have healthy livers. All 3D CT volumes were annotated manually by three experienced radiologists. The spatial resolution is 512×512 of each axial slice. The performance is evaluated on the publicly available 3D 3DIRCADb and CHAOS test dataset provided in the challenge without ground truth. Table 7.1 shows the dataset details.

7.4.2   Pre-Processing Dataset

The liver parenchyma is the area of interest for segmentation in CT volume. Focusing on the liver portion in CT images, the irrelevant details and organs are removed from the CT volume to clean the liver region for segmentation. The relative densities in the CT images are measured in Hounsfield Units (HU), ranging from −1,000 to 1,000. The radiodensities for the liver in CT images fluctuate from 40 to 50 HU [19].

The entire CT volume preprocessed slice-by-slice, as mentioned in Figure 7.4. In the first step, CT images resized into 256×256 to reduce the computational overheads on the network. Then, global windowing of HU values with the window of (−250, 200) applied to eliminate the unwanted details and tissues from CT images that ensure the clean liver area for segmentation. Afterward, the normalization applied to the data to represent it on the same scale [0, 1], which allows the network to converge fast. Lastly, an image enhancement step was performed to acquire an enhanced liver section for delineation. The preprocessing results are shown in Figure 7.5, which offers a clean liver section for segmentation.

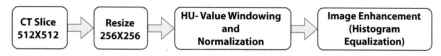

Figure 7.4 Preprocessing steps.

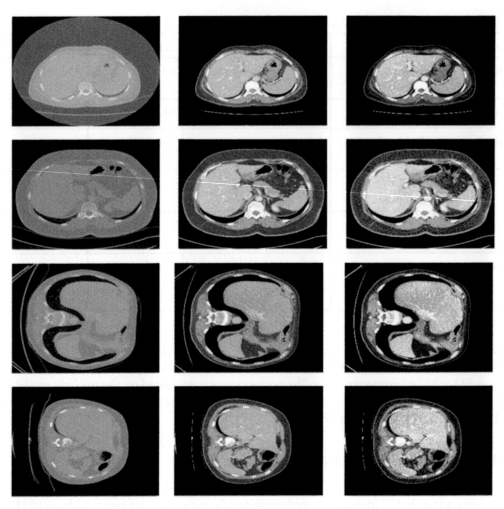

Figure 7.5 Preprocessing effect on input images (Rows 1 and 2, CHAOS dataset; Row 3, LiTS; and Row 4, 3DIRCADb dataset). The first column: resized (256 × 256) CT sample; the second column: HU windowing results; and the third column: the histogram equalized results.

7.4.3   Training Strategy

The network trained from scratch with Adam optimizer, 1×10^{-5} learning rate and a batch size eight was utilized. The training weights regularize using a weight decay of 1×10^{-5} to avoid overfitting.

7.4.4   Loss Function

The dice similarity coefficient (DSC) as a metric and a dice loss (L_{Dsc}) as a loss function for training, and it is the complement of the DSC [19] expressed as Equation (7.1).

$$L_{Dsc} = 1 - \frac{2\sum_{i=1}^{N} p_i \times g_i}{\sum_{i=1}^{N} P_i^2 + \sum_{i=1}^{N} g_i^2} \qquad (7.1)$$

where p_i is the binary predicted, g_i is the ground truth (GT), and N is the total voxels. It measures the similarity between two images and optimizes the network weight and loss accordingly.

7.4.5   Implementation Platform

The software platform utilized for the implementation is TensorFlow and Keras high-level artificial neural network library [20, 21]. The hardware platform was the following configuration: Intel(R)Xeon(R) CPU E5-16200, 16 GB RAM, NVIDIA GEFORCE TITAN-X GPU (12 GB memory), and Operating system—Windows 10.

7.4.6   Data Augmentation

Due to medical experts' unavailability in the medical domain, it is challenging and time-consuming to generate massive medical data with an annotation that limits deep learning in the medical domain. A large amount of data is required to avoid overfitting and better generalization of the new data to train deep neural networks. The small-size datasets are expanded by employing a data augmentation technique to train deep learning models. The data augmentation enables the use of deep learning on the small medical dataset. It permits enhancing the dataset by employing various transformations. The authors employed geometric transformations (rotation and scaling) and elastic deformation [22]. The data augmentation is helpful to diminish the overfitting issue during the training of the network and refine generalization ability on the unknown data.

7.4.7   Performance Metrics

The performance metrics utilized to assess the proposed model for liver segmentation are mentioned along with the minimum and maximum value and their implications in the segmentation performance evaluation illustrated in Table 7.2. These are the commonly utilized measures to evaluate the quality of segmentation results [23, 24]. The dice similarity coefficient (DSC), intersection of union (IoU), volumetric overlap error (VOE), and relative absolute volume difference (RAVD) are based on the volume overlap and relative size between GT and predicted result. The average symmetric surface distance (ASSD) and maximum symmetric surface distance (MSSD) are the surface distance metrics utilized for calculating the surface distance between GT and the predicted mask. The surface distance decides the boundary voxels and outliers in the predicted result. The A represents the GT, and B represents the predicted result.

Table 7.2 Performance metrics for liver segmentation quality evaluation.

Performance metrics	Formula	Implication
Dice similarity coefficient (DSC)	$DSC(A,B) = \dfrac{2|A \cap B|}{|A| + |B|}$	DSC = 1 perfect segmentation DSC = 0 worst segmentation
Intersection of union (IoU)	$IoU(A,B) = \dfrac{|A \cap B|}{|A \cup B|}$	IoU = 1 Perfect segmentation IoU = 0 worst segmentation
Volumetric overlap error (VOE)	$VOE(A,B) = \left(1 - \dfrac{|A \cap B|}{|A \cup B|}\right)$	VOE = 0 perfect segmentation VOE = 1 worst segmentation
Relative absolute volume difference (RAVD)	$RAVD = Abs\left(\dfrac{|B| - |A|}{|A|}\right)$	RAVD = 0 perfect segmentation RAVD = 1 worst segmentation
Average symmetric surface distance (ASSD)	$ASSD(A,B) = \dfrac{1}{|S(A)| + |S(B)|}\left(\sum_{S_A \in S(A)} d(S_A, S(B)) + \sum_{S_B \in S(B)} d(S_B, S(A))\right)$	ASSD = 0 mm perfect segmentation ASSD = Δ maximum value worst segmentation
Maximum symmetric surface distance (MSSD)	$MSSD(A,B) = max\left\{\max_{S_A \in S(A)} d(S_A, S(B)), \max_{S_B \in S(B)} d(S_B, S(A))\right\}$	MSSD = 0 mm perfect segmentation MSSD = Δ maximum value worst segmentation

Δ- No upper limit

7.5   Results

The proposed model trained from scratch and evaluated the performance using the performance measures mentioned in Table 7.2. The model performance is presented in Table 7.3. The multi-scale feature representation ability is explored by experimentation for different scale factors to leverage multi-scale feature characterization potential. The model's performance has evaluated by varying scaling factors s = 2, 4, and 8 of the R2N module. The experimentation performed on the two publicly available 3DIRCADb datasets offers significant complexity and variations and the CHAOS dataset with CT images of healthy liver volume. The network trained by varying scaling factors and evaluated the performance. The model shows the best performance for s = 4. The DSC, IoU, VOE, and RAVD are the significant measures utilized to analyze volume overlap between GT and predicted results. The ASSD and MSSD are the distance measures that decide the similarity between the surface voxels of GT and predicted results. The performance of the model is varying with the scaling factor of R2N. The DSC is the most utilized metric for analyzing the model's segmentation performance that decides the overlap between the GT and predicted volume. The proposed model shows the better DSC 97.3% ± 0.6% on the 3DIRCADb dataset and 96.4% ± 1% on the CHAOS dataset for s = 4. The detailed statistical analysis is presented graphically in Figure 7.6.

The model performance was validated for the liver segmentation on the CHAOS challenge test dataset. In the challenge, Task 2 is the segmentation of healthy liver from abdomen CT volumes. The submission results are available on the challenge leaderboard (https://chaos.grand-challenge.org; Team name: devidas.sggs submitted on October 7, 2020, 3:09 p.m.). The network trained for s = 4 shows better performance on the CHAOS validation dataset utilized while training; therefore, the same trained model was utilized for the test dataset. The performance on the leaderboard for the network trained for s = 4 is shown in the Table 7.4. The performance on each CT test set is presented graphically in Figure 7.7.

Table 7.3 Model performance on 3DIRCADb dataset for the different scaling factor.

Performance measures	Scaling factor (s)		
	s = 2	s = 4	s = 8
DSC	0.963 ± 0.012	0.973 ± 0.006	0.961 ± 0.008
IoU	0.931 ± 0.016	0.938 ± 0.013	0.935 ± 0.014
VOE	0.069 ± 0.016	0.062 ± 0.012	0.065 ± 0.015
RAVD	0.046 ± 0.019	0.059 ± 0.013	0.051 ± 0.017
ASSD (mm)	1.420 ± 1.491	0.710 ± 0.276	0.791 ± 0.292
MSSD (mm)	66.383 ± 23.18	63.037 ± 25.738	53.207 ± 26.560

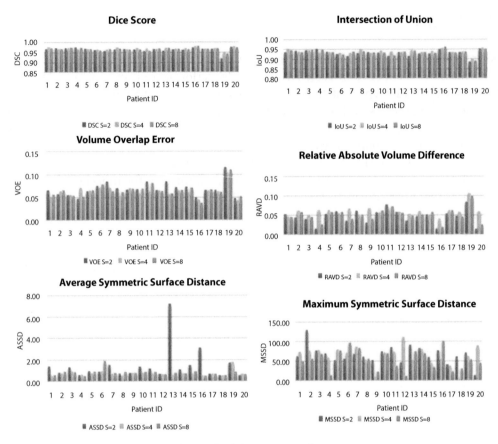

Figure 7.6 Results on the 3DIRCADb dataset for different statistical measures.

Table 7.4 Performance on CHAOS testing dataset.

Performance measures	CHAOS test CT dataset results scaling factor s = 4	Maximum score	Minimum score
DSC	0.964 ± 0.010	0.974	0.937
RAVD	3.794 ± 2.863	10.882	0.228
ASSD (mm)	3.831 ± 3.601	11.192	0.871
MSSD (mm)	121.751 ± 61.263	355.914	41.169

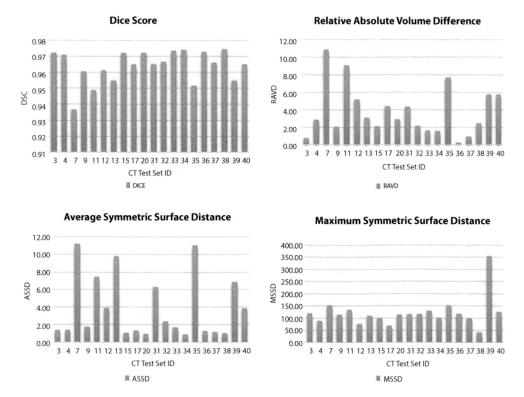

Figure 7.7 Results on the CHAOS test CT dataset.

The automatic segmentation of the liver is challenging because of its complex anatomical structure, varying liver shape and size, and less intensity difference in liver voxels and nearby abdomen organs. The liver boundaries are unclear because of the overlapping of adjacent organs. The proposed model performs effectively to segment complex liver parenchyma from the CT abdomen images with unclear liver boundaries, overlapped liver portions from the adjacent organs, and an adequately small liver region with more accuracy. The segmented sample mask on the test dataset (3DIRCADb dataset and CHAOS validation dataset) compared with the GT are presented in Figures 7.8 and 7.9. The result depicts that our proposed model has competence in the segmentation of the liver from the abdomen CT slices.

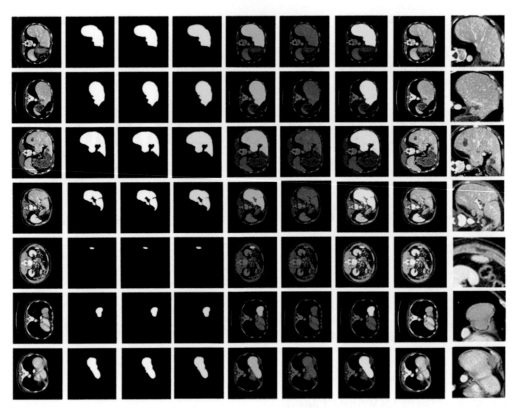

Figure 7.8 Segmented results on the 3Dircadb dataset. Column 1, input CT images; column 2, GT; column 3, segmented mask; column 4, overlap between GT and segmented mask (green color, GT; red color segmented mask; and yellow color, overlap); column 5, overlap between input CT image and GT; column 6, overlap between input CT image and segmented map; column 7, overlap between input CT image, GT, and segmented mask; column 8, the difference between GT and segmented mask on boundary voxels of the liver (green boundary for GT and red boundary for predicted mask); and column 9, the magnified liver region of eighth column images.

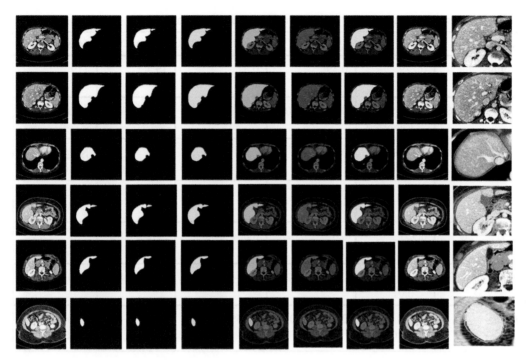

Figure 7.9 Segmented results on the CHAOS validation dataset. Column 1, input CT images; column 2, GT; column 3, segmented mask; column 4, overlap between GT and segmented mask (green color, GT; red color, segmented mask; and yellow color, overlap); column 5, overlap between input CT image and GT; column 6, overlap between input CT image and segmented map; column 7, overlap between input CT image, GT, and segmented mask; column 8, the difference between GT and segmented mask on boundary voxels of the liver (green boundary for GT and red boundary for predicted mask); and column 9, magnified liver region of eighth column images.

7.6   Result Comparison With Other Methods

The proposed network results compared with the state-of-the-art approaches utilized for liver delineation is illustrated in Tables 7.5 and 7.6. The dice score is a valuable metric utilized in numerous medical imaging segmentation, representing the overlap between GT and predicted mask. The DSC 0.973 and 0.964 on 3DIRCADb and CHAOS test dataset, respectively, achieved by the proposed model.

Table 7.5 Liver segmentation quantitative scores on 3DIRCADb dataset.

Methods	DSC	VOE	RAVD	ASSD	MSSD
Ronnebrger et al. [10]	0.729	0.39	0.87	19.4	119
Tang et al. [26]	Not Reported	0.087 ± 0.008	0.006 ± 0.025	1.37 ± 0.41	27.01 ± 7.28
Moghbel et al. [25]	0.9119	0.059	0.075	Not Reported	Not Reported
Christ et al. [27]	0.943	0.107	0.014	1.6	24
Li et al. [28]	0.951 ± 0.010	0.099 ± 0.028	0.004 ± 0.001	3.52 ± 0.88	9.35 ± 3.95
Seo et al. [29]	0.960 ± 0.011	0.097 ± 0.029	0.004 ± 0.001	3.11 ± 0.84	9.20 ± 3.43
Ours	**0.973 ± 0.006**	**0.062 ± 0.012**	**0.059 ± 0.013**	**0.710 ± 0.276**	**63.037 ± 25.738**

Table 7.6 Liver segmentation quantitative scores on CHAOS test set.

Methods	DSC	RAVD	ASSD	MSSD
Mulay et al. [30]	0.94 ± 0.03	Not Reported	Not Reported	Not Reported
Kavur et al. [31]	0.882	20.759	8.016	115.829
Ours	**0.964 ± 0.010**	**3.794 ± 2.863**	**3.831 ± 3.601**	**121.751 ± 61.263**

7.7 Discussion

Liver segmentation plays a vital role in many clinical applications. It is essential to make this process automated with a robust framework that will assist the medical experts in confirming the decision quickly during the diagnosis, treatment planning, and post-treatment assessment of the patient that saves the patient's life. The automatic segmentation of the liver is challenging due to its variable shape, similarities in the intensities with nearby organs, and the boundaries of the liver are ambiguous. This chapter presented the automatic segmentation of the liver with a deep learning model based on the multi-scale feature extraction and attention mechanism. The authors explored the multi-scale feature characterization potential of the R2N module. In UNet, the feature map resolution is reduced while downsampling because that critical information about the liver location is lost in every downsampling stage. The upsampling is performed by concatenating the feature map with respective downsampling stages for predicting the liver region from the encoded feature map. The downsampling approach of UNet is modified with a multi-scale framework with an attention mechanism to boost the segmentation performance. The authors utilized the multi-scale feature representation backbone R2N module in the network architecture instead of convolutional layers. The R2N module can abstract the more layer-wise granular features by improving CNN's receptive field, enhancing the subsequent downsampling layers' feature learning ability. The learning ability is further improved by fusing high-resolution features with low-resolution features. An attention layer is added to recalibrate the feature maps and refine skip-connection features to enhance the liver region's boundaries. It could improve the performance of the upsampling and segmentation quality. The results discussed in the above section indicate that the DMSAN can improve liver segmentation performance. The results validated with the CHAOS challenge test dataset that shows a better DSC score than the state-of-the-art algorithms utilized for liver segmentation.

As s- increases, multi-scale feature extraction ability and receptive field of the CNN improve that refines outcome. Therefore, s- can decide the feature extraction ability of the network. However, the s- increases moderately larger that cannot guarantee the performance upgradation. The experimental analysis indicates that s = 4 provides better performance than s = 2 but increases the scaling factor further s = 8 performance slightly degrading. It ensues because the R2N module can seize a suitable receptive field. If receptive fields in the R2N module previously cover the object in the image, then increasing s- can bound the network outcome [13]. Therefore, there is a trade-off between the value of the scaling factor and model outcome. It needs to pick up suitably to achieve improved segmentation.

Furthermore, the supervised training approach utilized to train the DMSAN for liver segmentation. It leads the network outcome to highly relies on the quality and quantity of the data. The upgradation in the model performance is highly possible by tuning the network hyper-parameters such as learning rate, batch size, scaling factor, and network learning policies.

7.8   Conclusion

In this chapter, the authors presented a DMSAN to segment the liver automatically from abdominal CT images. The proposed model exploited the multi-scale feature extraction capability of the R2N module. It enhances CNN's receptive field and extracts more granular features that augment the successive downsampling layers' learning ability. The network's feature extraction ability is refined by fusing high-resolution features with a low-resolution that explicitly enhances the liver region features. An attention layer recalibrated the feature map to upgrade the upsampling performance and achieved better segmentation performance. Automatic liver segmentation is challenging due to its anatomical structure and the introduction of noise during CT image acquisition. For the proposed method, the authors performed HU value windowing and image enhancement as preprocessing steps on the input CT images to make the liver region explicit and eradicate unwanted information and organs from the CT images.

The model trained end to end and demonstrated the network's potency by performing extensive experimentation and validation of the results on publicly available 3DIRCADb and CHAOS test CT datasets. The proposed model effectively segment the liver region from

CT images when s = 4. The dice score of the model is better than the state-of-the-art algorithms. The simple preprocessing steps applied would make it possible to apply the proposed algorithm for medical imaging application organ segmentation with distinct imaging modalities such as ultrasound, CT, and MRI. In the future, it is possible to extend this work for building an efficient algorithm for the automatic segmentation of liver tumors based on the liver segmentation for evaluation of liver tumor treatment planning.

Acknowledgement

The authors are highly grateful to the Faculty and Management of VPKBIET, Baramati, and VIIT, Baramati, for facilitating the resources required to accomplish the research work.

References

1. Gotra, A. *et al.*, Liver segmentation: indications, techniques and future directions. *Insights Imaging*, 8, 4, 377–392, 2017.
2. Moghbel, M. *et al.*, Review of liver segmentation and computer-assisted detection/diagnosis methods in computed tomography. *Artif. Intell. Rev.*, 50, 4, 497–537, 2018.
3. Wang, K. *et al.*, Automated CT and MRI liver segmentation and biometry using a generalized convolutional neural network. *Radiol. Artif. Intell.*, 1, 2, 180022, 2019.
4. Luo, S., Review on the methods of automatic liver segmentation from abdominal images. *J. Comput. Commun.*, 2, 02, 1, 2014.
5. Litjens, G. *et al.*, A survey on deep learning in medical image analysis. *Med. Image Anal.*, 42, 60–88, 2017.
6. Shen, D., Wu, G., Suk, H., Deep learning in medical image analysis. *Annu. Rev. Biomed. Eng.*, 19, 221–248, 2017.
7. Yamashita, R. *et al.*, Convolutional neural networks: an overview and application in radiology. *Insights Imaging*, 9, 4, 611–629, 2018.
8. Ueda, D., Shimazaki, A., Miki, Y., Technical and clinical overview of deep learning in radiology. *Jpn. J. Radiol.*, 37, 1, 15–33, 2019.
9. Shelhamer, E., Long, J., Darrell, T., Fully convolutional networks for semantic segmentation. *IEEE Trans. Pattern Anal. Mach. Intell.*, 39, 4, 640–651, 2017.
10. Ronnebrger, O., Fischer, P., Brox, T., U-net: Convolutional networks for biomedical image segmentation. *International Conference on Medical image computing and computer-assisted intervention*, Springer, Cham, 2015.
11. Xu, H. *et al.*, Automatic Segmentation of Liver CT Image Based on Dense Pyramid Network. *International Workshop on Multiscale Multimodal Medical Imaging*, Springer, Cham, 2019.
12. Sun, L. *et al.*, *A Multi-scale Attention Network for Kidney Tumor Segmentation on CT Scans*, University of Minnesota Libraries Publishing, 2019.
13. Gao, S. *et al.*, R2N: A new multi-scale backbone architecture. *IEEE Trans. Pattern Anal. Mach. Intell.*, 2, 43, 652–662, 2021.
14. Bilic, P. *et al.*, The liver tumor segmentation benchmark (lits). arXiv preprint arXiv:1901.04056, 2019.
15. Han, X., Automatic liver lesion segmentation using a deep convolutional neural network method. *arXiv preprint arXiv:1704.07239*, 2017.
16. 3DIRCADb: https://www.ircad.fr/research/3dircadb/.

17. Kavur, A.E., Selver, M.A., Dicle, O., Barış, M., Gezer, N.S., *CHAOS - Combined (CT-MR) Healthy Abdominal Organ Segmentation Challenge Data (Version v1.03) [Data set]*, Zenodo, Medical Image Analysis, Elsevier, 69, 101950, 2019, doi: 10.5281/zenodo.3362844 http://doi.org/10.5281/zenodo.3362844.

18. Kavur, A.E., Gezer, N.S., Barış, M., Conze, P.-H., Groza, V., Pham, D.D. *et al.*, CHAOS Challenge - Combined (CT-MR) Healthy Abdominal Organ Segmentation, arXiv preprint, https://arxiv.org/abs/2001.06535, Jan. 2020.

19. Jin, Q. *et al.*, RA-UNet: A hybrid deep attention-aware network to extract liver and tumor in CT scans, Frontiers in Bioengineering and Biotechnology, 8, 1471, 2020. *arXiv preprint arXiv:1811.01328*, 2018.

20. Chollet, F. *et al.*, Keras, 2015, Theano-based deep learning libraryCode: https://github.com/fchollet

21. Abadi, M. *et al.*, Software available from tensorflow. org: Large-scale machine learning on heterogeneous distributed systems. *arXiv preprint arXiv:1603.04467*, 9, 39, 2016.

22. Simard, P.Y., Steinkraus, D., Platt, J.C., Best practices for convolutional neural networks applied to visual document analysis. *Icdar*, 3, 2003, 2003.

23. Heimann, T. *et al.*, Comparison and evaluation of methods for liver segmentation from CT datasets. *IEEE Trans. Med. Imaging*, 28, 8, 1251–1265, 2009.

24. Yeghiazaryan, V. and Voiculescu, I., *An overview of current evaluation methods used in medical image segmentation*, Department of Computer Science, University of Oxford, 2015.

25. Moghbel, M. *et al.*, Automatic liver segmentation on computed tomography using random walkers for treatment planning. *EXCLI J.*, 15, 500, 2016.

26. Tang, W. *et al.*, DSL: Automatic liver segmentation with faster R-CNN and DeepLab, in: *International Conference on Artificial Neural Networks*, Springer, Cham, 2018.

27. Christ, P.F. *et al.*, Automatic liver and tumor segmentation of CT and MRI volumes using cascaded fully convolutional neural networks. *arXiv preprint arXiv:1702.05970*, 2017.

28. Li, X. *et al.*, H-DenseUNet: hybrid densely connected UNet for liver and tumor segmentation from CT volumes. *IEEE Trans. Med. Imaging*, 37, 12, 2663–2674, 2018.

29. Seo, H. *et al.*, Modified U-Net (mU-Net) with incorporation of object-dependent high level features for improved liver and liver-tumor segmentation in CT images. *IEEE Trans. Med. Imaging*, 39, 5, 1316–1325, 2019.

30. Mulay, S. *et al.*, Liver Segmentation from Multimodal Images Using HED-Mask R-CNN. *International Workshop on Multiscale Multimodal Medical Imaging*, Springer, Cham, 2019.

31. Kavur, A.E., Kuncheva, L.I., Selver, M.A., Basic Ensembles of Vanilla-Style Deep Learning Models Improve Liver Segmentation From CT Images. arXiv preprint arXiv:2001.09647, 2020.

32. Kushnure, D.T. and Talbar, S.N., MS-UNet: A multi-scale UNet with feature recalibration approach for automatic liver and tumor segmentation in CT images. *Comput. Med. Imaging Graph.*, 89, 101885, 2021.

8

AI-Based Identification and Prediction of Cardiac Disorders

Rajesh Karhe[1]*, Hemant Kasturiwale[2] and Sujata N. Kale[3]

[1]Shri Gulabrao Deokar College of Engineering, Jalgaon, MS, India
[2]Thakur College of Engineering and Technology, Kandivali (East), Mumbai, MS, India
[3]Department of Applied Electronics, Sant Gadge Baba University, Amravati, MS, India

Abstract

Electrocardiogram (ECG), a noninvasive technique, is used as a primary diagnostic tool for cardiovascular diseases. A cleaned ECG signal provides necessary information about the electrophysiology of the heart diseases and ischemic changes that may occur. It provides valuable information about the functional aspects of the heart and cardiovascular system. The objective of the work is to enhance arrhythmia analysis based on identification and prediction of cardiac disorder by using neural network classifiers. This analysis is devoted to decisions concerned with recognizing and classifying the patterns of the abnormal electrical signals of the heartbeats.

The detection of cardiac arrhythmias in the ECG signal consists of following stages: digitization of documented ECG images, detection of QRS complex in ECG signal, feature extraction from detected QRS complexes, and classification of beats using extracted feature set from QRS complexes using neural networks. In turn, automatic classification of heartbeats represents the automatic detection of cardiac arrhythmias in ECG signal. Hence, in this thesis, the automatic algorithms for classification of heartbeats to detect and classify cardiac arrhythmias in ECG signal are developed. Different neural network classification architectures with different functions are used to classify the cardiac arrhythmias. Several experiments are performed on the test dataset, and it is observed that feedforward neural network with "Trainlm" training function classifies ECG beats better as compared to other neural network classifiers under consideration. The neural network performance function "MSE" was found to be best for all experiments.

Keywords: ECG, feedforward neural network, PatternNet, CascadedForwardNet, Layrecnet, MIT-BIH, heart rate variability

---

**Corresponding author*: rajeshkarhe@yahoo.com

Tushar H. Jaware, K. Sarat Kumar, Ravindra D. Badgujar and Svetlin Antonov (eds.) Medical Imaging and Health Informatics, (141–164) © 2022 Scrivener Publishing LLC

8.1 Introduction

Medical practitioners always treat patients based on the previous analysis and previous symptoms. Although the heart care practitioner is providing the treatment based on present symptoms, it would be helpful to them if old ECG records are available. Old ECG documentations are being spoiled and not stored in proper electronics format. It is essential to obtain the digitization of old ECG records. During previous decades, ECG signals, which have been gathered by clinical systems, have not been reliably reported. Diagnostic representations of this type are often assumed to be correct and are treated as if they are correct when it comes to diagnosing patients' problems. In the future, it may be necessary to collect previous patient information in some instances. In certain circumstances, there is no other way. Manually analyzing the ECG old signals is the only option. Various common medical tools are available for the detection of abnormalities today, but current systems are unable to use historical signals for the detection of abnormal conditions. In addition, the majority of the ECG graphs is in need of repair or is too blurred to see. Converting these analog signals to comparable digital signals is a must; hence, by the inspection, tracing, and reconstruction operations, the analog signals must be preserved. By storing earlier cases and cases similar to those in the database, this helps build a database of past cases that may be utilized for additional research and treatment. Symptoms that occurred in the past can be detected with today's enhanced tools and parameters that have been recorded for long-term use are also available. Another advantage of digitizing the ECG signal is that it is simpler to provide digital ECG signals rather than scanned ECG signals. Today's numerous file formats may be easily obtained from electronic ECG readings. It will undoubtedly be beneficial to doctors and patients to use this rebuild.

This research aims toward digitization of ECG reports and analysis of same to detect arrhythmias using neural networks. Human heart is a four chambered muscular organ which pumps blood into arteries and circulates oxygen throughout the body. Hence, the pulsation of the heart called heartbeat is extremely important. This stimulus activates the heart rate. However, the heart rate may rise or fall outside the typical range. Arrhythmia is the term used to describe an abnormal heart rhythm. Arrhythmia is usually divided into two distinct categories: bradycardia (slow heartbeat) and tachycardia (rapid heartbeat). Arrhythmia is classified into two categories: bradycardia and tachycardia. When the heart rate falls down below 60 beats per minute (bpm), it is bradycardia, and when it rises higher than 100 bpm, it is tachycardia. Both types show different effects on the human body. Bradycardia causes drowsiness, fainting, sleepiness, and rare chances of cardiac arrest. However, tachycardia affects the pumping capability of the heart and generates the symptoms like chest pain and problem in breathing and may cause heart attack. It implies not all arrhythmias are not dangerous but most can damage heart and can cause death. Hence, sudden cardiac death is a growing concern in the world.

An electrocardiogram (ECG) instrument is used to detect these irregular heart rhythm patterns. This instrument quantifies the variance in electrical cardiac signal variations. As per the reports by American Heart Association (AHA) about 295,000 emergency medical services are treated out-of-hospital cardiac arrest, which occur in the United States. An automated system that is able to diagnose heartbeats and offer early detection of arrhythmia would greatly assist in preventing cardiac arrest and save thousands of lives. It would also benefit cardiologists in monitoring the heartbeat rates and deciding on the specific type of arrhythmia from the two categories mentioned above. A heartbeat can be symbolized as Q, R, S, T, and P wave beat morphology (normal and abnormal pattern) of different waves of ECG signals, which is considered for the arrhythmia detection. This analysis is aimed at heart rate variability (HRV) research decisions. Dijikstraw's shortest path technique is used to scan and digitize the ECG pictures. From the digitized ECG signal, both different statistical features and Harris corner features are retrieved.

This work was carried on neural network models of varying complexity and evaluates their capabilities. This training and testing is based on well-known MIT-BIH arrhythmia database extracts. The performance is also evaluated for the scanned ECG images to detect the arrhythmia ECG images.

8.1.1   Cardiac Electrophysiology and Electrocardiogram

An electrocardiogram, normally called as ECG, calculates the electrical activity of the heartbeat.

With every heartbeat, a wave is generated and due to it blood is pumped out from the heart.

The heart's electrical activity is tracked by ECG waveform and its dips and spikes will show the state of the heart as shown in Figure 8.1. The ECG waveform has positive and negative waves that are generated due to different deflection in each portion of heartbeat.

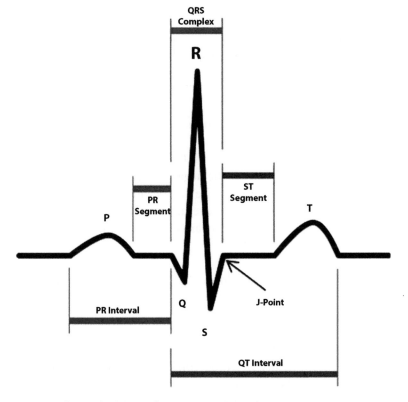

Figure 8.1 Generation of normal ECG signal.

Table 8.1 Normal ECG values for healthy person.

Feature	Association in the heart	Duration (s)	Amplitude (mV)
P wave	Triggering of the SA node and atrial depolarization	0.08–0.10	0.25
R wave	Representation of early ventricular depolarization	<0.04	1.60
Q wave	Result from left to right depolarization of the septum	0.04	25% of R wave
T wave	Ventricular repolarization	0.12–0.16	0.1–0.5
PR Interval	Impulse delay at the AV node and the depolarization of the atrium	0.12–0.20	
QR complex	Represents ventricular depolarization	0.06–0.10	
ST Interval	It should be isoelectric line and represents the beginning of ventricular repolarization	0.32	
RR Interval	The interval between the R wave and the next R wave in ECG wave	0.6–1.2	
QT Interval	Interval between starting of QRS complex to the end of T wave. Elongated QT interval leads to sudden death due to ventricular tachyarrhythmia	0.33–0.43	

P Wave: The P wave corresponds to atrial contraction and it also interprets depolarization of right and leftatrium.

QRS Complex: The QRS complex consists of Q wave, R wave and S wave and it indicates ventriculardepolarization. Q wave is the negative wave and that the R wave is the first positive wave of the complex. The S wave is the first negative deflection after the R wave.

T Wave: The QRS complex is followed by T wave, and it indicates ventricular repolarization.

Heart Rate: The heart rate is number of heartbeats per minute and is determined by sequence method.

The normal value of the different waveform of ECG is presented in Table 8.1.

8.1.2 Heart Arrhythmia

Cardiac problems arise when alterations in the production of electrical impulses or a decrease in the heart's contractility occur. A condition of the irregular pulse either too rapid or too sluggish is referred to as heart arrhythmia. Arrhythmia is the medical term for abnormal cardiac rhythms. If the heart does not move enough blood, then different bodily organs could be injured or do not perform properly. Upper and lower cardiac chambers can sometimes induce arrhythmias, but ventricular arrhythmias are life-threatening episodes. The factors like disease in coronary artery, changes in myocardium, damage from a heart attack, or healing process after heart surgery may cause arrhythmia. It may occur with a normal heart rate, bradyarrhythmias (slow heart rates below 60 bpm), or tachyarrhythmia (rapid heart rates above 100 bpm). Many arrhythmias have no symptoms and if symptoms persist the person may feel a gap between heartbeats, shortness of breath, or chest pain. Most of arrhythmias are not dangerous, but some may complain of stroke, others may have cardiac arrest result. An ECG analysis and Holter monitor could be helpful in the diagnosis of cardiac disorders.

8.1.2.1   Types of Arrhythmias

Sinus rhythm is a regular heart rhythm characterized by synchronized impulses propagating through the four chambers of the heart. Extra beats, supraventricular tachycardia, ventricular arrhythmias, and Brady arrhythmias are the four most prevalent kinds of arrhythmia. Figure 8.2 shows types of cardiac arrhythmias [25]. Arrhythmias, some of which, are well known, which include the following:

> Sinus Rhythm
> Normal sinus rhythm arises from the sinus node when it is normal cardiac beat. On the whole, the resting heart rate tends to be variable depending on the inputs to the sinus node
> Premature (Extra) Beats
> The most frequent arrhythmia, which has no symptoms, is called sinus arrhythmia. People will notice a strange sensation in the chest, as well as a distinct, uncomfortable heartbeat.
>> Premature atrial contraction (PACs): In this condition, generation of early extra beats occurs in theatria. This is a harmless condition and does not require treatment.
>> Premature ventricular contraction (PVCs): It is the most common type of arrhythmia, which may occur with and without a heart disease. It is a frisked heartbeat condition that may occur due to stress and use of nicotine or extensive exercise. Sometimes, heart disease or electrolyte imbalance causes PVCs.
> Supraventricular Arrhythmia
> This syndrome begins in the atria, where the heartbeats very quickly. Atrial fibrillation, atrial flutter, paroxysmal supraventricular tachycardia (PSVT), and Wolff-Parkinson-White (WPW) syndrome are the several forms of supraventricular arrhythmias.
>> Atrial fibrillation: It is having very fast and irregular heart rhythm. Chaotic activity in the atria causes abnormal contraction of heart due to a blood clot that causes a blockage in the blood vessel.
>> Atrial flutter: Fast contractions of the both atria with a regular pulse of 120 to 140 bpm. It commonly occurs in people with heart disease and after heart surgery within a week. In prolonged time, it converts to atrial fibrillation.
>> Paroxysmal Supraventricular tachycardia (PSVT): It begins and ends suddenly with rapid heart rate, originates from the ventricles.

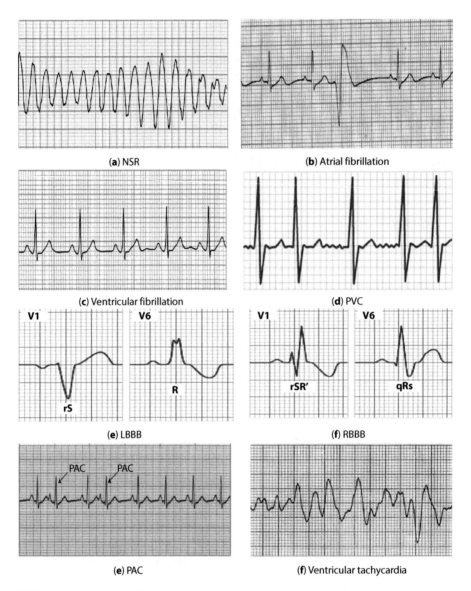

Figure 8.2 Types of cardiac arrhythmias.

WPW syndrome: It is a special type of PSVT with a life-threatening condition, the electrical signals travel from the atria to the ventricles along the extra pathway. It disturbs the rhythmicity of the heart with very fast of ventricular beat.

➤ Ventricular Arrhythmias

Ventricular flutter or tachycardia (V-tach) is the condition which indicates very rapid and constant contraction of the ventricles which is very dangerous; usually, it occurs prior to ventricular fibrillation.

Ventricular fibrillation (V-fb): This is an unpredictable condition of arrhythmia where the ventricles fire unsystematic impulses due to which the ventricles face a huge difficulty in pumping the blood to body parts, thereby putting the patient's life in danger. It can be treated with a defibrillator shock in order to prevent CPR (cardiopulmonary resuscitation.)

Bradyarrhythmias: This is a condition that arises due to improper electrical conduction system of the heart which leads to slowness of heart rhythms.

➢ Sinus Node Dysfunction

Sinus node dysfunction is problem that leads to a slower rhythm of heart. In order to remove or to get rid of this, patient may need a pacemaker.

➢ **Heart Block:** There is a condition that prevents the conduction channel of electrical impulse from being completed at the AV node or HIS-Purkinje system, often known as "heart block". In the case of a disturbance in the heart's conduction system, this condition is known as bundle branch block. RBBB or LBBB (LBBB). In RBBB, normal stimulation takes place in the left ventricle by the left bundle branch but the right ventricle is not precisely activated by impulses. Due to gradual conduction through the heart muscles, the QRS complex widens. In LBBB condition, the right ventricle contracts earlier that the left ventricle; hence, there are delays in left ventricular activation.

8.1.3   ECG Database

There are several publicly available databases where users can try out approaches used in studies that use ECG signals for analysis. ECG signal analysis can rely on the MIT-BIH databases widely.

In order to assess the performance of the method with us, the MIT/BIH rhythmic database is employed. The collection contains 48 records of ECG signals with two channels of 30 min recorded in the BIH Arrhythmia laboratory from 47 subjects between 1975 and 1979. A random range of 23 records is drawn from an array of four thousand ECG records from hospitals and outpatients and 25 from the same set with clinically relevant rhythmic. The other 25 are picked: 25 men between 32 and 89 and 22 women between 23 and 89 years of age. There are 116,137 QRS complex numbers in the database. Sample ECG signals are sampled with an 11-bit resolution of 360 samples per second in 10 mV and a passable band filter at 0.1–100 Hz. The database will be checked for timing and class information by an independent cardiologist. Five types of beats are most commonly employed in the MIT-BIH arrhythmic analysis database, e.g., left bundle branch block (LBBB), right bundle branch (RBBB), atrial premature contraction (APC), and ventricular premature contracting (VPC).

8.1.3.1   Association for the Advancement of Medical Instrumentation (AAMI) Standard

Five different arrhythmia conditions are described according to AAMI recommendations, and these conditions can be traced to different types of cardiac arrhythmia found in the MIT-BIH database as shown in Table 8.2. In this case, just 44 recordings from the database, out of the total of 48, are being used for the mix of five types of arrhythmia beats. It underlines the VEB classification challenge as well as the dilemma of separating the

Table 8.2 Description of AAMI standard beats as per MIT-BIH heartbeats.

AAMI standard beats	Description	MIT-BIH beats
N	Normal beat	Normal (N), right bundle branch block (RBBB), left bundle branch block (LBBB), nodal junction escape beats (NJE)
S	Supraventricular ectopic beats	Atrial premature contraction (APC), aberrated atrial premature beats (AAPB), nodal premature beats (NPB), supraventricular premature beats (SPB)
V	Ventricular ectopic beats	Premature ventricular contraction (PVC), ventricular escape beats (VEB)
F	Fusion beats	Fusion of ventricular and normal beats (FVN)
Q	Unclassifiable beats, including paced beats	Fusion of paced and normal beats (FPN), unclassified beats (U)

non-ventricular ectopic beats from the VEBs. The following five heartbeat types have been classified according to the AAMI standard: normally generated, supraventricular ectopic, ventricular ectopic, ectopic fusion, and miscellaneous beats (Q).

8.1.4 An Overview of ECG Signal Analysis

The ECG signal analysis has been one of the primary focuses in biomedical signal processing in the past forty decades. The rapid advancement of computer technology has made the topic of interest of ECG analysis in cardiac care activities all over the world. The computer-aided diagnosis system is a mimic to clinician and a reliable tool in application of routine and long-term cardiovascular disease (CVD) detection of ECG signals in the ICCU, or massive data processing as in the Holter recordings [32]. A tape to store large files of signals was used in Holter recorder, which is replaced by flash-type semiconductor memories to transfer to a workstation for post-recording analysis.

Computer technology has played important role in the development of high performance and accurate analysis of ECG signal in recent years. The biological exhibits complex dynamics and non-linear analysis, which is an important task in time-series analysis. The major steps of ECG signal analysis are given in Figure 8.3.

- Noise elimination from ECG signal using filters in pre-processing
- Detection of QRS complex and characteristic points from ECG signal
- Extraction and formulation of important feature sets
- Training the classifier
- Classification of cardiac arrhythmias

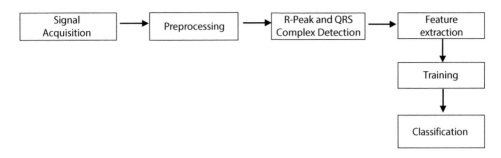

Figure 8.3 Block diagram of the arrhythmia detection and classification system.

The pre-processing stage is used to enhance the ECG signal for further analysis like QRS detection and classification. There are many interferences, like the baseline wanders, power line interference, and physiological artifacts. Interference from these diverse sources disrupts the ECG signal, and there are various strategies to remove it.

Two approaches are utilized to draw representative beats from the whole ECG record in system design, based on supervised and unchecked learning that results an automatic diagnosis process. Computer-aided diagnosis of ECG signal could be used for interpreting the cardiac disease more accurately.

8.2   Related Work

CVD analysis and diagnosis has relied heavily over many years on the ECG signal. Currently, CVD is the primary cause of death worldwide, and ECG is therefore highly demanded automatically and in real time. Most CVDs are enduring for a long time and require regular evaluations. The recurrence of treatment may vary depending on the severity of the infection. Even asymptomatic people should be routinely examined for cardiovascular health assessment when they reach a certain age. The essential evaluation boundary is the ECG follow, apart from the auscultation. ECG trace is mostly provided and a softcopy is not stored in print format. An annual ECG record is definitely necessary for a chronic CVD patient, and the frequency can increase to a daily record if the severity of the disease increases. With increasing records, there are opportunities for mishaps in administration and analysis.

Doctors need to analyze a patient's ECG fluctuations across a number of years. However, printed traces tend to disappear over time and prevent this task. Moreover, it will allow the provision of diagnostic help to extract ECG signals from printed trace reports. This is why and what ECG signals from scanned trace reports need to be digitized.

The literature review emphasizes on work done by researchers on analyzing different methods for prediction or classification of cardiac arrhythmia.

Lawson *et al.* [1] have presented one of the earliest methods for extracting and archiving 12 lead ECG signals from paper recordings that have suggested on automated waveform analysis by conversion of paper ECG recordings into digital ECG signals, and then, system is developed to evaluate measurement of ECG parameter. Scanned and original ECG signals are compared, and it is shows that there are no variations between them.

Badilini *et al.* [2] have executed a computer application developed for the conversion of paper ECG information to digital ECG documents using an image processing engine that is used to discover the underlying grid and in the end to extrapolate the ECG waveforms using a way based totally on active counter modeling.

Shen *et al.* [3] have advocated one-dimensional reconstruction of electronic signals by implementing spatial and frequency method on gray-level ECG chart that includes threshold segmentation and 2D Fourier transform method.

Chebil *et al.* [4] have suggested some improvements to the digitization method, such as selecting an appropriate image resolution during scanning and employing the community and median methods at some point during the extraction and digitization of the ECG waveform. The results show that the advanced software program preserved the ECG waveform's vital capabilities.

Sanroman-Junquera *et al.* [5] have proposed a four-stage automated approach based on digital image processing principles: 1. correction of the scanned image's orientation using eigenvector decomposition of the foreground pixel co-ordinates; 2. grid detection using cosine transforms on histogram vertical and horizontal projections; 3. identification of signal waveform using morpho-logical operators; and 4. to translate waveform in the image plane to the one-dimensional biomedical signal.

Paterni *et al.* [6] have advised a new approach to transform ECG from graph paper to digital signalwith the help of flatbed scanner and a mathematical operator called first-order absolute moment (FOAM). Then, a line detection technique is used to locate the ECG trace. Guojie *et al.* [7] have suggested K-means model to extracts ECG statistics from paper recording. The results show that there is separation of background grid and ECG waveform. It can be extracted by digitizing various ECG parameters that match upto 99%.

Widman *et al.* [8] have proposed an approach for maintaining fidelity of the signal in high error frequency region of the ECG signal and QRS complex by building a triangle approximation method that is successful but not completely automated.

Bhullar *et al.* [9] have suggested ways to store significant waveform data. In order toovercome problems such as thick line widths and random noise, a system is developed for the conversion ofwaveforms stored on paper, which are two-dimensional to a one-dimensional array of data values. To remove errors from these stored images, three digital image processing techniques are used. The first is a heuristic method, followed by pixel-based waveform thinning and data extraction from the thinned waveforms.

Feiwang *et al.* [10] have proposed an image based period detection method on different CVDs. Karsikas *et al.* [11] have developed a quantitative approach where they compared parameters that involve QRS and T wave area morphologies to assess the fidelity of the digitized ECG paper in comparison with directly digital gold standard.

Sucharita Mitra *et al.* [12] proposed the use in the digital time database using an automatic data extraction method created there to transfer ECG signals that are registered on paper. After detection of QRS complex, the ECG signal is calculated. Finally, Fourier discreetly transforms the data base to observe each ECG signal's frequency response characteristics.

A MATLAB-based technique, involving scanning, scaling, and skew correction, utilizes line contours to construct the recovered ECG signal followed by Ravichandran *et al.* [13].

Binary picture production utilizes the thresholding technique followed by interpolation and median filtering to remove thresholding salt and pepper noise. Results are validated with kappa statistics via direct comparison of RR, QTC, PR, QT, and QRS intervals.

Waits *et al.* [14] have suggested ways for converting paper ECG's into digital form and reviewed merits and demerits of the said algorithms, conversion algorithms, applications, and efforts of standardization. Rajani *et al.* [15] have developed an methodology to convert old ECG signals into digital form using three stages that include conversion of RGB image to grayscale image followed by removal of gridlines followed by enhancement of pixels.

Kumar *et al.* [16] have developed a method for translating ECG signals from ECG papers, and the results are compared to the MIT-BIH Normal Sinus Rhythm (NSR)/Arrhythmia database. The PR interval, heart rate QRS duration, QT interval, and RR interval are all compared, and 99% accuracy is achieved.

Jayaraman *et al.* [17] have proposed a novel method for obtaining the ECG morphological characteristics. The extraction of digital time-series signals and morphological functions was tested on a database of 25 paper data, and the accuracy is 95% and 97%, respectively.

Patil *et al.* [18] have discussed how to robustly handle numerous degradation issue encountered in ECG paper scanning using modified K-fill set of rules. The author extracted clinically essential parameter consists of heart rate with 97.33% of accuracy and abnormalities like tachycardia, bradycardia, and atrial flutter from the ECG paper using perceptual spectral centroid approach with 98.6% accuracy.

Harris *et al.* [19] have developed an algorithm for filtering of edge in an image called feature tracking algorithm. Nilanjan *et al.* [20] have compared Harris and Moravec corner detection for obtaining functions that are required to recognize and track object within a noisy image. Ryu *et al.* [21] have suggested an new corner less formula for the Harris corner detector which is used to analyze the corner angle.

Gueguen *et al.* [22] have designed an exclusive approach for evaluation of multi-scale corner and its detection by using Harris corner detector. Khleaf *et al.* [23] have developed image processing techniques for signal regeneration and feature extraction of ECG as a digital time series signal. The accuracy 98.25% is achieved. Stockbridge *et al.* [24] have suggested the points that need to be considered in ECG waveform extraction.

Niwas *et al.* [25] have used the artificial neural networks (ANNs) for classification of heartbeats of ECG, in which they accurately classify the heartbeat of ECG signals and evaluating features based on spectral entropy, RR intervals, and heartbeat intervals. The result shows classification of nine types of arrhythmia and normal heartbeat. Sayad *et al.* [26] have implemented 13 attributes for diagnosing heart diseases. In this methodology, multi-layer perceptron neural network along with training algorithmas backpropagation (BP) is used for prediction of risk of heart disease. Moavenian *et al.* [27] have proposed K-A (Kernel-Adatron) learning algorithm in order to support SVM (support vector machine) for classification of ECG arrhythmias. Using the BP learning algorithm, the classifier is compared to MLP (multi-layered perceptron).

8.3 Classifiers and Methodology

As ECGs are important parameters for prediction of heart disease, its preservation is of most importance. The old ECG documents need to be analyzed manually and there are chances of debasement of the documents. This research work focuses on analyzation and classification of previously documented ECG signal using ANN. The following steps briefly describe experiment in this research for arrhythmia detection and classification.

8.3.1   Databases for Cardiac Arrhythmia Detection

Different databases have been made available to evaluate the methodologies presented for analyzing ECG signals in investigations. In ECG signal analysis, the MIT-BIH databases are frequently utilized for many applications.

8.3.2   MIT-BIH Normal Sinus Rhythm and Arrhythmia Database

The ECG signals are downloaded and recorded through MIT-BIH Arrhythmia Database from PhysioBank, which is usually considered as a standard test bench for rhythm detection assessments.

In addition, research into rhythm analysis and related topics has been supported by laboratories at the Beth Israel Hospital in Boston (now the Beth Israel Deaconess Medical Center) and MIT since 1975. The MIT-BIH Arrhythmia Database and NSR were one of the first important outputs of this effort. The database is the first standard test material for rhythm detectors, generally available, and has been used to this end as well as for fundamental cardiac dynamic research at more than 500 sites worldwide. For performance evaluation, the MIT/BIH arrhythmia database is employed. It has 48 records, each one of which contains two-channel ECG signals selected from a 24-hour record of 47 persons for a 30-min period. The database contains 116,137 QRS complex numbers. Things are taken from 25 men between the ages of 32 to 89 and 22 women between the ages of 23 to 89 years and from the same male subject in the 201 and 202 records. The modified limb lead II and one of the modified leads V1, V2, V4, or V5 are included. Continuous ECGs are filtered to 0.1–100 Hz and then scans to 360 Hz, as well as NSR from male and female ages and sampled to 125 Hz. Continuous ECG is captured. Twenty-three of the recordings (100–124 numbered) are intended as a typical sample of clinical routine records and 25 records (200–234 numbers) include complicated, junctional, and superventricular rhythms. The database provides a timing annotation as well as class data confirmed by independent experts.

Distribution of records of MIT-BIH NSR and arrhythmia database is shown in Table 8.3.

Table 8.3 Distribution of records of MIT-BIH NSR and arrhythmia database.

Class	Record numbers
Normal Class	16272-16420-16483-16773-16795-17052-17453-18184-19088-19830
Arrhythmia Class	100-101-102-103-104-105-106-107-108-109-111-112-113-114-115-116-117-118-119-121-122-123-124-200-201-202-203-205-207-208-209-210-212-213-214-215-217-219-220-221-222-223-228-230-231-232-233-234

8.3.3 Arrhythmia Detection and Classification

This task is performed with detection of arrhythmias and normal sinus ECG signals by considering 55 ECG signals from MIT-BIH database. This project is intended to develop an effective arrhythmia detection system that will allow for improved heart diagnostic tests.

8.3.4 Methodology

MATLAB 2013a uses the approach for the detection of arrhythmias. Figure 8.4 illustrates the flowchart of the methods presented in order to detect rhythmic data from normal data. The image divides the entire process into three fundamental parts: QRST wave detection, extraction of features, and classification. The raw ECG data for QRST wave detection is available. It is possible to see. For the purposes of detecting ECG Q, R, S, and T peaks and preparing the processed signal for the following stage, the original ECG signal should be pre-processed. The next stage of the suggested model is the extraction of the feature that prepares the best input for the original signal. The method's final step is to classify the signal processed in normal and arrhythmic classes.

8.3.4.1 Database Gathering and Pre-Processing

- Obtain the standard arrhythmia ECG data from MIT-BIH laboratory and convert it in MATLAB readable format using PhysioNet ATM
- Obtain normal sinus ECG data from MIT-BIH laboratory and convert it in MATLAB readable format using PhysioNet ATM

8.3.4.2 QRST Wave Detection

In order to determine various peaks in an ECG signal, the QRST wave detection system uses state-machine logic. The company can deal with noise by neutralizing the noise by filtering high passes and walking through the base pass. In addition, see the criterion for stopping spike detection. The steps for QRST wave detection are as follows:

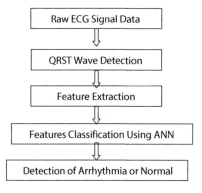

Figure 8.4 Steps of detection of arrhythmia.

1. Noise cancelation (filtering)
   • cutoff low frequency to get rid of baseline wander
   • cutoff frequency to discard high frequency noise
   • cutoff based on fs
   • band pass filtering
2. Enter state 1 (putative R wave)
3. Locate R by finding highest peak
4. Check if signal drops below the threshold to look for S wave
5. Enter S wave detection state 3 (S detection)
6. Enter state 4 possible T wave detection
   • See if the signal drops below mean
7. The detection of the S wave should result in the creation of a second threshold above and below the baseline of the signal, and only seek for a T wave to appear in between these two thresholds.

8.3.4.3 Features Extraction

Various features used for classification are as follows:

Heart Rate Variability: HRV is the time variation between consecutive cardiovascular sequences. The highest upward flux of a normal QRS complex in a conventional ECG is at the R wave peak (Figure 8.5), and the time of two adjacent R wave peaks is called the R-R interval. The ECG data is modified before HRV analyzes, and this is a process that requires removal of all beats that are not from the sinus node. This is called N-N (normal-normal) gap between adjacent QRS complexes caused by depolarizations in the sinusnode. HRV is measuring the N-N interval variability [28].

• **Mean RR interval:** The RR interval is the time between heartbeat PQRS complexes. To calculate the instantaneous heart rate, start counting QRS complexes, then divide by two. The time is one second between two R waves. RR intervals are uneven, whereas PQRST complexes are normal. The intervals

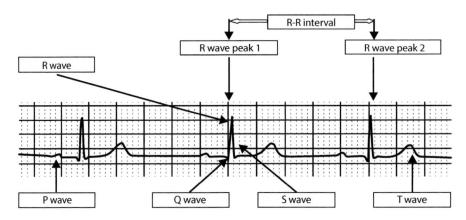

Figure 8.5 Heart rate variability.

between RRs do not exceed two typical RRs intervals. The vagal tone varies subsequent to the breath due to irregularities in RR intervals.

- **Root mean R-R interval square distance:** The RMSSD is a typical HRV index analysis that quantifies performance changes. Root mean square for successive RR differentials (RMSSD). The RMSSD value is standardized to the mean RR interval value in order to adjust its effect on the RR variability.
- **Number of R peaks in ECG that differ more than 50 ms:** The number of pairs of successive NNs that differ by more than 50 ms [29].
- **Percentage NN50:** The proportion of NN50 divided by total number of NNs.
- **Standard deviation of R-R series:** A value describing the degree of variation in a set of values is known as the standard deviation (also known as the lower case Greek letter sigma σ for the population standard deviation or the Latin letter s for the sample standard deviation).
- **Standard deviation of heart rate:** A low standard deviation indicates that the values tend to be close to the mean (also called the expected value) of the set, while a high standard deviation indicates that the values are spread out over a wider range [30].
- **Sample Entropy:** Entropy sampled (Entropy Sample) is an approximate entropy modification (ApEn) utilized for the assessment and diagnosis of sick conditions in physiologic time-series signals.
- **Power Spectral Entropy:** Random variables can be employed for an uncertain system to represent the system condition.

8.3.4.4   Neural Network

This research is carried out with the assistance of the neural network with several hidden neurons for classification of ECG. The two critical parameters required for neural network feature classification are as follows [31]:

a.   Input Vector
b.   Target Vector

a.   **Input Vector:** The feature vector is implemented as an input vector in this research. This 12 × 55 matrix of features indicates the amount of samples along each row, while the columns represent the features. A discussion of the input vector can be found as follows:
  - Number of rows = 12 (representing number of features of the samples)
  - Number of columns = 55 (representing number of respective samples taken for training, testing, and validation of neural network classifier).
  - Set-N-10 samples (normal patients)
  - Set-F-45 samples (arrhythmia patients)

b.   **Target Vector:** The results are implemented as a goal vector in this research. This vector consists of a 2 × 55 size matrix in which the rows show the target class and the column shows the number of specimens to test. The target vector overview has been discussed below.

- Number of rows = 2 (representing number of features of the samples)
- Class 1 - Normal Patient - (0)
- Class 2 - Arrhythmia Patient - (1)
- Number of columns = 55 (representing number of respective samples taken for training, testing, and validation of neural network classifier).

The overall classification is done using input vector and target vector with neural network.

8.3.4.5   Performance Evaluation

Evaluation of the performance of the system uses various neural network architectures as follows:

- PatternNet
- FeedforwardNet
- CascadedForwardNet
- Layrecnet

Evaluation of the performance for various numbers of hidden neurons.

- Total 55 ECG data subject are analyzed. This data is grouped in two classes, i.e., normal classand arrhythmia class and these classes are analyzed.
- The overall samples are divided into two categories:
  1) Training data: 70% of total dataset.
  2) Testing data: total dataset.

8.4   Result Analysis

8.4.1   Arrhythmia Detection and Classification

For the task, arrhythmias and normal sinus signals are identified using MIT-BIH database signals. The aim of this effort is to achieve a high performance cardiac diagnosis with an effective arrhythmia detecting system.

8.4.2   Dataset

Datasets used for evaluating the arrhythmia detection are MIT BIH of total 55 ECG samples as follows:

- a.   Arrhythmia ECG signals: 45
- b.   Normal ECG signals: 10

8.4.3   Evaluations and Results

Using MATLAB R2013a the overall classification is done using Neural Network Classifier. The design of the system is depicted in Figure 8.6.

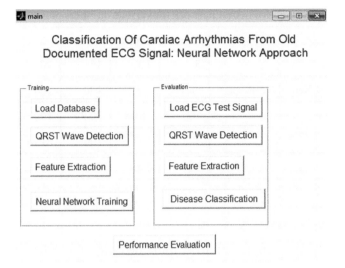

Figure 8.6 GUI designed for detection of arrhythmia using ECG.

Figure 8.7 shows the sample QRST wave detection for ECG signal.

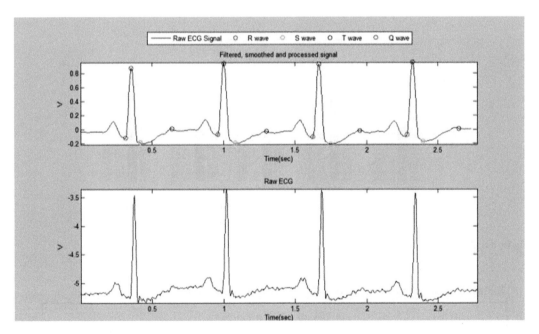

Figure 8.7 QRST wave detection.

8.4.4 Evaluating the Performance of Various Neural Network Classifiers (Arrhythmia Detection)

Table 8.4 shows the overall performance of the neural network, taking into consideration different topologies for neural networks for different hidden neurons. The trainings are "Trainlm" and neural network performance is "MSE". Trainings are examined here.

Table 8.4 Performance of neural network for various numbers of hidden neurons.

Classifiers	Number of hidden neurons				
	5	10	15	20	25
Feedforward Neural Network	98.18	100	100	100	100
PatternNet	100	98.18	90.90	100	100
CascadedForwardNet	100	100	100	81.81	92.72
Layrecnet	100	100	100	100	100

Figure 8.8 depicts the accuracy of arrhythmia detection for different neural network architectures.

The performance of the rhythmic detection is also tested for the time of implementation of various architectures in the neural network. Table 8.5 shows the runtime necessary for different topologies of the neural network.

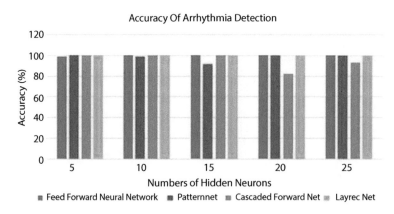

Figure 8.8 Accuracy of different neural network architectures for arrhythmia detection.

Table 8.5 Execution time in seconds for arrhythmia detection.

Classifiers	No. of hidden neurons				
	5	10	15	20	25
Feedforward Neural Network	0.2347	0.234	0.3109	0.252	0.2564
PatternNet	0.6034	0.3452	0.3393	0.3534	0.3813
CascadedForwardNet	0.3072	0.2305	0.2402	0.2432	0.2761
Layrecnet	0.6568	0.5818	0.6958	0.8336	0.9529

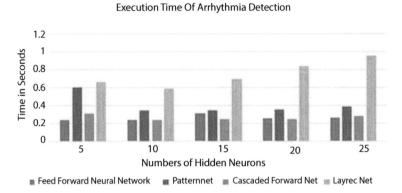

Figure 8.9 Execution time for arrhythmia detection.

As depicted in Table 8.5, feedforward neural network requires less execution time. Figure 8.9 shows the execution time for different neural network architectures considering number of hidden neurons as 5, 10, 15, 20, and 25.

8.5 Conclusions and Future Scope

An evaluation of the neural networks is made for each stage, in which a different neural network design and a different number of hidden neurons are considered, as well as different neural network training functions, different neural network performance functions, etc.

8.5.1 Arrhythmia Detection and Classification

This task is performed with detection of arrhythmia and normal sinus ECG signals by considering MIT-BIH database.

Table 8.6 shows average accuracy and the average execution time for various neural network architectures considering number of hidden neurons as 20 for detection of arrhythmia. It shows that feedforward neural network has average accuracy of 99.37% and less execution time of 0.241 seconds.

Table 8.6 Average accuracy and average execution time for arrhythmia detection.

Classifiers	Average accuracy (Percentage)	Average execution time (Seconds)
Feedforward neural network	99.37	0.241
PatternNet	97.54	0.404
CascadedForwardNet	83.62	0.312
Layrecnet	97.43	0.813

Table 8.7 shows the performance of Feedforward Neural network for different training functions. Feedforward neural network with "Trainlm" function requires the least execution time of 0.241 seconds andaccuracy of 99.37% is achieved; thus, it is the best training function for arrhythmia detection.

Table 8.8 shows the performance of feedforward neural network using "Trainlm" as training function. Here, the average accuracy for "MSE" as a performance function is 99.37% and the average execution time is 0.241 seconds.

The steps for arrhythmia detection and classification are as follows:

- An automated arrhythmia classification system is developed using statistical and morphological features extraction and neural network based classification tool.
- Total 55 samples are used. Out of which as 10 samples are Normal and 45 samples are of arrhythmia.
- Total 12 features for statistical and temporal features are selected to develop features input vector for classifier.
- The final step is to classify the processed signals into normal and arrhythmia class using neural network.

Table 8.7 Performances of feedforward neural network for different training functions.

	Feedforward net	
Training functions	**Average accuracy (Percentage)**	**Average execution time (Seconds)**
Trainlm	99.37	0.241
Trainbr	99.10	1.423
Trainscg	80.56	2.002
Trainrp	81.80	0.171

Table 8.8 Performance of feedforward neural network for different error functions.

	Feedforward neural network	
Error function	**Average accuracy (Percentage)**	**Average execution time (Seconds)**
MSE	99.37	0.241
SSE	93.72	0.372
SAE	98.99	0.412
MAE	80.41	0.314

The overall conclusion is as follows:

- For detection and classification of arrhythmia, feedforward neural network is the best classifier having maximum average accuracy of 99.37%.

From the study, it is verified that improvement in accuracy and execution time is achieved using the proposed algorithms. Our tool allows us to quickly and accurately scan ECGs with minimum human assistance, helping to identify arrhythmias.

8.5.2   Future Scope

Although this research work has been successful in addressing the problem of arrhythmia detection and classification from scanned ECG documents with the help of proposed modules. There is a scope for further research work on the following points:

- More types of arrhythmias and other heart diseases may be investigated.
- Emphasis may be given for detection of several features set of abnormal rhythms and also the manipulated images like similar fake images from the dataset.
- Time and storage consumption of ECG image database.
- In future, further research work can be preceded in the aforementioned aspects.

References

1. Lawson, W.T., Wagner, G.S., Startt-Selvester, R.S., Ybarra, G.A., New method for digitization and computerized analysis of paper recordings of standard 12-lead electrocardiograms. *Computers in Cardiology*, Institute of Electrical and Electronics Engineers, pp. 41–44, 1995.
2. Badilini, F., Erdem, T., Zareba, W., Moss, J., ECG Scan: a method for conversion of paper electrocardiographic printouts to digital electrocardio-graphic files. *J. Cardiol.*, 38, 310–318, 30 April 2005.
3. Shen, T.W., Tompkins, W.J., Hu, Y.H., Image processing on ECG chart for ECG signal Recovery. *Comput. Cardiol.*, 36, 725–728, 2009, ISSN 0276-6574.
4. Chebil, J., Al-Nabulsi, J., Al-Maitah, M., A Novel Method for Digitizing Standard ECG Papers, in: *International Conference on Computer and Communication Engineering*, Institute of Electrical and Electronics Engineers, pp. 1308–1312, 29 July 2008.
5. Sanroman-Junquera, M., Mora-Jimenez, Everss, E., Almendral-Garrote, J., Digital recovery of biomedical signals from binary images. *Signal Process.*, 92, 43–53, 2012.
6. Paterni, M., Belardinelli, A., Benassi, A., Carpeggiani, C., An automatic procedure to convert ECGs from graph paper to digital signals. Institute of Electrical and Electronics Engineers. Computer in Cardiology, pp. 263–266, 2002.
7. Shi, G., Zheng, G., Dai, M., ECG Waveform Data Extraction From Paper ECG Recording By K-means Method. *Computing in Cardiology*, pp. 797–800, 2011.
8. Widman, L.E. and Hines, L.S., Digitization of electrocardiograms by desktop optical scanner. *J. Electrocardiol.*, 24, 4, 325–338, October, 1991.

9. Bhullar, H.K., Fothergill, J.C., de Bono, D.P., Computer-based techniques for the optimal extraction of medical data from graphical paper records, in: *IEE Colloquium on Medical Imaging: Image Processing and Analysis,* Institute of Electrical and Electronics Engineers, 2002.

10. Wang, F., Mahmood, T.S., Beymer, D., Information Extraction from Multimodal ECG Documents, in: *10th International Conference on Document Analysis and Recognition, Institute of Electrical and Electronics Engineers,* pp. 381–385, 02 October 2009.

11. Karsikas, M., Huikuri, H., Perkiömäki, J.S., Lehtola, L., Seppänen, T., Influence of paper Electrocardiogram digitizing on T wave and QRS complex morphology parameters. *ANE,* 12, 4, 282–290, Oct 2007.

12. Mitra, S., Mitra, M., Chaudhuri, B.B., Generation of digital time database from paper ECG records and Fourier transform-based analysis for disease identification. *Comput. Biol. Med.,* 34, 551–560, 2004.

13. Ravichandran, L., Harless, C., Shah, A.J., Wick, C.A., Novel Tool for Complete Digitization of Paper Electrocardiography Data, in: *Medical imaging and Radiology,* vol. 1, Institute of Electrical and Electronics Engineers, 13 June 2013.

14. Waits, G.S. and Soliman, E.Z., Digitizing paper electrocardiograms: Status and challenges. *J. Electrocardiol.,* 50, 1–8, 2016.

15. Rajani, A., Digitization of Electrocardiography Data Sheet Through Image Processing Techniques. *IUP J. Electr. Electron. Eng.,* 9, 2, 116–120, 2016.

16. Kumar, V., Extracting Samples As Text From ECG Strips For ECG Analysis Purpose, in: *Fourth International Conference on Computational Intelligence and Communication Networks,* Institute of Electrical and Electronics Engineers, pp. 317–321, 06 December 2012.

17. Jayaraman, S. and Damodaran, V., An Improved Method for ECG Morphological Features Extraction From Scanned ECG Records. *4th International Conference on Bioinformatics and Biomedical Technology IPCBEE,* vol. 29, pp. 64–68, 2012.

18. Patil, R. and Karandikar, R.G., Digitization of documented signals using vertical scanning, in: *International Conference on Microwave, Optical and Communication Engineering,* Institute of Electrical and Electronics Engineers, , pp. 239–242, 2015.

19. Harris, C. and Stephens, M., *A combined corner and edge detector,* in: *Alvey Vision Conference,* pp. 147–151, Plessey Research Roke Manor, United Kingdom, The Plessey Company pic, 1988.

20. Dey, N., Nandi, P., Barman, N., A Comparative Study between Moravec and Harris Corner Detection of Noisy Images Using Adaptive Wavelet thresholding technique. *Int. J. Eng. Res. Appl. (IJERA),* 2, 1, 599–606, Jan-Feb 2012.

21. Ryu, J.B., Lee, C.G., Park, H.H., Formula for Harris corner detector. *Electron. Lett.,* 4, 3, 3, 180–181, February 2011.

22. Gueguen, L. and Pesaresi, M., Multi scale Harris corner detector based on Differential Morphological Decomposition. *Pattern Recognit. Lett.,* 32, 1714–1719, 2011.

23. Khleaf, H.K., Ghazali, K.H., Abdalla, A.N., Features Extraction Techniques For ECG Recording Paper. *International Conference on artificial Intelligence in computer science and ICT (AICS2013),* 26 November 2013.

24. Stockbridge, N., Points to consider in electrocardiogram waveform extraction. *J. Electrocardiol.,* 38, 319–320, 2005.

25. Issac Niwas, S. and Shantha Selva Kumari, R., Artificial Neural Network Based Automatic Cardiac Abnormalities Classification. *Proceedings of the Sixth International Conference on Computational Intelligence and Multimedia Applications (ICCIMA05),* IEEE, 2005.

26. Sayad, A.T. and Halkarnikar, P.P., Diagnosis of heart disease using neural network approach. *Int. J. Adv. Sci. Eng. Technol.,* 2, 3, 88–92, July-2014.

27. Moavenian, M. and Khorrami, H., A qualitative comparison of Artificial neural networks and support vector machines in ECG arrhythmias classification. *Expert Syst. Appl.*, 37, 3088–3093, 2010.

28. Kasturiwale, H. and Kale, S.N., Qualitative analysis of Heart Rate Variability based Biosignal Model for Classification of Cardiac Diseases. *Int. J. Adv. Sci. Technol.*, 29, 7, 296–305, 2020.

29. Karhe, R.R. and Kale, S.N., Neural network classifiers for cardiac arrhythmias from scanned ECG documents. *Int. J. Adv. Trends Comput. Sci. Eng.*, 8, 1.6, 549–555, 2019.

30. Kasturiwale, H.P. and Kale, S.N., BioSignal Modelling for Prediction of Cardiac Diseases Using Intra Group Selection Method. *Intell. Decis. Technol.*, 15, 1, 151–160, 1 Jan. 2021, 10.3233/IDT-200058.

31. Karhe, R.R. and Kale, S.N., Classification of Cardiac Arrhythmias using Feedforward Neural Network. 10, 5, 15–20, 2020.

32. Holter, N. J., New method for heart studies. *Science*, 134, 3486, 1214–1220, 1961.

9

An Implementation of Image Processing Technique for Bone Fracture Detection Including Classification

Rocky Upadhyay[1]*, Prakash Singh Tanwar[2] and Sheshang Degadwala[3]

[1]Computer Science and Engineering, Madhav University, Rajasthan, India
[2]Department of CSE and CSA, Madhav University, Rajasthan, India
[3]Department of Computer Engineering, SIE, Vadodara, Gujarat, India

Abstract

In the present time, an intense and regular issue is broken bones, which is a confound issue in any typical human that happens due to weighty mass of weight that is applied on bone or fundamental incident and, in fact, due to malignant growth of bone and osteoporosis. In this way, the specific improvement of bone break is huge perspectives in remedial field. From this exploration, X-shaft/ CT pictures are used for discovering split examination in object. The images dealing with the frameworks are useful for some advanced applications, for instance, science, security, satellite imagery, singular photo, and medication. The strategies of picture dealing with, for instance, picture overhaul, picture division, and feature extraction, are used for break acknowledgment framework. Picture processing techniques have been used in a wide arrangement of employments these days to redesign the idea of unrefined picture information. Picture division or ID of x-plate clinical imaging is standard and moves task in order to improve the finding and assessment result. A x-beam picture is one of the most settled photographic films that is commonly used in clinical investigation and treatment. A x-beam picture is an important technique for the specialists and authorities to choose and inspect the bone break, which is a huge reaction used for end, yet x-shaft conveys a solitary mid-extend quality picture, which will normally impact the information of the image. The standard purpose of this assessment is to perceive human bone break from x-ray pictures.

Keywords: Image processing, edge detection, noise removal, bone fracture, crack detection, x-ray, SVM

9.1 Introduction

Bone break is an essential issue even in most countries, and the amount of splits is extending quickly. Bone break can happen in view of a fundamental incident or different kinds of sicknesses. Thusly, fast and exact assurance can be hard to get accomplishment of any embraced cycle [2]. Despite the way that CT and MRI pictures gives improved quality tempers for live human organs in contrast with x-shaft pictures, at long last faster more

---

*Corresponding author: rko75316060@gmail.com

Tushar H. Jaware, K. Sarat Kumar, Ravindra D. Badgujar and Svetlin Antonov (eds.) *Medical Imaging and Health Informatics*, (165–178) © 2022 Scrivener Publishing LLC

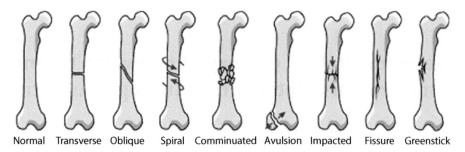

Normal   Transverse   Oblique   Spiral   Comminuated   Avulsion   Impacted   Fissure   Greenstick

Figure 9.1 Bone fracture types [1].

affordable, acknowledge more broad openness, and are less complex to use scarcely any requirements. Furthermore, the level of nature of x-shaft pictures is adequate joined the ultimate objective of bone break revelation [2].

Clinical picture handling is the mixture of different fields that incorporate software engineering, information science, organic science, and clinical science. Clinical picture calculation is a viable and furthermore a monetary design that guides during the age of appeared portrayals of the inside aspect of object by any human body for medical investigation as well as clinical conclusion. Removing particular that data is medically significant from the clinical picture is the primary goal of clinical picture handling. An area of clinical surmise has been seeing elevate in securing of clinical pictures as well as in its methods and skill of translation. Bone cracks are only the bursts which happen because of mishaps. There are numerous kinds of bone breaks, for example, typical, cross over, comminute, diagonal, winding, portioned, separated, affected, torus, and greenstick as shown in Figure 9.1 [1].

9.2   Existing Technology

These days, x-beam picture is broadly utilized for crack analysis and bone treatment as it gives exact outcomes and fast treatment. A few investigates have been recently accomplished for a similar reason. Various programming projects had been actualized to analyze break in human body [12, 13]. In this paper, crack determination is finished utilizing watchful edge discovery strategy. Picture processing utilizing shrewd edge location is executed, and also, it provides explicit results, yet the work can be altered, and more refined outcomes can be gotten. During the past analysis, the recognition administrator in term of edge, Sobel administrator, is utilized for the "edge distinguishing proof does not utilize boundary, for that picture acquired process will be improved more [11].

This work uses the Sobel operator. Figure 9.2 shows normal image with and without Sobel operator parameter.

9.2.1   Pre-Processing

This progression comprises of four stages, specifically editing, resizing, grayscaling, and honing, which will be obviously clarified in the following subsubsection [17–19].

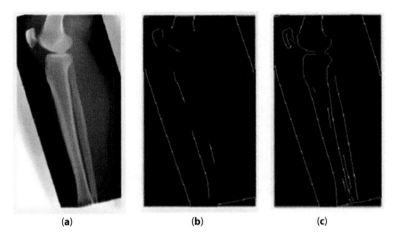

(a) **(b)** **(c)**

Figure 9.2 (a) Normal image. (b) Without sobel operator. (c) Using sobel operator.

- Cropping: It is led to get the locale of premium (ROI) and separate it from pointless territory of cruris picture.
- Resizing: This cycle is directed to make all pictures have a similar size. In this examination, we resize all the used picture information into more modest size, 100 × 400 pixels, to make the cycle run rapidly [17, 18].
- Grayscaling: After resizing the shading picture (has RGB parts), it will change into grayscale. The change from RGB into grayscale should be possible utilizing condition [17, 18].

$$G = \frac{R+G+B}{3} \tag{9.1}$$

- Sharpening: As the rule of high pass filter, honing is done to upgrade the picture quality and underline the edge of picture object.

9.2.2 Denoise Image

In the process, there were many unnecessary portions of picture may occur during x-ray scanning. This process will help out to making an adjustment or avoid from these various aspects, which are making any image dull. The dull or denoise image is never ideal for any conclusion in medical division, so some clear picture is required to getting proper picture. For this solution, we have below mentioned technology that will help to completing our requirements in different manners [20].

As per the picture appeared in Figure 9.3b, the image is full of noise. This image is never provided ideal result. Figure 9.3a is the original image. Somehow, some images are going through some unnecessary process or some images are dull by fetching. Ultimately, it is requiring some filtration process to remove this noise. For that, we have two filters are mentioned below and we will discuss it as on its work [14, 15].

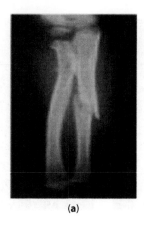 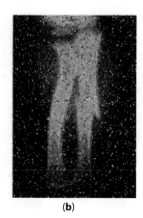

(a)   (b)

Figure 9.3 (a) Original image. (b) Noised image.

- Older Filter
- Mean Filter

For the process of masterminding in local stream, the request channels are mainly executing for them. In this process, local pixels are utilizing from low to high level of contrast. The required insight is the main measurement that is used for performing this kind of process. It is deployed specially for this work and responsibility [22–24].

9.2.3   Histogram

Histogram is a graph-oriented portrayal of different powers of a picture. A "histogram" including the little propagate has least difference and a by using wide, a wide propagate has a high-level differentiation. A picture that holds the histogram bunched at the least finish of the reach is dim and a histogram including the qualities grouped at the high-level finish of the reach relates to a splendid picture. It can likewise be changed by planning capacities, for example, stretch, slide a lot. In any case, these capacities would not create an ideal outcome. Histogram equalization is utilized to even out the picture with equivalent capacity [21].

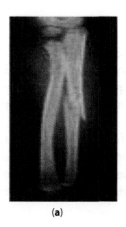 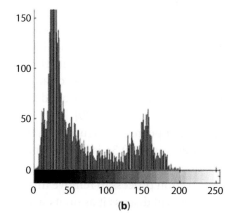

(a)   (b)

Figure 9.4 (a) Original image. (b) Noised image.

As shown in Figure 9.4a, the first image with normal input or original image for making any histogram and the second image is with some graphic-oriented histogram result, which you can clearly see in Figure 9.4b. Image enhancement process is used in this stream and makes the result as per appropriate requirements [30]. This method is used for differentiation different to any image which used for input or original [26].

9.3   Image Processing

Image processing technology uses the Canny edge algorithm.

9.3.1   Canny Edge

In this algorithm, mainly, edges are the most critical angle which gives vital data to examination of picture [2]. Cracks are essentially the blueprint that separates the article by using its experience. Distinguishing proof of crack is a significant typical cycle which is influenced from disintegration because of various fluctuating degree of commotion [2]. Watchful edge locator is a crack discovery administrator. For the expensive range of edges, it requires to utilize calculation in multi-stage [3]. Watchful the detection of edge calculation is demonstrated to initiate an ideal calculation for crack distinguishing proof. Its preferable picture is grayscale as information, measurements, and outcomes of that force appear in non-continuation mode.

There are mainly five different divisions in Canny edge detector [25, 27]:

1) Smoothing of input image by Gaussian filter
2) Finding gradients of the image
3) Non-maximum suppression
4) Double thresholding
5) Edge tracking

In this edge detection, various more area can be satisfying the outcomes:

1. Watchful has a superior identification (recognition standards). Shrewd strategy has the capacity to feature all the current edges that coordinate with the client decided boundary's edge [4].
2. Watchful has better confining way. Watchful can create least hole between identified crack and the genuine picture crack [4].
3. Evident reaction can be provided. Single reaction is for each crack. Ultimately, it makes less disarray tense recognition for the following picture. There will be direct impact of Canny edge detection during recognition of boundaries for every outcomes and edge discovery. Mainly, there are two boundaries [4]:
   (a) Gaussian deviate on standard value
   (b) Threshold value

-1	0	1
-2	0	2
-1	0	1

1	2	1
0	0	0
-1	-1	-1

Figure 9.5 Sobel operators in "Gx" and Gy.

Steps to perform the algorithm:

1. Eliminate all clamors on the picture by actualizing Gaussian channel. Subsequent to acquiring Gaussian channel, the subsequent picture that acquired will be least haze. The expectation of using the channel is to acquire the genuine crack in the picture. In the event that the given channel is not reflected, at times of its own commotion, it will be identified the crack [4].
2. After the detecting the crack by using existing operator, it will give the perfect sight or vision of the edges and distortions. Next is the work of Sobel operator (Figure 9.5) example:

The purpose of combining the result is to use or utilize both operators for fetching the actual data [4]:

$$[G] = [Gx] + [Gy] \tag{9.2}$$

3. Directives as per formula usage:

$$G = \sqrt{G2x} + \sqrt{G2y} \tag{9.3}$$

Identification utilizes two limits (greatest edge worth and least edge esteem). On the off chance that the matrix brilliant is greater than greatest edge, the matrix will be neglected as groundwork of picture. On the off chance that the pixel slope between greatest edge and least edge, the pixel will be acknowledged as an edge in the event that it identifies even separate edge pixel which is more than the most extreme limit [4].
4. Limit the developing edge line by applying non-greatest concealment. The cycle gives slimmer edge line [4].
5. Final step is to retrieve the machine level value of image matrix by administer two value of threshold.

9.4   Overview of System and Steps

9.4.1   Workflow

Framework outline of this task is talked about through stream diagram [28]. The stream outline clarifies the cycle stream from recognizing x-beam picture until delivering the bone crack discovery on the x-beam picture (Figure 9.6).

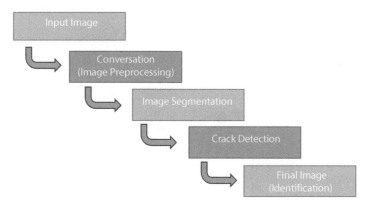

Figure 9.6 Workflow of main system.

The real work of the system is demonstrated as follows:

1. It will take medical image as an input for processing further.
2. In this step, we will perform tasks like, cleaning, filtering, or smoothening and binary form for making picture and result more accurate.
3. This step will provide segmentation of image for step.
4. By using, Canny detection and Sobel operators, this step will help to find out exact and maximum accurate edge detection of medical image for finding exact crack.
5. In final step, it will provide final detection of crack by red mark circle that will make easy to understand and conclude to any medical officer for further treatment.
➢ **Important factors of the system:**
  - Fast and efficient results.
  - High accuracy and fast conclusion.
  - Help lot for further treatments in serious issues of any object.

9.4.2   Classifiers

Order is the way toward perceiving, comprehending, and gathering thoughts and work into preset classifications or "sub-populaces". Using pre-sorted preparing datasets, AI programs utilize an assortment of calculations to characterize future datasets into classes.

Arrangement calculations in AI utilize input preparing information to anticipate the probability that ensuing information can be categorized as one of the foreordained classes. Perhaps, the most widely recognized an employment of order is sifting messages into "spam" or "non-spam".

9.4.2.1   *Extra Tree Ensemble Method*

As we observed from the couple of tree concepts, this is another expansion begged of decision tree.

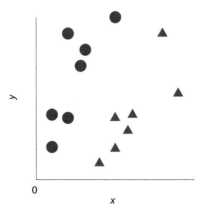

Figure 9.7 Various objects.

Basically, it is using the ensemble method that gives training sets or data random trees that are prepared. It is extremely randomized tree, where EXT is stands for extra and RA is stands for random Figure 9.7.

9.4.2.2   SVM

The SVM runs on the algorithm of training and classification of data in range of polarity, as an example in Figure 9.8. This classification uses the prediction policy to manipulate [28].

The example shows that we have two different objects with different colors that are normally considered as features of an object. This shows the work of classification into respective categories [29].

This vector machine made some separation process by assigning a hyperplane that provide best outcome. According to two dimensions, this is just a vertical line. Both sides are separated with different colors and shapes by hyperplanes or vertical lines. In case of sentiment analysis, answer may be in one word or sign like positive and negative (Figure 9.9) [26].

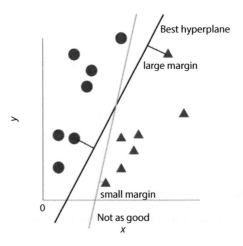

Figure 9.8 Hyperplane in SVM.

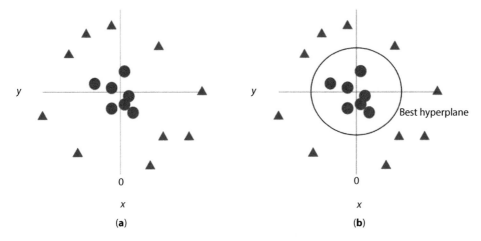

Figure 9.9 (a) Objects separation. (b) Selected best hyperplane.

9.4.2.3   Trained Algorithm

It is a hierarchical algorithm that works in mainly three principles which are explained step by step. It will show the solution of conditional situation and according to the appropriate selection further step is dependent.

1) For any sample, reliable classification should handle the higher level SVM.
2) If it is failed or reliably not classified by the higher-level SVM, then it should be passed to lower level SVM for the process.
3) The lower level SVM must have better level of performance that can handled passed sample for trained and prepared for higher level SVM.

9.4.3   Feature Extraction

The mind-boggling issue of dividing shape of bone in x-beam pictures can be decayed into a few divisible issues as pursues.

1) Highlight considering section is progression; fixed highlights ought to be chosen to acquire right congruity "bet'n" the focuses in the map book and the focuses in the objective picture. This is an imperative initial move that will influence the aftereffect of the accompanying advances.
2) Worldwide alignment is based on the highlight searches in the upper advance; worldwide arrangement is to decide a harsh arrangement "bet'n" the chart book and the picture as far as scaling, revolution, and interpretation. This progression is performed concerning the entire bone structure. Likewise, verbalizations between associated bones ought to be considered.
3) Neighborhood refinement local refinement is to precisely enroll the map book shapes to the limits of bones. It necessary to take into record the verbalization and states of bones. The examination fixture is to take care of every one of these smaller issues and afterward incorporate the calculations into an entire arrangement.

9.5   Results

This system takes x-ray as an info x-beam with vigilant edge discovery strategy. In Figure 9.10a, the client inserts the picture which is a x-beam picture of the bone. At that point, the framework will go through watchful edge location that incorporates Gaussian channel and edge identification.

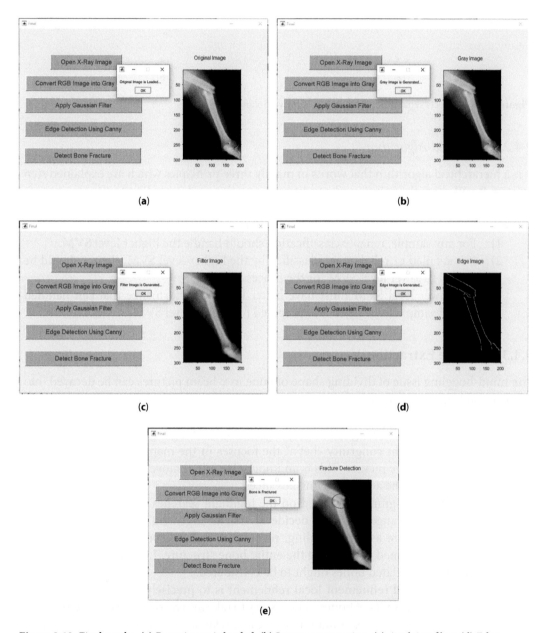

Figure 9.10 Final results. (a) Raw picture is loaded. (b) Image conversation. (c) Applying filter. (d) Edge image. (e) Born fracture identify.

Sobel administrator chased by non-most extreme concealment, and the yield acquired over this progression appeared in Figure 9.10b. In Figure 9.10c, the framework exhibits the yield by consolidating the yield of the outcome acquired in Figure 9.10b, by upsetting the first picture that is transferred by the client. Next, the framework identifies the area where it features the finish of boundary, which is shown in Figure 9.10d. In Figure 9.10e, the framework recognizes the cracked object as well as area of break.

9.5.1   Result Analysis

Evaluation is the first step for any normal fracture state that called binary. An analysis is totally depending on observer and from that mainly four possibilities comes out [16].

- (1)   TP represents correctly labeled.
- (2)   TN represents normal but nonfractured picture, which are correctly labeled.
- (3)   FP represents normal but nonfractured picture, which are incorrectly labeled.
- (4)   FN represents incorrectly labeled.

This performance is used for mainly accuracy, precision, sensitivity, and specificity.

$$\text{Accuracy} = \frac{TP + TN}{TP + TN + FN + FP} \tag{9.4}$$

$$\text{Precision} = \frac{TP}{TP + FP} \quad \text{Sensitivty} = \frac{TP}{TP + FN} \quad \text{Specificity} = \frac{TP}{TP + FN} \tag{9.5}$$

$$k = \frac{N \sum_{i=1}^{r} x_{ii} - \sum_{i=1} x_{i+} X \, x_{+i}}{N^2 - \sum_{i=1}^{r} x_{i+} X \, x_{+1}} \tag{9.6}$$

$$k = \frac{52 * (19 + 12 + 11 + 4) - [(19 * 23) + (12 * 14) + (16 * 11) + (5 * 4)]}{52 * 52 - [(19 * 23) + (12 * 14) + (16 * 11) + (5 * 4)]}$$

k=0.83=83%

By observing statistical data and its equation, we conclude 92% of accuracy, almost 100% of level of precision, 87% of sensitivity, and 100% of specificity by using number of input mages. Table 9.1 gives numerical data with four possible testing outcomes, which not included in Table 9.2.

Table 9.1 Numeric data of possible outcomes.

Stages	Broken	General
Broken	27	00
General	04	19

Table 9.2 Matrix for possible outcomes.

Stages	General	Broken
Broken	False Positive	True Positive
General	True Negative	False Negative

9.6 Conclusion

In this chapter, break concludable evidence is completed exploiting the Canny edge detection administrator. Finalized structure will be backing the medical supervisors with acquiring very precise results including lower egression and even with least timings. The system is tested over legal data. Utilizing Sobel administrator assists with improving the effectiveness of the framework and furthermore assists with diagnosing the hairline break all the more adequately. Since hairline break is fundamentally the crack that has different cracks consolidated, in this break, the total contortion of bone happens. Along these lines, at this worth, edges can be analyzed so that all the mutilations and joints are plainly obvious that help to expand the achievement pace of the framework. Alongside that, delicate processing procedures [5–9] and proper techniques [10] will likewise be researched to improve the grouping execution.

References

1. Upadhyay, R.S. and Tanwar, P., A Review on Bone Fracture Detection Techniques using Image Processing. *2019 International Conference on Intelligent Computing and Control Systems (ICCS)*, IEEE, 2019.
2. Mahajan, S.R., Zope, P.H., Suralkar, S.R., Review of An Enhance Fracture Detection Algorithm Design Using X-Rays Image Processing. *Int. J. Innov. Res. Sci. Eng. Technol.*, 1, 2, 141–146, 2012.
3. Petronas, Universititeknologi, Mean and Standard Deviation Features of Color Histogram using Laplacian Filter For Content-Based Image Retrieval. *J. Theor. Appl. Inf. Technol.*, 34, 1, 2011.
4. Johari, N. and Singh, N., Bone fracture detection using edge detection technique, in: *Soft Computing: Theories and Applications*, pp. 11–19, Springer, Singapore, 2018.
5. Gonzalez, R.C., Woods, R.E., Eddins, S.L., *Digital image processing using MATLAB*, Pearson Education India, 2004.
6. Ansari, I.A., Millie, P., Ahn, C.W., Robust and false positive free watermarking in IWT domain using SVD and ABC. *Eng. Appl. Artif. Intell.*, 49, 114–125, 2016.

7. Jauhar, S.K., Pant, M., Deep, A., An approach to solve multi-criteria supplier selection while considering environmental aspects using differential evolution. *International conference on swarm, evolutionary, and memetic computing*, Springer, Cham, 2013.

8. Ansari, I.A. and Pant, M., SVD watermarking: particle swarm optimization of scaling factors to increase the quality of watermark. *Proceedings of Fourth International Conference on Soft Computing for Problem Solving*, Springer, New Delhi, 2015.

9. Zaheer, H. *et al.*, A portfolio analysis of ten national banks through differential evolution. *Proceedings of Fifth International Conference on Soft Computing for Problem Solving*, Springer, Singapore, 2016.

10. Jauha, S.K. and Pant, M., Recent trends in supply chain management: A soft computing approach. *Proceedings of Seventh International Conference on Bio-Inspired Computing: Theories and Applications (BIC-TA 2012)*, Springer, India, 2013.

11. Smith, R. *et al.*, Detection of fracture and quantitative assessment of displacement measures in pelvic X-RAY images. *2010 IEEE International Conference on Acoustics, Speech and Signal Processing*, IEEE, 2010.

12. Lum, V.L.F. *et al.*, Combining classifiers for bone fracture detection in X-ray images. *IEEE International Conference on Image Processing 2005*, vol. 1, IEEE, 2005.

13. Chan, K.-P. and Fu, A.W.-C., Efficient time series matching by wavelets. *Proceedings 15th International Conference on Data Engineering (Cat. No. 99CB36337)*, IEEE, 1999.

14. Goswami, B. and Kr Misra, S., Analysis of various edge detection methods for x-ray images. *2016 International Conference on Electrical, Electronics, and Optimization Techniques (ICEEOT)*, IEEE, 2016.

15. Kaur, D. and Kaur, Y., Various image segmentation techniques: a review. *Int. J. Comput. Sci. Mob. Computing*, 3, 5, 809–814, 2014.

16. Upadhyay, R., Fracture Detection and Classification Using Machine Learning Approach. *J. Gujarat Res. Soc.*, 21, 6, 273–284, 2019.

17. Guan, B., Yao, J., Zhang, G., Wang, X., Thigh fracture detection using deep learning method based on new dilated convolutional feature pyramid network. *Pattern Recognit. Lett.*, 125, 521–526, 2019.

18. Kusche, C., Reclik, T., Freund, M., Al-samman, T., Kerzel, U., Id, S.K., Large-area, high-resolution characterisation and classification of damage mechanisms in dual-phase steel using deep learning. 1–22, 2019.

19. Chai, H.Y., Wee, L.K., Swee, T.T., Salleh, S.H., Ariff, A.K., Kamarulafizam, Gray-level co-occurrence matrix bone fracture detection. *Am. J. Appl. Sci.*, 8, 1, 26–32, 2011.

20. Tavares, J.M.R.S. and Fernandes, P.R., Special issue: 'CMBBE2018–15th international symposium on computer methods in biomechanics and biomedical engineering & 3rd conference on imaging and visualization. *Comput. Methods Biomech. Biomed. Eng. Imaging Vis.*, 8, 3, 231, 2020.

21. Cao, Y., Wang, H., Moradi, M., Prasanna, P., Syeda-Mahmood, T.F., Fracture detection in x-ray images through stacked random forests feature fusion. *Proc. - Int. Symp. Biomed. Imaging*, 2015-July, pp. 801–805, 2015.

22. Johari, N. and Singh, N., Bone fracture detection using edge detection technique. *Adv. Intell. Syst. Comput.*, 584, 11–19, 2018.

23. Chowdhury, A.S., Bhattacharya, A., Bhandarkar, S.M., Datta, G.S., Yu, J.C., Figueroa, R., Hairline fracture detection using MRF and gibbs sampling. *Proc. - IEEE Work. Appl. Comput. Vision, WACV 2007*, vol. 4, 2007.

24. Tanzi, L., Vezzetti, E., Moreno, R., Moos, S., X-Ray bone fracture classification using deep learning: A baseline for designing a reliable approach. *Appl. Sci.*, 10, 4, 2020.

25. Liu, J.E. and An, F.P., Image Classification Algorithm Based on Deep Learning-Kernel Function. *Sci. Program.*, 2020, 1, 2020.

26. Jauhar, S.K., Pant, M., Deep, A., An approach to solve multi-criteria supplier selection while considering environmental aspects using differential evolution. *Lect. Notes Comput. Sci. (including Subser. Lect. Notes Artif. Intell. Lect. Notes Bioinformatics)*, 8297 LNCS, PART 1, 199–208, 2013.

27. Shrestha, A. and Mahmood, A., Review of deep learning algorithms and architectures. *IEEE Access*, 7, 53040–53065, 2019.

28. Zhang, J., Xie, Y., Wu, Q., Xia, Y., Medical image classification using synergic deep learning. *Med. Image Anal.*, 54, 10–19, 2019.

29. Ebsim, R., Naqvi, J., Cootes, T.F., *Automatic detection of wrist fractures from posteroanterior and lateral radiographs: A deep learning-based approach*, vol. 11404 LNCS, Springer International Publishing, 2019.

30. Chung, S.W. *et al.*, Automated detection and classification of the proximal humerus fracture by using deep learning algorithm. *Acta Orthop.*, 89, 4, 468–473, 2018.

10

Improved Otsu Algorithm for Segmentation of Malaria Parasite Images

Mosam K. Sangole[1]*, Sanjay T. Gandhe[1] and Dipak P. Patil[2]

[1]Sandip Foundation's SITRC Nashik, Maharashtra, India
[2]Sandip Foundation's SIEM Nashik, Maharashtra, India

Abstract

Malaria is a severe worldwide medical issue that is accountable for approximately one million losses of life every year. Currently, many developing countries have an increasing number of children affected by this parasite, which results in the economic and social crisis. Malaria poses a threat to health if no immediate action is taken. With the large number of malaria cases diagnosed throughout the year, a fast and exact detection of malaria disease, which accelerates prompt treatment, is necessary to control spread of malaria disease. Microscopic detection of malaria from blood smear images manually takes too much time. Therefore, an automatic or semiautomatic technique needs to be developed to detect the *Plasmodium*-infected cell, thus providing the appropriate treatment to eradicate the outbreak. The most important stage in automatic detection of malaria disease is image segmentation. Many image segmentation techniques have been used in medical applications to segment infected RBC from malaria blood smear images. The Otsu segmentation method is a well-known automatic segmentation method in malaria blood smear image segmentation. This chapter proposed an improved Otsu method for segmentation of malaria parasite images. The quantitative results obtain from Accuracy, Sensitivity, Matthews correlation coefficient (MCC), Dice, Jaccard, and Structural Similarity Index (SSIM) prove that indeed the proposed improved Otsu algorithm is more effective than the Nobuyuki Otsu, valley-emphasis Otsu, and hybrid Otsu in medical image segmentation.

Keywords: Malaria, microscopic image segmentation, thresholding, Otsu, RBC, malaria parasite, Plasmodium

10.1   Introduction

Malaria is a contagious, widespread disease in tropical and subtropical areas, caused by a blood parasite of the genus *Plasmodium*. In recent decades, detection malaria disease becomes most exciting research projects because of the proposed alternatives to new

---

*Corresponding author: mosamleo@gmail.com

Tushar H. Jaware, K. Sarat Kumar, Ravindra D. Badgujar and Svetlin Antonov (eds.) Medical Imaging and Health Informatics, (179–194) © 2022 Scrivener Publishing LLC

automated detection methodologies. The segmentation of blood smear images is a big challenge in the field of image processing and analysis because of presence of noise, random background, illumination issues and overlapping objects [2–10]. Over the past few decades, many researchers have focused on automated technology as it is more accurate and efficient than traditional methods. An automated system for diagnosing a patient's disease is a faster procedure than a standardized technique using a microscope procedure.

Blood smear images must be segmented into the red blood cells (RBCs) to detect the malaria parasite. Image segmentation is a process of splitting pixels into two or more parts. Each pixel contains important features such as intensity, texture, and color. The main purpose of segmentation is to facilitate the representation of an understandable image. Numerous researches have proposed many techniques but no general technique for good segmentation still exists.

Automatic thresholding is significant method in the field of image segmentation. The basic idea of automatic segmentation is to automatically select an optimal value of gray-level threshold to separate items of interest in an image from the background.

Global thresholding is simple and easy automatic thresholding method to implement, but the result depends on good (uniform) illumination. Non-uniform illumination is generally not a problem in controlled lighting conditions. In such conditions, threshold is selected using global thresholding as it is simple and faster. Among the global thresholding methods, the Otsu technique (Otsu, 1979) [1] is a better way to select gray level threshold for common images in terms of uniformity and size measures.

10.2   Literature Review

Here, a few of the distinguished efforts made in the area of image segmentation of malaria blood smear images are briefly described.

Devi *et al.* [2] analyzed a set of different features to detect malaria-infected erythrocytes. In this paper, the stained parts were segmented using the Otsu's segmentation method. Unwanted stains and artifacts were then removed by morphological filtering and area thresholding respectively. Finally, marker-controlled watershed segmentation divides the overlapped blood cells into separate blood cells.

Knock *et al.* used machine intelligence to identify malaria parasite in thin blood smear image [3]. In this segmentation process, image was converted to L*a*b* color space. After that, the total pixels in an image was divided into three clusters using unsupervised K-means clustering. Foreground part of image belongs to first two clusters and the background part belongs to third cluster. Pixels of third cluster were replaced by black pixels.

Kaur and Walia proposed a hybrid form of ACO-SVM to classify malaria parasite [4]. For malaria image segmentation, basic ant colony optimization tool was suggested by authors in this paper.

Lorenzo-Ginori *et al.* [5] used digital image processing to classify *Plasmodium*-infected erythrocytes. In this process, segmentation was done in two steps. First, a rough segmentation was applied to the image intensity factor using Otsu's algorithm. Overlapped cell were then detected and segmented using weighted outer distance and marker-controlled watershed transform.

Madhu proposed a method of diagnosing malaria from microscopic blood images [6]. In this research, the author used segmentation method using Einstein t-conorm and a novel fuzzy type membership function to reveal part of the infected blood cell from microscopic blood smear images.

Pragya et al. [7] suggested a method for classification of malaria parasite using Chan–Vese Algorithm for segmentation and SVM as a classifier. The common method proposed for segmentation of malaria parasite is Chan–Vese [20], and the only purpose of using this algorithm is to segment image into areas with useful information.

Dawale and Baraskar implemented malaria detection technique using regional descriptors and PSO-SVM classifier [8]. In this paper, blood cells were segmented using region based and Otsu thresholding.

Manning et al. [9] used marker-based watershed segmentation technique for separating RBCs from background.

Hartati et al. [10] utilized Otsu's thresholding method to determine threshold automatically. The morphological closing and opening were then performed to remove the hole in the infected cell and to remove the unwanted artefacts.

Varma and Chavan used local binary pattern to detect malaria parasite in thick and thin blood smear images [11]. Here, authors used Otsu thresholding as a segmentation tool. For edge detection purpose, Sobel and Prewitt masks were used.

Sadiq et al. advised to select the optimal characteristics according to the Z-score to detect malaria-infected erythrocytes using supervised learning [12]. Canny edge detection was used to take out valuable information and significantly reduced the amount of data required for the process.

Kanojia et al. [13] performed image segmentation using Otsu global thresholding and watershed algorithm.

Devi et al. [14] had segmented all the stained components (i.e., erythrocytes and artifacts) using Otsu's thresholding method. After this, unwanted stained components were separated from the erythrocyte using morphological filter. Finally, clumped erythrocytes were separated using marker-controlled watershed algorithm.

Devi et al. [15] classified malaria-infected erythrocytes with the help of hybrid classifier. For segmentation of clump erythrocytes into individual erythrocyte, marker-controlled watershed segmentation was used by authors.

Elsalamony used neural networks to detect healthy and unhealthy RBC in human blood smears [16]. Watershed and morphological functions were used during the segmentation process.

Hung et al. used MP detector to segment parasite in Stained Blood Smears [17]. In this paper, Otsu's thresholding method was applied to select a threshold for segregating all the pixels into two clusters of parasites and background.

Somasekar et al. [18] used Fuzzy C-means (FCM) algorithm for extracting the malaria-infected cells from blood smear images with two clusters.

Tsai et al. recommended a method for detection and segmentation of malaria infected erythrocyte [19]. Here, Otsu's thresholding was used to select a threshold value for segmenting all pixels into two clusters of parasites and background.

From the above survey, we can say that majority of the researchers have used Otsu thresholding method for segmentation because of its ease of use and durability. In Otsu method, the threshold value is selected by maximizing the between-class variance of the histogram. This method is good for selecting threshold value of a histogram which is having bimodal or multimodal distribution. However, if the histogram is close to unimodal, then the method proposed by Otsu fails [1]. The main purpose of this research was to modify available Otsu method to select best threshold value and to evaluate the effectiveness of the suggested modified technique for segmentation of Malaria parasite images.

10.3   Related Works

Here, we begin by briefly introducing the Otsu method proposed by Nobuyuki Otsu in [20] to select the appropriate threshold for image segmentation. Let us assume that the pixels of a given image is denoted by gray levels having values [0, 1, 2, ..., L−1].

Let n_i = the total number of pixels having gray level i
$N = n_0 + n_1 + n_2 + ... + n_{L-1}$ = total pixels in that image

The probability of occurrence of gray level i is represented by Pi and given as

$$P_i = \frac{n_i}{N} P_i > 0 \qquad \sum_{i=1}^{L-1} P_i = 1 \tag{10.1}$$

The average gray level denoted by μ_T of the whole image is calculated as

$$\mu_T = \sum_{i=0}^{L-1} iP_i \tag{10.2}$$

In this method, threshold operation divides the total pixels into two classes C_0 and C_1 (e.g., foreground and background) at gray level t, i.e., C_0 represents pixels within levels {0, 1, 2,..., t} and C_1 represents pixels within levels {t + 1, t +2,....L−1}.

The probabilities of the two classes are

$$\omega_0 = P_r(C_0) = \sum_{i=0}^{t} P_i \tag{10.3}$$

$$\omega_1 = P_r(C_1) = \sum_{i=t+1}^{L-1} P_i \tag{10.4}$$

The two classes have mean values defined as

$$\mu_0 = \sum_{i=0}^{t} \frac{iP_i}{\omega_0} \tag{10.5}$$

$$\mu_1 = \sum_{i=t+1}^{L-1} \frac{iP_i}{\omega_1} \tag{10.6}$$

Then, $\omega_0\mu_0 + \omega_1\mu_1 = \mu_T$ and $\omega_0 + \omega_1 = 1$

Otsu showed that, for the threshold t, the between-class variance $\sigma_B{}^2$ of C_0 and C_1 is

$$\sigma_B{}^2 = \omega_0(\mu_0 - \mu_T)^2 + \omega_1(\mu_1 - \mu_T)^2 \tag{10.7}$$

$$\sigma_B{}^2 = \omega_0\omega_1(\mu_1 - \mu_0)^2 \tag{10.8}$$

$$\sigma_B{}^2 = \omega_0\mu_0{}^2 + \omega_1\mu_1{}^2 \tag{10.9}$$

The best possible threshold t^* can be calculated as

$$t^* = Arg \max_{0<t<L-1} \sigma_B{}^2 \tag{10.10}$$

$$t^* = Arg \max_{0<t<L-1} \{\omega_0\omega_1(\mu_1 - \mu_0)^2\} \tag{10.11}$$

10.4   Proposed Algorithm

When the overall distribution for a class C_k (k = 0 or 1) is heavy-tailed or skewed, compared with the average gray level, it is well known that the median value is a very robust and efficient estimate value [21], in which the authors find that the sum of the computed median value and the average can be used to replace the average.

The mean value μ_0 and μ_1 is replaced by the sum of median gray level m_0 and μ_0 of the foreground part C_0 and the sum of the median gray level m_1 and μ_1 of the background part C_1, respectively.

The between-class variance of the two parts C_0 and C_1 can be rewritten as $\sigma_B{}^2$

$$\sigma_B{}^2 = \omega_0\omega_1((m_1 + \mu_1) - (m_0 + \mu_0))^2 \tag{10.12}$$

For a single object, the best threshold value should be situated in the valley of the bimodal histogram [1], as shown in Figure 10.1.

At the threshold t, the probability of occurrence h(t) must be small. Using this concept, in [1] Hui-Fuang Ngai suggested a valley-emphasis technique, in which a threshold value would be selected which has probability of occurrence smallest. This maximizes the between-class variance. We applied this weighted approach to maximize the between class variance stated in Equation (10.12). The objective function now becomes

$$\sigma_B{}^2 = (1 - h(t))(\omega_0\omega_1((m_1 + \mu_1) - (m_0 + \mu_0))^2) \tag{10.13}$$

The best possible threshold is then chosen with the help of the equation as

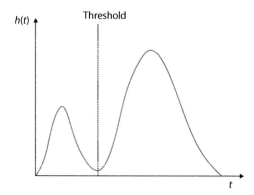

Figure 10.1 Best threshold value in histogram of all gray levels in an image [1].

$$t^\star = Arg \max_{0<t<L-1} \{(1-h(t))(\omega_0\omega_1((m_1+\mu_1)-(m_0+\mu_0))^2)\} \qquad (10.14)$$

In Equation (10.14), the first part $(1 - h(t))$ represents weight and the second part $(1 - h(t))(\omega_0\omega_1((m_1 + \mu_1) - (m_0 + \mu_0))^2)$ represents between class variance of the image. The value of threshold is selected such that the product of the two parts should have maximize value. For this, each part should have higher value at that particular time. For $(1 - h(t))$, the lower the value of h(t), the greater the value of weight $(1 - h(t))$. This ensures that for smaller h(t), the between class variance would have higher value. Thus, it chooses a threshold making the between class variance maximum value and also stays at the lower edge of the histogram. To achieve more accurate results, we have considered two adjoining gray values before and after the threshold value as obtained in Equation (10.14), in which the minimum of the five gray values is considered as the optimal threshold value $(t^\star)$.

10.5   Experimental Results

The improved Otsu algorithm is examined against the Otsu thresholding proposed by Nobuyuki Otsu in [20], valley-emphasis Otsu in [1], and hybrid Otsu thresholding in [21] considering Accuracy, Sensitivity, Matthews correlation coefficient (MCC), Dice, Jaccard, and Structural Similarity Index (SSIM). Standard images of Giemsa-stained malaria blood smear are collected from official standard website www.cdc.gov.us. These images are 300 × 300 in size. For experimentation purpose, we have used ImageJ software to obtain binary segmented images as ground truth. Experiments have been carried out using Intel(R) Core (TM)i5-7200 central processing unit @ 2.50 GHz, 8 GB RAM with MATLAB R2018a environment.

The parameters mentioned above are calculated as follows:

$$Accuracy = \frac{(TP+TN)}{(FN+FP+TP+TN)} \qquad (10.15)$$

$$Sensitivity = \frac{TP}{(TP+FN)} \tag{10.16}$$

$$Dice = \frac{2 \times TP}{(2 \times TP + FP + FN)} \tag{10.17}$$

$$MCC = \frac{(TN \times TP - FN \times FP)}{\sqrt{(FP+TP) \times (FN+TP) \times (FP+TN) \times (FN+TN)}} \tag{10.18}$$

$$Jaccard = \frac{Dice}{(2-Dice)} \tag{10.19}$$

where
  TP (True Positive): region segmented as mass that proved to be mass.
  FP (False Positive): region segmented as mass that proved to be not mass.
  FN (False Negative): region segmented as not mass that proved to be mass.
  TN (True Negative): region segmented as not mass that proved to be not mass.

The SSIM is depended on the calculation of three terms: luminance, contrast, and structural. The overall SSIM is obtained by following equation:

$$SSIM(m, n) = [l(m, n)]^\alpha \cdot [c(m, n)]^\beta \cdot [s(m, n)]^\gamma \tag{10.20}$$

where

$$l(m,n) = \frac{2\mu_m\mu_n + C_1}{\mu_m^2 + \mu_n^2 + C_1} \tag{10.21}$$

$$c(m,n) = \frac{2\sigma_m\sigma_n + C_2}{\sigma_m^2 + \sigma_n^2 + C_2} \tag{10.22}$$

$$s(m,n) = \frac{\sigma mn + C_3}{\sigma_m\sigma_n + C_3} \tag{10.23}$$

where μ_m and μ_n and are the local means, σ_m and σ_n are the standard deviations, and σ_{mn} is the cross-covariance for images m, n. respectively.

We have taken eight testing *Plasmodium* parasite images, and they are displayed in Figure 10.2. Figures 10.2a, b, c, d and e show the result of Original Otsu in [20], result of Valley-emphasis Otsu in [1], result of Hybrid Otsu thresholding in [21], and result of Proposed improved Otsu algorithm, respectively.

Tables 10.1 to 10.6 and Figures 10.3 to 10.8 give comparison of Accuracy, Sensitivity, MCC, Dice, Jaccard, and SSIM, respectively, of Otsu thresholding proposed by Nobuyuki Otsu in [20], valley-emphasis Otsu in [1], and hybrid Otsu thresholding in [21] with the proposed improved Otsu algorithm.

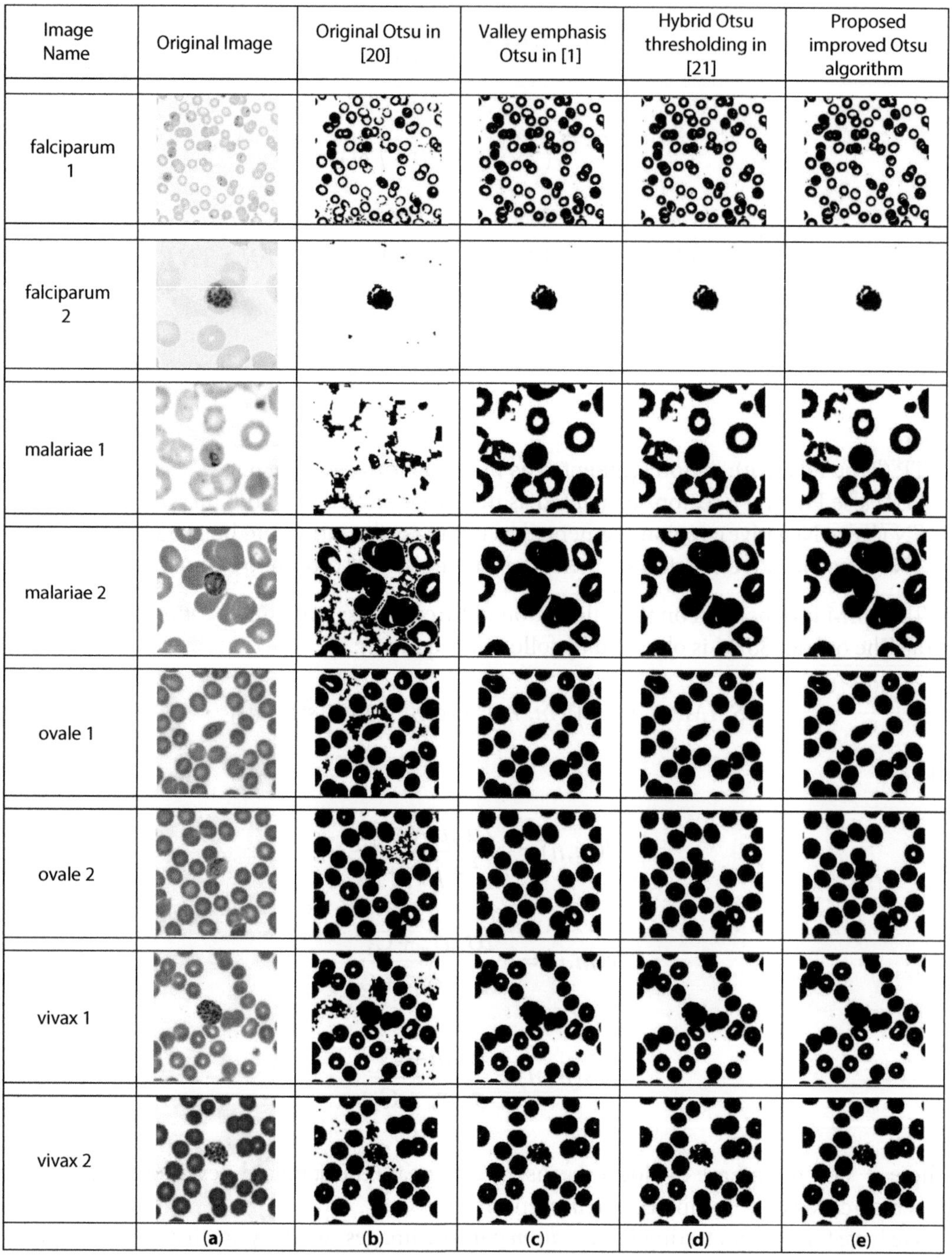

Image Name	Original Image	Original Otsu in [20]	Valley emphasis Otsu in [1]	Hybrid Otsu thresholding in [21]	Proposed improved Otsu algorithm
falciparum 1					
falciparum 2					
malariae 1					
malariae 2					
ovale 1					
ovale 2					
vivax 1					
vivax 2					
	(a)	(b)	(c)	(d)	(e)

Figure 10.2 (a) Original images. Segmentation of Plasmodium images using: (b) original Otsu in [20], (c) valley-emphasis Otsu in [1], (d) hybrid Otsu thresholding in [21], and (e) proposed improved Otsu algorithm.

From Tables 10.1 to 10.6 and Figures 10.3 to 10.8, we can notice that our improved Otsu algorithm is comparatively best with respect to the Otsu thresholding proposed by Nobuyuki Otsu in [20], valley-emphasis Otsu in [1], and hybrid Otsu thresholding in [21] considering Accuracy, Sensitivity, MCC, Dice, Jaccard, and SSIM.

Table 10.1 Comparison of accuracy of different Otsu methods with the proposed algorithm.

Image name	Accuracy			
	Original Otsu in [20]	Valley-emphasis Otsu in [1]	Hybrid Otsu thresholding in [21]	Proposed improved Otsu algorithm
Falci_1	0.90261111	0.98354444	0.983544444	0.99243333
Falci_2	0.99513333	0.99752222	0.997522222	0.99795556
Malariae_1	0.52931111	0.96747778	0.967477778	0.98212222
Malariae_2	0.81633333	0.99582222	0.996566667	0.99696667
Ovale_1	0.90732222	0.99752222	0.997522222	0.99763333
Ovale_2	0.95676667	0.99712222	0.997388889	0.99746667
Vivax_1	0.91181111	0.99682222	0.996822222	0.99763333
Vivax_2	0.97423333	0.99701111	0.997422222	0.99775556

Table 10.2 Comparison of sensitivity of different Otsu methods with the proposed algorithm.

Image name	Sensitivity			
	Original Otsu in [20]	Valley-emphasis Otsu in [1]	Hybrid Otsu thresholding in [21]	Proposed improved Otsu algorithm
Falci_1	0.98316493	0.97561989	0.97561989	0.992122582
Falci_2	0.99548816	0.99747063	0.997470633	0.997971949
Malariae_1	0.81137946	0.94902623	0.949026225	0.974020952
Malariae_2	0.73981943	0.9927021	0.994787214	0.996976584
Ovale_1	0.8524619	0.99661791	0.996617912	0.999275267
Ovale_2	0.94097902	0.99529138	0.996689977	0.998251748
Vivax_1	0.88160867	0.99509687	0.995096869	0.997906528
Vivax_2	0.96523722	0.99504512	0.995988911	0.996932696

Table 10.3 Comparison of MCC of different Otsu methods with the proposed algorithm.

Image name	Matthews correlation coefficient (MCC)			
	Original Otsu in [20]	Valley-emphasis Otsu in [1]	Hybrid Otsu thresholding in [21]	Proposed improved Otsu aalgorithm
Falci_1	0.7795812	0.96394291	0.963942909	0.98298615
Falci_2	0.90916273	0.95223015	0.952230154	0.95994258
Malariae_1	0.20281118	0.93344137	0.933441374	0.96237413
Malariae_2	0.64683602	0.99163805	0.993114465	0.99390721
Ovale_1	0.82012809	0.99504563	0.995045633	0.99527113
Ovale_2	0.91355138	0.9942362	0.994766706	0.99492419
Vivax_1	0.82507808	0.99337543	0.993375426	0.99504848
Vivax_2	0.94812141	0.99393735	0.99476612	0.99543826

Table 10.4 Comparison of Dice of different Otsu methods with the proposed algorithm.

Image name	Dice			
	Original Otsu in [20]	Valley-emphasis Otsu in [1]	Hybrid Otsu thresholding in [21]	Proposed improved Otsu algorithm
Falci_1	0.93102933	0.98754321	0.987543212	0.99432864
Falci_2	0.99749977	0.99872802	0.998728018	0.99895077
Malariae_1	0.68547118	0.97360947	0.973609471	0.98568976
Malariae_2	0.81106844	0.9960667	0.996772071	0.99715331
Ovale_1	0.90298117	0.99754899	0.997548993	0.99766486
Ovale_2	0.95402177	0.99697624	0.997259507	0.99734507
Vivax_1	0.92364819	0.99736799	0.997367985	0.99804399
Vivax_2	0.9769256	0.99734931	0.997715231	0.99801197

Table 10.5 Comparison of Jaccard of different Otsu methods with the proposed algorithm.

Image name	Jaccard			
	Original Otsu in [20]	Valley-emphasis Otsu in [1]	Hybrid Otsu thresholding in [21]	Proposed improved Otsu algorithm
Falci_1	0.87095872	0.97539295	0.975392949	0.98872124
Falci_2	0.99501201	0.99745927	0.997459269	0.99790373
Malariae_1	0.5214577	0.94857605	0.948576047	0.97178332
Malariae_2	0.68218262	0.99216422	0.993564913	0.99432279
Ovale_1	0.82312276	0.99510997	0.995109971	0.9953406
Ovale_2	0.91208568	0.99397071	0.994533994	0.9947042
Vivax_1	0.85812852	0.99474979	0.994749789	0.99609561
Vivax_2	0.95489204	0.99471263	0.995440879	0.99603182

Table 10.6 Comparison of SSIM of different Otsu methods with the proposed algorithm.

Image name	Structural similarity index (SSIM)			
	Original Otsu in [20]	Valley-emphasis Otsu in [1]	Hybrid Otsu thresholding in [21]	Proposed improved Otsu algorithm
Falci_1	0.56973174	0.86956772	0.869567719	0.918690449
Falci_2	0.96688912	0.98388874	0.983888739	0.986507926
Malariae_1	0.19096709	0.79199887	0.791998872	0.855417051
Malariae_2	0.47150844	0.93671379	0.939764215	0.942048997
Ovale_1	0.82312276	0.99510997	0.995109971	0.9953406
Ovale_2	0.78393649	0.93710559	0.939172269	0.940528808
Vivax_1	0.69053657	0.93943402	0.939434017	0.945918897
Vivax_2	0.86560977	0.9421802	0.944894203	0.945899065

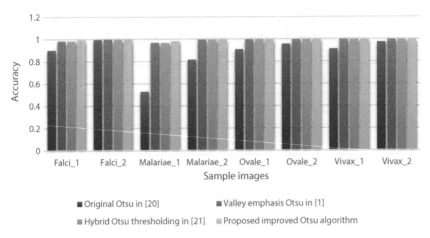

Figure 10.3 Comparison of accuracy of different Otsu methods with the proposed algorithm.

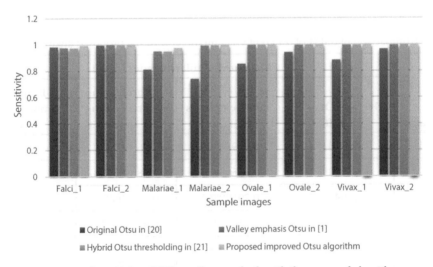

Figure 10.4 Comparison of sensitivity of different Otsu methods with the proposed algorithm.

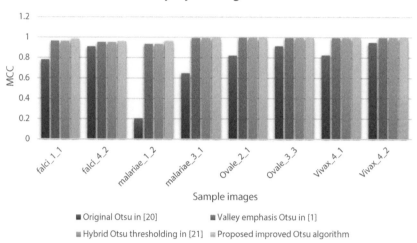

Figure 10.5 Comparison of MCC of different Otsu methods with the proposed algorithm.

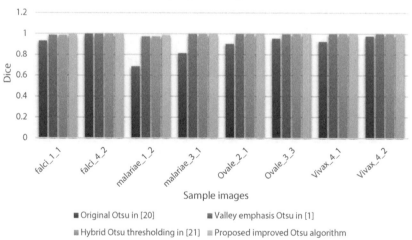

Figure 10.6 Comparison of Dice of different Otsu methods with the proposed algorithm.

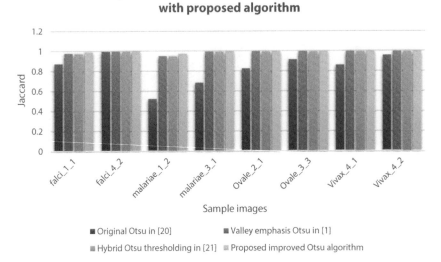

Figure 10.7 Comparison of Jaccard of different Otsu methods with the proposed algorithm.

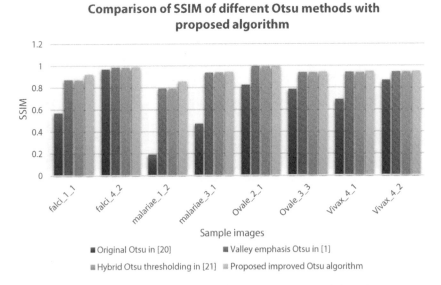

Figure 10.8 Comparison of SSIM of different Otsu methods with the proposed algorithm.

10.6 Conclusion

In this chapter, an improved Otsu algorithm is suggested depending on the concept of valley-emphasis technique provided by Hui-Fuang Ngai [1]. The proposed improved Otsu algorithm works excellently in segmenting the Giemsa stained malaria images. The quantitative results obtain from Accuracy, Sensitivity, MCC, Dice, Jaccard, and SSIM prove that indeed the proposed improved Otsu algorithm is more effective than the Nobuyuki Otsu in [20] valley-emphasis Otsu in [1] and hybrid Otsu thresholding in [21]. Thus, we conclude that, the suggested improved Otsu algorithm is effective and efficient to segment the malaria parasite in the blood cells.

References

1. Ng, H.-F., Automatic thresholding for defect detection. *Pattern Recognit. Lett.*, *27, Elsevier*, 1644–1649, 2006.
2. Devi, S.S., Singh, N.H., Laskar, R.H., Performance Analysis of Various Feature Sets for Malaria-Infected Erythrocyte Detection, in: *Soft Computing for Problem Solving, Advances in Intelligent Systems and Computing*, vol. 1057, pp. 275–283, © Springer Nature Singapore Pte Ltd, Singapore, 2020.
3. Nag, S., Basu, N., Bandyopadhyay, S.K., Application of Machine Intelligence in Digital Pathology: Identification of Falciparum Malaria in Thin Blood Smear Image, in: *Advancement of Machine Intelligence in Interactive Medical Image Analysis, Algorithms for Intelligent Systems*, pp. 65–97, © Springer Nature Singapore Pte Ltd, Singapore, 2020.
4. Kaur, D. and Walia, G.K., A Hybrid ACO-SVM Approach for Detecting and Classifying Malaria Parasites, in: *Computational Network Application Tools for Performance Management, Asset Analytics*, pp. 139–152, © Springer Nature Singapore Pte Ltd, Singapore, 2020.
5. Lorenzo-Ginori, J.V., Chinea-Valdes, L., Izquierdo-Torres, Y., Orozco-Morales, R., Mollineda-Diogo, N., Sifontes-Rodriguez, S., Meneses-Marcel, A., Classification of Plasmodium-Infected Erythrocytes Through Digital Image Processing, in: *CLAIB, IFMBE Proceedings*, vol. 75, pp. 351–360, © Springer Nature Switzerland AG, Singapore, 2020.
6. Madhu, G., Computer Vision and Machine Learning Approach for Malaria Diagnosis in Thin Blood Smears from Microscopic Blood Images, in: *Machine Learning for Intelligent Decision Science, Algorithms for Intelligent Systems*, pp. 191–209, © Springer Nature Singapore Pte Ltd, Singapore, 2020.
7. Pragya, Khanna, P., Kumar, S., Malaria Parasite Classification Employing Chan–Vese Algorithm and SVM for Healthcare, in: *Proceedings of First International Conference on Computing, Communications, and Cyber-Security (IC4S 2019), Lecture Notes in Networks and Systems*, vol. 121, pp. 697–711, © Springer Nature Singapore Pte Ltd, Singapore, 2020.
8. Dawale, D. and Baraskar, T., An Implementation of Malaria Detection Using Regional Descriptor and PSO-SVM Classifier, in: *Soft Computing and Signal Processing, Advances in Intelligent Systems and Computing*, vol. 898, pp. 213–222, © Springer Nature Singapore Pte Ltd, Singapore, 2019.
9. Manning, K., Zhai, X., Yu, W., Image Analysis Based System for Assessing Malaria, in: *CyberDI 2019/CyberLife 2019, CCIS*, vol. 1138, pp. 466–486, © Springer Nature Singapore Pte Ltd, 2019.
10. Hartati, S., Harjoko, A., Rosnelly, R., Chandradewi, I., Faizah, Performance of SVM and ANFIS for Classification of Malaria Parasite and Its Life-Cycle-Stages in Blood Smear, in: *SCDS 2018, CCIS*, vol. 937, pp. 110–121, © Springer Nature Singapore Pte Ltd, Singapore, 2019.

11. Varma, S.L. and Chavan, S.S., Detection of Malaria Parasite Based on Thick and Thin Blood Smear Images Using Local Binary Pattern, in: *Computing, Communication and Signal Processing, Advances in Intelligent Systems and Computing*, vol. 810, pp. 967–975, © Springer Nature Singapore Pte Ltd, Singapore, 2019.

12. Sadiq, M.J. and Balaram, V. V. S. S. S., OFS-Z: Optimal Features Selection by Z-Score for Malaria-Infected Erythrocyte Detection Using Supervised Learning, in: *Proceedings of the Second International Conference on Computational Intelligence and Informatics, Advances in Intelligent Systems and Computing*, vol. 712, pp. 221–234, © Springer Nature Singapore Pte Ltd, Singapore, 2018.

13. Kanojia, M., Gandhi, N., Armstrong, L.J., Pednekar, P., Automatic Identification of Malaria Using Image Processing and Artificial Neural Network, in: *ISDA 2017, AISC*, vol. 736, pp. 846–857, © Springer International Publishing AG, part of Springer Nature, Singapore, 2018.

14. Devi, S.S., Laskar, R.H., Sheikh, S.A., Hybrid classifier based life cycle stages analysis for malaria-infected erythrocyte using thin blood smear images, 2017.

15. Devi, S.S., Roy, A., Singha, J., Sheikh, S.A., Laskar, R.H., Malaria infected erythrocyte classification based on a hybrid classifier using microscopic images of thin blood smear, in: *Multimed Tools Appl.*, Springer Science+Business Media New York, 2016.

16. Elsalamony, H.A., Healthy and unhealthy red blood cell detection in human bloodsmears using neural networks, in: *Micron*, vol. 83, pp. 32–41, Elsevier, United Kingdom, 2016.

17. Hung, Y.-W., Wang, C.-L., Wang, C.-M., Chan, Y.-K., Tseng, L.-Y., Lee, C.-W., Tung, K.-C., Parasite and Infected-Erythrocyte Image Segmentation in Stained Blood Smears. *J. Med. Biol. Eng.*, 35, *Springer Taiwanese Society of Biomedical Engineering*, 803–815, 2015.

18. Somasekar, J. and Reddy, B.E., Segmentation of erythrocytes infected with malaria parasites for the diagnosis using microscopy imaging. *Comput. Electr. Eng.*, 45, Elsevier, 336–351, 2015.

19. Tsai, M.-H., Yu, S.-S., Chan, Y.-K., Jen, C.-C., Blood Smear Image Based Malaria Parasite and Infected-Erythrocyte Detection and Segmentation. *J. Med. Syst.*, 39, 118, Springer Science+Business Media New York, pp. 1–14, 2015.

20. Otsu, N., A Tlreshold Selection Method from Gray-Level Histograms. *IEEE Trans. Syst. Man Cybern.*, 9, 1, 62–66, 1979.

21. Suhas, S. and Venugopal, C.R., Hybrid Otsu Segmentation And Thresholding Of Medical Images With Separability Factor. *Int. J. Adv. Sci. Technol.*, 29, 11, 671–675, 2020.

11

A Reliable and Fully Automated Diagnosis of COVID-19 Based on Computed Tomography

Bramah Hazela*, Saad Bin Khalid and Pallavi Asthana

Amity School of Engineering & Technology Lucknow, Amity University, Noida, Uttar Pradesh, India

Abstract

Coronavirus or COVID-19 is an infectious disease that has been identified in humans. The symptoms range from mild to extremely severe when a person infected with COVID-19 may suffer from pneumonia. Chest imaging that may include radiography, computed tomography (CT), and ultrasound can be used for detecting thepresence of the virus. The certain distinctive factors that help differentiate COVID-19 from pneumonia are that COVID-19 affects both lungs as opposed to one and lungs may show a ground-glass appearance and abnormalities in liver et cetera. A drawback anyway about this method is that it requires an expert radiologist and provided the size of this pandemic, and the number of cases greatly outnumbers the radiologists. This paper aims to establish a proposal to a reliable, fully automated diagnosis powered by deep learning for diagnosis of COVID-19 from CT.

The approach is divided into three phases. The first phase is to look out for abnormalities in lungs. The second phase is to determine the presence of pneumonia using OpenCV for pointingout the regions of interest. The third is to distinguish COVID-19 from pneumonia proceeding on the guidelines mentioned above, which are both the lungs affected as opposed to one, and using the regions that were obtained using OpenCV, endorsing the potential presence of COVID-19.

The model, based on convolutional networks, takes advantage of TensorFlow 2.1 and Keras deep learning libraries since both were later integrated and can be used conjointly for the identification and the OpenCV library for image loading and preprocessing. Tenfold method is used for the division of training and test set, and the evaluation metric is accuracy.

The model was trained against a dataset of a thousand images (owing to the lack of x-ray images of patients affected with coronavirus), with images of normal versus abnormal lungs in a ratio of 1:1, and was tested for accuracy using the confusion matrix. It provided an accuracyof 86% in pointing out the abnormalities in lungs. Then, the identification of images with normal pneumonia versus those infected with coronavirus was done with an accuracy of 75%.

Keywords: COVID-19, pneumonia detection, lungs infection, deep learning, LeNet architecture, ultrasound images, CT scan

*Corresponding author: bramahhazela77@gmail.com

Tushar H. Jaware, K. Sarat Kumar, Ravindra D. Badgujar and Svetlin Antonov (eds.) Medical Imaging and Health Informatics, (195–208) © 2022 Scrivener Publishing LLC

11.1   Introduction

Several research studies have been performed in the subfield of machine learning that is well known as deep learning. Deep learning is being used as a source to help the medical personnel in the detection, prevention, and eradication of the COVID-19 pandemic. This research work aimed at the same with slight additions and alterations to the previous works.

The main objective of this work is the detection of COVID-19 using any of the three sources of medical imaging, i.e., ultrasound, computed tomography (CT) scan, or x-ray. CT scan proved to be slightly above too other two methods of detection, owing to lesser data available for ultrasound images. The network architectures used are the VGG-19, VGG-16, and the LeNet for different classification purposes.

11.2   Background

Based on samples from the lower respiratory tract, viral nucleic testing can be referred to as gold standard in diagnostics. Nevertheless, the availability of laboratory testing not to mention its quality in the infected region poses a challenge. Based on radiographical changes in CT for COVID-19, this paper hypothesizes the extraction of precise graphical functions of COVID-19 and therefore provision of a medical prognosis beforehand of the pathogenic look at is probably possible, hence saving critical time for control of disease. To look at the opportunity of the method proposed, 453 CT scan pictures of showed COVID-19 instances had been gathered alongside common viral pneumonia instances. The training set used 217 images, and the model used to establish the algorithm was the inception model. The performance was measured on accuracy, specificity, and sensitivity, giving back a score of 82.9%, 80.5%, and 84%, respectively. The external testing dataset scored 73.15 in accuracy, 67% in specificity, and 74% in sensitivity. The results highly compliment the value of deep learning for the extraction of radiological imaging features for COVID-19 diagnosis.

The work uses a modified version known as fine-tuned (M-Inception) network of the typical Inception network, having pretrained weights. The original inception part was not trained, and only the modified part was trained during the training phase. The distinction in class through Inception and M-Inception lies withinside the closing related layers. The dimensions of the capabilities had been decreased earlier than them attaining the final classification layer.

Initially, 99 patients were retrospectively enrolled for the grouping of viral pneumonia images, for developing a deep learning algorithm. This group, termed as COVID-19 negative, included 55 instances of regular pneumonia that have been identified earlier than the outbreak of COVID-19. The remaining 44 cases consisted of confirmed COVID-19 cases using nucleic testing and were termed as COVID-19 positive. A total of 453 representative images having 258 cases for COVID-19 negative and 195 for COVID-19 positive were reviewed and sketched by a couple of radiologists for analysis. The images were randomly divided into a testing set and training set. As an initial step, images were selected from each patient's image for the training randomly, in pairs of two to three while leaving the remaining images for testing. The training turned into 1,500 instances with a step size of 0.1. Generalization of the model and, for testing stability, utilization of a complete of 237 images was made to construct the model. The dataset comprising of 118 images from negative cases of COVID-19 and the rest of 119 from positive cases of COVID-19. The pictures last had been used for external validation. An AUC of 0.90 on the internal while 0.78 on the external was yielded after training by the algorithm. Making use of maximized threshold probability, specificity was 84.2% and 76.4%, and the sensitivity was 80.5% and 67.1%. The accuracy changed into 82.9% and 73.1%, the negative prediction value changed into 0.88 and 0.81, the Youden index changed into 0.69 and 0.44, and F1 rating changed into 0.77 [1].

In this paper, deep learning pretrained architectures were used as an automatic tool for detection of COVID-19 from the CT scan of chest. It utilized a SenseNet201-based deep transfer for the classification of the infected patients and non-infected patients. This model can extract the features through a convolutional neural structure through its own learned weights on ImageNet dataset. Large number of iterations evaluated the performance of DTL model on chest CT scan of COVID-19 patient, and it was found more accurate. COVID-19 classification model based on DTL was compared with different existing models on confusion matrix such as precision, F-1 measure, recall, sensitivity, and accuracy.

In another work, transfer learning model based on deep learning was designed with CNN and pretrained Dense Net model for the classification of COVID-19. This model was trained to classify the chest CT scans and validation accuracy received was 99.82%, 96.25%, and 97.40% that was found better when compared to deep transfer learning models as discussed in [2].

Now, CT scan facilities are to be had in maximum of the scientific institutions. In such institutions, the proposed model may be effortlessly employed for the testing of COVID-19 which can be taken as an alternative for diverse testing kits of COVID-19 as discussed in [2].

This paper employed an artificial intelligence–based system to diagnose pneumonia from CT scan images of patients through FCONet. FCONet model was developed through VGG-16, ResNet-50, Inception V3, or Xception. This test was conducted on 3993 CT scan images of patients suffering COVID-19, typical pneumonia, and ono-pneumonia from the public databases for the training and evaluation of the model from Won Kwang University Hospital, Italian Society of Medical and Interventional Radiology, and Chonnam National University Hospital. Testing and training was conducted on the data at the ration of 2:8, respectively. The model was also tested on the external dataset from low quality CT scan images [3]. Detection accuracy achieved from the low-quality CT images followed by Xception, Inception-v3, and VGG16 were 90.71%, 89.38%, and 87.12%, respectively. FCONet model based on a 2D deep learning framework showed good performance in the detection of Pneumonia patients when compared with VGG16, Xception, and Inception-v3. Performance was measured on the metric values of sensitivity, specificity, and accuracy in various models. When different models were tested for the detection COVID-19 pneumonia, accuracy is achieved as specified in Table 11.1.

Whereas Inception-v3–based FCONet model provided lower sensitivity, specificity, and accuracy for all groups of COVID-19 pneumonia as discussed in [3].

This study demonstrated the application of transfer learning from deep learning models on the x-ray images, CT scan, and ultrasound images. Initially, the test was performed to select the optimized VGG-19 model from the list of all popular models. Then, the model was selected that can provide good results for highly scarce and low in quality, challenging COVID-19 datasets. This paper also focuses on the lack of publicly available datasets and its

Table 11.1 Performance of different models.

	Sensitivity	Specificity	Accuracy
ResNet-50	99.58%	100%	99.87%
VGG-16	100%	99.64%	99.75%
Xception	97.91%	99.29%	98.87%

adverse effect on the trainability of the complex models. An image preprocessing phase has also been proposed in this paper to create a trustworthy dataset that would be used to train and test deep learning networks. This preprocessing step reduced the noise in the image so that network can easily detect the useful features for the classification of disease. This was used for all the images including CT scan image, x-ray image, and ultrasound images. It performed best with the ultrasound images with the accuracy of 100%, whereas accuracy of COVID-19 pneumonia detection with x-ray was 86%, and with CT scan was 84% [4].

Image preprocessing phase is important as the images that were used as dataset were in size and quality. Datasets were collected from variable resources. Data consisting of CT scan was publicly accessible COVID-CT dataset. Images were extracted by slicing CT scan images from a full scan of numerous discrete slices produced in helical pattern. Ultrasound images of COVID-19, pneumonia, and normal lungs were taken from POCOVID-Net dataset that is publicly accessible. This dataset was also highly diverse as the images in the dataset were sampled from the videos from different online sources. Images of chest x-ray of COVID-19 positive and negative patients were collected from COVID-19 image data collection that is publicly accessible. Hence, the dataset is highly variable in size and quality of images.

Speedy and actual diagnosis of COVID-19–suspected cases would help of arrangement of early treatment, helping the patient and early quarantine prevents the spread of disease. A software system, based on weakly supervised deep learning, was developed for 3D CT volumes for the detection of COVID-19. Lung region becomes segmented through a pre-trained UNet, and a segmented 3D lung region was fed right into a 3D network to test the presence of COVID-19 withinside the affected person. In this work, 499 CT volumes had been used for the training of network, and 131 CT volumes had been used for the trying out of data.

With the probability threshold of 0.5 for the classification of COVID-19–positive and COVID-19–negative patients, algorithm predicted the positive predictive value of 0.849, an accuracy of 0.901, and high negative predictive value of 0.982. A dedicated GPU was used to achieve the fast results and it took just 1.93 seconds to process one CT volume. Hence, a weakly supervised deep learning can predict the infectious probability; this easily trainable, high performance algorithm is beneficial to prevent the eruption of SARS-CoV-2 [5].

In this work, a deep 3D convolutional network is used for detecting COVID-19 with a network DeCoVNet from CT Volumes. A 3D lung mask is generated, which is divided into three stages for the input to DeCoVNet by pretrained UNet for clear illustration. These stages are as follows. First layer is a network stem, a vanilla 3D convolution with a kernel size of $5 \times 7 \times 7$, with a batch-norm layer and a pooling layer. Second layer has two 3D residual blocks or Res-blocks. A 3D characteristic map is passed into each a 3D convolution with a batch-norm layer and a shortcut connection containing a 3D convolution for dimension alignment in every Res-block. Third stage consists of a progressive classifier ProClf having 3D convolution layers with a fully connected layer having SoftMax activation function. This classifier can abstract information by 3D max pooling and output the possibility of patient being COVID effective. Here, 3D lung masks of chest CT volume were taken as input having less background information and thus improve the classification process. To obtain the 3D lung mask, the lung regions were segmented through unsupervised learning, and then, failure cases were removed. Remaining segmentation results were considered as ground truth masks. This process was done by frame-by-frame testing of trained 2D UNet without any temporal information.

A complete convolutional neural network technique to differentiate CT images of COVID-19 and non–COVID-19 patients has been proposed as CTnet-19 with the accuracy of 82.1%. Automated detection provides the facility of rapid screening that can prevent the outspread of virus. Image dataset of 738 photographs was gathered from COVID-19 CT dataset; images were split into training set, validation set, and test set in the ratio of 8:1:1. CT-10 was trained with image of length $128 \times 128 \times 3$, and 2D layer was transformed into 1D layer with two layers convolutional blocks and pooling layer with flatting layer. One-dimensional layer was fed into a layer of 256 neurons, where dimensions of the activation have been changed at each layer. Dropout of rate 0.3 was added in output layer with one neuron to classify the CT test pictures [6].

Images with a dimension of $150 \times 150 \times 3$ were used as input for VGG-16 model with 16 layers and five convolutional blocks. Each block having two to three convolutional layers and five max pooling layers. These layers are fully connected with consequent layers and a SoftMax layer. SoftMax layer can be replaced with sigmoid layer for binary classification.

For inception V3 model, image with resolution of $224 \times 224 \times 3$ was used with two dense layers of 1,000 and 500 neurons with L1 and L2 regularization set to 0.01.

Same process was done with DenseNet-169 model with 169 layers. Seventy-three images of size $224 \times 224 \times 3$ were used for this model.

11.3   Methodology

11.3.1   Models Used

In this work, initial phase consists of identifying the type of scanning performed to produce the image either through CT or through ultrasound images. Then, a comparison was performed between performance of LeNet architecture with Alex net architecture. It was found that the former was better in performance and, hence, it was selected for the implementation of the work.

11.3.2   Architecture of the Image Source Classification Model

LeNet architecture, as shown in Figure 11.1, shows two sets of convolutional layers, average pooling layers, and a flattening layer. These layers are further fully connected to two layers and finally with a SoftMax classifier. The initial is six feature maps convolutional layer or filters with size of 5×5 with a pace of one. Dimension of image followed by the captured

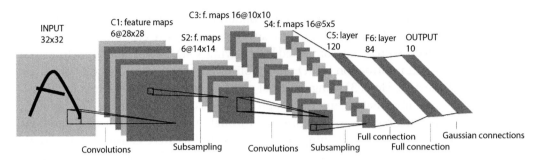

Figure 11.1 LeNet architecture.

picture passes through this layer change from (32 × 32 × 1) to (28 × 28 × 6). Then, these images are filtered with a size of 2 × 2 at a pace of two at the average pooling layer or subsampling layer and with the reduction of the image dimensions to 14 × 14 × 6. The third layer is a 16-feature map convolutional layer with size of 5 × 5 with a stride of 1. Out of 16 feature maps, 10 maps are connected to six feature maps of previous layer. The layer that follows the fourth layer is again an average pooling layer with a size 2 × 2 filter and with a stride of 2. Apart from the fact that it has 16 feature maps, this layer is like the second layer, so the output will be reduced to 5 × 5 × 16. The fifth layer constitutes a 120-feature fully connected convolutional layer with each of size 1 × 1. In C5, as shown in Figure 11.1, each having 120 is joint to all the 400 nodes (5 × 5 × 16) of the fourth layer as in S4. The sixth layer is of 84 units, which is, again, a dense fully connected layer (F6), as shown in Figure 11.1.

Then, after the source has been identified, the model goes forward toward the identification between the image of the normal lungs and COVID-19–affected lungs. This is done in three distinguished networks based on the source of the image that is to be classified.

For classifying the images coming from CT scan, the VGG-16 and Inception-v3 were the recommended version, so models based on these architectures were trained against the dataset from CT scan images and the VGG-16 model proved to have slightly better results and thus has been trained to fulfil the purpose of this work.

11.3.3   Architecture of the CT Scan Classification Model

The first two layers are convolutional layers of 64 channels with a 3 × 3 kernel size, 1 padding size, and a stride of 1. The input of this layer is an image with dimension 224 × 224. After those layers follows a max pooling layer of length 2 and a stride of 2, which gives and image output of size 112 × 112. After this are two convolutional layers with 128 channels, a 3 × 3 kernel with a stride of 1 followed by a max pooling layer of length 2 and a stride of 2. These layers give an image output of size 56 × 56. Following this comes three convolutional layers with 256 channels, a 3 × 3 kernel, and a stride of 1 followed by a max pooling layer of length 2 and a stride of 2. The output from these layers is an image of size 28 × 28. These are followed by three more convolutional layers with 512 256 channels, a 3 × 3 kernel and a stride of 1 followed by a max pooling layer of length 2 and a stride of 2. The output from these layers is an image of size 14 × 14. These are followed by four more convolutional layers with 512 × 256 channels, a 3 × 3 kernel, and a stride of 1 followed by a max pooling layer

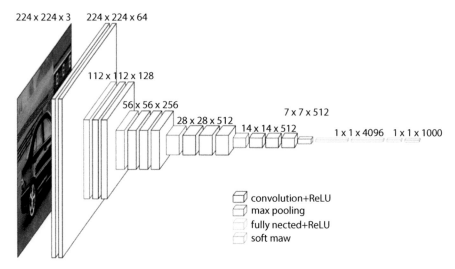

224 x 224 x 3   224 x 224 x 64

112 x 112 x 128

56 x 56 x 256

28 x 28 x 512

14 x 14 x 512

7 x 7 x 512

1 x 1 x 4096   1 x 1 x 1000

convolution+ReLU
max pooling
fully nected+ReLU
soft maw

Figure 11.2 VGG16 architecture.

of size 2 and a stride of 2. The output from these layers is an image of size 7×7. Finally, we have three fully connected layers followed by a SoftMax layer as depicted in Figure 11.2.

11.3.4   Architecture of the Ultrasound Image Classification Model

The first two layers are convolutional layers of 64 channels with a 3×3 kernel size, 1 padding size, and a stride of 1. The input of this layer is an image with dimension 224×224. These layers are followed by a max pooling layer of length 2 and with a stride of 2, which gives and image output of size 112×112. After this come two convolutional layers with 128 channels, a 3×3 kernel with a stride of 1 for our max pooling layer of length 2 with a stride of 2. These layers give an image output of size 56×56. Following this comes four convolutional layers with 256 channels, a 3×3 kernel with a stride of 1 for max pooling layer of length 2 with a stride of 2. The output from these layers is an image of size 28×28. These are followed by four more convolutional layers with 512×256 channels, a 3×3 kernel with a stride of 1 for max pooling layer of size 2 with a stride of 2. The output from these layers is an image of size 14×14. These are followed by four more convolutional layers with 512×256 channels, a 3×3 kernel with a stride of 1 for our max pooling layer of size 2 with a stride of 2. The output from these layers is an image of size 7×7. Finally, we have three fully connected layers followed by a SoftMax layer.

Lastly, for the classification of the images from x-rays, the VGG19 model again has been used as in Figure 11.3.

11.3.5   Architecture of the X-Ray Classification Model

The first two layers are convolutional layers of 64 channels with a 3×3 kernel size, 1 padding size, and stride is 1. The input of this layer is an image with dimension 224×224. These layers are followed by a max pooling layer of size 2 and with a stride 2, which gives and image output of size 112×112. After this comes two convolutional layers with 128

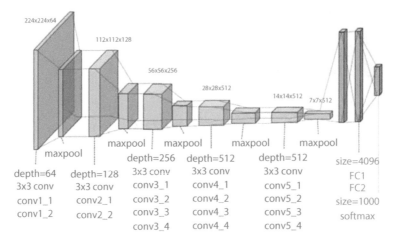

Figure 11.3 VGG19 architecture.

channels, a 3 × 3 kernel with a stride of 1 followed by a max pooling layer of size 2 with stride is 2. These layers give an image output of size 56X56. Following this comes four convolutional layers with 256 channels, a 3 × 3 kernel with a stride of 1 for our max pooling layer of length 2 with stride of 2. The output from these layers is an image of size 28 × 28. These are followed by four more convolutional layers with 512 × 256 channels, a 3 × 3 kernel, and a stride of 1 for our max pooling layer of size 2 with stride of 2. The output from these layers is an image of size 14 × 14. These are followed by four more convolutional layers with 512 × 256 channels, a 3 × 3 kernel, and a stride of 1 for our max pooling layer of size 2 and stride is 2. The output from these layers is an image of size 7 × 7. Finally, we have three fully connected layers followed by a SoftMax layer.

11.3.6 Dataset

In the training of the CT scan classification model, the dataset has been taken from publicly available dataset from Kaggle [7].

In the training of the x-ray detection model, the dataset has also been taken from publicly available dataset from Kaggle [8].

In the training of the ultrasound model, the dataset has been taken from a repository on GitHub [9].

11.3.6.1 Training

All classification models have been trained using mini batch gradient descent and to find the desired loss and accuracy in each case, Adam optimizer has been used. The models have been trained by the 10-fold method; in essence, the dataset was divided into training set and the testing set with 80% and 20%, respectively. Batches of size 32 have been used in the training of each of the models.

Optimization algorithm that is based on gradient descent is used for the reduction of cost function for the accurate prediction. It is an iterative algorithm that indicates the direction of increment.

Here, it is used to find in the valley in the minimum point and in opposite direction of the gradient. To minimize the loss, parameters are also updated in the negative gradient direction.

Optimizers replace the weight parameters to reduce the loss function. Loss function acts as guides to the terrain telling optimizer if it is moving withinside the right direction to attain the lowest of the valley, the worldwide minimum [10]. In this situation, we use the Adam optimizer. The Adam optimizer follows the below given equation

$$\theta_t + 1 = \theta_t - \frac{\alpha . \widehat{m_t}}{\sqrt{\widehat{v}} + \varepsilon}$$

where

$$\widehat{m_t} = \frac{m_t}{1 - \beta_1^t}$$

$$\widehat{v_t} = \frac{v_t}{1 - \beta_2^t}$$

$$m_t = (1 - \beta_1)g_t + \beta_1 m_{t-1} \text{ and}$$

$$v_t = (1 - \beta_2)g_t + \beta_2 v_{t-1}$$

where
α is the step size;
β_1 and β_2 are decay rates;
m_t is the first moment vector;
v_t is the second moment vector; and
t in the subscript is the timestep.
Initially, the timestep is initialized as zero.
For the timestep that is equal to zero, the foremost vector of moment and the second vector moment are also initialized as zero.

β_1 has the value of 0.9, β_2 holds the value of 0.999, and, as the timestep increases, both are raised to the powers of the timestep.

The exponential moving averages of the first moment gradient(mt) and the second moment squared gradient(vt) will be update via way of means of Adam algorithm.

Decay rates of these moving averages will be managed by hyperparameters as $\beta1$, $\beta2 \in [0, 1)$.

Moving averages are initialized as zero. This leads to estimation of moment that are biased around zero particularly during the initial timesteps. This initialization bias can be easily counteracted ensuing in bias-corrected estimates.

Finally, the parameters are updated.

11.4   Results

Model was trained on the X-ray images, CT-scan images, and ultrasound images. Figure 11.4 shows the loss in the CT scan and it shows the decreasing loss with increasing epochs. As the loss decreases, accuracy increases as shown in Figure 11.5.

For X-ray images also, same pattern was achieved as shown in Figures 11.6 and 11.7. Performance of the model on ultrasound images is also shown in Figures 11.8 and 11.9.

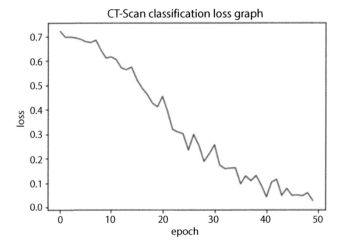

Figure 11.4 CT scan loss graph.

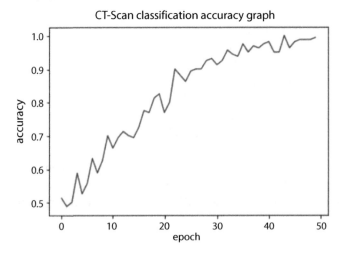

Figure 11.5 CT scan accuracy graph.

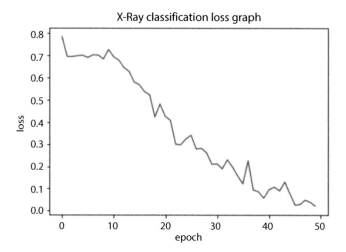

Figure 11.6 X-ray classification loss graph.

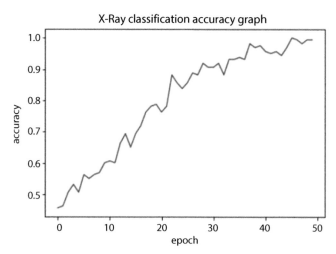

Figure 11.7 X-ray classification accuracy graph.

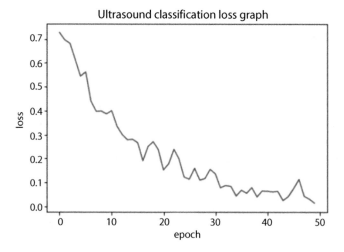

Figure 11.8 Ultrasound classification loss graph.

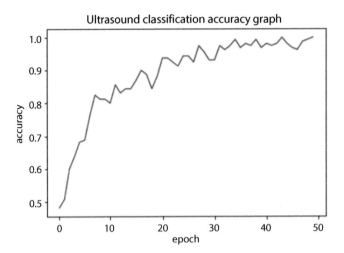

Figure 11.9 Ultrasound classification accuracy graph.

Table 11.2 Different networks and their performance in classification of images.

Model	Accuracy
VGG-19 for CT scan	96.3
VGG-19 for x-ray	94.2
VGG-16 for ultrasound	93

Comparison of the performance of the model on three types of images is shown in Table 11.2. It states that for the given model, highest accuracy for classification is achieved on CT scan images at 96.3%, where as accuracy for X-ray images is 94.2%, and ultrasound images is 93%.

11.5   Conclusion

The model has been built on compared classification architectures for best results and shows a high accuracy. It can be used with any of the three modes of imaging in essence: ultrasound imaging, CT scan, and x-rays, while also classifying where the image that needs be classified came from. This approach to first classify which source the image came from and then to proceed further with the classification whether the lungs are affected with COVID-19 or not not only makes the model's usage umbrella broader but also complements the performance metrics.

The datasets have been available through different media now because of the scale and time lapse of the pandemic. Training the model using accurate architectures and weights and using the correct optimization algorithm has proven to be of much help in gaining accuracy and reducing loss.

Different classification architectures were first compared to the most recommended ones, recommended by other works in the field and then used for the classification.

Initially, the network that classifies the source of image received is the LeNet classification architecture that was initially proposed for classifying small and distorted images. After this the other classification networks are used based on whether the image received was from Ultrasound, in which case the VGG-16 network trained on Ultrasound image dataset is used while if the image was received from either CT scan or x-ray, the VGG-19 model trained on respective datasets has been used.

Overall, the model can come in handy for making the process of detection easier, faster and safer and the human counterparts can be deployed for more complicated tasks.

References

1. Wang, S., Kang, B., Ma, J., Zeng, X., Xiao, M., Guo, J., Cai, M., Yang, J., Li, Y., Meng, X., Xu, B., A deep learning algorithm using CT images to screen for Corona virus disease (COVID-19). *European Radiology*, 31, 8, 6096–6104, 2021. https://doi.org/10.1007/s00330-021-07715-1

2. Jaiswal, A., Gianchandani, N., Singh, D. *et al.*, Classification of the COVID-19 infected patients using DenseNet201 based deep transfer learning. *J. Biomol. Struct. Dyn.*, https://www.tandfonline.com/doi/full/10.1080/07391102.2020.1788642

3. Ko, H., Chung, H., Kang, W. S., Kim, K. W., Shin, Y., Kang, S. J., Lee, J. H., Kim, Y. J., Kim, N. Y., Jung, H., Lee, J., COVID-19 Pneumonia Diagnosis Using a Simple 2D Deep Learning Framework With a Single Chest CT Image: Model Development and Validation. *J. Med. Internet Res.*, 22, 6, e19569, 2020. https://doi.org/10.2196/19569

4. Zheng, C., Deng, X., Fu, Q., Zhou, Q., Feng, J., Ma, H., Liu, W., Wang, X., "Deep Learning-based Detection for COVID-19 from Chest CT using Weak Label," medRxiv, 2020.2020.03.12.20027185v2.

5. Horry, M.J. *et al.*, COVID-19 Detection Through Transfer Learning Using Multimodal Imaging Data. *IEEE Access*, 8, 149808–149824, 2020. doi: 10.1109/ACCESS.2020.3016780., https://ieeexplore.ieee.org/document/9167243.

6. Shah, V., Keniya, R., Shridharani, A., Punjabi, M., Shah, J., Mehendale, N., Diagnosis of COVID-19 using CT scan images and deep learning techniques. *Emergency Radiology*, 28, 3, 497–505, June 2021.

7. Yang, X., He, X., Zhao, J., Zhang, Y., Zhang, S., Xie, P., COVID-CT-dataset: a CT scan dataset about COVID-19, 2020. arXiv preprint arXiv:2003.13865.

8. Cohen, J. P., Morrison, P., Dao, L., Roth, K., Duong, T. Q., Ghassemi, M., Covid-19 image data collection: Prospective predictions are the future, 2020. arXiv preprint arXiv:2006.11988.

9. Ebadi, A., Xi, P., MacLean, A., Tremblay, S., Kohli, S., Wong, A., COVIDx-US--An open-access benchmark dataset of ultrasound imaging data for AI-driven COVID-19 analytics. arXiv preprint arXiv:2103.10003. 2021.

10. Mishra, S., Chaudhary, N.K., Asthana, P., Kumar, A., Deep 3D Convolutional Neural Network for Automated Lung Cancer Diagnosis, in: *Computing and Network Sustainability*, 2019, https://link.springer.com/chapter/10.1007/978-981-13-7150-9_16.

12

Multimodality Medical Images for Healthcare Disease Analysis

B. Rajalingam*, R. Santhoshkumar†, P. Santosh Kumar Patra, M. Narayanan, G. Govinda Rajulu and T. Poongothai

Department of Computer Science and Engineering, St. Martin's Engineering College (Autonomous), Dhulapally, Secunderabad, Telangana, India

Abstract

Image fusion has grown as a powerful technique to enhance the aspects of the image, boosting its quality and making it more clear and descriptive, thanks to recent advancements in imaging technology and instrumentation. In medical assessment, using the specific quality of each image and combining them ensures precise diagnosis. The goal of this study is to see if a single domain radiological image can provide information about blood flow and metabolism. MRI and CT imaging offer information on the location and hard tissues. Organ functioning features can be seen in SPECT and PET imaging. As a result, the combined frame can more precisely localize disease. The fundamental aim for medical picture fusion is to improve disease diagnosis, reduce storage space, make clinical instruments more effective, enable accurate and effective distant assessment, and enhance the information content in a single image. To create hybrid algorithms for multimodal medical image fusion employing a mix of CT/MRI, MRI/PET, and MRI/SPECT medical imaging for better visual interpretation of diseases by radiologists for the goal of accurate diagnosis, therapy planning, and patient follow-up. The following are the goals of this study: 1. to contribute to multimodal medical picture fusion by creating novel hybrid algorithms; 2. to combine MRI pictures with CT, PET, and SPECT images in order to extract the relevant information from each multimodal medical imaging; 3. to employ hybrid fusion algorithms to fuse multimodal medical pictures for accurate diagnosis and precise localization of cancers and lesions; and 4. to create a generalized method that can be used to combine anatomical and functional pictures regardless of imaging modalities.

Keywords: Neurocysticercosis, neoplastic, astrocytoma, anaplastic astrocytoma, metastatic brochogenic carcinoma, Alzhimer's and mild Alzhimer's disease

---

**Corresponding author*: rajalingam35@gmail.com
†*Corresponding author*: santhoshkumar.aucse@gmail.com

Tushar H. Jaware, K. Sarat Kumar, Ravindra D. Badgujar and Svetlin Antonov (eds.) Medical Imaging and Health Informatics, (209–236) © 2022 Scrivener Publishing LLC

12.1 Introduction

12.1.1 Background

Medical imaging has long been regarded as the most important and crucial aspect of modern health treatment. Medical image processing is now an important part of the patient management system, from diagnosis to post-treatment analysis. The condition is diagnosed by imaging, which is a non-invasive method of gathering information about the human body organs. For obtaining data from impacted body areas, there are a variety of options. These are based on the physics employed during the acquisition. CT, MRI, PET, and SPECT are some of the imaging techniques used. Depending on the method of acquisition, each modality presents a different picture of the anomalies. The information relating to calcifications, bone structures, and tumor outline is notably provided by CT. For soft tissue anatomy, MRI is the best option. It clearly depicts the lesions. It aids in the diagnosis of disorders affecting the soft tissues, as well as the size of lesions. The pictures of PET and SPECT reveal aberrant metabolism in cancer-infected tissues. However, CT scans of soft tissues have weak contrast, and MRI scans cannot identify calcifications. The spatial and structural discrimination of PET and SPECT is extremely poor. A single medical picture modality is incapable of providing comprehensive and precise information. As a result, not every modality may display all of the relevant information about a specific condition. As a result, physicians always advise patients to undergo a variety of imaging modalities before making a definitive diagnosis. Almost majority health centers lack the ability to obtain combined details about multiple modalities using a single system. Because of the exorbitant expense of the technology, no hospital in India has hybrid modality imaging. Even if scanners become accessible, the cost of imaging will be too expensive for people. In the near future, such a facility may not be offered to patients from economically developing countries like India. A PET-CT scanner is a popular hybrid modality machine that works on the premise of overlaying both modality images. The new PET-MRI scanner is still in the works. As a result, there is a social and pressing demand for a software solution that can aggregate information from many imaging modalities in a single frame at a low cost. Multimodality medical image fusion is one such software solution (MMIF). It is the process of combining all important and complimentary information from two or more modality images to create a new enriched single frame. It should also assist radiologists in obtaining all anatomical structures from all modalities and improving visibility of anomalies.

Almost all modern healthcare practices benefit from multimodality medical image fusion. The method entails extracting complementary and relevant information from a variety of modality images. These attributes are blended using the appropriate fusion criteria to create a new image that is both better and more visually appealing. It is usually assumed that the resulting fused image is noise-free and free of misleading artifacts. The merged image should provide enough information for the radiologist to effectively delineate the infected tissues for treatment planning.

It should be a valuable tool for doctors in terms of accurate diagnosis, precise therapy, and study of the patient's response to treatment. The purpose of this thesis is to demonstrate the construction of hybrid algorithms for multimodality medical image fusion employing multiple fusion rules in order to improve the quality of fused images. The goal of this project is to create hybrid algorithms for clinical illness analysis. The two stages of the classic image fusion method are picture registration and fusion of pertinent features from the registered images. A method to fix the spatial misalignment between the different images is required for image registration. Compensation of variability caused by scale changes, rotations, and translations is common in data sets. When there is inter-image noise, missing features, or outliers in the images, the registration problem becomes more difficult. The fusion of features, on the other hand, entails the identification and selection of features with a focus on their relevance for a specific clinical evaluation aim.

The stages of medical image fusion methods are depicted in Figure 12.1. The MMIF mechanism is depicted in Figure 12.2. The practice of integrating numerous images from single or many imaging modalities to improve image quality for clinical applications is known as medical image fusion. Multimodal medical image fusion algorithms have proved to improve clinical accuracy significantly.

This chapter is organized as follows: In Section 12.1, the introduction to multimodal medical image fusion is presented. Section 12.1.1 gives the background and motivation for medical image fusion system. Section 12.3 discusses different types of multimodal medical images. Section 12.4 illustrates image fusion and levels of image fusion. Section 12.5 spells out the medical image fusion methods and reveals the list of diseases and their clinical relevance. Section 12.6 narrates the data sets and software used in this work. Section 12.7 explains the generalized medical image fusion. Section 12.8 describe the various fusion methods. Finally, Section 12.9 concludes the chapters.

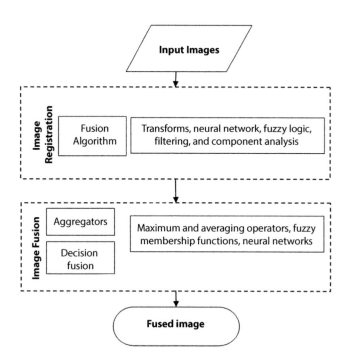

Figure 12.1 Stages of the medical image fusion.

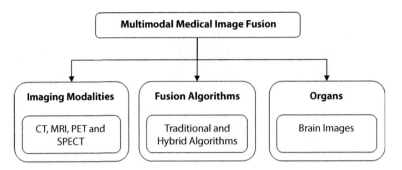

Figure 12.2 Multimodal medical image fusion.

12.2   Brief Survey of Earlier Works

Das *et al.* [12] suggested a unique NSCT and PCNN-based multimodal medical image fusion technique. To get better fusion outcomes, the suggested MIF technique takes advantage of both the NSCT and PCNN advantages. The suggested scheme's success in fusing multimodal medical pictures is demonstrated by subjective and objective examination of the findings, as well as comparisons with the state-of-the-art MIF technique. The proposed method by Shutao *et al.* [11] is a novel guided filtering-based weighted average strategy for fusion of the base and detail layers that takes full advantage of spatial consistency. The suggested method can achieve state-of-the-art performance for fusion of multispectral, multifocus, multimodal, and multiexposure images, according to the experimental results. Ganasala *et al.* [8] proposed NSST- and PCNN-based image fusion algorithms. The PCNN processing of both low-frequency and high-frequency subbands was motivated by normalized coefficient values, according to the authors. In comparison to alternative picture fusion approaches, visual and quantitative examination of experimental findings showed that the suggested method produces good fusion outcomes. The Laplacian pyramid–based fusion method, introduced by Li *et al.* [5], has been widely utilized for dissecting images into different sizes. The Laplacian pyramid, on the other hand, is thought to be incapable of accurately representing visual outline and contrast. The quality of the employed image can be greatly increased over that of traditional image quality assessment criteria, according to the visual and statistical assessments.

Using the adaptive PCNN and the Quantum-Behaved Particle Swarm Optimization (QPSO) algorithm, Xu *et al.* [15] suggested a method to merge multimodal medical pictures. The fused image was created using the fusion model's output. Finally, the suggested method is tested and verified using five pairs of multimodal medical images as experimental data. On the basis of NSCT, Gomathi *et al.* [9] suggested image fusion techniques for the merging of multimodal medical images. The performance parameters are compared to the experimental results on six pairs of medical photos. It is discovered that the suggested image fusion technique surpasses existing image fusion techniques in terms of image quantitative and qualitative results. Liu *et al.* [13] introduced a new multimodality medical image fusion technique that incorporates a gradient minimization smoothing filter and a PCNN. The suggested algorithm surpasses previous compared approaches in terms of both subjective and objective assessment, according to the experimental results on multiple data sets of CT and MRI scans. Chavan *et al.* [10] proposed a multimodality medical image fusion strategy employing a Nonsubsampled Rotated Complex Wavelet Transform to combine CT and MRI data from the same patient into a new slice (NSRCxWT). The forward NSRCxWT is used to extract complementary and edge-related features from both source modalities individually.

El-Hoseny *et al.* [2] study different medical image fusion approaches and explain their major benefits and drawbacks in order to design hybrid transform algorithms that improve the fused picture quality. Several quality indicators are used to assess both classic and hybrid fusion methods. This is advantageous, especially in terms of assisting with proper diagnosis and treatment applications. Murthy *et al.* [6] suggested a new method for improving the information richness of photos utilizing the Shearlet transform and the Singular Value Decomposition. For fusing, two distinct PET and MRI images are collected. The results reveal that the proposed strategy outperforms a number of progressive methods. Daniel *et al.* [1] proposed an OSMF for conventional GWO-based medical picture fusion. In multimodality fusion, the best mask provides more information.

For MR-SPECT, MR-PET, MR-CT, and MR: T1-T2 of brain images, the proposed OSMF is tested. The suggested technique outperforms other traditional pixel-based fusion techniques, according to the experimental data. Mehta *et al.* [7] proposed a modified fusion approach in which the wavelet coefficients produced after wavelet decomposition are decomposed using NSCT decomposition. Because of its edge-preserving quality, a guided filter was used for the fusion of high-frequency coefficients. The proposed technique's fusion response is also compared to that of previous fusion procedures, demonstrating the efficacy of the achieved fusion outcomes. Based on DT-CWT and the Modified Central Force Optimization approach, Heba *et al.* [3] proposed an efficient medical picture fusion system. The suggested optimized DT-CWT fusion system is put up against standard spatial and transform domain fusion techniques. Different fusion quality criteria are used to subjectively and objectively test and evaluate the proposed fusion system.

Heba *et al.* [4] provide an optimization-based contourlet image fusion method as well as a comparison analysis of the performance of both multiresolution and multiscale geometric impacts on fusion quality. The Modified Central Force Optimization and local contrast enhancement approaches are used to propose an optimal multiscale fusion technique based on the NSCT. The suggested optimized NSCT medical image fusion strategy based on the MCFO and histogram matching offers greater performance in terms of image quality, average gradient, and significantly more information in images, according to the experimental data. Using a moving frame–based decomposition framework and the NSST, Liu *et al.* [14] suggested a unique multimodality medical picture fusion technique. Experimental results show that the suggested method outperforms previous state-of-the-art methods in terms of both visual effects and objective criteria.

12.3   Medical Imaging Modalities

Different bands of the electromagnetic spectrum are used to collect medical pictures. Each modality is ideal for a certain purpose due to the great variety of sensors used for image acquisition and the physics that underpins them. Continuous efforts are made to increase image resolution, minimize acquisition noise, and extract more relevant information from the images. In this chapter, you will learn about the numerous types of medical imaging modalities. The fundamental concepts of CT, MRI, PET, and SPECT imaging are discussed.

12.3.1   Computed Tomography (CT)

The CT scan is a type of medical imaging that has had a significant impact on medical diagnosis and evaluation. CT scans are used to diagnose strokes and assess head injuries. A CT scan involves the patient lying in a tunnel-like equipment that rotates and captures x-rays from various angles.

These details are then fed into a computer, which combines them to create images of body slices or cross sections. They can also be merged to create a three-dimensional (3D) representation of a specific body part. Figure 12.3 depicts (a) the CT scan machine and (b) the neurocyticercosis disease–affected CT image.

12.3.2   Magnetic Resonance Imaging (MRI)

MRI is one of the most extensively utilized imaging modalities in medical investigations in trusted clinical settings, and it plays a vital role in the non-invasive diagnosis of brain malignancies. MRI is a sort of scan that produces detailed images of the inside of the body by combining powerful magnetic fields with radio waves. An MRI scanner is a huge tube with powerful magnets within. During the scan, the patients lie inside the tube. A MRI scan can be used to look at practically any region of the body, including the brain, bones, cranium, and blood vessels. MRI scans are used by doctors to diagnose a wide range of diseases, from torn ligaments to malignancies. Figure 12.4a shows an MRI image scanner, while Figure 12.4b shows an MRI image with metastatic bronchogenic carcinoma illness [16].

12.3.3   Positron Emission Tomography (PET)

PET imaging or a PET scan is a sort of nuclear medicine imaging. It demonstrates the functionality of organs and tissues. The structure of blood flow to and from organs is shown

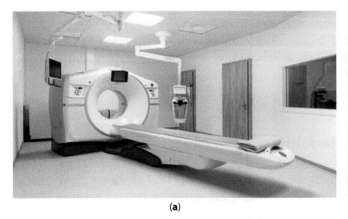
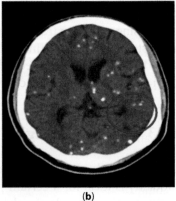

(a)   (b)

Figure 12.3 (a) CT scan machine. (b) Neurocysticercosis disease–affected CT image.

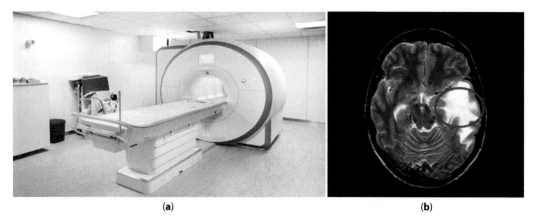

(a)   (b)

Figure 12.4 (a) MRI scan machine. (b) Metastatic bronchogenic carcinoma–affected MRI image.

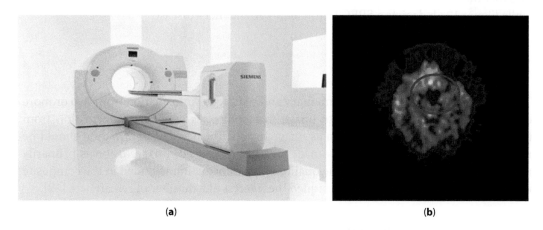

(a)   (b)

Figure 12.5 (a) PET scan machine. (b) Astrocytoma disease–affected PET image.

through these examinations. PET scans are used to diagnose cancer, heart disease, and brain illnesses such as CNS issues (CNS) [17]. The PET image scanner is depicted in Figure 12.5a, and the astrocytoma disease–affected PET image is depicted in Figure 12.5b.

12.3.4   Single-Photon Emission Computed Tomography (SPECT)

A nuclear imaging scan that combines CT with a radioactive tracer is known as a SPECT scan. It is commonly used to look at how blood flows through tissues and organs. Small amounts of radioactive materials are used in nuclear medicine imaging to diagnose, evaluate, and treat a range of disorders. Nuclear medicine examinations can reveal molecular activity and may be used to detect disease in its early stages. One of the most difficult difficulties in SPECT imaging is increasing sensitivity without lowering image resolution. It could be used to diagnose strokes, convulsions, stress fractures, infections, and spinal malignancies. A tracer is radio tagged before the SPECT scan, which means it emits gamma

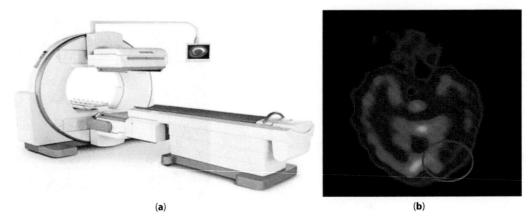

(a)   (b)

Figure 12.6 (a) SPECT scan machine. (b) Alzheimer's disease–affected SPECT image.

rays that the CT scanner can detect [18]. Figure 12.6a depicts a SPECT scanning machine, while Figure 12.6b depicts a SPECT afflicted by Alzheimer's disease.

12.4   Image Fusion

The technique of combining complimentary and redundant information from two or more different photos into one composite image that comprises enhanced information from the original source images is known as image fusion. The original information should be retained, and artifacts in the fused image should be reduced. Image fusion is primarily motivated by the need to increase the quality of the information included in the composite image. As a result, image fusion has piqued the interest of a number of researchers [19].

12.4.1   Different Levels of Image Fusion

The fusion process can be performed at three different processing levels. They are given as follows.

Figure 12.7 shows how the most common picture fusion methods are classified based on the source images' amount of processing and abstraction. The image fusion algorithms that are used in each fusion level are shown in the bottom branches. The pixel-level technique can be used to either the spatial or transform domains. Feature-level algorithms usually segment the image into contiguous sections and then use the properties of the regions to fuse them together. Image descriptions are merged using decision-level fusion methods.

12.4.1.1   Pixel Level Fusion

The procedure on each picture pixel is involved in the pixel level image fusion process. The simplest picture fusion technique simply averages the source images pixel by pixel. It creates a fused image from a series of pixels in source images by resolving the information content associated with each pixel. Fusion can be done in the spatial or frequency domains

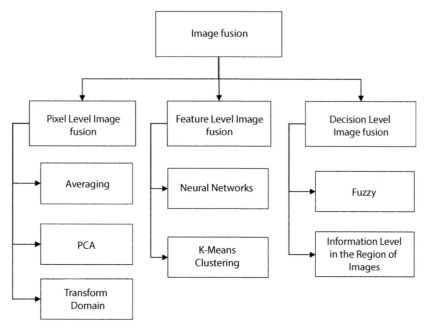

Figure 12.7 Different image fusion levels and methods.

at this level. However, this has unfavorable consequences, such as decreased contrast. A human observer can use pixel level picture fusion to quickly detect or distinguish prospective targets.

12.4.1.2   Feature Level Fusion

Feature level image fusion starts with feature extraction, which uses qualities like contrast, shape, size, and texture to identify features. The input photos are merged to create these related features.

12.4.1.3   Decision Level Fusion

At a higher level of abstraction, decision level fusion allows information from many images to be efficiently integrated. For information extraction and classification, the input photos are normally processed individually. To reinforce common interpretation, the gathered data might be integrated using decision rules. The optimum image fusion level is determined by the applications. Between the many stages of image fusion, there is a strong interconnection. To determine the individual pixels in the composite image at the pixel level, many fusion rules are used. To fuse the extracted features, the same procedures can be applied at the region level. Furthermore, decision-level fusion can make decisions based on the segmentation map established at the region level. Because the images utilized in pixel level fusion contain the actual measured quantities, the techniques are computationally efficient and simple to execute. Pixel-level–based approaches are used in the majority of picture fusion applications [20].

12.5   Clinical Relevance for Medical Image Fusion

In this research work, some of the disease-affected medical images are taken for the experimental work. The diseases are explained in the following sections.

12.5.1   Clinical Relevance for Neurocyticercosis (NCC)

The most severe type of the disease, neurocysticercosis, damages the brain and can be fatal. NCC is a preventable central nervous system parasite infection caused by the swine tapeworm *Taenia solium*. NCC is contracted by ingesting tiny eggs found in the feces of someone with an intestinal pig tapeworm. Neurocysticercosis is caused by these larvae, which can result in enormous cysts in the brain. The NCC-affected photos are shown in Figures 12.8a and b (CT and MRI) [21].

12.5.2   Clinical Relevance for Neoplastic Disease

Neoplasm is a disorder in which cells develop fast, resulting in the formation of abnormal tissues known as neoplasm. Tumors, or abnormal growths, can appear anywhere on the body. There are two types of tumors that can develop as a result of neoplastic disease: benign and malignant tumors. Noncancerous growths are benign tumors that grow slowly and are unable to spread to other tissues. Cancerous growth is defined as malignant tumors that rapidly grow and spread to many tissues and organs. The location of the neoplasm influences the symptoms of neoplastic illness. Symptoms of neoplastic diseases include anaemia, shortness of breath, stomach pain, persistent weariness, lack of appetite, chills, diarrhoea, and fever.

12.5.2.1   Clinical Relevance for Astrocytoma

The cancer astrocytoma is a form of brain cancer. They come from a specific type of glial cell called astrocytes, which are star-shaped brain cells in the cerebrum. This form of tumor

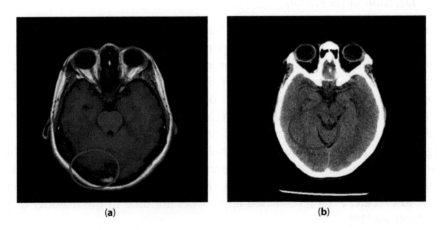

(a)   (b)

Figure 12.8 Neurocysticercosis disease–affected medical images. (a) CT. (b) MRI.

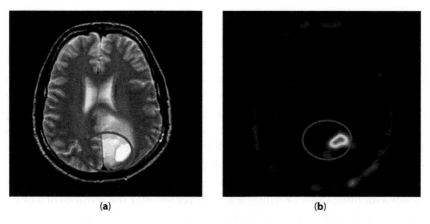

Figure 12.9 Astrocytoma disease–affected medical images. (a) MRI T2. (b) SPECT TC.

normally does not expand beyond the brain and spinal cord nor does it damage other organs. Seizures, headaches, and nausea can all be symptoms of astrocytomas in the brain. Astrocytoma can either be a slow-growing tumor or a malignancy that spreads swiftly. Consistent headaches, double or blurred vision, vomiting, loss of appetite, changes in temperament and personality, changes in thinking and learning abilities, new seizures, and gradual speech difficulty. Figures 12.9a and b depict medical images that have been changed by astrocytoma (MRI and SPECT).

12.5.2.2 Clinical Relevance for Anaplastic Astrocytoma

An anaplastic astrocytoma is a type of glioma that arises from star-shaped glial cells that support nerve cells but grows more quickly and aggressively than grade II astrocytomas. The appearance of these cells is not consistent. This form of brain tumor affects both men and women between the ages of 30 and 50. It has a greater impact on men than on women. The pictures impacted by the anaplastic astrocytoma disease are shown in Figures 12.10a and b (MRI and SPECT).

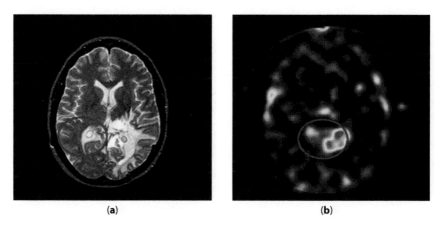

Figure 12.10 Anaplastic astrocytoma disease–affected medical images. (a) MRI T2. (b) SPECT TC.

12.5.2.3   Clinical Relevance for Metastatic Bronchogenic Carcinoma

Both the main and secondary malignancies of a lung carcinoma and a brain metastasis were surgically removed (combined operation). The goal of the study was to see how effective a combined operation for treating primary lung cancer and an apparent solitary brain metastasis was. From 1958 to 1976, 23 individuals with primary lung cancer and brain metastases had surgical resection. In all of the cases, neurological examinations revealed a single brain injury. The prognosis for lung cancer metastasis is poor, and the patient is usually deemed inoperable. The brain is particularly vulnerable to lung cancer metastasis; in postmortem studies, brain metastases occur in up to 48% of patients.

A considerable number of these individuals had an overt brain lesion at the time of the first lung lesion's identification, or a lung lesion develops after the removal of a brain metastasis. Although neuroradiological methods are usually accurate in detecting brain metastases, tiny multiple lesions may be missed. Images impacted by metastatic bronchogenic carcinoma disease are shown in Figures 12.11a and b (MRI and SPECT).

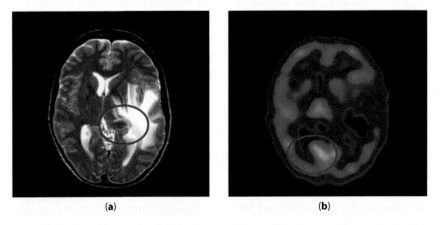

(a)   (b)

Figure 12.11 Metastatic bronchogenic carcinoma disease–affected medical images. (a) MRI T2. (b) SPECT TC.

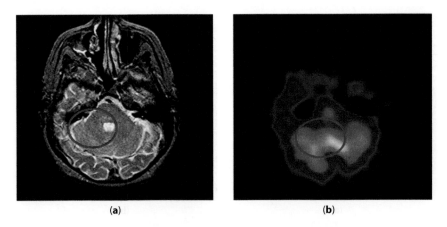

(a)   (b)

Figure 12.12 Alzheimer's disease–affected medical images. (a) MRI T2. (b) SPECT TC.

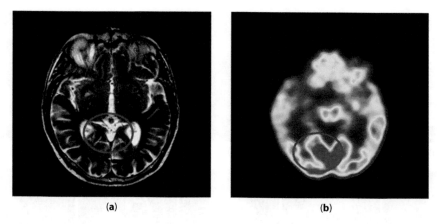

(a)   (b)

Figure 12.13 Mild Alzheimer's disease–affected medical images. (a) MRI T2. (b) PET FDG.

12.5.3   Clinical Relevance for Alzheimer's Disease

Alzheimer's disease is a type of dementia that causes memory loss and other mental skills to deteriorate over time. Alzheimer's disease patients may have mild disorientation and memory loss at initially. Persons with the condition may eventually forget crucial people in their lives and experience significant personality changes. Alzheimer's disease is responsible for 60% to 80% of dementia cases, according to the Alzheimer's association. The condition is most commonly detected after the age of 65. Figures 12.12a and b show the Alzheimer's disease–affected images (MRI and SPECT) and Figures 12.13a and b show the mild Alzheimer's disease–affected images (MRI and PET).

12.6   Data Sets and Software Used

Various medical imaging, including CT, MRI T1, MRI T2, SPECT T1, SPECT TC, SPECT CBF, PET, and PET FDG, were obtained for this study from the Harvard Medical School's total brain database [22] and the Radiopaedia internet database [23]. Medical photos were gathered from a database at Harvard Medical School, with variable spatial resolutions for distinct study sets. The finest recognizable element of a 3D object is the voxel (volume pixel or voxel), which is the 3D counterpart of a pixel. The spatial resolution of CT images is 512×512 and 256×256 voxels. MRI pictures are 512×304 voxels, 260×256 voxels, and 256×256 voxels in size, with a bit depth of 8 bits for grayscale images and 24 bits for color images. The case studies on the radiopaedia database are $1{,}024 \times 1{,}024$ voxels with an 8 bits per pixel format for both CT and MRI images, with intensity values ranging from 0 to 255. This research was carried out using MATLAB R2015a and Python 3.5 on a laptop computer with an Intel processor i5 2.50 GHz CPU and 4 GB RAM. The categories of multimodality medical images are shown in Figure 12.14 (a-j).

12.7   Generalized Image Fusion Scheme

The source modality images, registration of source images, fusion utilizing fusion rules, and visual quality evaluation of fused images are the four primary components of the

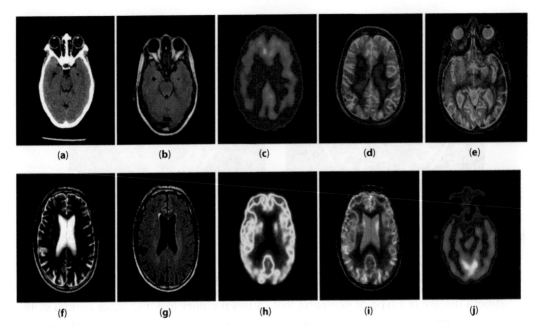

Figure 12.14 Categories of multimodality medical images. (a) CT. (b) MRI. (c) SPECT TC. (d) SPECT T1. (e) SPECT. (f) MRI T1. (g) MRI T2. (h) PET - FDG. (i) PET. (j) SPECT CBF.

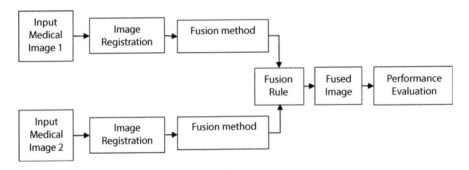

Figure 12.15 General block diagram of medical image fusion system.

generalized multimodality medical image fusion system. The general block diagram of a medical picture fusion system is shown in Figure 12.15.

12.7.1   Input Image Modalities

Different medical pictures are employed as pilot study data sets in this chapter. These photos are from the same patient and were taken at the same slice positions.

12.7.2   Image Registration

One of the necessary pre-processing processes that has a considerable impact on the fusion results is image registration. Image registration, also known as image alignment, is the process of exactly aligning the input images in order to get the best fusion results. It is impossible to achieve good fusion results if the input picture data sets are not aligned to each other, even if the fusion framework, scheme, and algorithm are optimal. As a result, prior to the main fusion process, it is important to align or register input images as much as feasible.

12.7.3   Fusion Process

One of the algorithms is used to decompose source modality images into the spectral domain. Anatomical structures in both modalities may be located or oriented differently. The physics of both input modalities' acquisition differs, resulting in differences in spatial resolution and size. However, these photos contain a wealth of information that must be merged. These fused images have a higher visual quality than the input modalities, making it easier for the radiologist to understand them. In comparison to source pictures, the fused images also provide a greater visibility of anomalies.

12.7.4   Fusion Rule

A fusion rule is proposed to preserve edges, lines, and contours of the fused image.

Maximum Fusion Rule

$$C_F = \begin{cases} C_i^1, if C_i^1 > C_i^2 \\ C_i^2, if C_i^1 < C_i^2 \end{cases} \tag{12.1}$$

Averaging Fusion Rule

$$C_F = \frac{1}{2}(C_i^1 + C_i^2) \tag{12.2}$$

where C_F is the combined coefficient, C_i^1 and C_i^2 are the coefficient of input images I_1 and I_2 at the ith level.

Weighed Averaging Fusion Rule

$$C_F = \frac{1}{2}(w_i^1 \times C_i^1 + w_i^2 \times C_i^2) \tag{12.3}$$

where weights of input images are I_1 and I_2 at i^{th} level w_i^1 and w_i^2, respectively.

12.7.5   Evaluation

Various sample study sets are used to test the proposed fusion strategies. The visual quality of the fused images is utilized to assess the performance and usefulness of the existing and planned algorithms. The fused pictures are assessed subjectively (qualitatively) with the help of experienced radiologists and objectively (quantitatively) by estimating fusion metrics. This paper also defines the subjective assessment criteria as well as the numerous fusion parameters utilized to estimate objective evaluation.

12.7.5.1   Subjective Evaluation

A radiologist is a significant figure in imaging patient care, who uses visual evaluation of images to make a diagnosis and develop a treatment plan for the patient. As a result, radiologists must assess the visual quality of the merged pictures. The subjective opinion of radiologists is also used to calculate the score for evaluating the suggested algorithms' performance. The radiologist is shown the identical fused images as well as the source images on a regular basis and asked to score the quality of the images using subjective ratings such as 0 for low content and 4 for excellent content in the fused image. As a subjective evaluation score, the average rating is used. The following are the image quality characteristics used to evaluate visual information in fused images.

- Image contrast.
- Visualization of anatomical structures.
- Lesion visualization.
- Confidence to delineate lesion or infected tissues.
- Usefulness of image for radiotherapy or treatment planning.

12.7.5.2   Objective Evaluation

Due to the lack of ground truth, fusion algorithms are evaluated using evaluation approach, which is a difficult undertaking. The parameters' values fluctuate when the study set changes. A large number of metrics allows for a variety of algorithm evaluations. The choice of fusion metrics, on the other hand, is the option of fusion application. These fusion measures are used to assess the visual quality. In this chapter, some of the fusion metrics/parameters employed in this research are presented. These characteristics are quite helpful in determining the objective quality of fused images: Factor 1: Fusion (FusFac); 2. Image Quality Index (IQI); 3. Edge Quality Measure; 4. mean Structural Similarity Index Measure (mSSIM); 5. Cross Entropy (CEn); 6. Mutual Information (MI); 7. Peak Signal-to-Noise Ratio (PSNR); and 8. Standard Deviation (STD).

12.8   Medical Image Fusion Methods

12.8.1   Traditional Image Fusion Techniques

As demonstrated in Figure 12.16, this study work implements many classic fusion techniques for medical photos.

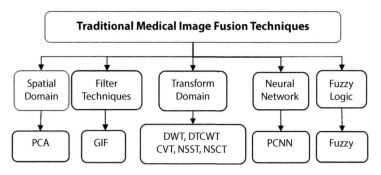

Figure 12.16 Traditional image fusion techniques.

12.8.1.1   Spatial Domain Image Fusion Approach

This method works directly with the pixels in the input images. To obtain the desired result, the pixel values are altered. Pixel averaging, maximum/minimum methods, Brovey methods, Principal Component Analysis (PCA), Intensity-Hue Saturation (IHS)–based methods, and high-pass filtering–based image fusion methods are among the spatial domain methodologies. Spatial domain techniques have the drawback of causing spatial distortion in the merged image. The transform domain technique effectively handles spatial distortions.

12.8.1.1.1   Principal Component Analysis

It is used to lower the dimension of input data without sacrificing quality. The number of correlated variables is divided by the number of uncorrelated variables to arrive at a total number of uncorrelated variables. The image's pixel data is calculated and subtracted from the mean value. The covariance matrix's eigenvalues, eigenvectors, and covariance matrix's covariance matrix's covariance matrix's covariance matrix's covariance matrix's covariance matrix.

12.8.1.2   Transform Domain Image Fusion Approach

The image in the spatial domain is first translated into the transform domain in this method. The inverse transform is utilized to obtain the resultant fused image once all of the fusion operations are completed in the transform domain. Discrete wavelet transform–based approaches, curvelet transform-based methods, contourlet transform-based methods, and Shearlet transform-based methods are all part of this approach. Image fusion techniques span from pixel averaging to state-of-the-art techniques like Multiscale Transform (MST)–based image fusion. The most often used transform domain image fusion algorithms are based on MST, which decomposes a picture into multiple scales and directional subbands. The fusion is done independently on a variety of scales and orientations. Discrete Wavelet Transform (DWT), Undecimated Wavelet Transform (UWT) also known as Dual-Tree Complex Wavelet Transform (DTCWT), Curvelet Transform (CVT), Non-Subsampled Contourlet Transform (NSCT), and Non-Subsampled Shearlet Transform are some of the most often used MSTs (NSST).

12.8.1.2.1   Discrete Wavelet Transform–Based Method

Wavelet-based approaches are the most generally used methods, which conduct multires-olution decomposition on each source image, then integrate all of these decompositions to produce a composite representation, and lastly reconstruct the fused image using an inverse multiresolution transform. Although DWT provides strong localization in both the time and spatial frequency domains, shift variance is one of its key limitations. Even modest shifts in the input photos cause significant changes in the wavelet coefficients of the image. In medical imaging, it is critical to keep track of where the data is stored. Inaccuracies may result from the shift variance.

In medical picture fusion, for example, edge information must be preserved, yet DWT-based fusion may result in specularities at the edges. A three-level iterative decomposition of a DWT is shown in Figure 12.17. In the first level of decomposition, the signal f(x) is decomposed into A1 and D1 subbands. A1 is further decomposed at the second level, yielding A2 and D2 subbands. Finally, in the third level of breakdown, A3 and D3 are subbands of A2.

12.8.1.2.2   Wavelet-Based Fusion Method

A linear transformation approach based on wavelet functions is the dual tree complex wavelet–based method. It can be used for picture compression, noise reduction, and satellite applications, among other things. Using the suitable fusion rule, the coefficients are fused.

12.8.1.2.3   Curvelet Transform–Based Method

It is used to represent images at various scales and perspectives. Because it uses a minimal number of coefficients, it can be utilized to deal with discontinuities. The input image is broken into curvelet coefficients, which are then fused together using the proper fusion method. The inverse discrete curvelet transform is utilized to create the final fused image.

12.8.1.2.4   Contourlet Transform–Based Method

NSCT is a shift-invariant MST that is quite effective. The unusual structure of NSCT, which includes two shift-invariant components, Nonsubsampled Pyramids (NSP) and Nonsubsampled Directional Filter Banks (NSDFB), confers shift invariance and redundancy, making it a better MST for image fusion algorithms. When the image has greater

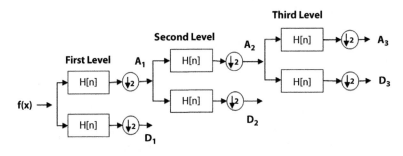

Figure 12.17 Three level decomposition of DWT.

dimensions, the problem of traditional NSCT-based image fusion methods is that they are computationally highly expensive.

12.8.1.2.5 Shearlet Transform–Based Method

Shearlet transform is a multiscale geometric analysis (MGA) method with a sophisticated mathematical framework. It is well-localized and decays quickly in the spatial realm. Shearlets follow the law of parabolic scaling. It has a lot of directional sensitivity. Every finer scale doubles the number of possible directions. However, the pseudo Gibbs phenomenon and other inefficiencies in the fusion findings are caused by the fact that it is not shift invariant. To address these flaws, a shift invariant version of the Shearlet transform known as NSST was created.

12.8.1.3   *Fuzzy Logic–Based Image Fusion Approach*

The fuzzy logic's conjunctive, disjunctive, and compromise features have been extensively studied in image processing and have been effective in picture fusion. For image fusion, fuzzy logic is used as a feature transform operator as well as a decision operator. The choice of membership functions and fuzzy sets that produce the best picture fusion is still a work in progress. When integrated with probabilistic methodologies such as fuzzy-neural network, fuzzy-genetic-neural network-rough set, fuzzy probability, and neuro-fuzzy wavelet, feature processing and analysis can be improved to better match the fuzzy space.

12.8.1.4   *Filtering Technique–Based Image Fusion Approach*

Edge-preserving filters have recently been a hot topic in image processing research. Edge-preserving smoothing filters like directed filter, weighted least squares, and bilateral filter can prevent ringing artifacts by avoiding blurring strong edges during decomposition. The guided filter, for example, is a newly proposed edge-preserving filter whose processing time is independent of the filter size. The guided filter is also qualified for other applications such as image matting, up-sampling, and colorization because it is based on a local linear model.

12.8.1.5   *Neural Network–Based Image Fusion Approach*

The Pulse Coupled Neural Network (PCNN) is a neural network inspired by biology. It is characterized by global coupling and neuronal pulse synchronization. Several publications in the recent literature have created image fusion algorithms based on the PCNN model that produce good results. They, on the other hand, have two drawbacks. The first is that the neuron is motivated by the value of a single pixel, whereas source images are sensitive to directional characteristics and edges. As a result, relying solely on single pixels is insufficient. The second reason is that the fundamental PCNN model is computationally difficult due to the vast number of parameters, making it unsuitable with Medical Image Fusion (MIF) applications. Furthermore, in image fusion techniques, the connecting strength coefficient of the fundamental PCNN model has a significant impact. It determines how the current neuron interacts with the surrounding neurons. In order to make computations

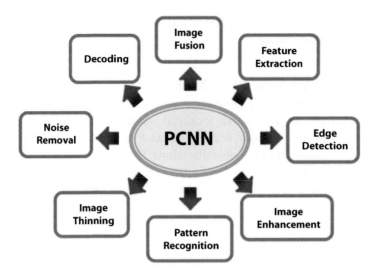

Figure 12.18 PCNN applications.

easier, it is usually treated as a fixed value. It is, nevertheless, an effective method for MIF applications.

12.8.1.5.1   PCNN Applications
PCNN is an active research topic in the field of artificial intelligence. PCNN is being utilized in building algorithms for various applications shown in Figure 12.18 shows the applications of PCNN.

12.8.2   Hybrid Image Fusion Techniques

Image fusion approaches used in the past have not been able to produce high-quality images. As a result, there is a pressing need to employ hybrid fusion approaches in order to attain this goal. The primary concept behind hybrid approaches is to combine two domain fusion techniques (spatial, neural network, filter, fuzzy logic, and optimization) to improve performance and image quality. Another option is to use two domain-based algorithms on the input images prior to the fusion process. These hybrid approaches improve picture characterization, handle curved shapes better, and improve the quality of fused details. The overall benefits of hybrid approaches include improved image visual quality and reduced image artifacts and noise. The flow diagram for the suggested hybrid medical image fusion approaches used in this study is shown in Figure 12.19.

12.8.2.1   *Transforms with Fuzzy Logic–Based Medical Image Fusion*

The initial contribution of this study is a DTCWT with NSST and NSCT hybrid fusion techniques based on Type 2 fuzzy logic. Because the wavelet transform does not represent long edges well and the NSCT does not represent minor characteristics like angles as well as the wavelet transform, these methods are offered for efficiently merging medical pictures. In the first step of the proposed approach 1, DTCWT is used to deconstruct the input images into

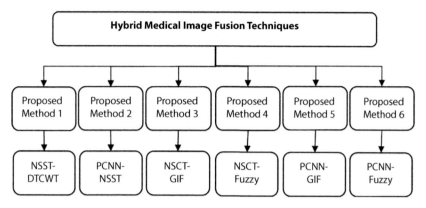

Figure 12.19 Hybrid image fusion techniques.

low and high-frequency components. The NSST is used on the DTCWT's low-frequency components. The NSST and DTCWT low-frequency components are merged using an average fusion technique. The maximal fusion rule is used to fuse the high-frequency components of NSST and DTCWT. The maximal fusion rule is used to fuse the high-frequency components of NSST and DTCWT. Inverse transforms with coefficients from all frequency bands are employed to create the merged image. In the proposed approach 2, the input images are first decomposed using NSCT to yield low and high-frequency components. On the low-frequency components of NSCT, phase congruency is used. The maximal fusion rule is used to fuse the high-frequency components of NSCT. Type 2 fuzzy logic approach is used to further address it. Inverse transforms with coefficients from all frequency bands are employed to create the merged image.

12.8.2.2   Transforms With Guided Image Filtering–Based Medical Image Fusion

The second contribution is the proposal of NSCT with GIF and GIF with PCNN-based hybrid fusion algorithms for efficiently merging medical pictures. In the proposed approach 3, the input images are first decomposed using NSCT to yield low and high-frequency components. On NSCT's low-frequency components, the averaging fusion rule is used. Maximum selection and averaging approaches merge the low and high-frequency components of NSCT. A guided image filtering approach is used to treat the high-frequency of NSCT. Inverse transforms with coefficients from all frequency bands are employed to create the merged image. In the proposed approach 4, the source images are first decomposed into low- and high-frequency components using guided image filtering. On low-frequency components, the averaging fusion rule with PCNN is used. On high-frequency components, the maximum fusion rule using PCNN is used. Image reconstruction with synthesizing the fused base image and detail image coefficients yields the fused image.

12.8.2.3   Transforms With Neural Network–Based Image Fusion

For image fusion, NSST with PCNN and NSCT with neuro fuzzy logic–based hybrid algorithms are proposed in the third contribution of this work. The PCNN has the property of global synchronization. NSST is used to decompose the input images into low and high frequency in the proposed approach 5. On low-frequency components, the averaging fusion rule with PCNN is used. On high-frequency components, the maximum fusion rule using PCNN is used. Inverse transforms with coefficients from all frequency bands are employed to create the merged image. In the suggested approach 6, the input images are first decomposed using NSCT. On low-frequency components, the averaging fusion rule with type 2 fuzzy logic is used. On high-frequency components, the maximum fusion rule using PCNN is used. Inverse transforms with coefficients from all frequency bands are employed to create the merged image.

The contributions of this research study are as follows:

In this work, the developed fusion techniques are tested for various MRI-CT, MRI-PET, and MRI-SPECT image fusion applications. The fusion results are evaluated for their effectiveness using subjective and objective fusion metrics. The radiologists evaluated the quality of fused images in comparison with source modalities. The subjective criteria are based on contrast, visualization of lesions, usefulness of image for contouring and treatment planning, etc. The radiologists have rated fused images on the scale of 0 (poor) and 4 (excellent). Radiologists have noticed a considerable improvement in visual quality and have given it a high rating for its applicability in clinical practice. For the proposed algorithms, the average subjective assessment value is quite near to 4 (excellent content).

In comparison to source modalities, the fused pictures employing suggested methods carry all necessary anatomical and functional features from both modalities, as well as superior visibility of anomalies. Estimating similarity or dissimilarity fusion parameters such as mutual information, standard deviation, fusion factor, structural similarity index metric, edge quality measure, image quality index, cross entropy, and PSNR are all part of the objective evaluation. The subjective score and objective fusion measures have a significant association, according to a comparison of fused images. All of the algorithms proposed produce the best fused images with the least amount of distortion and misleading artifacts. Tables 12.1, 12.2 and 12.3 show a comparison of various fusion factor, IQI, mSSIM, cross

Table 12.1 Performance metrics comparative analysis for different fusion methods.

(Proposed method 1 and 2) – Neurocysticercosis								
Metrics algorithm	FuFac	IQI	mSSIM	CE_n	EQM	MI	PSNR	STD
PCA	1.582	0.498	0.542	2.502	0.432	1.820	24.03	20.34
DWT	1.716	0.508	0.572	2.072	0.499	1.899	25.90	22.23
DTCWT	1.862	0.511	0.522	1.928	0.508	1.903	26.30	24.39
NSCT	2.012	0.530	0.549	1.898	0.537	2.030	28.60	26.50
NSST	2.162	0.552	0.575	1.807	0.571	2.230	29.88	28.34
Proposed 1 (DTCWT-NSST)	2.998	0.872	0.839	0.981	0.857	2.530	32.30	30.20
Proposed 2 (NSCT-Fuzzy)	3.201	1.021	0.962	0.887	0.982	2.630	34.20	32.39

entropy, EQM, MI, PSNR, and standard deviation performance measurement values for traditional and proposed hybrid fusion procedures.

Figure 12.20 shows the Sample screenshot for fuse the neurocysticercosis affected image using DTCWT-NSST and NSCT–fuzzy logic hybrid algorithms, Figure 12.21 shows the Sample screenshot for fuse the metastatic brochogenic carcinoma–affected image using NSCTGIF– and GIP-CNN–based hybrid algorithms and Figure 12.22 shows the Sample screenshot for fuse the astrocytoma affected image using NSST-PCNN and NSCT–neuro fuzzy logic–based hybrid algorithms.

Table 12.2 Performance metrics comparative analysis for different fusion methods.

(Proposed method 3 and 4) – Metastatic Bronchogenic Carcinoma								
Metrics algorithm	FusFac	IQI	mSSIM	CE_n	EQM	MI	PSNR	STD
PCA	1.154	0.462	0.423	1.511	0.451	1.962	29.05	32.10
DWT	2.265	0.558	0.548	1.481	0.508	2.049	32.39	34.50
GIF	2.412	0.542	0.595	1.322	0.549	2.402	35.55	37.20
PCNN	2.531	0.528	0.575	1.208	0.592	2.603	37.40	35.07
NSCT	3.612	0.701	0.670	0.969	0.722	2.952	39.58	38.81
Proposed 3 (NSCT-GIF)	4.142	0.920	0.941	0.567	0.898	3.502	46.62	42.10
Proposed 4 (GIF-PCNN)	4.020	0.940	0.939	0.529	0.930	3.650	45.72	44.10

Table 12.3 Performance metrics comparative analysis for different fusion methods.

(Proposed method 5 and 6) – Astrocytoma								
Metrics algorithm	FusFac	IQI	mSSIM	CE_n	EQM	MI	PSNR	STD
PCA	2.571	0.514	0.523	1.452	0.517	2.402	28.60	18.30
DWT	2.671	0.538	0.443	1.298	0.529	2.503	29.60	19.30
PCNN	2.712	0.554	0.585	1.389	0.534	2.603	29.65	23.54
NSCT	2.811	0.597	0.594	1.078	0.597	2.703	32.60	25.40
NSST	3.181	0.662	0.702	0.993	0.698	3.012	39.80	26.40
Proposed 5 (NSST-PCNN)	5.012	0.897	0.891	0.725	0.951	3.602	49.70	31.20
Proposed 6 (NSCT-Neuro fuzzy)	4.830	0.905	0.904	0.740	0.980	3.830	50.56	32.30

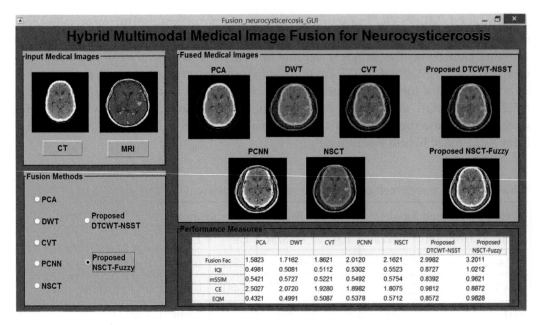

Figure 12.20 Sample screenshot for fuse the neurocysticercosis affected image using DTCWT-NSST and NSCT–fuzzy logic hybrid algorithms.

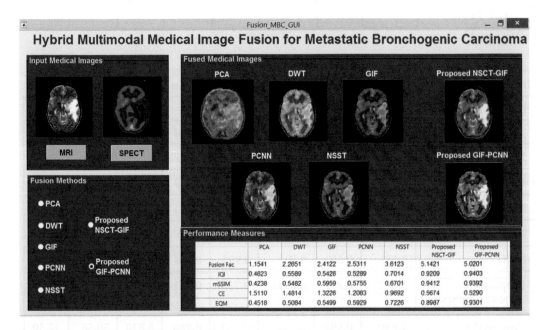

Figure 12.21 Sample screenshot for fuse the metastatic brochogenic carcinoma–affected image using NSCT-GIF– and GIP-CNN–based hybrid algorithms.

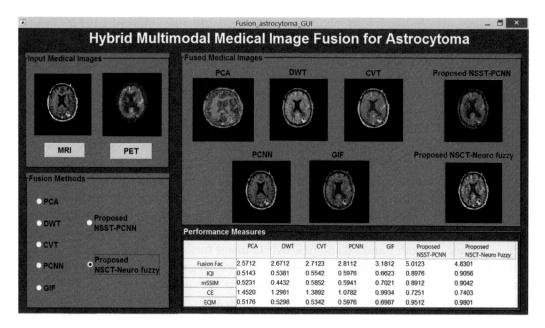

Figure 12.22 Sample screenshot for fuse the astrocytoma affected image using NSST-PCNN and NSCT–neuro fuzzy logic–based hybrid algorithms.

12.9   Conclusions

Multimodality medical image fusion combines upgraded versions of medical images into a single fused image that is free of distortion and visual artifacts while keeping complimentary and significant anatomical features from the source modality images. It is a software solution for when a single scanning equipment cannot capture all of the information about many modalities. This chapter proposes a variety of domain-based hybrid fusion algorithms. The proposed fusion schemes are applied in three different examples of disease diagnosis or treatment plans in patient management systems, such as neurocysticercosis diagnosis and stage analysis, degenerative and neoplastic disorders. The developed fusion approaches are put to the test in this chapter for diverse MRI-CT, MRI-PET, and MRI-SPECT image fusion applications. Subjective and objective fusion indicators are used to assess the effectiveness of the fusion findings. The radiologists compared the quality of the merged images to the source modalities. The subjective criterion is based on contrast, visualization of lesions, and the image's utility in contouring and treatment planning, among other things. The radiologists assessed the fused pictures on a scale of 0 (poor) to 4 (excellent).

The huge improvement in visual quality is noticeable, and radiologists have given it a high rating for its utility in clinical practice. The objective evaluation values for the proposed method 1 (DTCWT-NSST) are 4.851 for fusion factor and 0.861 for mSSIM, and 5.012 for fusion factor and 0.962 for mSSIM for the suggested method 2 (NSCT-Type 2 Fuzzy logic), respectively. The suggested method 1 (DTCWT-NSST) received a 3.5 out of 4 radiologist subjective evaluation score, whereas the proposed method 2 (NSCT-Type 2 Fuzzy) received a 3 out of 4 radiologist subjective evaluation score.

The proposed technique 3 (GIF-NSCT) has objective evaluation values of 4.191 for fusion factor and 0.941 for mSSIM, whereas the proposed method 4 (GIF-PCNN) has objective evaluation values of 4.020 for fusion factor and 0.939 for mSSIM. Suggested technique 3 (NSCT-GIF) receives a 3.5 out of 4 radiologist subjective evaluation score, whereas proposed method 4 (GIF-PCNN) receives a 3.5 out of 4 radiologist subjective evaluation score. The proposed technique 5 (NSST-PCNN) has objective assessment values of 5.012 for fusion factor and 0.904 for mSSIM, whereas the proposed method 6 (NSCT–neuro fuzzy) has objective evaluation values of 4.950 for fusion factor and 0.923 for mSSIM.

The proposed technique 5 (NSST-PCNN) received a 3.5 out of 4 radiologist subjective evaluation score, while the proposed method 6 (NSCT-Neuro Fuzzy) received a 3 out of 4 radiologist subjective assessment score. The proposed approaches' subjective criteria have been evaluated by radiologists. For our planned work as a whole, the average subjective evaluation score is 3.5. Several performance evaluation measures were used to investigate the performance of both standard and new hybrid image fusion approaches. There are subjective and objective evaluations. When compared to existing traditional methods, the proposed methods perform better on performance metrics such as fusion factor, cross entropy, IQI, edge quality measure, mutual information, PSNR, and cross entropy.

12.9.1   Future Work

1. The fused images can further be used for classification of diseases.
2. Other multimodality medical images like Ultrasonography (USG), Magnetic Resonance Angiography (MRA), and Nuclear Magnetic Resonance (NMR) can be included for the MMIF.
3. The fusion method can be further enhanced by combining more than one optimization methods like particle swarm optimization (PSO), Ant colony Optimization (ACO), Artificial Bee Colony (ABC), and Modified central force optimization (MCFO) along with Gray Wolf Optimization (GWO).
4. The deep learning approach can be preferred to fuse the features from both the modalities to make the system more robust, computationally efficient and reliable process, which will efficiently assist the radiologist or neurologist.

References

1. Daniel, E., Optimum Wavelet Based Homomorphic Medical Image Fusion Using Hybrid Genetic – Grey Wolf Optimization Algorithm. *IEEE Sens. J.*, 18, 16, 6804, 2018.
2. El-Hoseny, H.M., El Rabaie, E.-S.M., Abd Elrahman, W., Abd El-Samie, F.E., Medical Image Fusion Techniques Based on Combined Discrete Transform Domains. *IEEE 34th National Radio Science Conference*, vol. 34, p. 471, 2017.
3. El-Hoseny, H.M., Abd El-Rahman, W., El-Rabaie, E.-S.M., Abd El-Samie, F.E., Faragallah, O.S., An efficient DT-CWT medical image fusion system based on modified central force optimization and histogram matching. *Infrared Phys. Technol.*, Elsevier, 94, 223, 2018.
4. El-Hoseny, H.M., Abd El-Rahman, W., El-Shafai, W., Elm Rabaie, E.-S.M., Mahmoud, K.R., Abd El-Samie, F.E., Faragallah, O.S., Optimal multi-scale geometric fusion based on

non-subsampled contourlet transform and modified central force optimization. *Int. J. Imaging Syst. Technol.*, Wiley Periodicals, 29, 1, 4, 2018.

5. Du, J., Li, W., Lu, K., Xiao, B., An Overview of Multi-Modal Medical Image Fusion. *Neurocomputing*, 215, C, 3, 2016.

6. Narasimha, M.K.N. and Kusuma, J., Fusion of Medical Image Using STSVD. *Proceedings of the 5th International Conference on Frontiers in Intelligent Computing: Theory and Applications*, vol. 516, Springer, p. 69, 2017.

7. Mehta, N. and Budhiraja, S., Multimodal Medical Image Fusion using Guided Filter in NSCT Domain. *Biomed. Pharmacol. J.*, 11, 4, 937, 2018.

8. Ganasala, P. and Kumar, V., Feature-Motivated Simplified Adaptive PCNN Based Medical Image Fusion Algorithm in NSST Domain. *J. Digit. Imaging*, Springer, 29, 1, 73, 2015.

9. Gomathi, P.S. and Kalaavathi, B., Multimodal Medical Image Fusion in Non-Subsampled Contourlet Transform Domain. *Circuits Systems*, Sci. Res. Publishing, 7, 8, 1598, 2016.

10. Chavan, S., Mahajan, A., Talbar, S.N., Desai, S., Thakur, M., D'cruz, A., Non-subsampled rotated complex wavelet transform (NSRCxWT) for medical image fusion related to clinical aspects in neurocysticercosis. *Comput. Biol. Med.*, Elsevier, 81, 64, 2017.

11. Li, S., Kang, X., Hu, J., Image fusion with guided filtering. *Trans. Image Process.*, 22, 7, 2864, 2013.

12. Das, S. and Kundu, M.K., A Neuro-Fuzzy Approach for Medical Image Fusion. *IEEE Trans. Biomed. Eng.*, 60, 12, 3347, 2013.

13. Liu, X., Mei, W., Du, H., Multimodality medical image fusion algorithm based on gradient minimization smoothing filter and pulse coupled neural network, Biomed. *Signal Process. Control*, Elsevier, 30, 140, 2016.

14. Liu, X., Mei, W., Du, H., Multi-modality medical image fusion based on image decomposition framework and non-subsampled shearlet transform, Biomed. *Signal Process. Control*, Elsevier, 40, 343, 2018.

15. Xu, X., Shan, D., Wang, G., Jiang, X., Multimodal medical image fusion using PCNN optimized by the QPSO algorithm. *Appl. Soft Comput.*, Elsevier, 46, C, 588, 2016.

16. Rajalingam, B., Priya, R., Bhavani, R., Multimodal Medical Image Fusion Using Discrete Fractional Wavelet Transform (DFRWT) with Non-subsampled Contourlet Transform (NSCT) Hybrid Fusion Algorithm. *International Conference on Computational Vision and Bio Inspired Computing*, Springer, Cham, p. 1131, 2018.

17. Rajalingam, B., Priya, R., Bhavani, R., Comparative analysis of hybrid fusion algorithms using neurocysticercosis, neoplastic, Alzheimer's, and astrocytoma disease affected multimodality medical images, in: *Advanced Machine Vision Paradigms for Medical Image Analysis*, pp. 131–167, Elsevier, Academic Press, Cambridge, 2021.

18. Rajalingam, B., Priya, R., Bhavani, R., Santhoshkumar, R., Image Fusion Techniques for Different Multimodality Medical Images Based on Various Conventional and Hybrid Algorithms for Disease Analysis, in: *Applications of Advanced Machine Intelligence in Computer Vision and Object Recognition: Emerging Research and Opportunities*, pp. 159–196, IGI Global, Pennsylvania, 2020.

19. Rajalingam, B., Al-Turjman, F., Santhoshkumar, R., Rajesh, M., Intelligent multimodal medical image fusion with deep guided filtering. *Multimed. Syst.*, 1, 1, 2020.

20. Rajalingam, B. and Priya, R., Hybrid multimodality medical image fusion technique for feature enhancement in medical diagnosis. *IJESI*, 2, 52, 2018.

21. Rajalingam, B. and Priya, R., Multimodal medical image fusion based on deep learning neural network for clinical treatment analysis. *Int. J. ChemTech Res.*, 11, 06, 160, 2018.

22. Harvard Medical School, 2019. https://www.med.harvard.edu.

23. Radiopaedia.org, 2005. https://radiopaedia.org.

13

Health Detection System for COVID-19 Patients Using IoT

Dipak P. Patil[1]*, Kishor Badane[2], Amit Kumar Mishra[3] and Vishal A. Wankhede[4]

[1]SIEM Sandip Foundation, Nashik, Maharashtra, India
[2]Electrical Engineering, Head - Industry Institute Interaction, Amrutvahini College of Engineering Sangamner, Dist Ahmednagar, Maharashtra, India
[3]E & TC Department SIEM, Sandip Foundation, Nashik, India
[4]SNJBs SHHJB Polytechnic, Chandwad, India

Abstract

Currently, the entire planet is terrified of a virus known as COVID-19 (coronavirus). Its effects are so deadly that the whole world has been placed on lockdown. Vaccines for this virus are being developed by scientists and physicians all over the world. Machine learning, the Internet of Things (IoT), and artificial intelligence all play a role in detecting people who have been affected by coronavirus.

We have also operated in this direction and developed a system called "Health Detection System for COVID-19 Patients using IoT" which can identify coronavirus-infected people and create a database for easy monitoring. Our system named as "Health Detection System for COVID-19 Patients using IoT" can detect corona by measuring the temperature and oxygen level of the patient. The system will detect the temperature of person with the help of DHT sensor and the oxygen level with the help of MAX30100, which are interfaced with NodeMCU. Data will be uploaded on ThingSpeak server (cloud) through which it can be monitored.

The system is quite simple and very effective, especially at the hospital (ICU) where doctors can monitor patient from a distant place. Complete system cost around Rs 1,000/- (Rupees One Thousand Only).

Keywords: Arduino IDE, coronavirus, DHT, IoT, NodeMCU, MAX30100, proteus

13.1 Introduction

13.1.1 Overview

The healthcare sector is a large area of research that has seen major technological advancements. It is prohibitively expensive for those in need of healthcare services, especially in developing countries. In hospitals and other healthcare facilities, the health-monitoring infrastructure has grown dramatically, and portable health-monitoring systems based on

*Corresponding author: dipak.patil@siem.org.in

Tushar H. Jaware, K. Sarat Kumar, Ravindra D. Badgujar and Svetlin Antonov (eds.) *Medical Imaging and Health Informatics*, (237–252) © 2022 Scrivener Publishing LLC

emerging technology are attracting considerable interest in many countries around the world. The Internet of Things (IoT) has made it possible for healthcare to move away from face-to-face appointments and toward telemedicine.

As a consequence, this initiative is an attempt to solve a current health problem in society. The project's main goal is to provide a system for remote healthcare. This project proposes an intelligent IoT healthcare device that will continuously track a patient's health-related parameters as well as the state of the room in which they are currently located. Some sensors are used in this system to collect data from the patient and environment, such as a pulse sensor, body temperature sensor, room temperature sensor, blood oxygen sensor, ECG sensor, and room humidity sensor.

Patients' status is conveyed to medical staff through an online portal, which allows them to process and analyze the patients' current condition. The prototype would be well-suited for healthcare tracking, as shown by the system's efficacy. In the case of infectious disease, the system is very successful, including a novel coronavirus (COVID-19).

13.1.2   Preventions

Infection to corona can be reduced if we should do following things:

    a) Cover mouth and face with mask;
    b) Rub your hand with alcohol-based sanitizer;
    c) Stay home and only come out if it is very essential, or if you are feeling unwell. then stay home and maintain social distance.

13.1.3   Symptoms

General symptoms of coronavirus-affected person are as follows [10]:

Difficulty in breathing
Chest pain
Clean toast
Fatigue
Lose taste

13.1.4   Present Situation

Presently, there are 146,688,513 confirmed COVID-19 cases worldwide [9].

Figure 13.1 gives region-wise data of the patients suffering from novel coronavirus disease in various regions identified by world health organization [8]. Six regions such as America, Europe, Asia, Southeast Asia, Western Pacific, and Eastern Mediterranean are considered, and live updates of this regions are provided through this graphical dashboard [13].

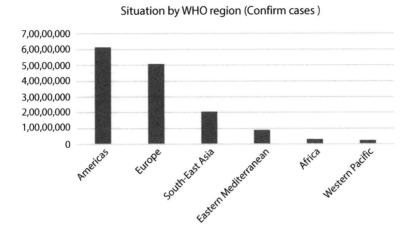

Figure 13.1 Region-wise COVID-19 data.

13.2   Related Works

Abdulrazaq *et al.* [2] offer a thermal imaging methodology using a thermal camera mounted on a smart helmet. The database is stored in the cloud via IoT. Because it includes a thermal camera and a smart helmet, the system is expensive. Rahman *et al.* [3] presented an IoT-based health monitoring system; the system may incorporate IoT, although it is still in the planning stages. The concept is still in the womb.

By giving a sneak guide for handling pandemic COVID-19, Singh *et al.* [4] emphasize the entire implementation of the well-known theory of IoT. They talked on how IoT can be used in healthcare. Singh *et al.* [5] explored the idea of combating the present COVID-19 pandemic by using the Internet of Medical Things (IoMT) technique, which would provide orthopedic patients with care. Gupta *et al.* [6] have worked on "Remote Health Monitoring System Using IoT". In this paper, authors have worked on some of the pitfalls of health monitoring system, which were not address by previous authors, i.e., they have considered machine learning and network secureness in this paper.

Swati and Chandana provided an insightful assessment and analysis [7] that contains various innovative cognitive IoMT applications to address the global health crisis. COVID-19 is a virus that infects people.

Patil *et al.* [8] proposed a system that will detect the temperature of person, i.e., one of the parameters that shows symptom of coronavirus.

13.3   System Design

13.3.1   Hardware Implementation

We have implemented a prototype of this system on NodeMCU. Block diagram of this has been shown in Figure 13.2.

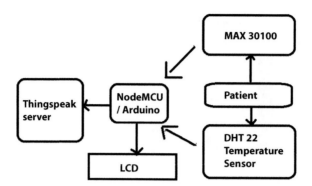

Figure 13.2 Block diagram of proposed system.

This system will detect the temperature and oxygen level of the patient. For temperature detection, DHT sensor is used, and for oxygen level measurement, MAX 30100 sensor is used. Here, we will see various parts of this system in detail.

13.3.1.1   NodeMCU

The following are the specifications of NodeMCU ESP8266:

Microcontroller: RISC Xtensa LX106 32-bit Tensilica CPU.
Voltage to operate: 3.3 V.
Voltage to input: 7–12 V.
Digital pins I/O (DIO): 16.
Input Analog Pins (ADC): 1.

13.3.1.2   DHT 11 Sensor

The system, as shown in Figure 13.3, consists of NodeMCU, which works with Arduino software (Arduino IDE).

Figure 13.3 NodeMCU [8].

Figure 13.4 DHT sensor [8].

Figure 13.4 shows DHT sensor. DHT sensor is used for sensing Temperature and Humidity. Its specifications are as follows:

Voltage service: 3.3- or 5-V DC.
Range of measurement: 20–95% RH; 0°C–50°C.
Resolution: 8-bit (humidity), 8 bit (temperature).

13.3.1.3   MAX30100 Oxygen Sensor

Figure 13.5 shows Max 30100 oxygen sensor. A Maxim's MAX30100 integrated pulse oximetry and a heart rate monitor are included in the heart rate click. It is an optical sensor that measures the absorbance of pulsing blood through a photodetector after emitting two wavelengths of light from two LEDs—a red and an infrared one. This particular LED color combination is designed to allow data to be read with the tip of one's finger.

Figure 13.5 MAX 30100 oxygen sensor [14].

A low-noise analog signal processing unit processes the signal before sending it to the target MCU through the mikroBUS I2C interface. Excessive motion and temperature changes will affect the readings, so developers of end-user applications should keep that in mind. Furthermore, too much pressure can constrict capillary blood flow, reducing the data's reliability. There is also a programmable INT pin. The device runs on a 3.3-V power supply.

13.3.1.4   ThingSpeak Server

ThingSpeak is IoT analytics platforms that allow visualizing, segregating, visualizing, and evaluating live cloud data sources. We can send out data to ThingSpeak device and also send alerts with instant visualization of live data.

Insertion into ThingSpeak: ThingSpeak is a free IoT database. Using a RESTful API, your computer or application will communicate with ThingSpeak, and it either keeps your data private or makes it available. In addition, ThingSpeak is used to analyze the data and act on it. Figure 13.6 shows ThingSpeak server webpage.

Channels on ThingSpeak: You start by creating a ThingSpeak channel once you have signed up and signed into ThingSpeak. There is a channel where you send the data to store. Each channel contains eight fields for any data type, three location fields, and one status field.

Steps involved in channel creation are as follows:

Build a channel

1. Sign in to ThingSpeakTM or create a new account using your MathWorks® account—Account to MathWorks.
2. Tap on > MyChannels.
3. Click on New Channel, on the Channels page.

Figure 13.6 ThingSpeak server webpage [8].

4. Check Fields 1–3 boxes next door. Enter the setting values for these channels.
5. Click At the bottom of the options, Save Tab. You will see those tabs now.

Figure 13.7 shows Channel Creation on Thingspeak server and Figure 13.8 shows API Key of channel on ThingSpeak. You will need proper read and write permissions when reading or writing data to your server using the ThingSpeak TM API or MATLAB® code. Because of API 16-digit key, we are reading and writing from a private computer to a server.

API Keys

- Click on > MyChannels.
- Choose the Update channel.
- Pick API Tab Keys

After signing-in using MathWorks account and creating a channel, we can have this window to set parameters of channel.

13.3.1.5   Arduino IDE

Arduino IDE is software in which we write program and upload programs to Arduino boards or NodeMCU.

Figure 13.9 shows Channel settings on ThingSpeak and Figure 13.10 shows Arduino IDE. Arduino Software (IDE) allows code writing and submission to server. This is operating on windows, Linux, and Mac OS X.

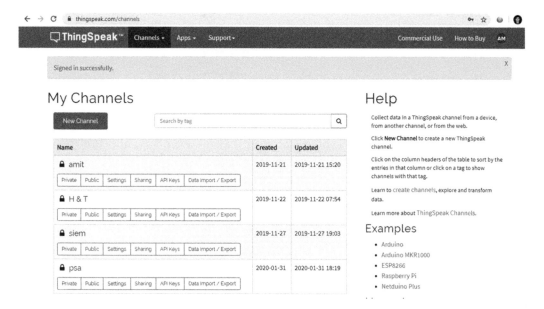

Figure 13.7 Channel creation on ThingSpeak server [8].

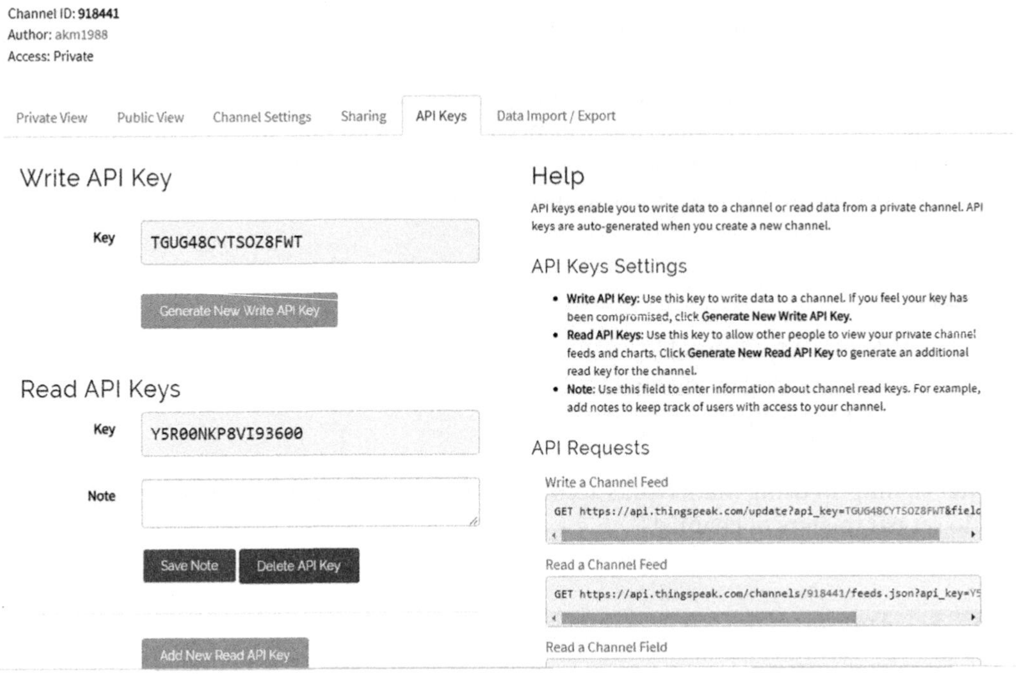

Channel ID: **918441**
Author: akm1988
Access: Private

Private View   Public View   Channel Settings   Sharing   API Keys   Data Import / Export

Write API Key

Key   TGUG48CYTSOZ8FWT

Generate New Write API Key

Read API Keys

Key   Y5R00NKP8VI93600

Note

Save Note   Delete API Key

Add New Read API Key

Help

API keys enable you to write data to a channel or read data from a private channel. API keys are auto-generated when you create a new channel.

API Keys Settings

- **Write API Key:** Use this key to write data to a channel. If you feel your key has been compromised, click **Generate New Write API Key**.
- **Read API Keys:** Use this key to allow other people to view your private channel feeds and charts. Click **Generate New Read API Key** to generate an additional read key for the channel.
- **Note:** Use this field to enter information about channel read keys. For example, add notes to keep track of users with access to your channel.

API Requests

Write a Channel Feed

GET https://api.thingspeak.com/update?api_key=TGUG48CYTSOZ8FWT&field

Read a Channel Feed

GET https://api.thingspeak.com/channels/918441/feeds.json?api_key=Y5

Read a Channel Field

Figure 13.8 API Key of channel on ThingSpeak [8].

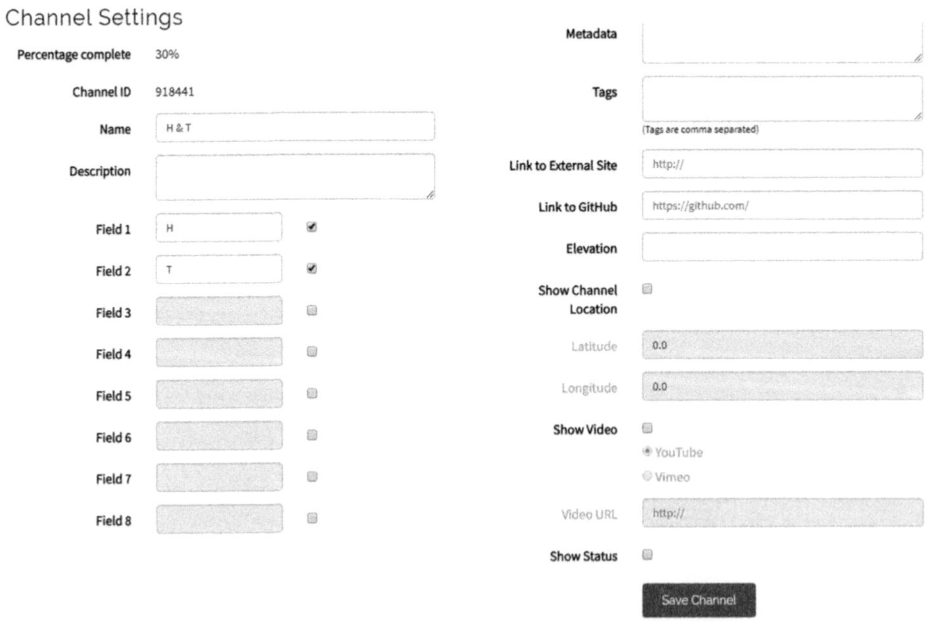

Channel Settings

Percentage complete   30%

Channel ID   918441

Name   H & T

Description

Field 1   H   ☑

Field 2   T   ☑

Field 3   ☐

Field 4   ☐

Field 5   ☐

Field 6   ☐

Field 7   ☐

Field 8   ☐

Metadata

Tags

(Tags are comma separated)

Link to External Site   http://

Link to GitHub   https://github.com/

Elevation

Show Channel   ☐
Location

Latitude   0.0

Longitude   0.0

Show Video   ☐
● YouTube
○ Vimeo

Video URL   http://

Show Status   ☐

Save Channel

Figure 13.9 Channel settings on ThingSpeak.

Figure 13.10 Arduino IDE [8].

13.4 Proposed System for Detection of Corona Patients

13.4.1 Introduction

Entire planet is terrified of a virus known as COVID-19 (coronavirus). PCR tests are used to detect COVID-19, but they are costly and out of reach for most countries. Hence, in order to find a solution to this problem, a cost-effective solution must be created. It is critical to design and build an efficient system based on IoT technique for accurate detection of the coronavirus. COVID-19 was first discovered in China, and it has had a negative impact on public health and the global economy, resulting in a global lockdown. COVID-19 is extremely contagious and spreads quickly around the world, making early detection critical. COVID-19 patients' lungs are damaged by a novel coronavirus. The lung periphery, subpleural field, and both lower lobes have the most damage. A screening system is needed to locate the exact location of the damage and to assist doctors in saving time and lives. Currently, the entire planet is terrified of a virus known as COVID-19 (coronavirus). It has such a lethal impact that it has put most countries on lockdown. When an infected person sneezes, the coronavirus spreads through the nasal saliva.

Several studies are being conducted to test the COVID-19 vaccine [10]. We have also operated in this direction and developed a system called "Health Detection System for COVID-19 Patients using IoT", which can detect coronavirus-infected people and create a database for easy monitoring.

IoT can be defined in many ways as follows [12]:

- Anything connected through Internet.
- Connectivity of Physical world with Computer System.

Examples of IoT [1] are wearable technologies, healthcare, and smart appliances.

For IoT implementation, various hardware such as Rasberry Pi and Arduino are available. Since Arduino has many drawbacks, such as requiring a separate ESP Module for Wi-Fi connectivity, our device has been implemented on NodeMCU. As a result, connectivity issues have arisen. The NodeMCU is a hardware framework with an ESP module built in (8266 module). We must be familiar with the requirements of the NodeMCU platform that we will be using in our system.

13.4.2   Arduino IDE

An open source, Arduino IDE, is a platform that supports NodeMCU. File required for interfacing NodeMCU with Arduino IDE is hidden. Hence, the path to unhide is as follows: C drive – Users – App Data – local – Arduino 15. In India, all devices have 9600 baud rate, and transmitter and receiver should have same baud rate. Hence, in programming, Serial begin (9600) has to be mentioned [8].

13.4.3   Hardware Implementation

The system shown in Figure 13.11 will detect coronavirus-affected person.

Components required to implement this system are as follows:

NodeMCU: 01
Connecting wires: 20
DHT sensor: 01
Oxygen sensor: MAX30100

It will work as follows: Our system is interfaced with NodeMCU (from Figure 13.3) that will detect the temperature and oxygen level of person with the help of DHT sensor (Figure 13.4) and MAX30100 (Figure 13.5). Data will be uploaded on ThingSpeak server (cloud) through which it can be monitored. The system is quite simple and very effective, especially

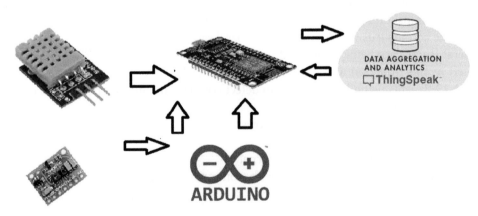

Figure 13.11 Block diagram of proposed system of "Corona Patient Detection and Monitoring".

at the hospital (ICU) where doctors can monitor patient from a distant place. Complete system cost around Rs 1,000/- (Rupees One Thousand Only).

13.5   Results and Performance Analysis

13.5.1   Hardware Implementation

13.5.1.1   Implementation of NodeMCU With Temperature Sensor

Table mentioned below consists of reading of Temperature on ThingSpeak server (from Figure 13.6, Figure 13.7, Figure 13.8). Figure 13.12 shows graphical representation of Temperature on ThingSpeak server (Figure 13.9 & Figure 13.10). Figure 13.13 shows interfacing of DHT sensor with NodeMCU.

Created_at	Entry_id	Temp in C
2019-11-22 08:15:01 IST	7	24
2019-11-22 08:15:18 IST	8	24
2019-11-22 08:15:38 IST	9	25
2019-11-22 08:15:56 IST	10	25
2019-11-22 08:16:13 IST	11	25
2019-11-22 08:16:49 IST	13	25
2019-11-22 08:17:06 IST	14	25

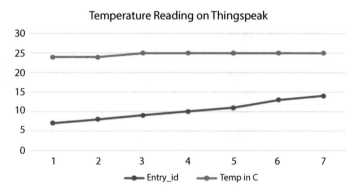

Figure 13.12 Graphical representation of temperature.

Figure 13.13 Interfacing of DHT sensor with NodeMCU [8, 11].

13.5.2   Software Implementation

13.5.2.1   *Simulation of Temperature Sensor With Arduino on Proteus Software*

Figure 13.14 shows the interfacing of Arduino with temperature sensor (LM 35). Figure 13.15 shows reading of temperature on virtual temperature. Figure 13.16 shows graphical representation of temperature shown on virtual terminal.

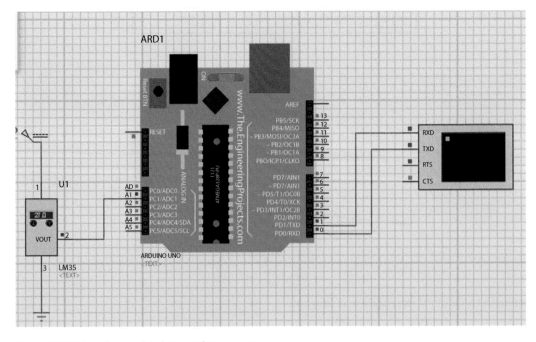

Figure 13.14 Interfacing of Arduino with temperature.

Figure 13.15 Result of temperature on virtual terminal.

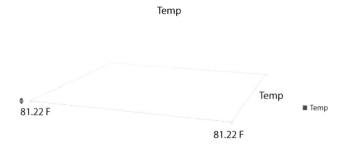

Figure 13.16 Graphical representation of temperature.

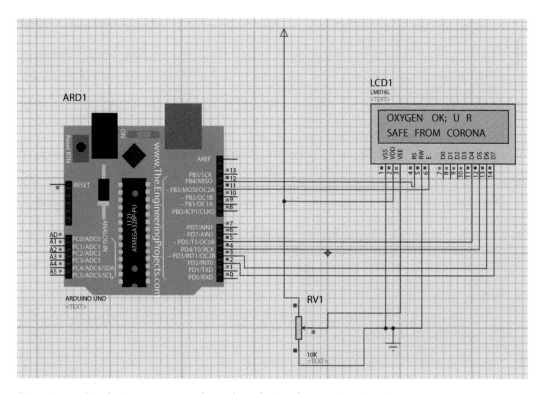

Figure 13.17 Simulation on Proteus software (Interfacing of LCD with Arduino).

13.5.2.2 Interfacing of LCD With Arduino

Figure 13.15 shows result of temperature on virtual terminal and Figure 13.16 shows graphical representation of temperature. Figure 13.17 shows interfacing of Arduino with LCD. A demo shown over here shows the message displayed on LCD "OXYGEN OK; U R SAFE FROM CORONA". Due to constraint of availability of hardware during lockdown, a small prototype in simulation has been shown.

13.6 Conclusion

Our system named as "Health Detection System for COVID-19 Patients using IoT" can detect corona by measuring the temperature and oxygen level of the patient. The system will detect the temperature of person with the help of DHT sensor and the oxygen level with the help of MAX30100, which are interfaced with NodeMCU. Data will be uploaded on ThingSpeak server (cloud) through which it can be monitored.

The system is quite simple and very effective, especially at the hospital (ICU) where doctors can monitor patients from a distance. Complete system cost around Rs 1,000/- (Rupees One Thousand Only).

References

1. Chamola, V., Hassija, V., Gupta, V., Guizani, M., A Comprehensive Review of the COVID-19 Pandemic and the Role of IoT, Drones, AI, Blockchain, and 5G in Managing Its Impact. *IEEE Access*, 8, 90225–90265, 2020.
2. Abdulrazaq, M., Zuhriyah, H., Al-Zubaidi, S., Karim, S., Ramli, R., Yusuf, E., Novel COVID-19 detection and diagnosis system using IoT based smart helmet. *Int. J. Psychosoc. Rehabil.*, 24, 2296–2303, 2020, 10.37200/IJPR/V24I7/PR270221.
3. Siddikur Rahman, Md, Peeri, N.C., Shrestha, N., Zaki, R., Haque, U., Hamidd, S.H.A., Defending against the Novel Coronavirus (COVID-19) outbreak: How can the Internet of Things (IoT) help to save the world? *Health Policy Technol.*, 9, 2, 136–138, 2020 Jun.
4. Singh, R.P., Javaid, M., Haleem, A., Suman, R., Internet of things (IoT) applications to fight against COVID-19 pandemic. *Diabetes Metab. Syndr.*, 14, 4, 521–524, 2020.
5. Singh, R.P., Javaid, M., Haleem, A., Vaishya, R., Al, S., Internet of Medical Things (IoMT) for Orthopaedic in COVID-19 Pandemic: Roles, Challenges, and Applications. *J. Clin. Orthop. Trauma*, 1–5, 2020 May 15.
6. Gupta, S., Dahiya, D., Raj, G., Remote Health Monitoring System Using IoT. *International Conference on Advances in Computing and Communication Engineering (ICACCE)*, 2018.
7. Swayamsiddha, S. and Mohanty, C., Application of Cognitive Internet of Medical Things for COVID-19 Pandemic. *J. Diabetes Metab. Syndr.*, 14, 5, 911–915, 2020 Jun 11.
8. Patil, D., Mishra, A., Javare, T., IOT based Automatic Corona Virus Detection and Monitoring System, in: *Health Informatics and Technological Solutions for Corona Virus (Covid 19)*, CRC press – Taylor and Francis, USA, 2021.
9. https://covid19.who.int/.
10. https://www.who.int/health-topics/coronavirus#tab=tab_1.
11. https://www.pce-instruments.com/english/slot/2/download/56251/datasheet-infrared-thermometer-pce-jr911.pdf.

12. https://www.who.int/health-topics/coronavirus#tab=tab_3.

13. https://covid19.who.int/?gclid=EAIaIQobChMIiZjat9Cc6gIVmiQrCh1qkw9GEAAYASAAE-gL1k_D_BwE.

14. https://www.google.co.in/search?q=max+30100+oxygen+sensor+specifications&-source=lnms&tbm=isch&sa=X&ved=2ahUKEwijtuPUu5zwAhW47HMBHWqaA4oQ_AUoAXoECAEQAw&biw=1536&bih=754#imgrc=10IalIb7DXxHUM.

14

Intelligent Systems in Healthcare

Rajiv Dey* and Pankaj Sahu

Electronics and Communication Department, BML Munjal University, Gurugram Haryana, India

Abstract

Intelligent systems are the man-made technologically advanced machines that acquire data from the sensors; do data analysis from the acquired data for feature extraction, classification, and decision making; and can learn from its past experience. These machines are integrated with various technologies that make them intelligent such as AI (artificial intelligence), machine learning, soft computing, expert systems, neural networks, and machine vision. This book chapter aims to briefly explore some of the well-known real life practical applications of the intelligent systems in healthcare domain where they show potential in effectively solving the real world problems so that the readers can be made aware about the intelligent healthcare technologies and there potential in this field. Moreover, it also explore about how these intelligent technologies are used in healthcare, there benefits and at last the chapter concludes with its future vision.

Keywords: Healthcare system, intelligent systems, robotic systems in healthcare, AI in healthcare, brain-computer–based healthcare systems, intelligent technologies in healthcare, remote health monitoring

14.1 Introduction

During the evolution of mother-nature, humanity has ever thought that artificial intelligence (AI)–based models can be developed that are unaffected from its surrounding environment. Later, researcher's community realized that imitating nature, better models of a system can be created as mother nature is the best ever architect that existed. This lead to researchers enhanced interest in this domain as a result problem solving reached another level. This nature inspired new perspective gave rise to a new computational technique also known as computational intelligence. Now, the question that arises is what are intelligent systems? Different people have different thoughts about intelligent system; some say it is a system having capability to acquire and analyze data and can also interconnect with other systems that can learn from self-experience and can adapt according to the changes in its surroundings. In short, these are the technologically advanced machines that can learn and reply to the environment. These capabilities of an intelligent system are shown in Figure 14.1.

In the age of modern mobile computing world, the biomedical industries has a vision to achieve two particular objectives [1].

---

*Corresponding author: rajiv.dey@iiitdmj.ac.in

Tushar H. Jaware, K. Sarat Kumar, Ravindra D. Badgujar and Svetlin Antonov (eds.) *Medical Imaging and Health Informatics*, (253–274) © 2022 Scrivener Publishing LLC

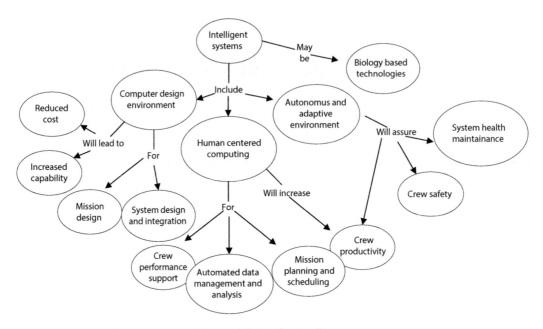

Figure 14.1 Pictorial representation of the capabilities of an intelligent system.

1. Accessibility of software application and medical data at any moment and any place.
2. Invisible and effort less computing

Due to the concepts such as electronic healthcare (e-healthcare) and e-health applications came into picture such as the systems that is able to acquire data from the medical devices/sensors, automatically process exchange the gathered knowledge with the other devices and take intelligent decisions. These applications are enabled with the feature of autonomy, i.e., user interaction for controlling and monitoring is not required, so that they can deliver right information and take right decision, action at right time [2]. Due to the availability of these technologies, a wide range of applications and services are made possible as follows:

a. Automated diagnosis
b. Emergency services and diagnosis
c. Personalized medicine
d. Remote home monitoring which comes under smart homes
e. Location-based medical services, etc.

The adoption of these latest technologies by the healthcare sector in implementing electronic healthcare services has enhanced its efficiency at cheap cost. The extensive use of internet-enabled smart phones capabilities has opened the way to the conception of smart electronic healthcare, which is believed to deliver the healthcare enmities using mobile communication [3]. Intelligent healthcare systems has amazing potential due to the enhanced use of the portable smart devices such as internet-enabled phones with GPS, various internet-enabled sensor modules having smart monitoring capabilities, etc., in the electronic healthcare systems, which is available 24/7. A wide variety of intelligent systems with various onboard technologies are deployed nowadays:

a. Particle swarm optimization (PSO)–based systems
b. Fuzzy logic–based systems
c. Deep learning–based systems
d. Neural network–based systems
e. Ant colony–based systems
f. Support vector machine–based systems
g. Evolutionary computing such as genetic algorithm–based systems
h. Clustering-based systems
i. Some hybrid systems including neuro-fuzzy and genetic-fuzzy–based systems.

The general domains of the latest intelligent systems include topics such as pattern recognition, AI, supervised, unsupervised learning, natural language processing (NLP), intelligent robotic system, swarm intelligence systems, intelligent system design, evolving clustering methods, and human computer interface. The details about intelligent systems can be found in Padhy *et al.* [4], Shin *et al.* [5], and Hopgood *et al.* [6]. With the practical application point of view these intelligent systems find a huge prospective in resolving the real life problems. For the readers to get an idea about the potential of these smart tools, the application domains of some of the well-known areas are mentioned briefly and can be found in the references mentioned therein:

a. Brain-computer interface (BCI)
b. Robotic systems
c. Voice recognition systems [7–8]
d. Remote health monitoring systems [9]
e. Internet of Things (IoT)–based intelligent systems [10–11]
f. Smart cities [12]
g. Smart grids [13]
h. Fuzzy and neural network based control systems [14], etc.

Among the above mentioned areas, some of the applications related to health monitoring are discussed in the following.

14.2   Brain Computer Interface

A BCI is an intelligent hardware used to acquire brain signals also known as electro encephalogram EEG, analyzes them, and converts them into such a form so as to control an output device to perform some desired action. The BCI systems are strictly restricted to use the signals produced by the central nerves system; thus, it does not consumption the brain's neuromuscular pathways of peripherals such as nerves and muscles. This can also be confirmed through an example that a voice-activated or a muscle activated system such as electromyogram (EMG) cannot be considered as BCI. Moreover, an EEG device cannot be considered as BCI as it only records the brain signals and does not produce an output to control that can control a device [15–17].

14.2.1 Types of Signals Used in BCI

According to Jerry *et al.*, any type of brain signals can be used for BCI such as electrical signals by neuronal post synaptic membrane. This signal is obtained by the polarity changes in the activation potential or ion-gated channels. The Herger Berger is the person who invented scalp EEG in 1929 which is a measure of the above discussed signals [19]. The advantage of scalp EEG is that it is simple and easy to implement. However, the scalp recorded signals get highly attenuated upon passing through the skull and scalp. Therefore, new technologies such as small intracortical micro arrays can be can be implanted on the cortex.

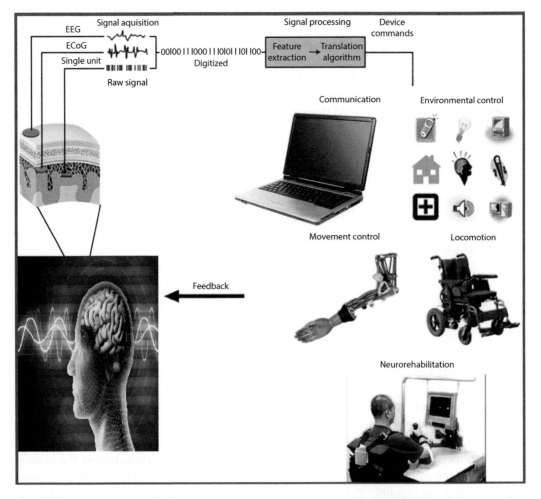

Figure 14.2 Representation of BCI components, recording the brain signals using the electrodes connected on the scalp or the cortical region or within the brain. These signals are first filtered and amplified, and then, it is passed through high resolution the A to D convertor; after this, features are extracted from these digital signals; further, it is classified using a variety of classification algorithms. The classified signals are then used for generating commands [18].

14.2.2   Components of BCI

To achieve the task of identifying the features of the brain signals which shows the user's intensions and to translate it in real time into device commands, the BCI as shown in Figure 14.2 is divided in following four sections:

1. The data acquisition section
2. Feature extraction section
3. Feature classification section
4. Device output section

(i) Data acquisition: It is a device used to measure physical parameter (brain activity using sensors that may be fitted on the scalp or inserted inside the brain) that improves the quality of signals either by amplification, attenuation, or filtering. This device converts the signals in such a form so it can be used in a digital device, e.g., a computer for further processing. Types of brain signal data acquisition methods are shown in Figure 14.3.

(ii) Feature extraction: Feature extraction is a process of dimensionality reduction to detect specific signal characteristics such as features related to person's intent from an unnecessary content and represent them in a compressed form appropriate to convert it into output commands. These features should strongly match with the person's intent as most of the brain events are either momentary or oscillatory.

(iii) Feature classification: The signal features obtained after feature extraction are passed through some specialized classification algorithm to convert features into commands. The classification algorithms used should be dynamic so that it can accommodate the sudden changes in the extracted features.

(iv) Device output: The commands generated from classification algorithms are used to derive the outdoor device to provide functions such as robotic arm movement, robot movement, and cursor control.

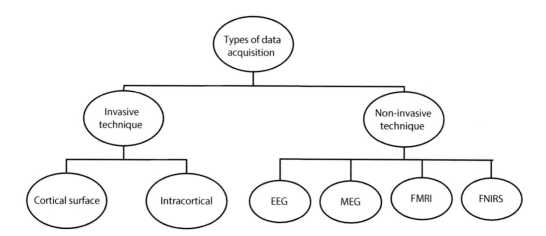

Figure 14.3 Data acquisition methods.

14.2.3   Applications of BCI in Health Monitoring

Brain signals can be used in a variety of ways in the health monitoring including prevention, detection, diagnosis, and rehabilitation [20].

(i) Prevention [21]: BCI can be used to prevent the habits of a human such as smoking, alcoholism, and motion sickness. Various brain allied studies have been established on the detection of consciousness level detection system. In the work of Hanafiah *et al.*, the effect of smoking and consuming alcohol on brain is well studied. This study is important in the healthcare domain to prevent some human conditions caused due to excess consumption of smoking and alcohol such as loss of alertness, loss of function, etc.

(ii) Detection and diagnosis [22–23]: Mental health monitoring feature of BCI has been deeply studied in predicting and forecasting the health related issues such as sleep disorders (narcolepsy), brain tumors, disorders of brain, and epileptic seizure.

(iii) Rehabilitation and restoration [24]: Mobility rehabilitation can be considered as a physical rehabilitation is used for the patients with mobility issues such as disability and physical disorders. The mobility rehabilitation helps the patients in recovering from loss of function and regaining their previous levels of mobility. BCI can be used to detect the movement changes using frames comparison approach of a coma patient taking treatment in the hospitals [25].

14.3   Robotic Systems

Nowadays, robots can be found everywhere from home to local hospitals. The advantages of robots in medicine can be used to help in relieve the medical officials from their regular tasks, so that they can invest their time on more critically ill patients. It also helps in making medical procedures safer, effective and less costly. Moreover, robots can be used in performing complicated surgery in tiny places of the body and carriage dangerous substances [27–30]. Some studies shows that robotic systems can be used in rehabilitation of hand after brain stroke [31]. A detailed study can be found in [26] in perspective of the use of robotics in pre-, intra-, and postsurgical applications in mitigating the infectious contamination and support patient's supervision in surgical environment as shown in Figure 14.4.

14.3.1   Advantages of Surgical Robots

Implementation of robots for surgical procedure can benefit the surgeon by supporting them in improving the safety while doing surgery and to make the entire procedure more efficient which in turn the time and cost both gets reduced when running a surgical room.

Implementation of machine learning models and data analytics [26]: For mastering, the surgery personal experience plays an important role and even the surgeons learn from their own experience by sometimes looking at their own video of previous surgical operations. In the future, the systems may have the feature of automated data recording and its analysis. In implementation of AI and deep learning models, these systems explore the novel

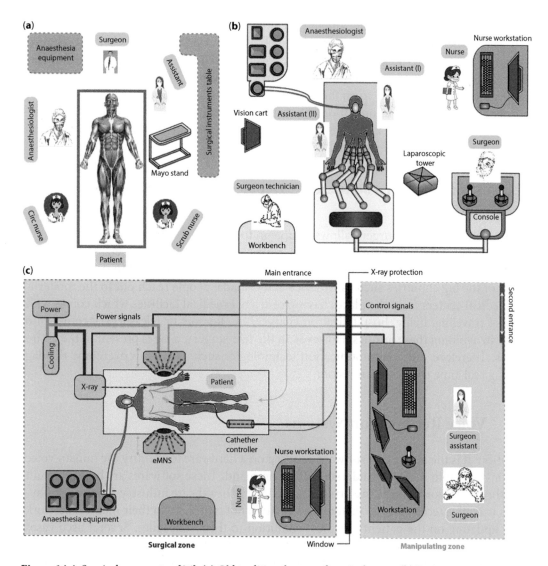

Figure 14.4 Surgical room setup [26]. (a) Old traditional setup of surgical room. (b) Recent operative room setup for surgical operations where the surgeon is directing the robot remotely to conduct operations, therefore as compared to point (a). Lesser number of team members is required for the coordination. (c) Latest wireless robotic surgery where no person is needed for close monitoring of the patient. The surgeon sits on a control station directing the robot to perform the surgical operations remotely.

possibilities in the surgery domain reducing the complications and enhancing the safety. These modern technologies such as virtual and augmented reality–based simulators have opened a new way of training and gauging the surgeons [32].

14.3.2   Centralization of the Important Information to the Surgeon

Various industrial sectors such as automobiles or aviation the operating persons such as drivers and pilots get the important relevant data to perform a particular task from a central console. On the other hand, the surgeons acquire this information from their colleagues such as anesthesiologist, retrieving images such as x-rays and CT scans on the separate devices to locate the critical structures and convert those images into the surgical operations. These stages are time consuming and obstruct the surgical flow as for each of the tasks the surgeon need to see away from the operative filed which ultimately delayed the process and also increase the cost of operation substantially. Therefore, implementation of centralization can play a vital role in providing the necessary information at a common platform which will reduce the burden on surgeons [33].

14.3.3   Remote-Surgery, Software Development, and High Speed Connectivity Such as 5G

Additionally, the remote surgery allows a surgeon to perform a surgery from a far location which is beneficial during wars, pandemics, restricted medical facilities, etc. However, on the other hand, remote surgery also have some consequences associated to it, for example, in case of the big countries such as America and Canada, people reach out to the modernized medical centers from the places having restricted medical facilities which comes with a cost of traveling, living, hospitalization charges, etc. Remote or tele-surgery comes into picture in avoiding these hurdles. However, in the tele-surgery, a lag is present in the entire process. Therefore, latest communication technologies such as 5G can overcome this lag enabling real-time signal transmission.

14.4   Voice Recognition Systems

Definition: It is the ability of a software running on a hardware to identify the human voice and convert it into machine understandable command. These softwares are basically built upon the NLP algorithm and are primarily used in the healthcare industry. Doctors or physicians used this technology to dictate there written notes to share in their medical network or for updating on the patient's medical condition to their colleagues. Several used cases related to voice recognition systems can be found in the literature, e.g., medical transcription [34] for recording the patients' medical report (EMR). Numerous companies, nowadays, are offering AI-based voice recognition software to clinicians and hospitals. These software helps the clinicians in many ways, e.g., it converts there speech into text note to update on the patient's health condition in their databases.

14.5   Remote Health Monitoring Systems

This concept in the field of telemedicine denotes to methods and ways such the clinicians and medical professionals can remotely consult with the patient, diagnose, and treat them. The main aim of remote health monitoring is to provide timely delivery of medical services over remote locations where medical facilities are restricted. The concept of remote health monitoring system nowadays looks feasible to be implemented in the field of medicine due to the advancement of the modern technologies such as 5G, cloud computing, and data storage facilities. It plays an important role in prioritizing the patients suffering from multiple chronic disorders and provides them high quality healthcare facilities. Therefore, it can be concluded that in remote health monitoring the clinicians basically monitors the patients based on the priority and severity of the medical condition thereby provide instant feedback based on the real-time data analysis to the patients. The remote health monitoring studies can be categorized into three parts [35].

   (i) Patent triage
  (ii) Service delivery to the patients
 (iii) Prioritization of the patients

(i) Patient triage [33]: Selecting a patient based on the severity of disease is known as triage. A variety of studies have been done on this topic some studies focused on inside triage [35], while the others have focused on the outside triage [36].

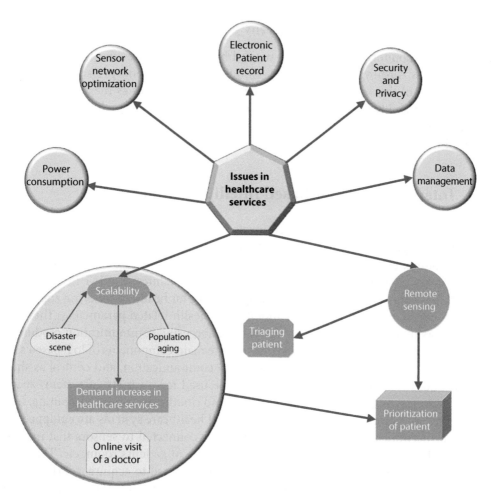

Figure 14.5 Organization of healthcare showing scalability issue [35].

(ii) Service delivery to the patients: Many studies have been aimed at developing an alert emergency based service that can give an alarm to the caregiver to provide fast response in case the important signs becomes irregular [37]. Multiple services are offered nowadays that provide guidelines for prevention, drugs prescription, and tele-recommendations. Some studies have introduced a new concept of elder caregiver, the service will connect medical clinic with the remotely located home of the elder [37]. Furthermore, some studies suggest prescribing medicines drug and its related dosage.

(iii) Prioritization of patients: This feature is basically a server-based (i.e., including cloud and IoT) patient prioritization approach in which the patients are prioritized on the basis of their medical conditions and if necessary transport them to the nearby hospital. The prioritization application consists of two steps: In the first step, a variety of sensors are used to gather information about the patient's health condition on the basis of which the decision has been taken about the health status. In the second step the application sends the patient's data using communication channel such as LTEFemo network to the related healthcare center for prioritization [38].

14.5.1   Tele-Medicine Health Concerns

Remote health monitoring is seemingly needed by the people specifically for the chronic diseases such as cardiovascular disorder, blood sugar, high blood pressure, and cancer. These are some of the serious matters for the healthcare services as they are the cause of mortality and disability. There are several issues and challenges in the tele-healthcare monitoring, among those the most crucial one is the scaling problem and its taxonomy is shown in Figure 14.5.

14.6   Internet of Things–Based Intelligent Systems

IoT is a technological revolution which connects any objects internally using internet. Some of the possible applications of IoT are health monitoring system, smart grid, smart parking, smart agriculture, etc. The incredible use of IoT is in the healthcare management system providing data of health and environmental conditions facilities. The IoT is a network of physical things connected through internet, specifically, for health monitoring applications the sensors can be used on devices for monitor the health related parameters. These connected sensors then send the data to a remote location using communication module and internet for further processing. The following are the main components of IoT-based smart healthcare systems that are sensing, identification, communication, and control as shown in Figure 14.6. IoT-based smart healthcare can be used for a variety of systems such as emergency services, big data, remote monitoring, and cloud-based smart computing. In the domain of telemedicine system, the IoT-based smart healthcare systems are equipped with body sensor networks, which includes special nodes connected to sensors that monitors health related data of patients, to check air conditioning of patient's room, etc. The microcontroller boards connected to these sensors are programmed to acquire a variety of data such as temperature and humidity. The technologies such as 3G, 4G, LTE, 5G, and internet make the data monitoring task easier and to send it to remotely situated medical healthcare professional such as doctors and nurses. It is helpful in acquiring and storing patients' data

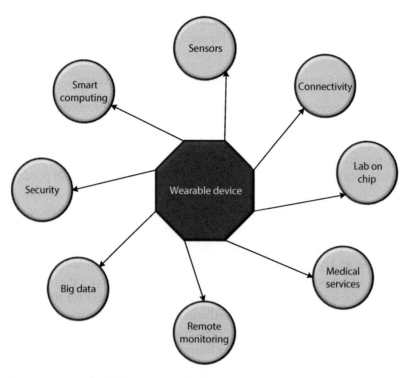

Figure 14.6 Basic components of IoT-based smart healthcare system.

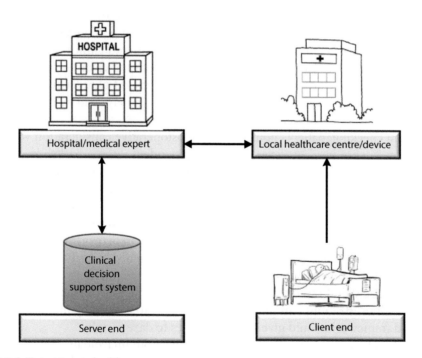

Figure 14.7 IoT structure in healthcare.

using store-and-forward approach so that the stored data can be used at any time anywhere. The IoT services and its role are shown in Figure 14.7.

14.6.1   Ubiquitous Computing Technologies in Healthcare

In the age of the pervasive and versatile computing world, the biomedical informatics has the vision to achieve two explicit objectives:

1. The programing application's accessibility.
2. Clinical data anyplace and whenever and the imperceptibility of processing.

Both previously mentioned objectives lead to the demonstration of inescapable processing ideas and highlights in electronic well-being (e–well-being) applications. The biomedical applications and their interfaces that consequently want to handle information given by clinical gadgets and sensors, trade information, and settle on insightful choices in a given setting are unequivocally attractive. Regular client associations with such applications depend on independence, staying away from the requirement for the client to control individual activity, so they are contextualized and modified, conveying the perfect data and choice at the perfect second. All the above inescapable processing highlights add esteem in present-day unavoidable e-medical services frameworks.

These innovations can uphold an extensive scope of utilizations and presidencies including portable area-based clinical benefits, telemedicine, patient observing, crisis reaction, and the executives, inescapable admittance to clinical information, and customized checking. Remote innovation empowers the rescue vehicle workforce to send continuous digital data about a patient's situation to a clinic though in transit. At times, paramedics can recover the patient's clinical history with known hypersensitivities or past conditions from the clinic data set electronically. In clinical offices outfitted with the remote neighborhood (LANs), specialists and teams can audit and refresh a patient's clinical history from any region utilizing a handheld gadget. Entering expressive data and electronically taking notes dispose the requirement for tedious manual transcription and blunder related to written by hand guidelines. Likewise, doctors can produce and remotely send medicines to a drug store; additionally, it saves time and builds precision.

With distant checking, patients going through postoperative consideration who are not, at this point in intense peril however are as yet dependent upon a backslide or different entanglements can be securely moved before to different units inside a medical clinic. Many can move to less expensive helped care offices or even get back additional rapidly. Medical care suppliers can utilize area-based following administrations to manage old patients or those with psychological instabilities who are mobile yet limited to a specific territory. For instance, a helped care office could utilize sensors connected in network and radiofrequency ID identifications to restraint staff individuals when an assigned security zone is vacated by the patients. Organization or satellite situating innovation additionally can be utilized to rapidly and precisely find remote supporters in a crisis and convey data about their area. Vicinity data administrations can guide portable clients to a close-by medical care office; voice-enacted frameworks could give such guidelines to daze people.

The patient and medical care suppliers would profit from unavoidable access to lifetime medical data. During the registration process, for instance, patients could utilize a handheld gadget to transfer their medical record and protection information into their medical care supplier's information base, diminishing the exertion needed to enter such nitty-gritty data physically. On the other hand, such data could be downloaded from a web server with authenticity verification. The patients could similarly utilize cell phones to refresh their own what is more, family clinical data and doctor contacts, get alarms to take endorsed prescriptions, check for medicine cooperation's, or powerfully alter limitations on who can get to their well-being information. Remote specialist co-ops or medical services suppliers could utilize such abilities to make any data they store sharable just with the client's assent. Various convenient gadgets are accessible that can recognize certain clinical conditions— beat rate, pulse, breath liquor level, etc., from a client's touch. Plentiful such capacities could be incorporated into a handheld remote gadget that likewise comprises the client's medical history. It might even be conceivable to recognize certain relevant data, for example, the client's degree of nervousness, in light of keystroke designs. In the wake of examining information input, the gadget could communicate an alarm message to a medical services supplier, the closest clinic, or then again a crisis framework if fitting.

The advancement of inescapable medical services frameworks is a promising region for business associations dynamic in the well-being observing area. The considered inescapable foundation sets out various business open doors for players like crisis clinical help organizations, the telecom administrators, insurance agencies, and so forth The inescapable worldview makes added an incentive for every one of these entertainers in the business chain. As of now, the savvy arrangement of value medical care is a vital issue all through the world since medical care faces a huge subsidizing emergency because of the expanding populace of more established individuals and the return of sicknesses that ought to be controllable. The inescapable medical services frameworks are fit for assaulting every one of these challenges in a proficient, omnipresent, and practical way. Unavoidable equipment and programming are progressively getting cost-moderate, it can be introduced and worked in various locales (as often as patients possible visited), can be interfaced to a wide assortment of clinical data frameworks (e.g., patient data sets, clinical files), accordingly including various entertainers. Consequently, the unavoidable e-health frameworks present genuinely adaptable engineering covering an extensive range of commercial jobs and models.

14.6.2 Patient Bio-Signals and Acquisition Methods

An expansive meaning of a sign is a "quantifiable sign or portrayal of a genuine wonder", which in the field of bio-signals, alludes to discernible realities or improvements of organic frameworks or living things. To remove and archive the significance or the reason for a sign, a doctor may use straightforward assessment methods, like estimating the human body temperature or then again need to move toward exceptionally particular and at times meddling gear, like an endoscope. Following sign procurement, doctors go on to a second step, that of deciphering its significance, generally after some sort of sign improvement or "pre-handling", that isolates the caught data from commotion and sets it up for specific preparing, order and choice support calculations.

Bio-signals need a digitization step to be changed over into a reformist construction. This cycle begins with invigorating the rough sign in its basic construction, which is then dealt with into a straightforward (A/D) converter. Since the PCs cannot manage or store persevering data, the underlying advance of the change technique is to make a discrete-time game plan from the straightforward sort of the essential sign. This progression is acknowledged as "reviewing", and it is proposed to make a gathering of potentials inspected from the primary straightforward signs at presumed extends, which can reliably replicate the basic sign waveform. Quantization is the second step of digitization, which immediately manages the inspected assessments of the elementary sign and makes a sign, which is both momentarily and quantitatively discrete; from this, it can be inferred that the fundamental characteristics are changed over and encrypted by properties, for instance, bit distribution and worth reach. Fundamentally, quantization maps the tried sign to an extent of characteristics that is both negligible and capable for estimations to work with. The most prominent bio-signals used in unavoidable prosperity applications are summarized in the Table 14.1.

Table 14.1 Types of biomedical signals in health monitoring system.

Biomedical measurements (Broadly Used Biosignals)	Voltage range	Number of sensors	Information rate (b/s)
ECG	0.5–4 m	5–9	15,000
Heart sound	Extremely small	2–4	120,000
Heart rate	0.5–4 m	2	600
EEG	2–200 μ	20	4,200
EMG	0.1–5 m	2+	600,000
Respiratory rate	Small	1	800
Temperature of the body	0–100 m	1+	80

Figure 14.8 Electromyogram (EMG), gyroscope, and accelerometer sensors to monitor stroke [39].

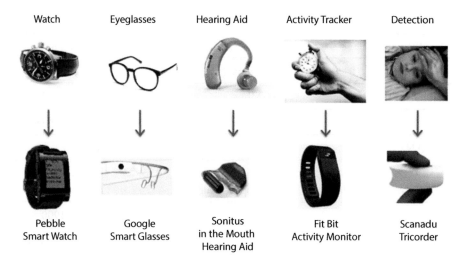

Figure 14.9 Wearable sensor devices for medical application.

Notwithstanding the previously mentioned bio-signals, patient physiological information (e.g., body development data dependent on accelerometer esteem), and setting mindful information (e.g., area, climate, and age bunch data) have likewise been utilized by inescapable well-being applications.

With regard to inescapable medical care applications, the securing of biomedical signs is performed through exceptional gadgets (for example sensors) joined on the patient's body as shown in Figure 14.8 or wearable gadgets as shown in Figure 14.9.

14.6.3 Communication Technologies Used in Healthcare Application

The two most fundamental empowering advances to wearable technology: on-body (wearable) and off-body associations. Late mechanical innovations have made possible another period of little, astounding, and portable registering gadgets. A wearable PC ought to be nearly nothing and sufficiently light to easily adjust inside pieces of clothing. Rarely, it is associated with decorations such as a belt, watch, or spectacles. A huge feature in wearable management systems is the way the gadgets are interconnected and share data. The off-body network partners with various frameworks that the client does not wear or convey on and it relies upon a Wireless Local Area Network (WLAN) establishment, whereas an on-body network, i.e., Wireless Personal Area Network. (WPAN) which is defined as IEEE 802.15 standard interfaces the actual gadgets; the other subsystems such as computers, sensors, and peripherals run at exceptionally designated mode. Table 14.2 shows the characteristics of distant accessibility and compact frameworks organization propels, correspondingly, that are associated to off-body and on-body. The most relevant technology for the unpreventable e-prosperity structures is IEEE 802.15.4, such as Bluetooth and ZigBee. The advancement of Bluetooth was at first proposed in 1994, by Ericsson, as a choice as opposed to joins associated mobile phone enhancements. It is a distant advancement that was used to enable any electrical contraption to pass on in the free ISM 2.5-GHz (grant-free) repeat band. It grants gadgets like cellphones, PDAs, headsets, and reduced PCs to grant and propel data to one

Table 14.2 Pervasive health systems applicable wireless technologies [40].

Technology	Data rate	Range	Frequency
IEEE 802.11a	54 Mbps	150 m	5 GHz
IEEE 802.11b	11 Mbps	150 m	2.4-GHZ ISM
Bluetooth (IEEE 802.15.1)	721 Kbps	10-150 m	2.4-GHZ ISM
HiperLAN2	54 Mbps	150 m	5 GHz
HomeRF [Shared Wireless Access Protocol (SWAP)]	16 Mbps (10 Mbps for ver. 2)	50 m	2.4-GHZ ISM
DECT	32 Kbps	100 m	1880-1900 MHz
PWT	32 Kbps	100 m	1920-1930 MHz
IEEE 802.15.3 (high data rate wireless personal area network)	11–55 Mbps	1–50 m	2.4-GHZ ISM
IEEE 802.16 (Local and Metropolitan Area Networks)	120 Mbps	City limits	2-66 GHz
IEEE 802.15.4 (low data rate wireless personal area network	250, 20, and 40 Kbps	100–300 m	2.4-GHz ISM, 868 MHz
ZigBee			915-MHz ISM
IrDA	4 Mbps (IrDA-1.1)	2 m	IR (0.90 μm)

another deprived of the prerequisite for wires or connections to interface the gadgets with each other.

It has been explicitly planned as a minimal effort, low size, and low power radio development that is particularly fit for the short extent of a Personal Area Organization (PAN). The essential features of Bluetooth are as follows:

1) Real-time information moves regularly possible between 10 and 15 m.
2) Aid of highlight point remote associations without links, similarly as highlight multipoint relationship with enable offhand close by far off associations.
3) Information Movement at the rate of 400 kb/s evenly or 700–150 kb/s of data disproportionately.

On the other hand, ZigBee (IEEE 802.15.4 standard) is made as a very less informed rate arrangement with multi month to multi-year battery life and less complexity. It is required to work in an unlicensed worldwide repeat band. The most limit data rates for each band are 250, 40, and 20 kbps, independently. The 2.4-GHz band works worldwide while the sub–1-GHz band works in North America, Europe, and Australia. Unavoidable clinical consideration structures set high mentioning necessities concerning energy, size, cost, adaptability, organization, and incorporation. Fluctuating size and cost goals clearly achieve relating moving cutoff focuses on the energy open, similarly as on enlisting, accumulating, and correspondence resources. Low force requirements are significant in like manner from prosperity deliberations since such structures run close or within the body. Versatility is other huge matter for unavoidable e–well-being requirements considering the way that of the possibility of customers and applications and the simplicity of the accessibility to other open distant associations. Both "off-body" and individual domain associations ought not have seen (LoS) necessities. The distinctive correspondence modalities can be used in different manners to build up a certifiable correspondence association. Two normal structures are framework-based organizations and promotion hoc networks. Portable impromptu organizations address complex frameworks that comprise of remote versatile hubs, which can unreservedly and powerfully self-arrange into self-assertive and impermanent, "impromptu" network geographies, permitting gadgets to flawlessly between network in territories with no previous correspondence framework or unified organization. The powerful scope of the sensors joined to a sensor hub characterizes the inclusion space of a sensor hub. Accompanied by inadequate inclusion, just pieces of the space of interest are enclosed by the sensor hubs. Accompanied by thick inclusion, the space of interest is totally (or totally) enclosed by sensors. The level of inclusion likewise impacts data preparing calculations. High inclusion is a key to strong frameworks and might be abused to expand the organization lifetime by changing repetitive hubs to power-saving rest mode.

14.6.4   Communication Technologies Based on Location/Position

Situating of people gives medical services applications the capacity to offer administrations like management of older patients or those with psychological instabilities who are walking however confined to a specific region. Besides, helped care workplaces are able to utilize network sensors and radio frequency ID recognizable pieces of proof to inform office laborers when patients left to a doled out security zone. Organization or satellite situating innovation additionally could be utilized for a rapid and precise finding of remote endorsers in a crisis and convey data about their area. Nearness data administrations can guide portable clients to a close-by medical services office. Area-based well-being data administrations can help find individuals coordinating with blood classifications, organ contributors, etc.

Situating methods can be carried out in two ways: self-situating and distant situating. In the primary methodology, gear that the client employments (for example, a movable miniature terminal, or a labeling gadget) utilizes signals, communicated by the doors/radio wires (which can either be earthly or satellite) to figure its self-position. All the more explicitly, the situating collector puts together the fitting sign estimations from topographically conveyed transmitters and utilizes these estimations. Advancements based on satellite technologies such as the Global Positioning System (GPS) technology or earthbound foundation based (such as utilizing the cellphone identification number of a bought-in portable terminal). The subsequent strategy is far off situating. For this condition, the individual is often located by estimating the signs heading bent and from a group of collectors. Much more unequivocally, the beneficiaries, which can be introduced at any rate one districts, measure a sign beginning from, or reflecting off, what to be found. Such sign appraisals has to be used to choose the length similarly as heading of the individual radio advances, and sometime later, the advantageous terminal region is dealt with from mathematical relationship; on an essential level, a solitary evaluation makes a straight-line locus from the distant beneficiary to the cell phone. The other Angle of Arrival (AOA) assessment will yield a subsequent straight route, the intersection point reason for the two lines giving the fix position for this development. Time deferral could be, in like manner, be utilized. As electromagnetic waves (EM) travel at the speed of light in free space, the distance among two centers could be steadily evaluated by reviewing the time delay of a radio wave sent among them. The abovementioned strategy is appropriate for the satellite frameworks.

14.7   Intelligent Electronic Healthcare Systems

14.7.1   The Background of Electronic Healthcare Systems

The systems administration applications can know about the presence and qualities of the client's exercises as well as conditions. In quickly evolving situations, for example, the ones considered in the fields of versatile, inescapable, or omnipresent processing, frameworks need to adjust their conduct in light of the present conditions and the dynamicity of the climate they are drenched in [41]. A framework is setting mindful on the off chance that it can separate, decipher, what is more, use setting data and adjust its usefulness to the current setting of utilization. The test for such frameworks lies in the intricacy of catching, addressing, and handling context-oriented information. To catch setting data for the most part some extra sensors, as well as projects, are required. The way setting mindful applications utilize setting can be classified into the three after classes: introducing data and administrations, executing assistance, and labeling caught information. Introducing data and administrations alludes to applications that by the same token present setting data to the client, or utilize setting to propose fitting determinations of activities to the client. Consequently, carrying out a help portrays applications that trigger an order, or reconfigure the framework for the client as per setting changes. Appending setting data for later recovery alludes to applications that label caught information with significant setting data.

14.7.2   Intelligent Agents in Electronic Healthcare System

Clever specialists can be seen as self-governing programming (or equipment) develops that is proactively engaged with accomplishing a foreordained assignment and simultaneously responding to its current circumstance. As per [42], specialists are prepared to do the following:

- performing assignments (in the interest of clients or different specialists).
- associating with clients to get directions and give reactions.
- working self-sufficiently without direct intercession by clients, including checking the climate and following up on the climate to bring about necessary changes.
- showing insight to decipher checked occasions and form suitable choices.

Specialists can be proactive (regarding having the option to show objective coordinated conduct), receptive (having the option to react to changes in the climate, including recognizing and imparting to different specialists), and independent (forming choices and controlling their activities free of others). Keen specialists can be likewise considered as friendly elements that can speak with different specialists utilizing a specialist correspondence language during the time spent completing their errands.

14.7.3   Patient Data Classification Techniques

Information or data arrangement is a significant issue in an assortment of designing and logical trains such as science, brain research, medication, promoting PC vision, and man-made reasoning [43]. Its primary item is to group objects into various classifications or classes. Contingent upon the application, these items could be pictures or sign waveforms or any sort of estimations of the ones needed to be characterized. Given a particular information highlight, its characterization may comprise of one of the accompanying two assignments: a) directed grouping in which the input design is recognized as an individual from a predefined class; b) unaided arrangement in which the example is appointed to an until-now obscure class.

In quantifiable information demand, input information is tended to by a great deal of "n" highlights, or characteristics, seen as a section vector of n-dimension. The request structure is worked in the following two modes: planning and course of action. Data pre-processing and preparing can be moreover acted to area the case of interest from the establishment, dispose of fuss, normalize the model, and some other movement that contributes in describing a negligible depiction of the plan. During readiness mode, the segment assurance module will track down the suitable features for tending to the data plans in the meanwhile the classifier is set up to fragment the component space. The analysis way allows a maker to improve the preprocessing and feature extraction/assurance strategies. In the portrayal mode, the pre-arranged classifier assigns the data guide to one among the model classes reasonable ward on the conscious features. There is a colossal area of set up request methodologies, going from conventional quantifiable techniques, similar to straight and determined backslide, to the neural association and tree-based procedures [e.g., feed-forward networks, which consolidates multi-layer wisdom, Radial Basis Function (RBF), Self-Organizing Guide/Korhonen-Networks, and, in the future, Support Vector Machines].

Different kinds of cross-breed–wise frameworks are neuro-fluffy versatile frameworks which can include a versatile fluffy regulator and an organization-based indicator. With regard to shrewd unavoidable well-being frameworks, input characterization information can be both biomedical signs, physiological, and context-oriented information. Created arrangement results can contain data concerning the situation with a patient, proposed conclusion, standards of conduct, and so forth.

14.8   Conclusion

Intelligent healthcare systems play a vital role in day today life of humans and is used for remote monitoring of health parameters such as heart rate, blood pressure, ECG, and EEG. Technologies such as 3G, 4G, LTE, and 5G help healthcare systems to store and transport the acquired data at remote locations where the specialized health professionals such as doctors and nurses are available. In this book chapter, a comprehensive review of such type of intelligent healthcare system has been presented. The review included brain computing–based, robotic, and IoT-based healthcare systems with the intent that the readers of this book chapter gets benefitted by reading this chapter.

References

1. Varshney, U., *Pervasive Healthcare Computing*, p. 288, Springer, US, 2009.
2. Birnbaum, J., Pervasive information systems. *Commun. ACM*, 40, 2, 40–41, 1997.
3. Rani, S., Ahmed, S.H., Shah, S.C., Smart health: A novel paradigm to control the chickungunya virus. *IEEE Internet Things J.*, 6, 2, 1306–1311, 2019.
4. Padhy, N.P., *Artificial Intelligence and Intelligent Systems*, p. 631, Oxford University Press, United Kingdom, Feb. 15, 2005.
5. Shin, C. and Xu, Y., *Intelligent Systems: Modeling, Optimization, and Control*, 1st ed, p. 456, CRC Press, Boca Raton, 2009.
6. Hopgood, A., *Intelligent Systems for Engineers and Scientists*, 3rd ed, p. 301, CRC Press, Boca Raton, Jan. 12, 2012.
7. Rajput, A.A. and Nanavati, N., *Speech in Mobile and Pervasive Environments*, p. 352, Wiley U.S, United States, 2012.
8. Schmitt, W. and Minker, A., *Towards Adaptive Spoken Dialog Systems*, 1st ed, p. 254, Springer Verlag, New York, 2013.
9. Bandopadhaya, S., Dey, R., Suhag, A., Integrated healthcare monitoring solutions for soldier using the internet of things with distributed computing. *Sustain. Comput. Inf. Syst.*, Elsevier, vol. 26, 100378, 2020.
10. McEwen, H. and Cassimally, A., *Designing the Internet of Things*, 1st ed, p. 313, Wiley, Hoboken, 2013.
11. Holler, D., Tsiatsis, J., Mulligan, V., Avesand, C., Karnouskos, S., Boyle, S., *From Machine-to-Machine to the Internet of Things: Introduction to a New Age of Intelligence*, p. 327, Academic Press, Cambridge, Massachusetts, 2014.
12. Batty, M., *The New Science of Cities*, p. 520, MIT Press, Cambridge, Nov. 2013.
13. Sha, K., Alatrash, N., Wang, Z., A Secure and Efficient Framework to Read Isolated Smart Grid Devices. *IEEE Trans. Smart Grid*, 8, 6, 2519–2531, 2017.
14. Bai, D., Zhuang, Y., Wang, H., *Advanced Fuzzy Logic Technologies in Industrial Applications*, 1st ed, p. 342, Springer, London, 2006.
15. Dayan, L. and Abbott, P., *Theoretical Neuroscience: Computational and Mathematical Modeling of Neural Systems*, p. 526, MIT Press, Cambridge, 2005.
16. Wolpaw, E.W. and Wolpaw, J., *Brain-Computer Interfaces: Principles and Practice*, 1st ed, p. 419, Oxford University Press, United Kingdom, 2012.
17. Allison, A., Dunne, B.Z., Leeb, S., Del, R., Millán, R., Nijholt, J., *Towards Practical Brain-Computer Interfaces: Bridging the Gap from Research to Real-World Applications*, p. 423, Springer, Heidelberg Oct. 12, 2012.
18. Shih, J.J., Krusienski, D.J., Wolpaw, J.R., Brain-computer interfaces in medicine. *Mayo Clin. Proc.*, 87, 3, 268–279, 2012.
19. Berger, H., Über das Elektrenkephalogramm des Menschen - Dritte Mitteilung. *Arch. Psychiatr. Nervenkr.*, 94, 1, 231–23316–60, 1931.
20. Abdulkader, S.N., Atia, A., Mostafa, M.S.M., Brain computer interfacing: Applications and challenges. *Egypt. Inform. J.*, 16, 2, 213–230, 2015.

21. Hanafiah, Z.M., Taib, M.N., Hamid, N.H.A., EEG pattern of smokers for Theta, Alpha and Beta band frequencies. *2010 IEEE Student Conference on Research and Development (SCOReD)*, pp. 320–323, 2010.

22. Selvam, V.S. and Shenbagadevi, S., Brain tumor detection using scalp EEG with modified Wavelet-ICA and multi layer feed forward neural network. *Proc. Annu. Int. Conf. IEEE Eng. Med. Biol. Soc. EMBS*, pp. 6104–6109, 2011.

23. Sharanreddy, B. and Kulkarni, P.K., Detection of Primary Brain Tumor Present in EEG signal using Wavelet Transform and Neural Network. *Int. J. Biol. Med. Res.*, 4, 1, 2855–2859, 2013. [Online]. Available: www.biomedscidirect.com.

24. Sreedharan, S., Sitaram, R., Paul, J.S., Kesavadas, C., Brain-computer interfaces for neurorehabilitation. *Crit. Rev. Biomed. Eng.*, 41, 3, 269–279, 2013.

25. Sellakumar, S., Manonmani, A., Arivalagan, M., Lavanya, M., Coma patient monitoring using brain computer interface. *Int. J. Psychosoc. Rehabil.*, 24, 3, 3701–3710, 2020.

26. Zemmar, A., Lozano, A.M., Nelson, B.J., The rise of robots in surgical environments during COVID-19. *Nat. Mach. Intell.*, 2, 10, 566–572, 2020.

27. Liu, K.C., Wang, D., Tan, L., *Design and control of intellegent robotic systems*, p. 491, Springer, Heidelberg, 2009.

28. Mutlu, B. and Forlizzi, J., Robots in organizations: The role of workflow, social, and environmental factors in human-robot interaction. *HRI 2008 - Proc. 3rd ACM/IEEE Int. Conf. Human-Robot Interact. Living with Robot*, pp. 287–294, 2008.

29. Romeo, L., Petitti, A., Marani, R., Milella, A., Internet of robotic things in smart domains: Applications and challenges. *Sensors (Switzerland)*, 20, 12, 1–23, Jun. 12, 2020.

30. Afanasyev, I. *et al.*, Towards the internet of robotic things: Analysis, architecture, components and challenges. *Proc. - Int. Conf. Dev. eSystems Eng. DeSE*, pp. 3–8, Oct. 20, 2019.

31. Baniqued, P.D. *et al.*, Brain–computer interface robotics for hand rehabilitation after stroke: a systematic review. *J. Neuroeng. Rehabil.*, 18, 1, 1–25, 2021.

32. Dunkin, B., Adrales, G.L., Apelgren, K., Mellinger, J.D., Surgical simulation: A current review. *Surg. Endosc.*, 21, 3, 357–366, 2007.

33. Visarius, H., Gong, J., Scheer, C., Haralamb, S., Nplte, L.P., Man-Machine Interfaces in Computer Assisted Surgery. *Comput. Aided Surg.*, 2, 2, 102–107, 1997.

34. Mejia, N., Voice Recognition in Healthcare – A Brief Overview. https://emerj.com/ai-sector-overviews/voice-recognition-healthcare.

35. Mohammed, K., II *et al.*, Real-Time Remote-Health Monitoring Systems: a Review on Patients Prioritisation for Multiple-Chronic Diseases, Taxonomy Analysis, Concerns and Solution Procedure. *J. Med. Syst.*, 43, 7, 2019.

36. Niswar, M. *et al.*, The design of wearable medical device for triaging disaster casualties in developing countries. *2015 5th Int. Conf. Digit. Inf. Process. Commun. ICDIPC 2015*, pp. 207–212, 2015.

37. Gómez, J., Oviedo, B., Zhuma, E., Patient Monitoring System Based on Internet of Things. *Proc. Comput. Sci.*, 83, 90–97, 2016.

38. Hindia, M.N., Rahman, T.A., Ojukwu, H., Hanafi, E.B., Fattouh, A., Enabling remote health-caring utilizing IoT concept over LTE-femtocell networks. *PloS One*, 11, 5, 1–17, 2016.

39. Malan, D., Fulford-Jones, T., Welsh, M., Moulton, S., Codeblue: An ad hoc sensor network infrastructure for emergency medical care. *International Workshop on Wearable and Implantable Body Sensor Networks*, pp. 12–14, 2004.

40. Doukas, C. and Maglogiannis, I., Intelligent pervasive healthcare systems. *Stud. Comput. Intell.*, 107, 95–115, 2008.

41. Khedo, K.K., Context-aware systems for mobile and ubiquitous networks. *Proc. Int. Conf. Networking, Int. Conf. Syst. Int. Conf. Mob. Commun. Learn. Technol.*, 123, 2006.

42. Fox, J., Beveridge, M., Glasspool, D., Understanding intelligent agents: Analysis and synthesis. *AI Commun.*, 16, 3, 139–152, 2003.

43. Zhai, J.H., Zhang, S.F., Wang, X.Z., An overview of pattern classification methodologies. *Proc. 2006 Int. Conf. Mach. Learn. Cybern*, pp. 3222–3227, August 2006.

15

Design of Antennas for Microwave Imaging Techniques

Dnyaneshwar D. Ahire[1]*, **Gajanan K. Kharate[1] and Ammar Muthana[2]†**

[1]Matoshri College of Engineering and Research Centre, Nashik, Maharashtra, India
[2]Department of Communication Networks and Data Transmission, The Bonch-Bruevich Saint-Petersburg State University of Telecommunications (SPBSUT), St. Petersburg, Russia

Abstract

The present epidemic of coronavirus (COVID-19) was originated in Wuhan, China, on 31 December 2019. After that, it spread worldwide, and continues to this day. Its affects are deadly and keeps all countries around the world in lockdown. Countries are fighting with it by keeping lockdown and by developing vaccines to save human life. Due to this pandemic situation, people who have other diseases are in fear to go to hospitals because of infections. Many medical devices are available to monitor ourselves at home itself, like oximeters, thermometer, blood pressure monitoring devices, and blood sugar monitoring devices. If similar devices were available for breast cancer detection, it would help many women to save their lives and get treatment in time. This chapter focuses on such technology that is known as microwave imaging technology, where wideband antennas play a vital role. The design of such antennas is a challenge for researchers; here, few of the designs of ultra-wideband antenna are presented.

Keywords: UWB, FCC, VSWR, COVID-19, FCC, patch antenna, microstrip

15.1 Introduction

Precise diagnosis of the diseases is foremost issues in today's leading biomedical field for human being. Well-timed finding of life-threatening diseases like cancer, tuberculosis, and brain tumors is still a challenging task and boundless necessity of society. Preceding decades show that the main cause of death is cancer. After heart diseases, numerous kinds of cancers are the key reason for early death. The cancer cases in India are likely to be 13.9 lakh in 2020 and possibly will rise up to 15.7 lakh by 2025. The number of breast cancer patients is contributing 2 lakhs (14.8%) and the number of cervix cancer patients is contributing 0.75 lakh (5.4%) among women, whereas the number of patients for gastrointestinal tract is contributing 2.7% for both men and women. One out of 28 woman is probable to develop breast cancer through her lifetime [1]. It is a diseases characterized

---

*Corresponding author: dnyaneshwar.ahire@matoshri.edu.in
†Corresponding author: muthanna.asa@spbgut.ru

Tushar H. Jaware, K. Sarat Kumar, Ravindra D. Badgujar and Svetlin Antonov (eds.) *Medical Imaging and Health Informatics*, (275–302) © 2022 Scrivener Publishing LLC

by the outgoing growth and spread of abnormal cells. If the spread of abnormal cells is not controlled, then it can result in death. Breast cancer is most serious type of cancer and second leading cancer that affects many women which occur in the prime of their lives. Breast cancer is a proliferation of malignant cells that arises in the breast tissue, specifically in the terminal ductal-lobular unit. It can be possible to prevent the undesired growth of malignant tissues in human body if they are being detected early and accurately [2–4]. Various methods exist to detect malignant tissues inside human body. However, these methods are limited due to their false positive and false negative diagnosis. Likewise, these techniques are trustworthy, and individual is not feeling ease while experiencing it. Microwave imaging (MI) is one of the upcoming innovations to beat every one of these limitations and give an answer to detect malignancy at the very early stage to keep the life of person [5–9].

15.1.1 Overview

With the advent of a tremendous update and upgrade in communication technology, it becomes challenging to supply the demand of an unprecedented rise in the bandwidth of the services. One of the major applications in the medical field, where wideband microstrip patch antenna (MPA) is a suitable candidate on which the specialist can rely for the diagnosis of malignant tissues in at an early stage. Federal Communications Commission (FCC) recommends ultra-wideband (UWB) that is approximate for early detection of malignant tissues in the human body. FCC has defined the standard of a 7.5GHz (from 3.1 to 10.6 GHz) bandwidth for UWB wireless communications. Microwave signals have shown a great usefulness in a wide variety of applications. Owing to their penetrative nature in the human body, one of the useful applications of all is the use of microwave signals to see through dielectric structures. MI is a competent investigative modality for non-invasive imagining dielectric properties of human bodies. Growing attention toward this field has been paid during this era. Many application areas in the biomedical field have been cited. Medical imaging is considered as the most effective way of diagnosis of malignant tissues, where x-ray, mammography, and magnetic resonance imaging (MRI) are the leading methodologies; however, those are not appropriate for the bulky scale screening program. False-negative rate and false-positive rate to detect malignancies using mammography is up to 15%. Many a times, there is a need to go for the incisive biopsy to verify a diagnosis. MI possibly would be quite inexpensive and has big potential to overcome limitations of existing methodologies. MPA used in biomedical devices help the specialist medical professionals to diagnose the fatal disease. With this objective to contribute in the designing miniaturized MPA for biomedical applications, research work is carried out. We have designed and developed a wideband candidate suitable for the biomedical application, which is significantly appropriate due wide bandwidth and desired radiation pattern. The research is directed toward the design and development of wideband MPA followed by testing, analysis, and validation. In this research work, the designs of various wideband MPAs are presented. Varieties of probe and microstrip line feed wideband patch antenna designs have been presented. Probe feed design achieves bandwidth up to 2.43 GHz. Furthermore, to enhance bandwidth, microstrip feed line technique is applied which helps to overcome the problem of inductive effect of probe. Further, monopole wideband antennas have been proposed. Slotting and defective ground structure techniques are used to improve bandwidth.

Length of current flow has been modified and increased by incorporating rounded corner shape cutted to the lower side of radiating patch. Rounded corner shape cutted to the upper corner of partial ground plane has been introduced which helps to match impedance. Samples of design have been presented, and results of simulated and fabricated designs are observed and analyzed. The novel key-shaped oval slotted antenna with rounded corner and a groove-shaped notch in the partial ground is implemented. Implemented design resonates from 3.20 to 20.46 GHz, which covers FCC-defined UWB, suitable for biomedical applications. Measurement has been carried out for simulated and fabricated designs.

15.2   Literature

MPAs are used in various biomedical applications. It has been studied that, for biomedical application, wideband MPAs are required. Various bandwidth enhancement techniques are also studied and reviewed. It is observed that bandwidth is directly proportional to the thickness of substrate used; however, it may increase the overall volume of MPA. For biomedical applications, compact, light-weight, and low profile MPAs are desired. Therefore, low thickness substrates are studied. It has been observed that, using slotting, stacking techniques bandwidth can be enhanced. However, as the bandwidth is limited due to probe inductance, microstrip feed line technique is one of the techniques used to cope up with the problem of bandwidth limitation to some extent. The papers from various researchers of high repute journals are reviewed.

MI is a technique that has been advanced from older detecting techniques in order to estimate hidden objects in a structure using electromagnetic (EM) waves in microwave system (i.e., ~300 MHz to 300 GHz). The use of MI in biomedical applications was first demonstrated by Larsen and Jacobi et al. in the late 70s, and they designed a basic water immersed antenna for biomedical applications [7]. This was the first time where someone has started the use of a biological object with microwaves, to create images of the internal structures of the body. Recently, researchers suggested the use of MI for breast tumor detection, in particular the biomedical application, offering a promising trade-off between imaging resolution and tissue penetration. MI for biomedical is currently a very capable technology for wireless communications having characteristics of very high speed, high precision radars, and imaging systems [8]. MI for biomedical application has established a massive attention because it has the ability to access the breast for imaging. The breast imaging technique develops the signal scattering from the object, when the object is scanned by an EM signal. MBI uses small amount of power and larger wavelength signals as compared to existing technique x-ray mammography, to acquire facts about breast tissues, and assures a harmless and more correct technique for regular breast scanning. The signal spreading by an object is determined by on numerous factors, including the surroundings, signal power, and the material dielectric characteristics of the object. This technique is applied to discover the malignant tumor in the breast by means of microwave signals. To reduce the effect of signal replication from the breast skin, a new methodology of keeping the antenna in-contact with the breast skin has made an attempt. In this technique, the skin is treated as a layer of the antenna substrate, and the upshot of having the antenna in contact with the skin is involved in the antenna design [9]. In the earlier years' substantial progress has been made by means of microwaves for breast cancer finding. MI can be well defined as sighted the internal structure of an object by enlightening the object with small power EM wave at microwave frequencies. In this passive, hybrid and active methodologies to breast cancer finding are being researched. Such approaches would be valuable to patients as both ionizing radiation and breast compression are easily avoided. By considering the requirements of scattered microwave signal reflected from malignant tissue; FCC has allotted unlicensed UWB range of frequencies from 3.1 to 10.6 GHz for various biomedical applications. Antennas are an integral part of the wireless communication system; it attracts the minds of researches to have some modification in the present design technology to achieve better performance characteristics. The basic goal of antenna design with higher performance includes wide bandwidth which covers basically UWB range along with size reduction which was obtained by various techniques such as slotting, metamaterial, defective ground structure, and various feeding techniques. To transmit UWB signals, antenna must have a high level, which is used as transmitter and receiver. This condition thus restricts the class of antenna that can be developed. The existing antennas used for breast cancer detection have been nothing but a compact microstrip antenna [11].

15.2.1   Microstrip Patch Antenna

A new class of omnidirectional antenna has been discussed, and these are wraparound microstrip antennas, flat thin microstrip antennas, and A-phased array that consists of flat (or curved) thin microstrip antennas. These antennas have capability of producing expectable and nearly perfect omnidirectional coverage (R.E. Munson, 1974) [12]. Microstrip antennas ideally suited to applications, which require low-profile antenna elements or conformal arrays at frequencies from UHF up to S band, have been discussed by the researcher [13]. A novel technique to examine a microstrip antenna which includes demonstrating the antenna by acceptable wire grid immersed in a dielectric medium and then using Richmond's response preparation to estimate the piecewise currents on the wire grid divisions has been showed by Pradeep K. Agrawal and M. C. Bailey in 1977. This method will support as an exceptional tool to design microstrip antennas [14]. In 2011, Custodio Peixerio has presented historic perspective of development of MPA. Basically, a survey on MPA carried out initially along the evolution since last 40 years. It has been observed that since last 30 years the research development in MPA increased rapidly [15]. The evaluation of three popular designs of MPAs, i.e., rectangular, square, and hexagonal, has been done by experimentation conducted by Vinita Mathur and Dr. Manisha Gupta in year 2014. Designing initiates with the design of patches and, after that, its analysis. All MPAs have been analyzed using high-frequency structure simulator (HFSS) and dealt benefits such as low-profile constructions, frivolous, suitable gain, and small in size [16]. The researchers concluded the following:

- Same radiation pattern is observed in rectangular and square patches.
- Feed line impedance value is taken as 50 Ω having good input/output matching value of the antennas.
- The throughput of optimized hexagonal shape antenna is much enhanced in comparison to that of a regular rectangular and square patch antenna.
- Substrate having high loss tangent value is used, and simulated parameters are observed.

Many more feeding techniques have been used as follows:

- Probe feed technique of MPA
- Use of slotting and stacking methods on MPA
- Microstrip Line Feed techniques

15.2.2   Early Detection of Breast Cancer and Microstrip Patch Antenna for Biomedical Application

Breast cancer grows from breast tissues. Symptoms of breast cancer might a lump in the breast, a variation in breast figure, lumpiness of the skin, fluid start to come out from the nipple, a newly inverted nipple, or a red or scaly patch of skin. X-ray mammography method is used to discover the breast cancer. However, the main drawback in this method is the ionizing radiation level from x-rays, which causes cell death, cell change, and fatal destruction inside the body. Hence, the MI method is planned to acquire the details about breast tissues using antenna structure. In 1999, Susan C. Hagness, Allen Taflove, and Jack E. Bridges have designed a novel UWB microwave radar technology to discover and image at very early-stage, malignant tumors that are every so often undetectable to x-rays. In the present work, basically, the technique and initial results of three-dimensional finite-difference time-domain (FDTD) simulations have been carried out. The work mainly emphasizes on the design of a single resistively loaded bowtie antenna element of a planned confocal sensor array. The sensor array of dynamic range comprises of such elements fit in with existing microwave equipment to discover lesser cancerous tumors typically missed by x-ray mammography [59].

UWB, a new class of antenna, is a short-range communications methodology, which sends the signal in the form of short pulses. These earlier military tools have extended a lot of popularity among researchers and the wireless engineering. UWB has also offered extraordinary data rates at short distances with small power, as it has wide resolution bandwidth. A rectangular monopole on one side of an FR4 substrate of thickness 1.6 mm and relative permittivity 4.4 with the partial ground plane located on the other side has been practically studied and experimented. The antenna gave excellent performance for UWB system, ranging from 3.7 to 13.8 GHz. Width of the half-done ground, feed line width, and its position played an important role for appropriate frequency band [75]. In 2008, J. Rashed-Mohassel and N. Ghassemi have presented an aperture coupled patch antenna with a rectangular antenna located on above of two slots on ground area with U-shaped feed line for UWB application. The patch and slots have been separated by an air gap and a material with low dielectric constant and relative permittivity of 2.2. There was a 50-Ω feed line which was divided into two 100-Ω feed lines by a two-way microstrip power divider under the ground plane. Simulation results show that the antenna has VSWR less than 2 for 5.3 to 13.2 GHz [76].

15.2.3   UWB for Microwave Imaging

For the proposed antenna, rectangular patches are used; one is a rectangular ring and second one is a small rectangular patch. Ring patch that is rectangular in shape is used for radiation and small rectangular patch is for coaxial probe feed. Small circular shape slot on radiating patch will enhance the bandwidth. However, we cannot increase more and more area of hole, to increase the bandwidth of an antenna. Antenna has a return loss less than −9.5-dB loss from frequency range of 4.4 to 8.42 GHz, and bandwidth is of 4.02 GHz. This large bandwidth is beneficial for taking image with high resolution, and it is also beneficial in fast signal processing. This antenna has 66.44 % impedance bandwidth, so it is UWB antenna, as we are all familiar that UWB devices have at least 20% impedance bandwidth [78].

In 2014, M. Aziz ul Haqand and M. Arif Khan have proposed an patch antenna with the ring slots on FR-4 substrate an fed through a microstrip feed line by optimizing the width and the position parameters of the feed line along with the width of the partial ground structure. The main antenna is made up of of four circular rings. Circular patch antennas have widespread use in wireless transceiver applications [79].

15.3   Design and Development of Wideband Antenna

15.3.1   Overview

MPA is a low profile, narrowband, wide pillar radio antenna created by scratching receiving antenna component design in metal follow attached to a protecting dielectric substrate, for example, PCB with a metal layer clung to an opposite side of substrate which shapes a ground plane. MPA is also called as printed reception apparatus as it is specifically imprinted onto circuit board. Essentially, a miniaturized scale microstrip antenna is only a metallic fix suspended over a ground plane. It is built on dielectric substrate utilizing a procedure like lithography. Patch antenna in its easiest arrangement comprises transmitting patch on one side of a FR4 dielectric substrate and ground plane on opposite side. Main working drawbacks of patch antenna are small productivity, low power, high Q and false radiations from feed point, and limited transfer speed. The general objective of configuration is to accomplish particular execution attributes at planned operating frequency. In the event that MPA can accomplish these general objectives, then the principal choice is to choose reasonable antenna structure. Rectangular antenna can be planned utilizing accompanying methodology. Substrate selection: First step to design antenna is to pick suitable substrate of suitable thickness and loss tangent. Thicker substrate's actuality and mechanically durability will build the radiated power, diminish conductor loss, and enhance impedance bandwidth. Transmission Line Model: Transmission line model is simplest model to understand the execution of a MPA. The operation of this model is mainly founded on comparable magnetic current circulation everywhere the patch edges [24]. The patch is represented by two conductors that are isolated by dielectric having thickness in terms of wavelength. Patch width has slight effect on the frequency and radiation pattern on microstrip antenna. It affects the input resistance and bandwidth. The patch width should be selected to obtain good radiation efficiency. Suggested value is that $1 < W/L < 2$ [24]. Patch length determines the resonant frequency.

The effective patch length L_{eff} is given by

$$L_{\text{eff}} = \frac{c}{2f_r \sqrt{\epsilon_{r_{eff}}}} \tag{15.1}$$

Additional line length ΔL is given by

$$\frac{\Delta L}{h} = 0.412 \frac{\left(\epsilon_{ref}f + 0.3\right)\left(\dfrac{w}{h} + 0.2264\right)}{\left(\epsilon_{ref}f - 0.258\right)\left(\dfrac{w}{h} + 0.8\right)} \tag{15.2}$$

where w is width of patch and h is thickness of substrate.

Effective dielectric constant is given by

$$\epsilon_{ref}f = \frac{\left(\epsilon_r + 1\right)}{2} + \frac{\left(\epsilon_r - 1\right)}{2\sqrt{1 + 12\left(\dfrac{h}{w}\right)}} \tag{15.3}$$

Patch length value is given by

$$L = L_{eff} - 2\Delta L \tag{15.4}$$

Patch width is given by

$$W = \frac{c\sqrt{\dfrac{2}{1 + \epsilon_r}}}{2f_r} \tag{15.5}$$

The resonating frequency is given by

$$f_r = \frac{c}{2(L + 2\Delta L)\sqrt{\epsilon_{reff}}} \tag{15.6}$$

15.3.2   Design of Rectangular Microstrip Patch Antenna

The geometry of a rectangular microstrip fabricated patch antenna is shown in Figures 15.1 and 15.2. The structure has been planned in utilizing a substrate FR4 having dielectric constant of 4.4, loss tangent of 0.02, thickness of 1.59 mm. The transmitting patch is sustained by a 50-ohm microstrip probe feed. The radiating rectangular microstrip patch and probe feed are set on top side of the substrate and the ground plane set on the other side of the radiating patch. The antenna design is simulated and enhanced by the full wave EM recreation programming CADFEKO suite, utilizing the method of moment. Feed purpose of coaxial feed strategy is 6.7 mm on x-axis.

Figure 15.1 Fabricated rectangular microstrip patch in antenna radiating patch.

Figure 15.2 Fabricated rectangular microstrip patch in antenna ground plane.

For the design of rectangular MPA, the width and the length of the microstrip patch and of the substrate are calculated using the following equations. These parameters are the functions of resonance frequency, dielectric constant of the substrate, height of the substrate, and velocity of light.

$$W = \frac{c\sqrt{\dfrac{2}{1+\epsilon_r}}}{2f_r} \tag{15.7}$$

$$L_{eff} = \frac{c}{2fr\sqrt{\epsilon_{reff}}} \tag{15.8}$$

$$\epsilon_{reff} = \frac{(\epsilon_r+1)}{2} + \frac{(\epsilon_r-1)}{2\sqrt{1+12\left(\dfrac{h}{w}\right)}} \tag{15.9}$$

$$\frac{\Delta L}{h} = 0.412 \frac{\left(\epsilon_{reff} + 0.3\right)\left(\dfrac{w}{h} + 0.2264\right)}{\left(\epsilon_{reff} - 0.258\right)\left(\dfrac{w}{h} + 0.8\right)} \tag{15.10}$$

The resonance frequency is $f_r = 2.45$ GHz, dielectric constant of the substrate is $\varepsilon_r = 4.4$, and thickness of the substrate is $h = 1.59$ mm. The antenna has been designed, and the parameters are calculated as $W_p = 37.26$ mm, $L_p = 29.21$ mm, $W_{sub} = 46.36$ mm, and $L_{sub} = 37.82$ mm.

15.3.3   Design of Microstrip Line Feed Rectangular Microstrip Patch Antenna

In the probe feed technique, the inductance of the probe dominates the capacitance of the patch that limits the bandwidth of the antenna. This problem can be overcome up to certain extent by providing the capacitive strip. This problem can be solved by using line feed technique.

The simple line feed rectangular MPA radiating patch and ground plane is as shown in Figures 15.3 and 15.4, respectively. Here for the rectangular microstrip patch the input is provided by a thin line. It is comprised of radiating patch (length $L_p = 28$ mm and width $W_p = 37$ mm) and substrate (length $L_{sub} = 70$ mm, width $W_{sub} = 70$ mm, and thickness $h = 1.59$ mm). Microstrip feed line has length $F_l = 30$ mm and width $F_w = 3$ mm. The radiating patch is fed by 50-ohm microstrip line. CADFEKO, the full wave EM simulation software, is utilized to simulate and optimize the antenna.

Characteristic impedance Z_0 can be calculated as

$$Z_0 = \frac{60}{\sqrt{\varepsilon_{re}}} \ln\left(\frac{8h}{W} + \frac{W}{4h}\right) for \frac{W}{h} \leq 1 \tag{15.11}$$

$$Z_0 = \frac{120\pi}{\sqrt{\varepsilon_{re}\left[\dfrac{W}{h} + 1.393 + 0.667\ln\left(\dfrac{W}{h} + 1.444\right)\right]}} for \frac{W}{h} \geq 1 \tag{15.12}$$

For given Z_0 and ε_{re}, the W/h ratio can be found as

$$\varepsilon_{re} = \frac{\varepsilon_r + 1}{2} = 2.7 \tag{15.13}$$

For $z_0\sqrt{\varepsilon_{re}} = 50\sqrt{2.7} = 82.15 < 89.91 \ i.e.A < 1.52$

$$\frac{W}{h} = \frac{2}{\pi}\left[B - 1 - \ln(2B - 1) + \frac{\varepsilon_r - 1}{2\varepsilon_r}\left\{\ln(B - 1) + 0.39 - \frac{0.61}{\varepsilon_r}\right\}\right] \tag{15.14}$$

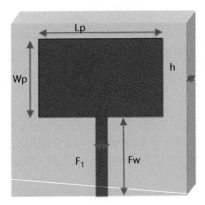

Figure 15.3 Microstrip line feed rectangular microstrip patch in antenna radiating patch.

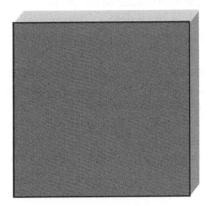

Figure 15.4 Microstrip line feed rectangular microstrip patch in antenna ground plane.

$$A = \frac{Z_0}{60}\sqrt{\frac{\varepsilon_r + 1}{2}} + \frac{\varepsilon_r - 1}{\varepsilon_r + 1}\left(0.23 + \frac{0.11}{\varepsilon_r}\right) \tag{15.15}$$

$$B = \frac{60\pi^2}{Z_0\sqrt{\varepsilon_r}} \tag{15.16}$$

$$B = 5.64$$

After putting the value of B

$$\frac{W}{h} = 1.94$$

$$h = 1.59mm$$

So,

$$W = 3.01 \ mm$$

These are the calculated values of length and width of microstrip line feed.

Frequency domain performance of microstrip line feed rectangular MPA is observed, and detail discussion of the results is presented. It resonates at four frequencies, and it has a bandwidth in the range of 100 to 240 MHz, but the gain is low.

15.3.4   Design of Microstrip Line Feed Rectangular Microstrip Patch Antenna with Partial Ground

To improve the radiation pattern of MPA and to avoid the radiation due to microstrip line which is used for the feeding, the concept of partial ground has been introduced. The geometrical structure of the microstrip line feed rectangular MPA with partial ground radiating patch and ground plane is as shown in Figures 15.5 and 15.6, respectively.

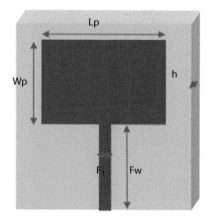

Figure 15.5 Microstrip line feed rectangular microstrip patch antenna in partial ground radiating patch.

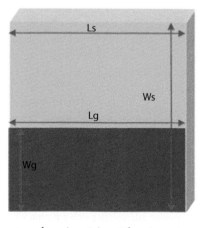

Figure 15.6 Microstrip line feed rectangular microstrip patch antenna in partial ground plane.

The structure has patch (length L_p = 28 mm and width W_p = 37 mm), substrate (length L_{sub} = 70 mm, width W_{sub} = 70 mm, and thickness h = 1.59 mm), and partial ground (length L_g = 28 mm and width W_g = 70 mm). Microstrip feed line has length F_l = 30 mm and width F_w = 3 mm. The radiating patch is fed by a 50-ohm microstrip line. With proposed geometry, bandwidth obtained is 1.23 GHz with positive gain of 2.34 dB.

15.3.5 Key Shape Monopole Rectangular Microstrip Patch Antenna with Rounded Corner in Partial Ground

By increasing the radius of the curves, the length of the smoothened curve is increased which results in increase in the bandwidth. If the length of the smoothened curve increased beyond certain limit, the effective length of the current decreases, which deteriorates the radiation pattern. This problem has been resolved by creating the notches over the radiation patch. In the key shape monopole rectangular microstrip patch antenna (RMPA) with rounded corner in partial ground, one notch is created on the top of the patch and two notches are created on lateral sides as shown in Figures 15.7 and 15.8, respectively.

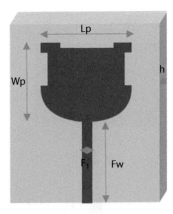

Figure 15.7 Key shape monopole rectangular microstrip patch antenna with rounded corner in partial ground radiating patch.

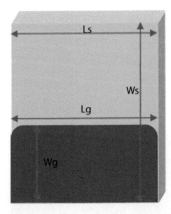

Figure 15.8 Key shape monopole rectangular microstrip patch antenna with rounded corner in partial ground, ground plane.

The key shape monopole is fed through a microstrip line, which is appended to a coaxial link through a standard 50 ohm, SMA connector for input signal transmission. The width of the microstrip feed line is settled at 3 mm and length is of 16.01 mm. On the base side of the substrate, a leading halfway ground plane with upper corners is fit as a fiddle, with length of 15.01 mm and width of 30 mm. Partial ground structure corners are made roundabout fit as a fiddle with a sweep of $3mm$ and lower corners of radiating patch are made smoother with a radius of $5mm$. Addition to this, there are notches on radiating that has vertical notch (length L_v = 5 mm and width W_v = $1mm$) and horizontal notch (length L_h = $1mm$ and width W_h = $10mm$).

The fabricated key shape monopole rectangular microstrip patch with rounded corner in partial ground is shown in Figures 15.9 and 15.10, respectively. The input impedance of the antenna has been calculated; it is a function of dimensions of top notch, lateral notches, the dimensions of the base rectangular patch, and the relative dielectric constant of the substrate used. For this calculation, the effect of smoothness of the curve on impedance has been assumed as insignificant. The following equations are used for the calculations.

Figure 15.9 Fabricated key shape rectangular microstrip patch with rounded corner in partial ground radiating patch.

Figure 15.10 Fabricated key shape rectangular microstrip patch with rounded corner in partial ground, ground plane.

$$Z_{in} = \frac{Z_{TL}.Z_P}{Z_{TL} + Z_P} \tag{15.17}$$

where Z_p is the impedance of base rectangular patch and Z_{TL} is the total impedance of the notches.

$$Z_p = \frac{1}{\dfrac{1}{R1} + j\omega C1 + \dfrac{1}{j\omega L1}} \tag{15.18}$$

where R_1, C_1, and L_1 are the resistance, capacitance, and inductance of the base rectangular patch.

$$R_1 = \frac{Q}{\omega_r.C_1} \tag{15.19}$$

$$C_1 = \frac{\varepsilon_e \varepsilon_0 L_p W_p}{2h}\left(\cos\frac{\pi * x_0}{L}\right)^{-2} \tag{15.20}$$

$$L_1 = \frac{1}{\omega_r^2.C_1} \tag{15.21}$$

$$Q = \frac{C\sqrt{\epsilon_e}}{4.f_r.h} \tag{15.22}$$

$$f_r = \frac{1}{2\pi\sqrt{L_1 * C_1}} \tag{15.23}$$

where h = thickness of substrate, ϵ_e = effective dielectric constant, x_0 = feed point location along x axis, and ε_0 = permittivity of free space

$$Z_{TS} = \frac{Z_{vl}.Z_{hl}}{Z_{vl}. + Z_{hl}} \tag{15.24}$$

where Z_{vl} is an impedance of the side notches and Z_{hl} is an impedance of the top notch.

$$Z_{vL} = R_{vL} + jX_{vl} \tag{15.25}$$

$$Z_{hl} = R_{hL}. + jX_{hl} \tag{15.26}$$

$$R_{Vl} = 60 \left[\begin{array}{l} C + \ln(k.L_V) - C_i(k.L_V) + \frac{1}{2}\sin(k.L_V).(s_i(2k.L_V) + 2s_i(k.L_V)) \\[2mm] + \frac{1}{2}\cos(k.L_V)\left[c - \ln\frac{(k.L_V)}{2} + C_i(2k.L_V) - 2C_i(k.L_V) \right] \end{array} \right] \tag{15.27}$$

where L_v = length of vertical slot and k is propagation constant

$$X_{Vl} = 30 \left[\begin{array}{l} 2s_i(k.L_V) + \cos(k.L_V).\left(2s_i(k.L_V) - s_i 2(k.L_V)\right) \\[2mm] -\sin k.L_V \left[2C_i(k.L_V) - C_i 2(k.L_V) - C_I \frac{Ka^2}{2L} \right] \end{array} \right] \tag{15.28}$$

$$R_{hl} = 60 \left[\begin{array}{l} C + \ln(k.L_h) - C_i(k.L_h) + \frac{1}{2}\sin(k.L_h).(s_i(2k.L_h) + 2s_i(k.L_h)) \\[2mm] + \frac{1}{2}\cos(k.L_h)\left[c - \ln\frac{(k.L_h)}{2} + C_i(2k.L_h) - 2C_i(k.L_h) \right] \end{array} \right] \tag{15.29}$$

$$X_{hl} = 30 \left[\begin{array}{l} 2s_i + \cos(k.L_h).\left(2s_i(k.L_h) - s_i 2(k.L_h)\right) \\[2mm] -\sin k.L_h \left[2C_i(k.L_h) - C_i 2(k.L_h) - C_I \frac{Ka^2}{2L} \right] \end{array} \right] \tag{15.30}$$

where L_v = length of vertical slot, L_h = length of horizontal slot, and k is propagation constant

$$S_i(x) = \int_0^x \frac{\sin x}{x} .dx$$

$$C_i(x) = -\int_x^\infty \frac{\cos x}{x} .dx$$

For the designed dimensions, the input impedance has been calculated.

$$Z_{in} = 60.10 + 12.56i \text{ ohm}$$

Magnitude of Z_{in} = 61.39 ohm

The results of the simulated antenna and fabricated antenna have been observed. Due to the increase in length of the current by creating the notches and smoothness at the corners, bandwidth has increased up to 10.05 GHz. It also resonates at two frequencies; it has a stable radiation with moderate gain. It is also found that impedance is near to the expected value for the resonating frequencies. However, it is observed just above the higher resonance frequency the reflection coefficient is slightly more than −10 dB.

15.4   Results and Inferences

15.4.1   Overview

Planar and printed probe feed antennas are most widely used in applications like Wi-Fi, Wi-Max, and WLAN. Techniques like slotting and stacking adopt to enhance the performance and convert design into wideband antenna suitable for biomedical application. The designs of antenna are discussed and the performance of the designed antennas have been presented and discussed in this chapter. The parameters used to define the performance of the MPA are reflection and VSWR bandwidth, far-field radiation pattern, E and H plane co- and cross-polarization, surface current distribution, and impedance of the patch. These parameters are also observed by varying the dimensions and position of the slot and discussed under the heading of Parametric Analysis.

15.4.2   Rectangular Microstrip Patch Antenna

The rectangular MPA is designed at L_p = 29.2 mm, W_p = 37.26 mm, L_{sub} = 37.82 mm, W_{sub} = 46.36 mm, and h = 1.59 mm. It is simulated using CADFEKO simulation software. The results of the simulated antenna are presented here and sample results are compared with fabricated antenna.

15.4.2.1   *Reflection and VSWR Bandwidth*

Simple rectangular patch antenna is designed and simulated at resonance frequency 2.45 GHz. The plot of reflection coefficient vs. frequency and the plot of VSWR vs. frequency are obtained as shown in Figures 15.11 and 15.12, respectively.

From Figure 15.11, it is found that the designed antenna has a resonance frequency f_r = 2.4563 GHz and reflection coefficient of −71.2643 dB, the reflection bandwidth of 66 MHz in the frequency band of 2.424 to 2.492 GHz. From Figure 15.12, it is observed that VSWR is below 2, which is measured at −10dB value of reflection coefficient and VSWR bandwidth is 71 MHz in the frequency band of 2.422 to 2.493 GHz.

The reflection coefficient of the fabricated antenna is observed to be −35dB, which is not matching with the simulated results, and resonance frequency is tuned at 2.45 GHz, which is matching with the simulated results.

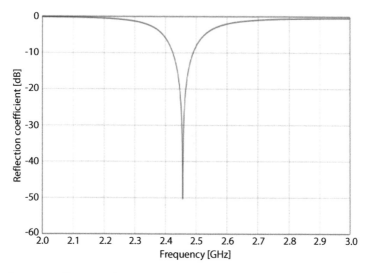

Figure 15.11 Reflection coefficient vs. frequency of rectangular microstrip patch antenna.

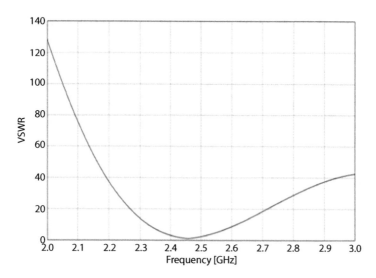

Figure 15.12 VSWR vs. frequency of rectangular microstrip patch antenna.

15.4.2.2   Surface Current Distribution

The surface current distribution pattern of the simulated rectangular MPA at the resonance frequency 2.45 GHz is shown in Figure 15.13.

It is observed that surface current is linearly distributed at 2.45 GHz and the radiating patch current distributed linearly over entire radiating patch.

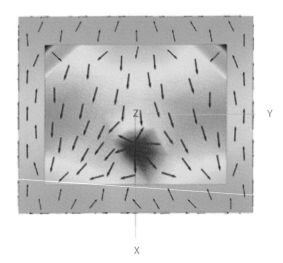

Figure 15.13 Surface current distribution on radiating patch at 2.45 GHz of rectangular microstrip patch antenna.

15.4.3   Microstrip Line Feed Rectangular Microstrip Patch Antenna with Partial Ground

The microstrip line feed rectangular MPA with partial ground is designed at L_p = 28 mm, width W_p = 37 mm, L_g = 28 mm, W_g = 70 mm, L_{sub} = 70 mm, W_{sub} = 70 mm, and h = 1.59 mm; microstrip feed line has length F_l = 30 mm and width F_w = 3 mm. It is simulated using CADFEKO simulation software. The results of the simulated antenna are presented here.

15.4.3.1   Reflection and VSWR Bandwidth

Microstrip line feed rectangular MPA with partial ground is designed and simulated. The plot of reflection coefficient vs. frequency and the plot of VSWR vs. frequency are obtained as shown in Figures 15.14 and 15.15, respectively.

From Figure 15.14, it is found that the microstrip line feed rectangular MPA with partial ground is resonating at single frequency. The resonance frequencies are f_{r1} = 2.08 GHz, and the corresponding reflection coefficient is −12.34 dB. The reflection bandwidth is 1.23 GHz, in the frequency band of 1.71 to 2.94 GHz.

From Figure 15.15, VSWR is observed below 2 in the frequency band of 1.68 to 3.58GHz; bandwidth is 1.9 GHz.

15.4.3.2   Surface Current Distribution

The surface current distribution pattern of the simulated microstrip line feed rectangular MPA with partial ground, resonating at frequency of 2.08 GHz, is shown in Figure 15.16.

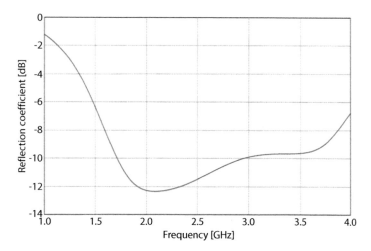

Figure 15.14 Reflection coefficient vs. frequency of microstrip line feed rectangular microstrip patch antenna with partial ground.

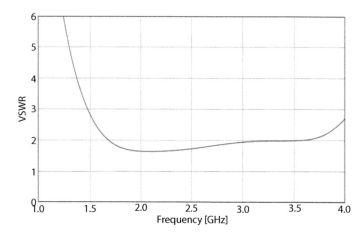

Figure 15.15 VSWR vs. frequency of microstrip line feed rectangular microstrip patch antenna with partial ground.

It is observed that surface current is linearly at resonance frequencies 3.77 GHz, while for resonance frequency 2.08 GHz.

15.4.3.3   Inference

It is resonating at single frequency, and the bandwidth up to 1.9 MHz. It has a moderate gain.

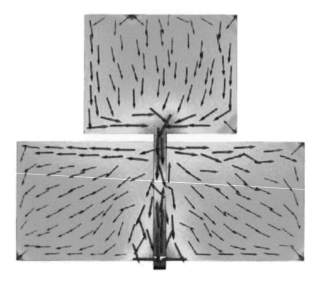

Figure 15.16 Surface current distribution on radiating patch of microstrip line feed rectangular microstrip patch antenna with partial ground at 2.08GHz.

15.4.4 Key Shape Monopole Rectangular Microstrip Patch Antenna with Rounded Corner in Partial Ground

The key shape monopole rectangular microstrip patch antenna with rounded corner in partial ground is designed at L_p = 12.7 mm, W_p = 15.2 mm, L_{sub} = 39 mm, W_{sub} = 30 mm, F_1 = 16.01 mm and width F_w = 3 mm, r_p = 5 mm, r_g = 3 mm, W_v = 1 mm, L_v = 5 mm, and W_h = 10 mm. It is simulated using CADFEKO simulation software. The results of the simulated antenna are presented here and sample results are compared with fabricated antenna.

15.4.4.1 Reflection and VSWR Bandwidth

The plot of reflection coefficient vs. frequency and the plot of VSWR vs. frequency of modified lower corner rounded monopole rectangular MPA with rounded corner in partial ground are shown in Figures 15.17 and 15.18, respectively.

From Figure 15.17, it is found that the key shape monopole rectangular MPA with rounded corner in partial ground is resonating at two frequencies. The resonance frequencies are f_{r1} = 3.86 GHz and f_{r1} = 10.44GHz and the corresponding reflection coefficients are −28.62 dB and −20.74 dB. The reflection bandwidth is 9.90GHz in the frequency band of 3.25 to 13.14 GHz. From Figure 15.18, VSWR is observed below 2 in the frequency band of 3.22 to 13.25 GHz, and VSWR bandwidth is of 10.05 GHz.

15.4.4.2 Surface Current Distribution

The surface current distribution patterns of the simulated key shape monopole rectangular MPA with rounded corner in partial ground at the resonance frequencies of 3.86 and 10.44 GHz are shown in Figures 15.19 and 15.20, respectively.

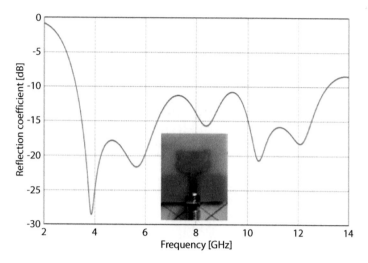

Figure 15.17 Reflection coefficient vs. frequency and of key shape monopole rectangular microstrip patch antenna with rounded corner in partial ground.

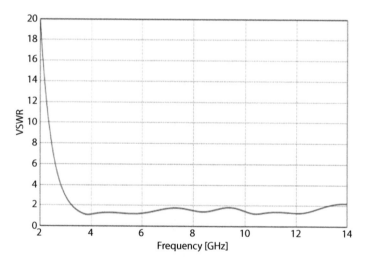

Figure 15.18 VSWR vs. frequency and of key shape monopole rectangular microstrip patch antenna with rounded corner in partial ground.

It is observed that surface current is linearly distributed at resonance frequencies 3.86 GHz, while for resonance frequency 10.44 GHz, the flow of current is erratic over entire radiating patch.

15.4.4.3   Results of the Fabricated Antenna

The reflection coefficient of the fabricated antenna is observed to be −24 and −21 dB, which is not matching with the simulated results, and resonance frequency is tuned at 4.38 and 10.01GHz, which is not matching with the simulated results. Reflection bandwidth is of 9.09 GHz, which is not match with simulated results. The comparative results of fabricated antenna and simulated antenna in terms of reflection coefficient vs. frequency are shown in

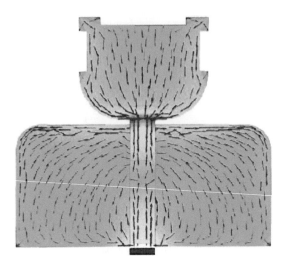

Figure 15.19 Surface current distribution on radiating patch key shape monopole rectangular microstrip patch antenna with rounded corner in partial ground at 3.86GHz.

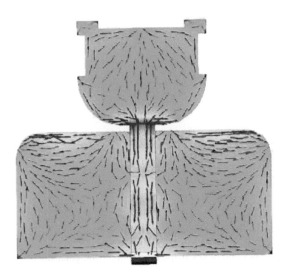

Figure 15.20 Surface current distribution on radiating patch key shape monopole rectangular microstrip patch antenna with rounded corner in partial ground at 10.44GHz.

Figure 15.21. Resonance band frame starts at 3.58GHz, and it is up to higher resonance of 12.67GHz, total bandwidth is of 9.09 GHz, and it is matching with simulated results.

15.4.4.4   Inference

It is resonating at two frequencies, and the bandwidth is up to 10.05GHz. It has a moderate gain, slightly degraded radiation pattern, and more smoothness of surface current.

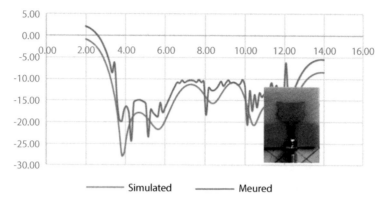

Figure 15.21 Simulated and measured reflection coefficient vs. frequency of key shape monopole rectangular microstrip patch antenna with rounded corner in partial ground.

15.5 Conclusion

This chapter presents the conclusions of the undertaken research work which is discussed in the preceding chapters and the further research avenues are listed out.

The fatal disease, which is cancer, is the major cause of death all over the world. Among the different categories, breast cancer shares the major percentage in females. For the timely and precise diagnosis, the researchers have suggested the new method, referred as MI. In MI technique, the WB antenna plays the key role in MI technique. Hence, the research work is mainly focused on the design of wideband MPA.

EM CADFEKO simulation tool is being used to simulate the designed MPA and selected antennas have been fabricated using FR4 substrate. CADFEKO provides the design based on two independent factors: equivalent magnetic current around the patch and electric current circulation on surface of the patch. The electric current circulation on surface of the patch has been used to design the antennas. This technique is also classified as integral equation methods and differential equation methods. The integral equation method has been selected for the design. Integral equation method uses Maxwell's equation to formulate the EM problems in term of unknown currents.

The design and simulation start from basic reference rectangular patch antenna with probe feeding. The simulated results are observed in relations of resonance frequency/frequencies, reflection coefficient, bandwidth, radiation pattern, and distributions. The problem of probe feeding has been overcome by using microstrip line feeding technique.

For the further improvement in bandwidth, monopole antenna has been designed with microstrip line feeding. The results are observed in terms of resonance frequency/frequencies, reflection coefficient, bandwidth, radiation pattern, and current distributions. The microstrip line feed monopole MPA has been modified as monopole lower corner rounded rectangular patch antenna with half-done ground, monopole lower corner rounded rectangular patch antenna with curved corner in partial ground, monopole modified lower corner rounded rectangular patch antenna with half-done ground, monopole key-shaped rectangular MPA with half-done ground, monopole key-shaped slotted rectangular microstrip antenna with half-done ground, and monopole key-shaped oval slotted rectangular MPA with rounded corner and half notch in partial ground. For these designs, the achieved bandwidth ranges from 5.03GHz to 10.05GHz with moderate gain.

This designed antenna is suitable candidate for MI technique, which will help to save many lives.

References

1. Fear, E.E. and Hagness, S.C., Enhancing Breast Tumor Detection with near field Imaging. *IEEE Microwave Mag.*, 3, 1, 48–56, March 2002.

2. Carr, K.L., Microwave Radiometry: Its importance to detection of cancer. *IEEE Trans. Microw. Theory Tech.*, 37, 12, 1862–1869, December 1999.

3. Shahira Banu, M.A., Vanaja, S., Poonguzhali, S., UWB Microwave Detection of Breast Cancer Using SAR. *Energy Efficient Technologies for Sustainability (ICEETS), 2013 International Conference on*, IEEE, 2013.

4. Liu, J., Xue, Q., Wong, H. *et al.*, Design and Analysis of A Low Profile and Broadband Microstrip Monopole Patch Antenna. *IEEE Trans. Antennas Propag.*, 61, 1, 11–18, January 2013.

5. Osman, H.A., Abdallah, E.A., Abdel Rahim, A.A., A novel compact circular disk Microstrip antenna for wireless application. *Prog. Electromagn. Res., PIER*, 4, 7, 761–766, 2008.

6. Deshmukh, A.A. and Ray, K.P., Compact Broadband E-Shaped Microstrip Antennas. *IEEE Electron. Lett.*, 41, 18, 989–990, 2005.

7. Joisel, Mallorqui, J., Broquetas, A., Geffrin, J.M., Joachimowicz, N., Iossera, M.V., Jofre, L., Bolomey, J.-C., Microwave Imaging Techniques for Biomedical Applications. *IEEE Instrumen. Measure. Tech. Conf.*, 1999.

8. Karli, R. and Ammor, H., Miniaturized UWB Microstrip Antenna With T-Slot for Detecting Malignant Tumors by Microwave Imaging. *Int. J. Microw. Opt. Technol.*, 9, 3, 214–220, May 2014.

9. Shrestha, S., Agarwal, M., Reid, J., Varahramyan, K., Microstrip Antennas for Direct Human Skin Placement for Biomedical Applications. *PIERS Proceedings*, Cambridge, U.S.A, 6 July 2010, pp. 926–931.

10. Adnan, S., Abd-Alhameed, R.A., Hraga, H.I. *et al.*, Microstrip Antenna for Microwave Imaging Application. *Progress In Electromagnetic Research Symposium Proceedings*, Marrakesh, Morocco, 22 March 2011, pp. 431–434, J. Eichler.

11. Jacobi, J.H., Larsen, L.E., Hast, C.T., Water-Immersed Microwave Antennas and Their Application to Microwave Interrogation of Biological Targets. *IEEE Trans. Microwave Theory Tech.*, 27, 70–78, Jan./ 1979.

12. Munson, R.E., Conformal microstrip antennas and microstrip phased arrays. *IEEE Trans. Antennas Propag.*, AP-22, 74–78, Jan. 1974.

13. Howell, J.Q., Microstrip antennas. *IEEE Trans. Antennas Propag.*, 23, 90–93, Jan. 1975.

14. Agrawal, P.K. and Bailey, M.C., An analysis technique for microstrip antennas. *IEEE Trans. Antennas Propag.*, AP-25, 756–759, Nov. 1977.

15. Peixeiro, C., *Microstrip Patch Antennas: An Historical perspective of the development*, IEEE, pp. 684–688, 2011.

16. Mathur, V., *Comparison of Performance Characteristics of Rectangular, Square and Hexagonal Microstrip Patch Antennas*, 14 January 2014, IEEE, 978-1-4799-6896.

17. Pan, S.-C. and Wang, K.-L., Dual-frequency triangular microstrip antenna with a shorting pin. *IEEE Trans. Antennas Propag.*, 45, 12, 1889–1891, Dec 1997.

18. Park, J., Na, H-g, Baik, S.H., Design of a Modified L-probe fed Microstrip Patch Antenna. *IEEE Antennas Wirel. Propag. Lett.*, 3, 117–119, 20042004.

19. Bhan, C., Dwivedi, A.K., Mishra, B., Kumar, A., Quad Bands U-shaped Slot Loaded Probe Fed Microstrip Patch Antenna. *IEEE Second International Conference on Advances in Computing and Communication Engineering*, 2015.

20. Shanmuganatham, T., Design of Multi Utility Multi Band Microstrip Calculator Shaped Patch Antenna Using Coaxial Feed. *IEEE International Conference on Computer, Communication, and Signal Processing (ICCCSP)*, 2017.

21. Pues, H. and Capelle, A.V., Accurate transmission-line model for the rectangular microstrip antenna. *Proc. IEEE*, 131, 6, 334–340, December 1984.

22. Sze, J.Y. and Wong, K.L., Slotted Rectangular Microstrip Antenna for Bandwidth Enhancement. *IEEE Trans. Antennas Wirel. Prorog. Lett.*, 48, 1149–1152, August 2000.

23. Weigand, S. and Huff, G.H., Analysis and Design of Broad-Band Single-Layer rectangular U-Slot Microstrip Patch Antennas. *IEEE Trans. Antennas Propag.*, 5 1, 3, 457–468, 2003.

24. Lu, J.-H., Design of Single-Layer Slotted Circular Microstrip Antennas. *IEEE Trans. Antennas Propag.*, 51, 5, 1126–1129, may 2003.

25. Wu, J.W., 2.4/5-GHz dual-band triangular slot antenna with compact operation. *Microw. Opt. Technol. Lett.*, 45, 81–84, 2005.

26. Deshmukh, A. and Kumar, G., Compact broadband U slot-loaded rectangular microstrip antennas. *Microwave Opt. Technol. Lett.*, 46, 6, 556–559, 2005.

27. Lotfi Neyestanak, A., Hojjat Kashani, F., Barkeshli, K., W-shaped enhanced-bandwidth patch antenna for wireless communication. *Wirel. Pers. Commun.*, 43, 4, 1257–1265, 2007.

28. Yang, S.-L.S., Frequency Reconfigurable U-Slot Microstrip Patch Antenna. *IEEE Antennas Wirel. Propag. Lett.*, 7, 127–129, 2008.

29. Ansari, J.A. and Dubey, S.K., Analysis of U Slot loaded Patch for Dual Band Operation. *Int. J. Microw. Opt. Technol.*, 3, 2, 80–84, April 2008.

30. Jolani, F., Dadgarpour, A.M., Hassani, H.R., Compact M– slot folded patch antenna for WLAN. *Prog. Electromagn. Res. Lett.*, 3, 35–42, 2008.

31. Deshmukh, A.A. and Ray, K.P., Compact Broadband Slotted Rectangular Microstrip Antenna. *IEEE Antennas Wirel. Propag. Lett.*, 8, 1410–1413, 2009.

32. Islam, M.T., Shakib, M.N., Misran, N., Broadband E-H shaped microstrip patch antenna for wireless systems. *Prog. Electromagn. Res.*, 98, 163–173, 2009.

33. Ghalibafan, J., Attari, A.R., Kashani, F.H., A new dual-band microstrip antenna with U-shaped slot. *Prog. Electromagn. Res. C*, 12, 215–223, 2010.

34. Ansari, J.A., Yadav, N.P., Mishra, A., Kamakshi, Singh, A., *Broadband Rectangular Microstrip Antenna Loaded with a Pair of U-Shaped Slot*, IEEE, ©2010, 978-1-4241-8541-3/10/$26.00.

35. Ansari, J.A., Mishra, A., Yadav, N.P., Singh, P., Dualband slot loaded circular disk patch antenna for WLAN application. *Int. J. Microw. Opt. Technol.*, 5, 3, 124–129, MAY 2010.

36. Ansari, J.A., Mishra, A., Vishvakarma, B.R., Half U- slot loaded semicircular disk patch antenna for GSM mobile phone and optical communication. *Prog. Electromagn. Res. C*, 18, 31–45, 2010, 2011.

37. Agarwal, V.K., Shaw, A.K., Kr. Das, M., Mukherjee, J., Mandal, K., A Novel Compact Dual Frequency Microstrip Antenna. *Proc. Technol.*, 4, 427–430, 2012.

38. Sharma, R., *Trapezoidal Patch with H and V Shaped Slot Loaded Microstrip Antenna*, IEEE, ©2013, 978-1-4799-1 607-8/1 3/$31.00.

39. Chen, Y., Yang, S., Nie, Z., A Compact Dual-Polarized Double E-Shaped Patch Antenna with High Isolation. *IEEE Trans. Antennas Propag.*, 58, 7, 2442–2447, Aug. 2013.

40. Chakraborty, U., Kundu, A., Chowdhury, S.K., Bhattacharjee, A.K., Compact Dual-Band Microstrip Antenna for IEEE 802.11a WLAN Application. *IEEE Antennas Wirel. Propag. Lett.*, 13, 407–410, 2014.

41. Moosazadeh, M. and Kharkovsky, S., Compact and Small Planar Monopole Antenna with Symmetrical L- and U-Shaped Slots for WLAN/WiMAX Applications. *IEEE Antennas Wirel. Propag. Lett.*, 13, 388–391, 2014.

42. Consul, P., Triple Band Gap Coupled Microstrip U-Slotted Patch Antenna using L-Slot DGS for Wireless Applications. *International Conference on Communication, Control and Intelligent Systems (CCIS)*, 2015.

43. Thatere, A. and Zade Dwejendra Arya, P.L., Bandwidth Enhancement of Microstrip Patch Antenna using 'U' Slot with Modified Ground Plane. *International Conference on Microwave, Optical and Communication Engineering*, December 18–20, 2015.

44. Deshmukh, A.A. and Kumar, G., Compact Broadband Stacke Microstrip Antennas. *Microwave Opt. Technol. Lett.*, 48, 1, 538–541, January 2006.

45. Islam, M.T., Misran, N., Shakib, M.N., Yatim, B., Wideband Stacked Microstrip Patch Antenna for Wireless Communication. *IEEE International Symposium on Parallel and Distributed Processing with Applications*, 2008.

46. Kahrizi, M., Sarkar, T.K., Maricevic, Z.H., Analysis of a wide radiating slot in the ground plane of a microstrip line. *IEEE Trans. Microwave Theory Tech.*, MTT-41, 29–37, Jan. 1993.

47. Chen, W.-S., Wong, K.-L., Wu, C.-K., Inset microstripline-fed circularly polarized microstrip antennas. *IEEE Trans. Antennas Propag.*, 48, 1253–1254, 2000.

48. Chen, D. and Cheng, C.H., A Novel Ultra-Wideband Microstrip-Line Fed Wide-Slot Antenna. *Microwave Opt. Technol. Lett.*, 48, 4, 776–777, April 2006.

49. Tseng, L.-Y. and Han, T.-Y., Microstrip-Fed Circular Slot Antenna for Circular Polarization. *Microwave Opt. Technol. Lett.*, 50, 4, 1056–1058, April 2008.

50. Liu, W.-C., Wu, C.-M., Dai, Y., Design of Triple-Frequency Microstrip-Fed Monopole Antenna Using Defected Ground Structure. *IEEE Trans. Antennas Propag.*, 59, 7, 2457–2463, July 2011.

51. Wang, Y., Fathy, A.E. *et al.*, Novel Compact Tapered Microstrip Slot Antenna for Microwave Breast Imaging. *IEEE Trans. Antennas Propag.*, 2119–2122, 2011.

52. Sung, Y., Bandwidth enhancement of a microstrip line-fed printed wide-slot antenna with a parasitic center patch. *IEEE Trans. Antennas Propag.*, 60, 1712–1217, 2012.

53. Yang, W. and Zhou, J., A Single Layer Wideband Low-Profile Tooth-like-slot Microstrip Patch Antenna Fed by Inset Microstrip Line. *2013 International Workshop on Antenna Technology (iWAT)*, pp. 248–251.

54. Park, R.C., *Implementation of Long Microstrip Line-fed Antenna for WLAN Applications*, IEEE, 2013.

55. Chandel, R., Gautam, A.K., Kr. Kanaujia, B., Microstrip-Line Fed Beak-Shaped Monopole-Like Slot UWB Antenna with Enhanced Band Width. *Microw. Opt. Technol. Lett.*, 56, 11, 2624–2627, November 2014.

56. Aneesh, M., Ansari, J.A., Singh, A., Kamakshi, Sayeed, S.S., Analysis of Microstrip Line Feed Slot Loaded Patch Antenna Using Articial Neural Network. *Prog. Electromagn. Res. B*, 58, 35–46, 2014.

57. Ansari, J.A., Vermal, S., Verma, M.K., Agrawal, N., A Novel Wide Band Microstrip-Line-Fed Antenna with Defected Ground for CP Operation. *Prog. Electromagn. Res. C*, 58, 169–181, 2015.

58. Henderson, K.Q. and Latif, S.I., A Microstrip Line-Fed Multi-Resonant Slot Antenna in the 4G/LTE Band for Smartphones. *Milcom 2016 Track 1 - Waveforms and Signal Processing*.

59. Hagness, S.C., Taflove, A., Bridges, J.E., Three Dimensional FDTD Analysis of a Pulsed Microwave Confocal System for Breast Cancer Detection: Design of An Antenna Array Element. *IEEE Trans. Antennas Propag.*, 47, 5, 783–791, May 1999.

60. Nilavalan, R., Craddock, I.J. *et al.*, Wideband microstrip patch antenna design for breast cancer tumor detection. *IET Microw. Antennas Propag.*, 1, 2, 277–281, 2007.

61. Stang, J.P., Joines, W.T. *et al.*, Tapered Microstrip Patch Antenna Array for Microwave Breast Imaging. *Microwave Symposium Digest, 2008 IEEE MTT-S International*, IEEE, 2008.

62. Yu, J., Yuan, M., Liu, Q.H., A Wideband Half oval patch antenna for breast imaging. *Prog. Electromagn. Res., PIER*, 98, 1–13, 2009.

63. Mudar, A., Aguilar, M. *et al.*, Dual Band Miniaturized Patch Antennas for Microwave Breast Imaging. *IEEE Antennas Wirel. Propag.*, 9, 268–271, 2010.

64. Gibbins, D., Klemm, M., Craddock, I.J., Leendertz, J.A., Preece, A., Benjamin, R., A Comparison of a Wide Slot and A Stacked Patch Antenna for the Purpose of Breast Cancer Detection. *IEEE Trans. Antennas Propag.*, 58, 3, 665–674, March 2010.

65. Bassi, M., Caruso, M. *et al.*, An integrated Microwave Imaging Radar with Planar Antennas for Breast Cancer Detection. *IEEE Trans. Microw. Theory Tech.*, 61, 5, 2108–2118, May 2013.

66. Banu, S., Viswapriya, A., Yogamathi, R., Performance Analysis of Circular Patch Antenna for Breast Cancer Detection. *4th ICCCNT-2013*, India, July 4-6, 2013.

67. Çalışkan, R. *et al.*, A Microstrip Patch Antenna Design for Breast Cancer Detection. *World Conference on Technology, Innovation and Entrepreneurship -Science direct*, @2015.

68. Scarpello, M.L., Kurup, D., Rogier, H., Design of an Implantable Slot Dipole Conformal Flexible Antenna for Biomedical Applications. *IEEE Trans. Antennas Propag.*, 59, 10, 3556–3564, October 2011.

69. Yang, W., Ma, K., Yeo, K.S., Lim, W.M., Kong, Z.H., A Compact Dual-Band Meander-line Antenna for Biomedical Applications. *IEEE MTT-S International Microwave Workshop Series on RF and Wireless Technologies for Biomedical and Healthcare Applications*, 2013.

70. Akowuah, B.Y., Kallos, E., Palikaras, G., A Novel Compact Planar Inverted-F Antenna for Biomedical Applications in the MICS band. *IEEE the 8th European Conference on Antennas and Propagation*, 2014.

71. Liu, C., Guo, Y.-X., Xiao, S., Capacitively Loaded Circularly Polarized Implantable Patch Antenna for ISM Band Biomedical Applications. *IEEE Trans. Antennas Propag.*, 62, 5, 2407–2417, May 2014.

72. Mahalakshmi, N. and Thenmozhi, A., Design of hexagon shape bow-tie patch antenna for implantable bio-medical applications. *Alexandria Eng. J.*, 56, 235–239, 2017.

73. Bouazizi, A., Nasri, N., Zaibi, G., Samet, M., Kachouri, A., A Novel Implantable Planar Inverted-F Antenna for Biomedical Applications. *2015 12th International Multi-Conference on Systems, Signals & Devices*.

74. Dinesh, S. and Vivek, P.R., Design of Implantable Patch Antenna for Biomedical Application. *IEEE Sponsored 2nd International Conference on Innovations in Information Embedded and Communication Systems ICIIECS*, 2015.

75. Zahirul Alam, A.H.M., Rafiqul Islam, Md., Khan, S., Design and Analysis of UWB Rectangular Patch Antenna. *Pacific conference on applied electromagnetics proceedings*, December 4–6, 2007.

76. Rashed-Mohassel, Slot Coupled Microstrip Antenna for Ultra-Wideband Applications in C and X Band. *Prog. Electromagn. Res.*, 3, 15–25, 2008.

77. Jiang, W. and Che, W., A Novel UWB Antenna with Dual Notched Bands for WiMAX and WLAN Applications. *IEEE Antennas Wirel. Propag. Lett.*, 11, 293–296, 2012.

78. Singh, S.K. and Singh, A.K., UWB Rectangular Ring Microstrip Antenna with Simple Capacitive Feed for Breast Cancer Detection. *Progress in Electromagnetics Research Symposium*, Beijing, China, March 23–27, 2009.

79. Aziz ul Haq, M. and Arif Khan, M., A Multiple Ring Slot Ultra-Wideband Antenna (MRS-UWB) For Biomedical Applications. *IEEE Conference publication*, pp. 56–60, 2014.

80. Ping, L.C. and Chakrabarty, C.K., Bending Effect on Ultra-Wideband (UWB) Microstrip Patch Antenna Performance. *Int. J. Microw. Opt. Technol.*, 9, 5, 2336–2344, September 2014.

81. www.antenna-theory.com

82. www.cancer.org

16

COVID-19: A Global Crisis

Savita Mandan[1] and Durgeshwari Kalal[2]*

[1]Department of Microbiology, R C Patel Institute of Pharmaceutical Research and Development, Shirpur, MS, India
[2]Department of Pharmaceutical Chemistry, R C Patel Institute of Pharmaceutical Research and Development, Shirpur, MS, India

Abstract

Coronavirus is a kind of COVID infection having a place with the family Coronaviridae. The infection is thought to start from bats and was spread to individuals through an obscure medium in Wuhan, China. Preferably, the condition is spread by inward breath or close association with infected drops that have an incubation period somewhere in the range of 2 to 14 days. Today, there are a large number of infections and passing that have emerged as a result of the sickness. Besides, an indications of illness induce a high level of anxiety, cough, sneezing, a painful throat, difficulty breathing, and sluggishness. Also, the conclusion of the illness starts with social affair like upper and lower respiratory tract of infected person. Additionally, in initial stage, x-rays of the chest and a CT scan are used. In essence, there is no specific treatment and cure for the disease, which demands the urge to prevent the infection from spreading. Outstanding counteraction systems are used for the infected people, appropriate hand hygiene, ventilation, and use of individual protective equipment. Along these lines, this paper gives top to bottom COVID-19 data, as it pertains to the illness, disease transmission, research, clinical highlights, detection, treatment, and prevention.

Keywords: COVID-19, x-ray, CT scan, SARS, pandemic, outbreak, MERS

16.1 Introduction

COVIDs are large spectrum of illnesses that can lead to sickness in living creatures or humans. In people, a few COVIDs are likely to affect respiratory contaminations originating in normal viral to more serious diseases like SARS and MERS, which are acronyms for Severe Acute Respiratory Syndrome and Middle East Respiratory Syndrome, respectively. COVID illness is caused by the most recently discovered COVID-19 [1].

Coronaviruses are a retrovirus implicated in social and vertebrates diseases. Coronaviruses are siblings of Coronavirinae sub-family of Coronaviridae family as well as Nidovirales order [2]. In 2019, COVID-19 coronavirus emerged recently with an burst of

Corresponding author: durgeshwari.kalal@gmail.com

Tushar H. Jaware, K. Sarat Kumar, Ravindra D. Badgujar and Svetlin Antonov (eds.) *Medical Imaging and Health Informatics*, (303–316) © 2022 Scrivener Publishing LLC

atypical viral pneumonia in city Wuhan of China, followed by a pandemic outbreak. In December 2019, before the Wuhan pandemic in China, this novel virus and sickness were unknown. COVID-19 has become a pandemic, disturbing several nations around globe [3].

COVIDs are discovered in avian and mammalian species. They are simulated after each other in morphology and synthetic construction. For perspective, people's COVIDs and dairy cattle's COVIDs are antigenically similar. There is no evidence, nonetheless, that person COVIDs can be communicated by animals. In creatures, different COVIDs attack a wide range of tissues and result in a variety of infections, yet they have only been shown to produce moderate upper respiratory contaminations in humans, for example, normal colds. In rare cases, gastrointestinal COVID has already been associated with episodes of inflammatory bowel syndrome in children [4].

16.1.1   Structure

A COVID gets its name from the fact that it is not a magnifying glass. The term crown denotes "crown". When closely examined, the round infection has a "crown" a protein called peplomers extending distant to its middlein each direction. These are the proteins aid in infectious disease with distinguishing whether it is capable of contaminating its host [5].

COVID virions range in shape from round to pleomorphic. The envelope is densely packed with glycoproteins that project from it and contains a network protein center inside which is encased a solitary strand of positive-sense RNA (Mr 610 6) related to nucleoprotein. Some COVIDs additionally contain a hem agglutinin-esterase protein [6].

The envelope glycoproteins are responsible for connection to the host cell and furthermore convey the primary antigenic epitopes, especially the epitopes perceived by killing antibodies. Round and pleomorphic envelopes carrying single-beamed RNA that is associated with a nucleoprotein within a matrix protein in a capside [7].

16.1.2   Classification of Corona Virus

The COVIDs have been originally assembled on the Coronaviridae family premise. On electron microscopy, the glycoprotein-studded envelope seems to have a crown or radiance. That kind of grouping has since been confirmed by extraordinary highlights of the infection's science and replication. Human COVIDs are broadly classified into two groups: 229E-like and OC43-like. These contrast in both antigenic determinants and refined prerequisites. 229E-like COVIDs might ordinarily be detached in human early stage fibroblast culture, and OC43-like viruses can be separated or adapted to development in nursing mouse cerebrum. There is virtually no antigenic cross-response between these two types. They cause undefined pandemics of infection [8].

16.1.3   Types of Human Coronavirus

Human coronavirus was first distinguished during the 1960s. There are four primary sub-groupings of coronaviruses, known as alpha, beta, gamma, and delta. These are dispersed in seven subtypes of corona that can virulent for individuals:

General human coronavirus

1. 229-E formalized (alpha COVID)

2. NL-63 (alpha COVID)
3. OC-43 (beta COVID)
4. HKU-1 (beta COVID)
5. MERS-CoV is the fifth most common cause of death in the United States
6. SARS-CoV is an acronym for Severe Acute Respiratory Syndrome Corona
7. SARS-CoV-2 is a virus that causes severe respiratory illness. Individuals all throughout the planet regularly get contaminated with human coronavirus 229E, NL63, OC43, and HKU1 [9, 10].

16.1.4   Genome Organization of Corona Virus

Coronaviruses have the biggest genomes about 26.4–31.7 kb among all RNA infections that have been identified, containing G+C substance inconsistent between 32% and 43%. There are various amounts of lesser ORFs available among various monitored qualities, *viz.*, spike, ORF1ab, layer, envelope, as well as nucleocapsid, and below to nucleocapsid gene in distinct coronavirus lineages. The genome of a virus comprises special illustrates, among them an extraordinary N-terminal part within spike protein. Genes of most important primary proteins all around coronaviruses arise as S, E, M, and N in the 5′–3′ request [12–14].

A normal CoV contains no less than six ORFs in its genome. Aside from Gamma COVID nsp1 lakes, the primary ORFs (ORF1a/b), around 66% in contexts of entire length of the genome, encode 16 nsps (nsp1-16). ORF1a and ORF1b have a frameshift in the middle of which generates two polypeptides: pp1a and pp1ab. These polypeptides are handled by chymotrypsin-like protease (3CLpro) encoded by a virus or primary protease (Mpro), and also a couple of 16 nsps of papain-like protease. Every one of the primary and adornment proteins are interpreted from the sgRNAs of CoVs. Four primary underlying proteins contain spike (S), layer (M), envelope (E), and nucleocapsid (N) proteins are encoded by ORFs 10 and 11 on the 33% of the genome close to the 3′-end. Other than these four principle underlying proteins, distinctive CoVs encode unique primary and adornment proteins, like HE protein, 3a/b protein, and 4a/b protein. These develop proteins are responsible for a few significant capacities in genome support and infection replication [11, 15, 16].

The coronavirus layer contains three or four viral proteins. The film (M) glycoprotein is the most abundant main protein; it ranges the layer bilayer numerous times, leaving a small NH2-terminal region outside the infection and a lengthy COOH end for example cytoplasmic space within the virion. The spike protein (S), a type I film glycoprotein, is responsible for the formation of peplomers. In reality, S protein is the primary inducer of deadly antibodies. There are proteins between the envelope with an atomic association that in all likelihood decides the development and piece of the coronaviral film. M assumes a key element of the infection-particle arrangement without S. COVID produces spikeless, non-infectious virions, containing M without S, from the viewpoint of tunicamicin [14, 16, 17].

16.1.5   Coronavirus Replication

The sign of the COVID record seems to be the production of different mRNAs with subgenomic layouts for the genome's two finishes. The record are recognizable because of the interaction between mRNAs of subgenome size and COVID duplication is just the cycle during which RNA of genomic size, which also acts as an mRNA, is supplied. The age of subgenomic mRNAs therefore comprises an uneven cycle of records. COVID genomic RNA with approximately 30,000 nucleotides encodes the infection proteins, non-structural protectins which are essential for viral RNA combination, which we refer to as replicase-transcriptase proteins, and non-structural proteins which, however, are superfluous for infectious cell culture replication, give *in vivo* a particular benefit. We shall refer to this as explicit proteins of specialization. Nucleocapsid protein (N) is related with viral RNA union, something like one explicitly defined protein, nonstructural protein 2 (nsp2), and one main protein [17, 18].

The interpretation of the genomic RNA interferes with the production of the Coronavirus replicase-transcriptase protein characteristics. In Open Perusing 1a (ORF1a), the replicase transcriptase proteins are joined as two large polyproteins, pp1, and pp1ab. They are originally combined as pp1a as well as pp1ab. The pp1ab synthesis contains the intended ribosomal contours of ORF1a. The virus encoded proteinases (PL Pro) and the chymotrypsin-like folding of the polyprotein during or after amalgamation are split into 16 protectins by viruses; nsp1 is coded in nsp11a, ORF1, and nsp12 is encoded in nsp16 by ORF1b. Replica transcriptase proteins collect into the complex layer-bound replication record together with other virals proteins and perhaps cell protein. Such buildings are found in perinuclear regions and connected to two folding film vesicles. The transmitted hydrophobic regions of nsp3, nsp4, and nsp6 are accessible and may moor at the early stage of the RTC scheme the incipient polyproteins pp1a/pp1ab to layers [18–20].

16.1.6 Host Defenses

The viruses enter the host cell, and the uncoated genome is interpreted and interpreted. The mRNAs structure an interesting "settled set" sharing a typical 3′-end. New virions structure by growing from cell membranes [21, 23].

The indication of neutralizer in nasal and serum discharges is lagged by goal of infection. Resistance fades inside a little while. Despite the fact that mucociliary action is proposed to clear the aviation routes of particulate material, COVIDs can effectively contaminate the shallow cells of the ciliated epithelium. Simply around 33% to one portion of contaminated people foster indications. Nevertheless, interferon can secure against contamination, yet its significance is not known. Since COVID contaminations are normal, numerous people have explicit antibodies in their nasal emissions, and these antibodies can ensure against contamination. The vast majority of these antibodies are coordinated against the surface projections and stop the infectivity of the infection. Cell-intervened resistance and sensitivity may assume a part [24–26].

16.2 Clinical Manifestation and Pathogenesis

Corona viruses attack the respiratory lot by means of the nose. After an incubation period of around 3 days, they cause the manifestations of a typical cold, including nasal check, sniffling, runny nose, and only from time to time hack. The infection settle in a couple days, during which infection is shed in nasal discharges. There is some proof that the respiratory

COVIDs can cause illness of the lower airways routes; however, it is think that this is because of direct invasion. Other indication of infection, for example, numerous sclerosis have been attributed to these viruses. Corona viruses cause intense and gentle upper respiratory disease, i.e., common cold.

Transmission is normally through airborne beads to the respiratory tract. In cells of the ciliated epithelium, the viruses locally proliferate, producing cell damage and irritation. Persons with COVID-19 will get the illness from many other persons. The disease is generally transferred by droplets in the nose or mouth from each one person with COVID-19 hacking, wheezing, or conversation. Such drops are nearly hefty, do not move too much or you will fall to the earth. Persons might have COVID-19 from an individual who is tinged with the illness in these beads. This is the reason stay somewhere around 1 meter from all others. These beads may arrive on articles as well astopsnearby individual like tables, door handles, as well as guardrails. Individuals may get contaminated by contacting the items, surfaces, and afterward contact one's nose, mouth, or eye, during that time. Coronavirus infection on plastic and hardened steel may continue for as long as 72 hours, on copper less than 4 hours, and on cardboard less than 24 hours [27].

16.2.1   Symptoms

The utmost renowned side effects of COVID-19 is dry hack, fever, as well as sluggishness. Different side effects that are more uncommon and may influence a few patients incorporate hurts also, torments, nasal clog, cerebral pain, conjunctivitis, sore throat, looseness of the bowels, lost smell or taste, as well as skin rash with toe or finger staining. Such side effects often are mild as well as constantly beginning. A few group become contaminated yet as it were have exceptionally gentle side effects.

The overwhelming majority recover from the illness need medical care. About one in five people receiving COVID-19 are really ill and have difficulties relaxing. Well-settled people as well as those with clinical problems, such as cardiac and lung complications, sugar problem, high blood pressure, and otherdisease, are now significant of danger of creating genuine sickness. Though, anybody may hold onto COVID-19 as well as become genuinely sick. Individuals at any age experiencing fever with hack related to windedness, chest agony, pressing factor, or loss of discourse or development should look for clinical consideration right away [25, 28].

16.2.2   Epidemiology

The study of disease transmission of COVID colds has been minimal contemplated. Floods of contamination go through networks throughout the cold weather months, and frequently cause little flare-ups in families, schools, and so on Resistance does not endure, and subjects might be re-tainted, at times inside a year. The example accordingly varies from that of rhinovirus contaminations, which top in the fall and spring and for the most part inspire long- enduring invulnerability. Around one out of five colds is expected to COVIDs. The infection is typically sent through breathing of tainted beads; however, it might likewise be sent by the hands to the mucosa of the nose or eyes [22, 23].

16.3   Diagnosis and Control

Fast and from the get-go research facility determination of COVID-19 is the primary focal point of treatment and control. Sub-atomic tests are the reason for affirmation of COVID-19, in any case, serological tests for SARS-CoV-2 are generally accessible and play a progressively critical part in understanding the study of disease transmission of the infection and in distinguishing populaces at higher danger for disease [29, 30]. Epidemiological components are available to help you decide who to test. This incorporates anybody who has been in close touch to a patients having a COVID-19 confirmation center within 14 days beginning or a background marked by movement from influenced geographic areas inside 14 days of manifestation inception. Point-of-care tests enjoy the benefit of fast, exact, convenient, minimal expense, and vague gadget prerequisites, which offer incredible assistance for infection analysis and discovery [31].

16.3.1   Molecular Test

Coronavirus caused colds in no individual may be clinically distinguished from various colds. The analysis of the research center might be based on immune system responses titers in mixed serum. The infection is difficult to untie. Currently, nucleic acid hybridization testing using PCR. Polymerase chain reaction testing, (PCR) trusted source remains the essential COVID-19 diagnostic testing strategy [21–23].

WHO advises that both the top respiratory pathways (*viz.*, nasso, oropharyngeal, sputum, or endotracheal suction or bronchosalveolar lavage) as well as lower respiratory routes should be collected. Specimens and BAL samples in patients correctly ventilated as lower respiratory system tests seem to stay more positive for a longer duration. BAL samples should be used only for the exact ventilation of patients. The sample needs a 4°C capacity. The improvement of the inheritance material separating from the salivation or bodily fluid example is achieved at the research institution by means of a reverse polymerase chain reaction (RT-PCR). If the inherited material is suitable, the the aim is to monitor the sections of a CoV hereditary code. Tests utilized depend on the underlying quality arrangement and probes used on the initial gene sequence [32, 33].

Might the test result be positive, the test will be repeated additional inspection. The evaluation of the research center should be re-assessed for viral freedom in patients with affirmed COVID-19 determinations before observation is provided. The accessibility of investigations performed on which nation a person resides in practically every day when access is expanded [32, 33].

16.3.2   Serology

In spite of the various immunizer tests planned, serological to presentdetermination has restrictions in both particularity as well as affectability. Once again, there are different test findings. A CDC test investigation from the US Vaccine Research Center at the National Health Institutes is ongoing. This test appears to be more than 99% specific with a 96% affectability. The most helpful strategy for research facility conclusion is to gather matched sera and to test by ELISA for an ascent in antibodies against OC43 and 229E.

Complement fixation tests are insensitive, and different tests are not advantageous and can be utilized uniquely for one serotype [32, 34].

Exploration is furnishing many with a wealth of knowledge about the work of serology. It has been demonstrated, for example, that there is no cross-reactivity between autoantibodies derived from blood testing of individuals with immune system illness and SARS-CoV-2 antibodies. By and by, additional explorations required to clarifying a few perspectives of the matter. Serologic, be that as it may, can have a significant job in expansive based observation. Specifically [34]

1. If IgG antibodies provide protection against future SARS-CoV-2 illness.
2. In terms of antibody defense titer.
3. Concerning the duration of the protection.

16.3.3   Concerning Lab Assessments

In the beginning phase of the infection, an ordinary or diminished complete white blood cell tally (WBC) as well as a diminished lymphocyte tally may be illustrated. It is possible to differentiate the expanded advantages of liver chemical, muscle compounds, lactate dehydrogenase (LDH), as well as C-responsive protein. Unless there is a bacteria overlay, a normal procalcitonin value is discovered. Increased neutrophil to lymphocyte ratio (NLR) as well as the ratio from platelet to lymphocyte might be its outflow of fiery storm, as well as d-NLR (nutrophil checks separated from WBC's tally briefs). Revision of such lists is an excellent pattern outflow [35].

16.3.4   Significantly Improved D-Dimer

D-dimer value is increased in critically ill patients; blood lymphocytes diminished tenaciously, as well as research center modifications of multi-organ lopsidedness, and furthermore show high amylase, coagulation issues, and so on, which are found [36, 37].

16.3.5   Imaging

Chest x-ray evaluation: Because the infection manifests as pneumonia, diagnostic imaging plays a critical role in the analytic dialogue, decision-making, and follow-up. In detecting early lung abnormalities and the underlying stages of infection, standard radiographic evaluation (X-beam) of the chest has a poor affectability. It is possible that it will be completely negative at this point. The chest x-ray evaluation for the most part displays reciprocal multifocal alveolar opacities in the advanced stages of illness, which tend to convert up to the complete haziness of the lung. Pleural emission can be associated [38].

16.3.6   HRCT

Due to the high technique affectability, the strategy for decision in the study of pneumonia of the coronavirus even at the subsequent phases is the chest figured tomography (CT), in special high-gage CT (HRCT) [38, 39].

16.3.7 Lung Ultrasound

Ultrasound methodology may permit assessing development of infection, with frequent evidence of subpleural consolidations, from a core interstitial patterns to the white lung. It should be done within the suspicion and within the early 24 hours every 24/48 and may be useful for patient monitoring, mechanical ventilation adjustment decisions, and signs of tilted positioning [40, 42]. The basic sonographic features are pleural lines that often get thicker, sporadic, and pathogens to the point that they look almost discontinuous. There is no dependable clinical strategy to recognize COVID-19 colds from colds brought about by rhinoviruses or more uncommon specialists. For research purposes, virus can be refined from nasal swabs or washings by inoculating organ culture of human fetal or nasal tracheal epithelium. A sample is might be gathered from swab of nose or on the other hand the rear of throat, or suction liquid from the lower respiratory parcel or take a salivation or feces test [41, 42].

16.4 Control Measures

Although antiviral treatment has been endeavored, the treatment of coronavirus colds stays demonstrative. The chance of transmission can be decreased by rehearsing clean measures. Normal cold treatment is suggestive, and no particular medicines are available. Cleaning practices reduce the transmission rate [28]. On the off chance that anyone have been in close contact with somebody with COVID-19, that might be infected. Close contact implies that one live with or have been in settings of less than 1 meter from the individuals who have the sickness. In these cases, it is ideal to remain at home [8]. Attend the health facility like wear the medical masks. If conceivable, keep something like 1 meter far off from others and do not contact surfaces with your hands. In the event that it is anything but a kid who is wiped out help the youngster adhere to this counsel. Isolate implies limiting exercises or separating people who are not ill themselves yet may have been presented to COVID-19. The objective is to forestall spread of the illness when individuals simply foster manifestations. Segregation implies separating people who are ill with side effects of COVID-19 and might be infectious to prevent the spread of the disease. This can assist to prevent the spread of sickness from individuals with COVID-19 before they feel sick or have symptoms. Quarantine can mean remaining at a particular facility or remaining at home [33].

1. Watch for common signs and symptoms, like fever, hack, or brevity of breath, remain at home for 14 days.
2. Keep distance around 6 feet, or 2 meters, among yourself as well as other people.
3. Stay away from others, however, much as could reasonably be expected, particularly individuals at high hazard of genuine sickness. Wear a mask if contact with others.
4. Isolate yourself in your house if you feel unwell. Call your doctor if indications deteriorate.
5. Physical separating implies being genuinely separated. WHO suggests keeping something like 1-meter distance from others. This is an overall measure

that everyone should take regardless of whether they are well with no known openness to coronavirus [28, 33].

16.4.1   Prevention and Patient Education

We can decrease the shots at being contaminated or spreading COVID-19 by taking some straightforward insurances:

1. Keep no less than 1-meter distance among yourself as well as other people. They display little fluid droplets from their nose and lips, which may carry illness, whenever someone hacks, sniffs, or speaks. In case you go too closer, you will be able to remove the balls as well as COVID-19 if the person is unwell [43].
2. Try not to go to packed full places. Where individuals meet up in swarms, you are bound to come incloserinteraction with somebody suffering with COVID-19, it is merely possible to maintain 1-meter distance [8].
3. Clean hands frequently and thoroughly with an alcohol-based hand sanitizer or rinse hands using water and cleansers. Cleaning your palms by water as well as soap or utilizing a sanitizer containing alcohol destroys any viruses that may be on your hands ([10].
4. For symptoms like cough, fever, or inhalation difficulties, get medicinal care immediately. However, if possible, contact ahead of time as well as obey the directions of your local health department.
5. Make certain that individuals in your surrounding should maintain hygiene in all respect. This entails shielding your nose as well as mouth using paper or bended elbow whenever users sniffle or hack. Then, immediately dispose the used tissue as well as clean your hand. Infection is transmitted via beads. By maintaining hygiene in respiration, one can protect surrounding individuals against illnesses like the common cold, influenza, as well as COVID-19 [33, 44].
6. Stay home and hole up even with minor manifestations like hack, cerebral pain, until you recover from a mild fever. Request that someone deliver you groceries. On the off chance that you need to take off from your home, wear a cover to try not to taint others. Avoiding interaction with each other will protect them against possible COVID-19 as well as other diseases.
7. Try not to contact mouth, nose, and eyes. Hands make touch with a variety of surfacesas well as may pick what is more, pick up infections. When your hands become contaminated, the illness might spread to your mouth, nose and eyes. The pathogen can then penetrate your body as well as contaminate you [43].
8. Keep forward-thinking on the most recent data from confided in sources, like WHO or your nearby and public well-being specialists. Neighborhood and public specialists are ideal put to direct on what individuals in your space ought to do to ensure themselves.

9. Coronavirus infection can get by for as long as 3 days on hardened steel as well as on plastic, under a day on cardboard and less than 4 hours on copper, so stay away from to contact such kind of article [44].

16.5   Immunization

Immunizations help our body's safe framework fight against infection quicker and that is just the beginning viably, shielding us from genuine illnesses. The immunization triggers a reaction from our immune system that helps our body fight off and hold the data of viruses so it can attack it again returns in the body. It likewise invests with dependable insusceptibility and provide long lasting immunity [44, 45].

There are three things for a vaccine: first, the well-being; second, the immunogenicity; and, third, the adequacy [44, 45].

16.5.1   Medications

Currently, no COVID-19 medication is provided, and no remedy is available. Antibiotics are not very much in effect in the face of viral contaminations like COVID-19. Specialists trying an assortment for potential medicines. FDA has approved the usage of crisis remedies for the treatment of COVID-19. The United States public health institutions later proposed dexamethasone for those with severe COVID-19 who require additional oxygen. The FDA also granted approval of crises for better plasma therapy for COVID-19 treatments. The FDA too has approved the authorization of emergency need for COVID-19 plasma convalescent treatment. Steady considerationsare pointed toward easing manifestations as well as may include pain reliefs like acetaminophen or ibuprofen, medicine, or cough syrup [45].

The point of treatment is to oversee and decrease manifestations until you have recuperated. The vast majority—around 80%—have an asymptomatic or gentle contamination which can be treated at home. One in five people who contract COVID-19 will require emergency clinic care. Around 15% of cases experience an extreme contamination requiring oxygen to help with respiratory side effects. In addition, 5% experience basic contaminations, requiring ventilation. Those at a higher danger of extreme or basic contaminations incorporate more seasoned individuals and those with fundamental ailments. For most popular contaminations, including influenza and the normal chilly, basic painkillers such as paracetamol and NSAIDs (non-steroidal calming drugs) such as ibuprofen are broadly suggested [46–50].

In the event that vibe wiped out you should rest, drink a lot of liquid, and eat nutritious food. Stay in a separate room from other relatives, and utilize a devoted restroom if conceivable. Clean and sanitize often contacted surfaces. Everybody should keep a solid way of life at home. Keep a sound eating routine, rest, stay dynamic, and make social contact with friends and family through the telephone or web. Youngsters need extra love and consideration from grownups during troublesome occasions. Keep to standard schedules and plans, however, much as could reasonably be expected. It is entirely expected to feel miserable, pushed, or befuddled during an emergency. Conversing with individuals you trust, like loved ones, can help. On the off chance that you feel overpowered, converse with a well-being specialist or advisor [51].

16.6   Conclusion

The novel coronavirus spread so quickly that it has changed the mood of the globe. Regardless of whether from the perspective of a solitary nation or multilateral levels, the immovability of worldwide relations has been set under test. The most evident results incorporate monetary downturn, an emergency of worldwide administration, exchange protectionism, and expanding isolationist feeling. From individuals to individuals, social and travel trades have all been limited. COVID-19 does not have a specific therapy at this time. Significantly higher rates of spread of such an illness among individuals, its outbreaks too, the premise of its reproduction and structure, and, moreover, of pathogenicity to discover a means to unusual treatment or to prevent it is vital to recognize. Due to its similarity with its family, the virus has been attempted to construct COVID-19 medications and anticorps. In COVID-19, differences seem to be as lengthy as the spike is larger probably going toward assume a significant part in the pathogenesis and treatment of this infection. In any case, distinguishing the particular molecular facts of virus may be useful in accomplishing treatment objectives.

References

1. https://www.who.int/health-topics/coronavirus#tab=tab_1
2. Pal, M., Berhanu, G., Desalegn, C., Kandi, V., Severe Acute Respiratory Syndrome Coronavirus-2 (SARS-CoV-2): An Update. *Cureus.*, 12, 3, e7423, 2020.
3. Ramphul, K., Ramphul, Y., Park, Y., Lohana, P., Dhillon, B.K., Sombans, S., A comprehensive review and update on severe acute respiratory syndrome coronavirus 2 (SARS-CoV-2) and Coronavirus disease 2019 (COVID-19): what do we know now in 2021? *Arch. Med. Sci. Atheroscler. Dis.*, 6, e5–e13, 2021.
4. Tyrrell, D.A.J. and Myint, S.H., Coronaviruses, in: *Medical Microbiology*, 4th, vol. Chapter 60, S. Baron (Ed.), p. PMID: 21413266, University of Texas Medical Branch at Galveston, Galveston TX, 1996.
5. Wrapp, D., De Vlieger, D., Corbett, K.S., Torres, G.M., Wang, N., Van Breedam, W., Roose, K., van Schie, L., Hoffmann, M., Pöhlmann, S., Graham, B.S., Callewaert, N., Schepens, B., Saelens, X., McLellan, J.S., VIB-CMB COVID-19 Response Team, Structural Basis for Potent Neutralization of Betacoronaviruses by Single-Domain Camelid Antibodies. *Cell.*, 181, 5, 1004–1015.e15, 2020.
6. Mousavizadeh, L. and Ghasemi, S., Genotype and phenotype of COVID-19: Their roles in pathogenesis. *J. MicrobiolImmunol. Infect.*, 54, 2, 159–163, 2021.
7. Banerjee, N. and Mukhopadhyay, S., Viral glycoproteins: biological role and application in diagnosis. *Virusdisease*, 27, 1, 1–11, 2016.
8. Tyrrell, D.A.J. and Myint, S.H., Coronaviruses, in: *Medical Microbiology*, 4th, S. Baron (Ed.), University of Texas Medical Branch at Galveston, Galveston, TX, 1996.
9. Ye, Z.W., Yuan, S., Yuen, K.S., Fung, S.Y., Chan, C.P., Jin, D.Y., Zoonotic origins of human coronaviruses. *Int. J. Biol. Sci.*, 16, 10, 1686–1697, 2020.

10. Latif, A.A. and Mukaratirwa, S., Zoonotic origins and animal hosts of coronaviruses causing human disease pandemics: A review. *Onderstepoort. J. Vet. Res.*, 87, 1, e1–e9, 2020.

11. Atkins, J.F., Loughran, G., Bhatt, P.R., Firth, A.E., Baranov, P.V., Ribosomal frameshifting and transcriptional slippage: from genetic steganography and cryptography to adventitious use. *Nucleic. Acids Res.*, 44, 7007–78, 2016.

12. Kelly, J.A. *et al.* Structural and functional conservation of the programmed -1 ribosomal frameshift signal of SARS coronavirus 2 (SARS-CoV-2). *J. Bio. Chem.*, 295, 31, 10741–10748, 2020.

13. Perlman, S. and Netland, J., Coronaviruses post-SARS: update on replication and pathogenesis. *Nat. Rev. Microbiol.*, 7, 439–50, 2009.

14. Wu, A., Peng, Y., Huang, B., Ding, X., Wang, X., Niu, P., Meng, J., Zhu, Z., Zhang, Z., Wang, J. *et al.*, Genome composition and divergence of the novel coronavirus (2019-nCoV) originating in China. *Cell Host Microbe*, 27, 325–8, 2020.

15. Zhu, N., Zhang, D., Wang, W., Li, X., Yang, B., Song, J., Zhao, X., Huang, B., Shi, W., Lu, R. *et al.*, A novel coronavirus from patients with pneumonia in China, 2019. *N Engl. J. Med.*, 382, 727–33, 2020.

16. Kim, D., Lee, J.-Y., Yang, J.-S., Kim, J.W., Kim, V.N., Chang, H., The architecture of SARS-CoV-2 transcriptom. *Cell-Press*, 181, 4, 988865, 2020:2020.2003.2012.

17. Chen, N., Zhou, M., Dong, X., Qu, J., Gong, F., Han, Y., Qiu, Y., Wang, J., Liu, Y., Wei, Y. *et al.*, Epidemiological and clinical characteristics of 99 cases of 2019 novel coronavirus pneumonia in Wuhan, China: a descriptive study. *Lancet*, 395, 507–13, 2020.

18. Bergmann, C.C. *et al.*, Coronavirus infection of the central nervous system: host–virus stand-off. *Nat. Rev. Microbiol.*, 4, 121–132, 2006.

19. Masters, P.S., The Molecular Biology of Coronaviruses. *Virus Res.*, 66, 193–292, 2006.

20. Sola, I. *et al.*, RNA-RNA and RNA-protein interactions in coronavirus replication and transcription. *RNA Biol.*, 8, 2, 237–248, 2011.

21. Gwaltney, J.M., Jr, C.OMMA Virology and immunology of the common cold. *Rhinology*, 23, 265, 1985.

22. Myint, S., Johnstone, S., Sanderson, G., Simpson, H., An evaluation of 'nested' RT-PCR methods for the detection of human coronaviruses 229E and OC43 in clinical specimens. *Mol. Cell Probes.*, 8, 357–364, 1994.

23. Sanchez, C.M., Jimenez, G., Laviada, M.D. *et al.*, Antigenic homology among coronaviruses related to transmissible gastroenteritis virus. *Virology*, 174, 410, 1990.

24. Schmidt, O.W., Allan, I.D., Cooney, M.K. *et al.*, Rises in titers of antibody to human coronaviruses OC43 and 229E in Seattle families during. *Am. J. Epidemiol.*, 123, 862, 1975–1979, 1986.

25. Spaan, W., Cavanagh, D., Horzinek, M.C., Coronaviruses: structure and genome expression. *J. Gen. Virol.*, 69, 2939, 1988.

26. Tyrrell, D.A.J., Cohen, S., Schlarb, J.E., Signs and symptoms in common colds. *Epidemiol. Infect.*, 111, 143–156, 1993.

27. Subbarao, K. and Mahanty, S., Respiratory Virus Infections: Understanding COVID-19. *Immunity*, 52, 6, 905–909, 2020.

28. Lee, Y., Min, P., Lee, S., Kim, S.W., Prevalence and Duration of Acute Loss of Smell or Taste in COVID-19 Patients. *J. Korean Med. Sci.*, 35, 18, e174, 2020.

29. Lau, S.K.P., Woo, P.C.Y., Yip, C.C.Y., Tse, H., Tsoi, H., Cheng, V.C.C., Lee, P., Tang, B.S.F., Cheung, C.H.Y., Lee, R.A. *et al.*, Coronavirus HKU1 and Other Coronavirus Infections in Hong Kong. *J. Clin. Microbiol.*, 44, 2063–2071, 2006.

30. Singhal, T., A Review of Coronavirus Disease-2019 (COVID-19). *Indian J. Pediatr.*, 87, 281–286, 2020.

31. COVID-19 Dashboard by the Center for Systems Science and Engineering (CSSE) at Johns Hopkins University (JHU). Available online: https://coronavirus.jhu.edu/map.html.

32. World Health Organization Advice on the Use of Point-Of-Care Immunodiagnostic Tests for COVID-19. Available online: https://www.who.int/news-room/commentaries/detail/advice-on-the-use-of-point-of-care-immunodiagnostic-tests-for-covid-19.

33. Coronavirus Disease 2019 (COVID-19) Guidelines for Clinical Specimens. *U.S. Centers for Disease Control and Prevention (CDC)*, Accessed March 21, 2020. https://www.cdc.gov/coronavirus/2019-nCoV/lab/guidelines-clinical-specimen.

34. Vandenberg, O., Martiny, D., Rochas, O., van Belkum, A., Kozlakidis, Z., Considerations for diagnostic COVID-19 tests. *Nat. Rev. Microbiol.*, 19, 3, 171–183, 2021.

35. Azkur, A.K., Akdis, M., Azkur, D., Sokolowska, M., van de Veen, W., Bruggen, M.C., Immune response to SARS-CoV-2 and mechanisms of immunopathological changes in COVID-19. *Allergy*, 75, 1564–1581, 2020.

36. Kermali, M., Khalsa, R.K., Pillai, K., Ismail, Z., Harky, A., Life Sciences, The role of biomarkers in diagnosis of COVID-19 - a systematic review. *Life Sci.*, 254, 117788, 2020.

37. Chen, G., Wu, D., Guo, W., Cao, Y., Huang, D., Wang, H., Clinical and immunological features of severe and moderate coronavirus disease 2019. *J. Invest. Clin.*, 130, 2620–2629, 2020.

38. Caruso, D., Zerunian, M., Polici, M., Pucciarelli, F., Polidori, T., Rucci, C., Chest CT features of COVID-19 in Rome. *Italy. Radiol.*, 296, E79–85, 2020.

39. Farias, L.P.G., Strabelli, D.G., Sawamura, M.V.Y., COVID-19 pneumonia and the reversed halo sign. *J. Bras. Pneumol.*, 46, 1–8, 2020.

40. Yang, Y., Yang, M., Shen, C., Wang, F., Yuan, J., Li, J., Laboratory Diagnosis and Monitoring the Viral Shedding of SARS-CoV-2 Infection. *The Innovation*, 1, 1–7, 2020.

41. Vieira, L.M., Emery, E., Andriolo, A., COVID-19: laboratory diagnosis for clinicians. An updating article. *Sao Paulo Med. J.*, 138, 259–266, 2020.

42. Peixoto, A.O., Costa, R.M., Uzun, R., Fraga, A.M.A., Ribeiro, J.D., Marson, F.A.L., Applicability of lung ultrasound in COVID-19 diagnosis and evaluation of the disease progression: A systematic review. *Pulmonology*, S2531–0437(21)00050-7, 27, 6, 2021.

43. Conly, J., Seto, W.H., Pittet, D., Holmes, A., Chu, M., Hunter, P.R., WHO Infection Prevention and Control Research and Development Expert Group for COVID-19. Use of medical face masks versus particulate respirators as a component of personal protective equipment for healthcare workers in the context of the COVID-19 pandemic. *Antimicrob. Resist. Infect. Control.*, 9, 1, 126, 2020.

44. Chou, R., Dana, T., Jungbauer, R., Weeks, C., McDonagh, M.S., Masks for Prevention of Respiratory VirusInfections, Including SARS-CoV-2, in Healthcare andCommunity Settings: A Living Rapid Review. *Ann. Intern. Med.*, 173, 7, 542–555, 2020.

45. Samudrala, P.K., Kumar, P., Choudhary, K., Thakur, N., Wadekar, G.S., Dayaramani, R., Agrawal, M., Alexander, A., Virology, pathogenesis, diagnosis and in-line treatment of COVID-19. *Eur. J. Pharmacol.*, 883, 173375, 2020.

46. Chen, N., Zhou, M., Dong, X. *et al.*, Epidemiological and clinical characteristics of 99 cases of 2019 novel coronavirus pneumonia in Wuhan, China: a descriptive study. *Lancet*, 395, 507–13, 2020.

47. Huang, C., Wang, Y., Li, X. *et al.*, Clinical features of patients infected with 2019 novel coronavirus in Wuhan, China. *Lancet*, 395, 497–506, 2020.

48. Wang, D., Hu, B., Hu, C. *et al.*, Clinical Characteristics of 138 Hospitalized Patients With 2019 Novel Coronavirus-Infected Pneumonia in Wuhan, China. *JAM*, 323, 11, 1061–9, 2020.

49. Chan, J.F., Yuan, S., Kok, K.H. *et al.*, A familial cluster of pneumonia associated with the 2019 novel coronavirus indicating person-to-person transmission: a study of a family cluster. *Lancet*, 395, 514–23, 2020.

50. Hu, Z., Song, C., Xu, C. *et al.*, Clinical characteristics of 24 asymptomatic infections with COVID-19 screened among close contacts in Nanjing, China. *Sci. China Life Sci.*, 63, 706—11, 2020 Mar 4.

51. Uzunova, K., Filipova, E., Pavlova, V., Vekov, T., Insights into antiviral mechanisms of remdesivir, lopinavir/ritonavir and chloroquine/hydroxychloroquine affecting the new SARS-CoV-2. *Biomed. Pharmacother.*, 131, 110668, 2020.

17

Smart Healthcare for Pregnant Women in Rural Areas

D. Shanthi

Infromation Technology, Maturi Venkata Subba Rao Engineering College, Hyderabad, India

Abstract

The conditions of villages in India have improved the last few decades; however, people are migrating from village to rural towns where there are insufficient healthcare facilities. The need now is to create "smart villages" and "smart rural towns". In developing countries have high incidences of neonatal, infant, child mortality, and malnutrition. Governments, aid agencies, and NGOs have taken a range of steps over time to minimize child mortality, infant mortality, hunger, and maternal mortality. In addition to the government's initiatives across different schemes, science and technology must be harnessed for their solution. Physical and intellectual development is affected by malnutrition among children. In the long term, malnutrition impacts overall production and the country's economic growth. Neonatal, child mortality, and malnutrition suggest that adequate maternal care raises birth weight to minimize infants' low birth weight. Their maternal health development feature explains that it is necessary to have an early onset of prenatal care and a minimum number of prenatal care visits to improve both mothers and unborn children's health.

Keywords: Smart villages, healthcare, pregnant women, government, Anganwadi, LDA, SDD

17.1 Introduction

Over 800 women worldwide move on preventive causes identified with pregnancy, and 20% are from India. This is reported annually that 44,000 women have died in India cause of avoidable causes related to childbirth. The astonishing thing indicates that maternal deaths per 100,000 live births have decreased from 212 in 2007 to 167 in 2013. Via different schemes, UNICEF, the Government of India, and various state governments contributed to this reduction. Mothers have higher death rate in the most minimal monetary section [1]. These deaths occur only because of the lack of services, and most of them are treatable. In developed countries, virtually all maternal deaths (99%) occur and women die in pregnancy and childbirth as a result of complications. During pregnancy, most of those complications arise and are treatable. The main complications responsible for

Email: dshanthi01@gmail.com

Tushar H. Jaware, K. Sarat Kumar, Ravindra D. Badgujar and Svetlin Antonov (eds.) *Medical Imaging and Health Informatics*, (317–334) © 2022 Scrivener Publishing LLC

almost 75% of all maternal deaths are severe bleeding, infections, childbirth complications, etc. Poverty, distance, lack of knowledge, insufficient resources, and cultural traditions are other significant problems because women cannot take proper medication during pregnancy and childbirth. Therefore, required efforts should provide pregnant women with timely and quality health assistance that will contribute to the birth of healthy children [2, 3].

A commonly used public health measure is the infant mortality rate (death within the first year of life) per 1,000 live births. In developing countries, it is one digit. It is 2.1 in Japan, 3.9 in the UK, and 5.8 in the USA, as per the statistics for 2014. The rate of infant mortality in India, however, is very high. According to the Press Information Bureau, the GOI is 34 in 2016, 31.4 in 2017, 29.7 in 2018, and 28.3 in 2019. It is at its lowest in Goa at 8 and 31 in Telangana State [4]. India is a developed country, but there are still some rural areas below the poverty line. These individuals are also not qualified and do not have the minimum knowledge of nutritious foods. Thus, our nation is suffering from many problems, and neonatal, baby, child mortality, and malnutrition are significant problems. The other major problem is usually in rural areas where access to hospitals is restricted, and due to limited access to registered physicians, patients frequently receive incorrect diagnoses [5, 6].

As per the World Health Organization, prenatal care consists of four visits to pregnant women's healthcare facilities and health professionals. The four antenatal treatments assure adequate diet, vitamin intake, acceptable vaccine, exercise, negative behavioral adjustment, and institutional delivery. Pregnancy, both physically and emotionally, is one of the most vulnerable times of a woman's life. Right treatment during pregnancy is essential for the health of the mother and the welfare of the unborn child [7–9]. Medicines, as well as healthy habits and care and parenting skills, are needed during pregnancy. Antenatal care is an umbrella term used to describe the medical procedures and care carried out during pregnancy. It is critical that in promoting prenatal care, this program's success leaves no room for doubt. Prenatal care is a vital strategy for achieving public health priorities, key goals for health, and the Millennium Development Goals (MDGs) [9]. The healthcare facility and trained health workers will prepare delivery during four antenatal visits, understand risk signs during pregnancy through multiple physical assessments, and change risky habits and advise on healthier diets. For normal delivery, the state health workers can operate. In the literature, it is well known that there are lower rates of maternal and child mortality and positive pregnancy outcomes among those women who received four antenatal treatment. The best use of prenatal care is related to the weight and gestational age of babies. In literature, children of mothers who have not obtained prenatal healthcare are reported to die twice as often during childhood as children of prenatal mothers [10]. Preterm births and babies with low birth weight contribute to death in neonates and children. Despite the evidence that prenatal care is linked to favorable birth outcomes, cost-effectiveness is not an easy step. Since there was a considerably greater incidence of low and meager birth weight, premature delivery, transfers to acute care, and early mortality for women who did not receive prenatal treatment, the cumulative impact of an absocare facility on total care has been substantially higher [11]. This paper is aimed mainly at exploring the effects of babies' prenatal care in India. The word antenatal treatment is used to describe the procedures and treatments to be taken during pregnancy. Prenatal care is a central strategy to meet public health priorities, primary health goals, and MDGs.

- Significant health problems:
  The fundamental issues facing women in rural areas are (a) a lack of awareness of the signs of risk, (b) the absence of a household decision maker, (c) a woman's low financial status, (d) costs involved, (e) past unsatisfactory experience with the healthcare system, and (f) poor standard of care perceived. All these challenges bring on life-threatening conditions for rural women.

17.2   National/International Surveys Reviews

From three National Family Health Surveys, we collected secondary data. In various states in India, data is collected from NFHS1 (1992 to 1993), NFHS2 (199 to 1999), and NFHS3 (2005 to 2006). The International Institute for Population Science provides various health indicators withstate-level health data. We analyzed data from three surveys related to prenatal care [12].

17.2.1   National Family Health Survey Review-11

AUTHORS: Kamla Gupta, Prof., IIPS.
In 1992 to 1993, the National Family Health Survey(1), India's first broad demographic and health survey, was carried out. It provided data on 89,777 married women from 88,562 families in the 13 to 49 age group. It covered 99% of India's total population in 24 states. NFHS(I)'s primary objective was to collect data on fertility rates, family size patterns, demand for family planning products, family planning awareness, and various family planning methods. To obtain breastfeeding and food supplement details, the undesired fertility level, health services before delivery, collect data on child nutrition and well-being, vaccination, infant mortality, and neonatal mortality rates. The other aim of NFHS(1) was to gain knowledge of fertility rates, family planning, and understanding of socioeconomic and demographic health indicators for children and mothers [13, 14]. For all nations, the questionnaire used for NFHS(1) was the same, but additional knowledge was gathered to learn about some countries' particularities. The NFHS(1) questionnaire included questions relating to people's propensity from Rajasthan to marry girls, questions about awareness of AIDS, sex-determination tests in Punjab, and foreign migration from Punjab and Kerala [15].

17.2.2   National Family Health Survey Review-2.2

AUTHORS: Prof. Sulabha Parasuraman, IIPS Parasuraman,
NFHS(2's) primary goal was to include projections of birth rates, the family planning system, infant and child mortality rates, maternal and child health, and the health services available, obtaining information on women's status, education and living conditions

in society, reproductive and family planning programs, women's health issues, domestic violence, and atrocities against them. In NFHS(1), information on the weight of children is collected only, while in NFHS(2), information on eligible women is collected, knowing their nutritional level is as per NFHS(2).

One of the aims of NFHS(2) was to test blood through the Hemocu system to learn about the levels of hemoglobin among women and children under 3 years of age and learn about the incidence of anemia in India as a whole. To have an additional examination carried out in the two metropolitan cities of Mumbai and Delhi to assess the levels of lead in the blood of children less than 3 years of age. NFHS(2)'s goal was also to understand the quantity of iodized salt used by families in India for cooking.

17.2.3   National Family Health Survey Reviews-3

AUTHORS: Dr. P. Arokiasamy, IIPS

Each successive round of the NFHS has two unique objectives: a) to provide the critical health and family welfare data required for policy and program purposes by the Ministry of Health and Family Welfare and other agencies, and b) to provide information on important emerging health and family welfare issues. NFHS(3), such as NFHS(1) and NFHS(2), offers estimates of significant family welfare and health measures by context characteristics at national and state levels to achieve the first of these two goals; and measure patterns at the federal and state level in family welfare and health measures over time. Perinatal mortality, male participation in family welfare, reproductive health of teenagers, high-risk sexual activity, education in family life, healthy injections, tuberculosis and malaria; slum and non-slum dwellers' family welfare and health conditions in eight cities (Chennai, Delhi, Hyderabad, Indore, Kolkata, Meerut, Mumbai and Nagpur); and global, Uttar Pradesh and five high HIV prevalence countries (Andra Pradesh, Karnataka, Maharashtrá, Manipur, and Tamil Nadu) have HIV prevalence among adult women and males.

17.3   Architecture

An Android application that tracks the baby's daily progress and according to the doctor's prescription will be established in the proposed operation, which would solve the above problems. The proposed algorithms to be developed include displaying specifics of the diet chart and vaccine that the pregnant woman must adopt during her pregnancy time. This app also offers via SMS notifications required physical exercises that a pregnant woman must follow for a healthy and safe delivery. In risky cases, it often consists of several steps to be taken. The Android application will continuously facilitate all the requisite details about the fetus (baby) transition until 40 weeks. The checkup records of pregnant women were obtained with safe parameters from Anganwadi workers. Any anomalies reported are sent to the health department to take prompt action (and the individual woman). The model has been built on a zonal basis and could be applied to the national level. The app also provides timely information for easy accessibility and better care concerning the nearest Anganwadis, maternity hospitals, along with their contact details [17] which is shown in Figure 17.1.

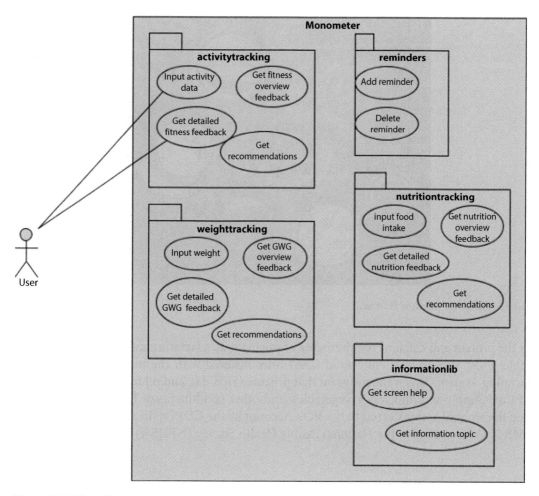

Figure 17.1 Block diagram.

17.4 Anganwadi's Collaborative Work

Over the years, with differential approaches across the states, the Anganwadi Services Scheme under Umbrella ICDS has developed, and there are many examples of groundbreaking and influential models introduced by state governments that have shown positive results and have the potential to be scaled up [18].

17.5 Schemes Offered by Central/State Governments

17.5.1 AAH (Anna Amrutha Hastham)

Under this scheme, in all Anganwadi centers, Andhra Pradesh's government offers one daily meal to pregnant and nursing women (AWCs), see the Figure 17.2. A full meal consists of rice, dal with green onions, vegetables, eggs, and 200 ml of milk for a minimum period of 25 days per month. A complete meal can meet 40% of the day's calories and 40%

Figure 17.2 Anna Amrutha Hastham.

of the protein and calcium requirements of pregnant and lactating mothers each day. The tablet must also be Iron Folic Acid (IFA) Administered with the meal to pregnant and lactating women. This is the program that procures rice, dal, and oil from the Department of Civil Supply and milk, eggs, vegetables, and other condiments at DPC approved rates, and the amount is transferred to the VO's Account by the CDPOs. In Andhra Pradesh, the IMR is 35, according to the National Family Health Survey (NFHS 4) for 2015 to 2016, 20

Figure 17.3 Arogya Laxmi Program.

in urban areas and 40 in rural areas. In addition, 58.6 were anemic children aged between 6 and 59 months, and 52.9% were pregnant women aged between 15 and 49 years [11].

17.5.2   Programme Arogya Laxmi

There are, therefore, critical opportunities for the prevention of malnutrition to address the nutrition requirements of pregnant and lactating women. In particular, the need to change ICDS nutrition was noticed as the take-home ration (THR) given to pregnant and nursing women under ICDS is not only too minimal; all families are also shared which is shown in Figure 17.3.

The government of Telangana has introduced the Arogya Laxmi Program in this regard, which involves the spot feeding of a complete meal for pregnant and breastfeeding women at the Anganwadi center, in compliance with the IFA (Iron and Folic Acid) tablet administration. On 1 January 2013, the program was launched with the ICDS program's most harmful health and nutrition [11].

17.5.3   Balamrutham-Kids' Weaning Food from 7 Months to 3 Years

Weaning food is distributed monthly for boy children from 7 months to 3 years in packages of 2.5 kg. The children get two eggs in a week at the AWC on an ICDS food model for a span of 7 months to 3 years under the ICDS and the Balamrutham packet. The children also get the two eggs a week on an ICDS food-model. In the critical period of 7 months to 3 years, Balamrutham is expected to serve as significant supplementary nutrition for the child and help avoid chronic malnutrition and advise the mother in IYCF practices. Balamrutham is a dense calorie food for weaning meals, minimizes malnutrition, and provides food of supervised feeding for malnourished children [11] which is shown in Figure 17.4.

17.5.4   Nutri TASC (Tracking of Group Responsibility for Services)

This surveillance system allows for close monitoring of pregnant women, nursing mothers, children under one year of age, and malnourished children under 5 years of age to benefit from nutrition services. The NutriTASC ha been created to monitor nutrition services for

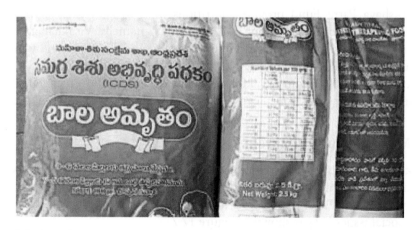

Figure 17.4 Bala Amrutham.

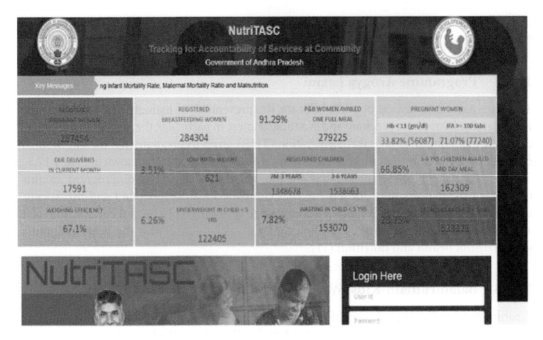

Figure 17.5 Tracking of group responsibility for services.

mothers and infants, to promote and monitor health services to ensure close monitoring of all high-risk pregnant women, to provide exceptional care, and to supervise malnourished children under 5 years of age, teenage girls, and pregnant women. Name-based monitoring objectives are to monitor nutrition services and promote the delivery of healthcare services among beneficiaries; enhance the nutritional status of children under 5 years of age, pregnant, and lactating mothers; and achieve the desired objectives of reducing the rate of infant mortality, the ratio of maternal mortality and malnutrition among women and children [11]. Tracking of accountability services at community is shown in Figure 17.5.

17.5.5   Akshyapatra Foundation (ISKCON)

M/s. The Akshaya Patra Fund provides nutritious food to all groups of beneficiaries, covering 42,580 beneficiaries, in four ICDS projects, namely, Visakhapatnam (U): I, Visakhapatnam (U): II, Anakapalli and Sherlingampalli. The recipes given by the foundation include Rice Kichidi, Sweet Pongal, Dhalia, Rice Kheer, Veg Kichidi, and Sweet Dhalia. Both snacks, such as Kala Channa or kommu Senagalu, are given to recipients for 4 days with 25 g and 2 days per week boiled eggs [11]. Akshaya patra is shown in Figure 17.6.

17.5.6   Mahila Sishu Chaitanyam

The 1-week IEC Campaign involves a combined effort from various stakeholders. We urge women and children, primary and secondary education, elected officials, electronic press, etc., at the village/business and local level to increase visibility and disseminate nutrition, health, and social issues [11] as shown in Figure 17.7.

Figure 17.6 Akshaya Patra Foundation.

Figure 17.7 Mahila Sishu Chaitanyam.

17.5.7   Community Management of Acute Malnutrition

A Memorandum of Understanding has been signed by the Department of Women and Child Development with Jamshedji Tata Trust and UNICEF to implement the Nandurbar District Community Management of Acute Malnutrition ("CMAM Project"). This initiative aims to improve the survival and development results of an estimated 11,500 SAM (Severe Acute Malnutrition) children in all six blocks of the Nandurbar District and compare the products of three nutrition protocols: recipes from MNT/RUTF, SF, and ARF [11].

17.5.8   Child Health Nutrition Committee

A Memorandum of Understanding was formed to create a Mumbai Child Health and Food Commission to improve health and nutrition in informal urban settings by the Department of Women and Child Development and Society for Nutrition, Education, and Health (SNEHA) [11] shown in Figure 17.8.

17.5.9   Bharat Ratna APJ Abdul Kalam Amrut Yojna

APY Abdul Kalam (Figure 17.9), Amrut Yojna is approved for one hot and cooked nutritious food in tribal areas by the Department of Women and Child Development, Government of Maharashtra. In 16 provinces with predominant tribal communities, the scheme is placed in place by AWCs that come under the Women and Child Department. The scheme replacing the previous "THR," which supplied lactating or expectant moms with purely or update packages in tribal state regions [11].

Figure 17.8 Child Health Nutrition Committee.

Figure 17.9 APJ Abdul Kalam.

17.6 Smart Healthcare System

There are essential issues worldwide given the recent high healthcare costs and an aging society's growing cost. Implementing cost-cutting initiatives is, therefore, one of the most relevant developments in healthcare today. One way to achieve cost savings is to make healthcare institutions more efficient, for example, by reducing the number of days of hospital stays, reducing expensive treatment services and the amount of personal consultations. Prevention is often provided by early identification of people at risk and recommendations for preventing expensive hospital admission. It is also necessary to encourage people to keep their lifestyle safe [20, 21].

In the modern world, people and many people, especially young people, feel more and more responsible for their safety; they want to make health or sickness decisions.

Figure 17.10, explains the goal of this project is to develop a mobile app for women in rural areas during pregnancy. Appropriate child care is vital both for maternal health and parental health. A key objective of healthy mothership and child survival is increasingly qualified care at birth.

The key problem facing women in rural areas is the lack of awareness of the signs of danger of the family, the absence of the decision-maker, the woman's low status, the expense of previous unsatisfactory experience with the health system, and the presumptuous low quality of treatment. These are all issues that endanger women with lives.

The project's goal was to establish a health monitoring system to allow a rural pregnant woman to communicate with an almost complete doctor/doctor. The risk of childbearing females' death is rising due to analphabetism in women and the lack of access to health facilities in many rural areas. The project's primary goal is to reduce costly hospitalization by continuous patient health surveillance in the early stages and avoid certain risks. In this project, the health monitoring system continuously monitors the pregnant lady's temperature and heart rate and GSM sends details to gynecologists on the remote site via their cell phone when fluctuations occur [23, 24].

This system also allows the patient to listen to the doctor's recommendations and dietary prescriptions. The health monitoring unit acts as this device, but the patient can hear the doctor's instructions and diet prescriptions. The audio recording and playback chip is used to accomplish this. Anganwadi will collect the information and uploaded in the app, so that it will generate complete report of the patient. Figure 17.11 shows the system architecture of smart health care system.

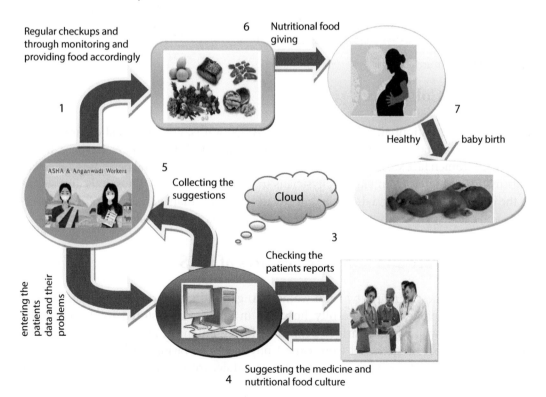

Figure 17.10 Working procedure.

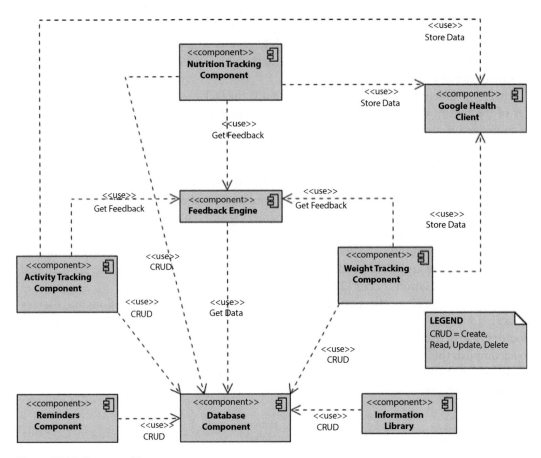

Figure 17.11 System architecture.

17.7   Data Collection

In the form of questionnaires by rural women, Anganwadis, governmental organizations, government hospitals, and maternity hospitals in villages and stored in the database, information on women face various problems during antenatal and neonatal periods is collected. Information gathered from expert physicians in various well-known hospitals and stored in the database concerning a diet schedule, treatment steps, management of different situations and exercises in the pre and post-pregnancy periods shall be collected [25].

17.8   Hardware and Software Features of HCS

In the form of questionnaires by rural women, Anganwadis, governmental organizations, government hospitals, and maternity hospitals in villages and stored in the database, information on women face various problems during antenatal and neonatal periods is collected. Information gathered from expert physicians in various well-known hospitals and stored in the database concerning a diet schedule, treatment steps, management of different situations and exercises in the pre and post-pregnancy periods shall be collected. Information on women facing various challenges throughout the prenatal and neonatal periods is collected in the form of questionnaires by rural women, Anganwadi's, governmental organizations, government hospitals, and maternity hospitals in villages and saved in the database. Information about a food regimen, therapeutic steps, and management of different scenarios, and exercises in the pre- and post-pregnancy periods will be collected from expert physicians in several well-known hospitals and saved in the database.

17.9   Implementation

17.9.1   Modules

- Pre-processing of data
- Product features extraction
- Psychological measurement of the consumer
- Analysis of emotions.

Rural women do not know the value of proper medicine. Health expenses are also too costly. The body systems use critical parameters including heart rate, temperature, and kicking.

17.9.2   Modules Description

17.9.2.1   Data Preprocessing

We build preprocessing data in the first module. Scoring data collection we received from http://www.yelp.com. We include this data as the device input. The data set contains data set for product products, a dataset for user reviews and user feedback. We must distinguish information from datasets and assessments. Our approach is aimed at seeking useful hints from analysis and predicting the ratings of social users. This module extracts features of the product from the consumer review corpus first and then introduces the method of defining social users' sentiment. The set of data is a factor group.

- Similarity of emotions

17.9.2.2   Component Features Extraction

- We extract product features from textual feedback with LDA in this module. We want mainly the product features, including individuals and specific product/item/service attributes. LDA is a Bayesian model used to model the relationship between feedback, subjects and words.
- We first consider each user's analysis as a word set without considering the order to construct the vocabulary. Then, we filter out the following terms: "Stop Words," "Soft Words," "Stop Words," and "Stop Words."
- A stop word may be defined as a word with the same probability of occurrence in non inquiry documentation as in the related documents. For example, the Stop Words may be some prepositions, articles, pronouns, and so on. The input text is transparent and does not interfere much with the generation of subjects afterword filters. The vocabulary V is used to construct all the

specific terms; each word has a label. We have a few frequent words from each subject. Nevertheless, we have to screen out the noisy characteristics of the candidate by using adjective terms and their frequencies at the context corpus.

17.9.2.3   User Sentimental Measurement

Inside this module, the Sentiment Degree Dictionary (SDD) develops five different levels with 128 terms. Level 1 includes 52 phrases, the highest level of feeling like "most" and "best" words. In addition, 48 words in level 2, meaning a greater degree of emotion, such as "better" and "very" words. Level 3 includes 12 words, including "more" and "such". The terms "a little", "a bit", and "more or less" are in level 49 phrases. In level 5, there are seven words like "less" or "bit" or "not too". We have also developed the negation dictionary (ND) by gathering commonly used negative prefix terms like "no". These terms reverse the polarity of words of thought.

17.9.2.4   Sentiment Evaluation

First, the initial analysis is divided by the punctuation mark into several clauses. We first look up the SD dictionary for each clause to find the feeling terms before the product characteristics. A positive word for score +1.0, while a negative word for score −1.0 is assigned. Second, we discover the words of the sentiment grade based on the SDD dictionary and consider the words of the sentiment graduation to increase the sentiment. Finally, we search the negative word prefix based on the ND dictionary and apply a negative control factor with a default value of +1.0. An unknown number of negative prefix terms in the specified zone precedes the word sentiment; we reverse the polarity of feeling and set the coefficient to −1.0 [26].

The following is listed in each sentiment factor:
The similarity of consumer feeling

- We equate our method's output with existing Yelp dataset models. In RPS, k is the user dimension and latent item vectors In the objective function.
- The test results indicate the high precision of RPS. We also display the significance of social friend variables in the recommender method (i.e., CircleCon2b and PRM) and unique characteristics (i.e., EFM).

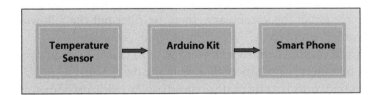

Figure 17.12 Block diagram.

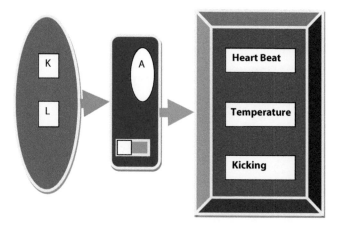

Figure 17.13 User reviews of the home_service.

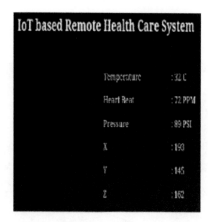

Figure 17.14 IoT-based smart healthcare system.

17.10   Results and Analysis

- Rural women do not know the value of proper medicine. Health expenses are also too costly. The body systems use critical parameters including heart rate, temperature, and kicking.
- Alerts are highlights of our method. It is helpful to collect more health information about pregnant women in rural areas. A mobile healthcare system that focuses on prenatal identification to reduce fetal and maternal mortality rate.
- A fetal heart monitor monitors a baby's pulse. Signals are processed by an instrumentation amplifier and then filtered the required frequency band. A signal is given to the Arduino that exceeds a specific threshold. The heart rate sensor tracks heartbeats and exact this is given as an input to Arduino shown in Figures 17.15 and 17.16.

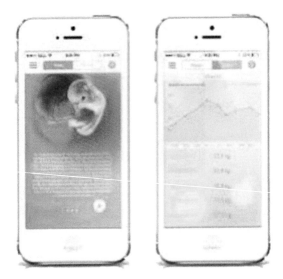

Figure 17.15 Working stage of the app.

Figure 17.16 Baby is kicking.

The temperature is input to the ADC of the friend ARM board. There are 10 ADC (Analog-to-Digital Converter) channels on this production package. We are using a 12-bit ADC to calculate temperature as seen in the block diagram shown in Figures 17.12 & 17.13.

This friendly ARM kit allows for easy growth. The role "readadc" reads a digital value from an analogue input pin and returns the analogue value. The role returns a raw digital data of the analogue input signal. This must be normalized.

It can be hard to say when your baby has moved. If the mother has a second or third child, then she knows to be more discerning in the diagnosis of colic. Babies vary between being alert and sleepy at various times of the day. They are most involved between 9 p.m. and 1 a.m. as trying to sleep. This is due to fluctuating blood sugar levels. Babies often respond to sound or touch and can kick your partner if you snuggle too close in bed. A sample report shown in Figure 17.14.

17.11 Conclusion

In this chapter, the knowledge from social users' feedback proposes a recommendation model. We incorporate similarity of user feeling, interpersonal feeling and the credibility of things into a single factoring process to fulfill the prediction task. We use the feeling of social users to suggest user tastes in particular. Moreover, we create a new relationship called the influence of interpersonal feeling between the user and friends, representing user friends' influence from a nostalgic point of view. Moreover, as long as we receive textual analysis, we can calculate the consumer's feeling quantitatively and use the distribution of sentiment among users to deduce the reputation of the object.

The results of the experiment indicate that the three sentimental variables contribute significantly to the rating forecast. In comparison to current approaches to real-world data collection, it illustrates significant changes. We should consider more linguistic laws in our future work when interpreting the meaning and incorporate more fine-grained emotion analysis into the feeling dictionaries. We can also adapt or construct other hybrid factoring models to integrate sentence-level analysis, tensor factorization, or profound learning techniques.

References

1. Zoric, A.C. and Ilic, S., PC Based Electrocardiography & Data Acquisition. *TELSIKS*, IEEE, pp. 619–622, September 28-30, 2005.
2. Yang, X., Steck, H., Liu, Y., Circle-based recommendation in online social networks, in: *Proc. 18th ACM SIGKDD Int. Conf. KDD*, New York, NY, USA, pp. 1267–1275, Aug. 2012.
3. Jiang, M., Cui, P., Liu, R., Yang, Q., Wang, F., Zhu, W., Yang, S., Social contextual recommendation, in: *Proc. 21st ACM Int. CIKM*, pp. 45–54, 2012.
4. Jamali, M. and Ester, M., A matrix factorization technique with trust propagation for recommendation in social networks, in: *Proc. ACM conf. RecSys*, Barcelona, Spain, pp. 135–142, 2010.
5. Fu, Z., Sun, X., Liu, Q. *et al.*, Achieving Efficient Cloud Search Services: Multi-Keyword Ranked Search over Encrypted Cloud Data Supporting Parallel Computing. *IEICE Trans. Commun.*, 98, 1, 190–200, 2015.
6. Ganu, G., Elhadad, N., Marian, A., Beyond the stars: Improving rating predictions using Review text content, in: *12th International Workshop on the Web and Databases (WebDB 2009)*, pp. 1–6.
7. Xu, J., Zheng, X., Ding, W., Personalized recommendation based on reviews and ratings alleviating the sparsity problem of collaborative filtering. *IEEE International Conference on e-business Engineering*, pp. 9–16, 2012.
8. Qian, X., Feng, H., Zhao, G., Mei, T., Personalized recommendation combining user interest and social circle. *IEEE Trans. Knowl. Data Eng.*, 26, 7, 1763–1777, 2014.
9. Feng, H. and Qian, X., Recommendation via user's personality and social contextual. *Proc. 22nd ACM International Conference on Information & Knowledge Management*, pp. 1521–1524, 2013.
10. Fu, Z., Ren, K., Shu, J. *et al.*, Enabling Personalized Search over Encrypted Outsourced Data with Efficiency Improvement. *IEEE Trans. Parallel Distrib. Syst.*, 1–1, 2015.
11. https://www.nipccd.nic.in/file/reports/bestprac.pdf

12. Aziiza, A.A. and Susanto, T.D., Ministry of Communications and Informatics, Buku Panduan Penyusunan Masterplan Smart City, *IOP Conf. Ser.: Mater. Sci. Eng.*, 722 012011, 2020, Jakarta: Organisasi.

13. Wilkoff, B.L., Auricchio, A., Brugada, J., Cowie, M., Ellenbogen, K.A., Gillis, A.M. *et al.*, HRS/EHRA Expert Consensus on the Monitoring of Cardiovascular Implantable Electronic Devices (CIEDs): Description of Techniques, Indications, Personnel, Frequency Ethical Considerations. *Europace*, 10, 707–25, 2008.

14. Fajrillah, Mohamad, Z., Novarika, W., Smart city vs smart village. *Jurnal Mantik Penusa*, 22, 1, 1–6, 2017.

15. Novi, R. and Ella, S., Pengembangan Model Smart Rural Untuk Pembangunan Kawasan Perdesaan di Indonesia. *J. Borneo Administrator (JBA)*, 15, 1, 41–58, 2019.

16. Rachmawati, R., Pengembangan, Smart Village Untuk Penguatan Smart City Dan Smart Regency. *Jurnal Sistem Cerdas*, 01, 02, 12–18, 2018.

17. *Republic of Indonesia, Law Journal*, 6, 3, 1–103, 2014.

18. Holmes, J. and Thomas, M., Introducing the Smart Villages Concept. *Int. J. Green Growth Dev.*, 1, 2, 151–154, 2015.

19. Natarajan, G. and Kumar, D.L.A., Implementation of IoT based Smart Village for the Rural Development. *Int. J. Mech. Eng. Technol.*, 8, 8, 1212–1222, 2017.

20. Gao, T., Greenspan, D., Welsh, M., Juang, R.R., Alm, A., Real Time Patient Monitoring System Using Lab view. *Int. J. Sci. Eng. Res.*, 11, 6, 5561–5595, April-2012.

21. Syaodih, E., Smart Village Development. *The 9th International Conference of Rural Research and Planning Group*, pp. 22–33, 2018.

22. Ahlawat, J., Smart Villages, Information Communication Technology and Geographical Information System. *Inter. J. Curr. Trends Sci. Tech.*, 7, 8, 20232–20238, 2017.

23. Muke, A.M. and Nilesh S, U., Use of Advanced Technology in Developing Smart Villages. *Int. J. Res. Eng. Sci. Technol.*, 03, 04, 1–6, 2017.

24. Bozzon, A., Houtkamp, J., Kresin, F., De Sena, N., de Weerdt, M., From Needs to Knowledge. A reference framework for smart citizens initiatives, Amsterdam Institute for Advanced Metropolitan Solutions, Netherlands, 2015.

25. Gaur, A., Scotney, B., Parr, G., McClean, S., Smart city architecture and its applications based on IoT. *Proc. Comput. Sci.*, 52, 1, 1089–1094, 2015.

26. Correia, L.M. and Wünstel, K., Smart Cities Applications and Requirements. *NetWorks European Technology Platform*, 2011.

27. Dirks, S. and Keeling, M., *A vision of smarter cities: How cities can lead the way into a prosperous and sustainable future*, New York, 2009.

18

Computer-Aided Interpretation of ECG Signal—A Challenge

Shalini Sahay[1][*] and A. K. Wadhwani[2][†]

[1]EC Department, SIRT, Bhopal, India
[2]EE Department, MITS, Gwalior, India

Abstract

Signals acquired from a patient, i.e., bio-signals, are used to predict the health of patient. One such bio-signal of principal significance is the electrocardiogram (ECG). Any irregular conduction in the ECG signal is a symptomatic measure of a malfunctioning of the heart, named an arrhythmia condition. Because of the included complexities, for example, absence of human skill and high likelihood to misdiagnose, long term observing dependent on PC supported finding. There exist different computer aided methods for arrhythmia finding with their own advantages and impediments. CAD systems hold the promise of reducing cost and at the same time improving the accuracy of ECG based diagnosis. The cost reduction arises from the fact that human labour is replaced by machine work.

The interpretation of Electrocardiography (ECG) signals is difficult, because even subtle changes in the waveform can indicate a serious heart disease. Furthermore, these waveform changes might not be present all the time. As a consequence, it takes years of training for a medical practitioner to become an expert in ECG-based cardiovascular disease diagnosis. In addition, human interpretation of ECG signals causes interoperator and intraoperator variability. ECG-based Computer-Aided Diagnosis (CAD) holds the promise of improving the diagnosis accuracy and reducing the cost. The same ECG signal will result in the same diagnosis support regardless of time and place. The heart muscle pumps blood to vital organs, which is indispensable for human life. Congestive heart failure (CHF) is characterized by the inability of the heart to pump blood adequately throughout the body without an increase in intracardiac pressure. The symptoms include lung and peripheral congestion, leading to breathing difficulty and swollen limbs, dizziness from reduced delivery of blood to the brain, as well as arrhythmia. Coronary artery disease, myocardial infarction, and medical co-morbidities such as kidney disease, diabetes, and high blood pressure all take a toll on the heart and can impair myocardial function. CHF prevalence is growing worldwide. It afflicts millions of people globally, and is a leading cause of death. Hence, proper diagnosis, monitoring and management are imperative. Electrocardiography (ECG) is inexpensive and widely accessible, but changes are typically not specific for CHF diagnosis. A properly designed computer-aided detection (CAD) system for CHF, based on the ECG, would potentially reduce subjectivity and provide quantitative assessment for informed decision-making.

Keywords: Computer-aided detection system, congestive heart failure, arrhythmia intracardiac, statistical analysis, interoperator, computational techniques

*Corresponding author: shalinisahay2020@gmail.com
†Corresponding author: wadhwani_arun@rediffmail.com

Tushar H. Jaware, K. Sarat Kumar, Ravindra D. Badgujar and Svetlin Antonov (eds.) *Medical Imaging and Health Informatics*, (335–358) © 2022 Scrivener Publishing LLC

18.1   Introduction

According to the World Health Organization, cardiovascular diseases (CVDs) are a major cause of death, accounting for 30% of all fatalities globally his means a primary detection of risky subjects and a enhanced knowledge about the mechanisms of disease is required for improvement in diagnostics and therapy. Electrocardiogram (ECG) recordings are frequently utilized as a standard method for treatment in hospitals. ECG records are used to record the propagation of the electrical heart signal on the surface of the body. In consequence, many operational or electrophysiological anomalies in the heart are marked with an ECG and can help diagnose heart disease. It is a non-invasive recording which are voltages varying with time that doctors use to check the health of their patients' hearts. The electrical activity of the heart is recorded during the cardiac cycle by the potential difference between a number of electrodes linked to various locations of the body's surface.

Electrocardiography is a technique for measuring electrical activity throughout time. Electrodes positioned on the chest surface and on the leg (limb leads) record changes in electrical potential difference (voltage) during depolarization and repolarization of the cardiac fibers [1]. Contractile cardiac muscle cells are the sources of electrical potentials (cardiomyocytes). The ECG waveform is displayed on a computer screen or printed onto graph paper that runs at a constant speed. Electrocardiography's benefits include its low cost, instant availability, and ease of use.

There are six electrodes included in a standard 12-lead ECG that are placed on the surface of chest, two on the wrists, and two on the legs. The total amplitude of the heart's electrical potential is then acquired and recorded over time from 12 different angles ("leads"). During each heartbeat, a healthy heart has a precise order of polarization and depolarization. It begins in the sinoatrial (SA) node and travels via the atrium to the atrioventricular (AV) node and, finally, to the ventricles. The graph of normal ECG features is shown in Figure 18.1. This non-invasive process generates an ECG that is a voltage-to-time characteristic graph. This non-invasive procedure is called an ECG, which shows the voltage versus the time. Every ECG is formed by regular PQRST complexes that represent a activity of cardiac series of various durations.

Particularly, one complex has the following:

1. P wave (atrial contraction)
2. QRS-complex (ventricles contraction)
3. T wave (relaxation of the ventricles)

The length of PQRST may vary according to the heart rate [2]. The most common method for calculating the RR interval is to express the length as the distance between two subsequent R peaks.

18.1.1   Electrical Activity of the Heart

The ECG interprets the electrical action of the heart over a definiteduration of time. The ECG signal is a diagnostic tool for monitoring and recording electrical activity, as well

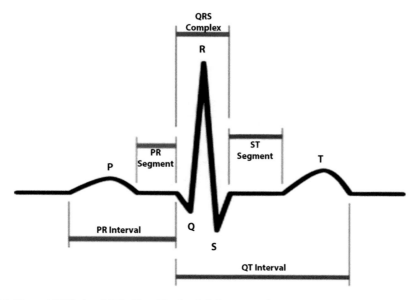

Figure 18.1 Normal ECG signal (File:SinusRhythmLabels.svg 2019).

as determining the rhythm and invariability of heartbeats. The intervals and amplitudes described by the ECG's characteristics are where the majority of the clinically valuable information is found. An ECG signal has a frequency range of [0.05–100] Hz and a dynamic range of [1–10] mV. The ECG signal has five peaks and valleys, each identified with a letter of the alphabet: P, Q, R, S, and T. The precise and dependable detection of the QRS complex, as well as the T and P waves, is critical for an ECG analyzing system's high performance [3, 4]. The P wave indicates the activation of the heart's upper chambers, the atria, while the QRS wave (or complex) and T wave reflect the heart's lower chambers, the ventricles. HRV testing has been demonstrated to provide an indication of cardiovascular health in some instances. In medical applications, heart problems and their diagnosis using an ECG are more important. Electric activity excitation wave originates in the node of SA and precedes every heart contraction. Electrical waves propagate via the atria and reach the AV node. The ventricular muscle tracing, like the SA node tracing, reveals no consistent resting potential. The spontaneous depolarization and repolarization of the SA node offer a unique and miraculous pacemaker stimulus that activates the atrium and AV node, which transmits the current of activation to activate the ventricular muscle tracking through the pacemaker branches. The spontaneous depolarization and repolarization of the SA node creates the unique and miraculous pacemaker stimulus which activates the atria and the AV node leads the activation of the ventricular muscle mass through the bundle branches. Heart cells outside the SA node usually do not spontaneously depolarize, so they must be stimulated. The radial spread of activation from the SA node is seen in Figure 18.2.

The cardiac cycle is divided as in two types: diastole [when muscles of heart (myocardium) rests and supply blood] and systole (when the heart muscle contracts and blood pump out). The action potential is a method by which a cell's membrane potential, or its

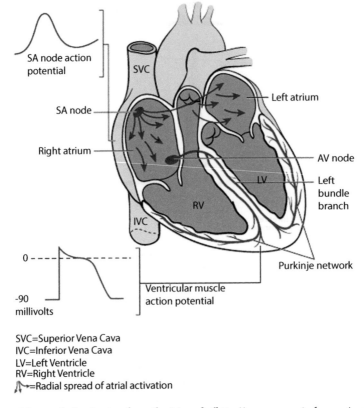

SA node action potential

SVC

SA node

Right atrium

Left atrium

AV node

LV

Left bundle branch

RV

IVC

Purkinje network

0

-90 millivolts

Ventricular muscle action potential

SVC=Superior Vena Cava
IVC=Inferior Vena Cava
LV=Left Ventricle
RV=Right Ventricle
⌁=Radial spread of atrial activation

Figure 18.2 The axial spread of activation from the SA node (http://www.cancerindex.org/medterm/medtm8.htm).

relative potential to the surrounding extracellular fluid, increasesrapidly and falls, causing individual muscle cells to contract. Ions such as Na+, Ca2+, and K+ flows inside and outside causing depolarizing and then repolarizing the cell's membrane from resting state negative charge.

Broadly, every individual action potential will cause an charge in nearby excitable cells, causing a depolarization and repolarization impulse to propagate across the heart. Pacemaker cells in the heart's SA node, which "set the tempo," cause depolarization during a healthy heartbeat. This then travels through the atrium, the AV node, the His bundles, the Purkinje fibers, and, lastly, the ventricles.

18.2 The Cardiovascular System

It is a complicated closed hydraulic system that transports oxygen, carbon dioxide, a variety of chemical substances, and blood cells, among other things. The heart is alienated into right and left portions structurally. The atrium and ventricle are two chambers in each portion. There are four valves in the heart (Figure 18.3). Between the right atrium and the ventricle is the Tricuspid valve, also known as the right AV valve. It is made up of three cusps or flaps. It stops blood from flowing backward from the right ventricle through right atrium. Between the atrium ventricle situated in left is the Bicuspid Mitral or left atrio-ventricular valve. There are two flaps or cusps on the valve. This prevents blood from returning to the right ventricle [5]. Between the left ventricle and the aorta is the aortic valve. It is built similarly to a pulmonary valve. This valve stops blood from returning from the aorta to the left ventricle.

There are three layers to the heart wall:

(i) The pericardium, known as heart's exterior layer. It avoids friction when heart beats by keeping the outside surface wet.

(ii) The heart's main layer is myocardium. It is the heart's major muscle, and it is consisting of short cylindrical fibres. Those muscle contracts and relaxes in a rhythmic pattern throughout one's life.

(iii) The heart's inner layer is the endocardium, which provides a smooth surface for flowing blood through it. Blood veins, which are hollow tubes, transport blood to different regions of the body.

Blood vessels are divided into two categories.

(i) Arteries: These are blood vessels with strong walls that convey blood enriched with oxygen.

(ii) Veins: These blood vessels are thin walls that convey deoxygenated blood.

The heart is a four-chamber muscular pump that pumps blood via the circulatory system's blood arteries (Figure 18.3) and sends blood to all regions of the body. It beats roughly 72 times per minute (for a healthy adult in average) and sends blood through the body. It works like two two-stage pumps that are functionally separate but synchronized. The first stage (atrium) of each pump collects blood from the hydraulic system and transports it to the second stage (the ventricle). During this technique, in pulmonary circulation heart pumps blood through the lungs andto the rest of the body through the systemic circulation. Deoxygenated venous blood is transported from the right ventricle to the lungs via the pulmonary artery, where it is oxygenated and expelled carbon dioxide. The pulmonary veins carry the arterial (oxygenated) blood to the left atrium. The blood is pumped through blood vesselsin systemic circulation that are rather elastic. The branches of aorta and its arteries, carry blood from the left atrium to the left ventricle, then expelled into the body. Arterioles (tiny arteries) transport blood to capillaries in the tissues, where oxygen and chemical compounds are given up and carbon dioxide and combustion products are taken out, Several channels carry blood from various parts of the body back to the heart. It usually flows directly from the capillaries' venous side to either the superior or inferior vena cava, which both discharge into the right atrium [6]. The coronary arteries are two small but crucial arteries that deliver blood to the heart. They emerge from the aorta, which runs directly

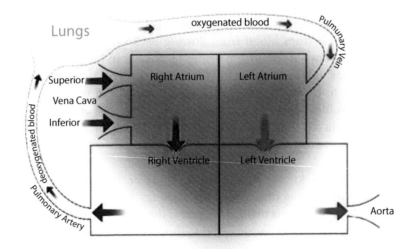

Figure 18.3 The circulatory system of the heart (https://www.cmsfitnesscourses.co.uk/blog/the-structure-and-function-of-the-heart).

above the heart. Myocardial infarction, which can be fatal, happens when they get blocked due to coronary thrombosis. Heart rate is regulated by the nervous system and action taken up automatically. The pump's efficiency, speed, and pattern of fluid flow are all controlled by these.

The circulatory system is the body's transportation system, carrying water, food, oxygen, and other essentials to tissue cells while simultaneously removing spoil. The blood cell diffuses into the interstitial fluid through the capillary wall, causing this to happen.

The waste products like carbon dioxide from the interstitial fluid also flow through the capillary wall and through the blood cell. Cardiovascular system is assessed using haemodynamic measurements, as well as measuring the electrical action of the heart muscle (electrocardiography) and listening to heart sounds (phonocardiography). To assess the heart's performance as a pump, measurements of cardiac output (the blood pumped by the heart per unit time), blood pressure, blood flow rate, and blood volume are collected at throughout the circulatory system at different locations [7, 8].

18.3   Electrocardiogram Leads

Electrical activity in the heart causes currents to travel throughout the body, resulting in potential differences that may be measured across the skin's surface. Electrodes are conductive pads that are placed on the skin's surface. A lead is made up of two electrodes that detect the difference in voltage between their connection points. A depolarization wave moving near to a lead causes a deflection which is positive, and so on. The axis that a lead measures determines its amplitude and direction of reflection. By merging several leads, complete view of the heart's three-dimensional conduction can be spotted diagonally in numerous axes. Then, most common ECG system is the 12-lead system.

1. The limb leadsare I, II, and III. On the limbs, electrodes which are three placed: left arm (LA), right arm (RA), and left leg (LL) (LL). Leads I = LA–RA, II = LL–RA, and III = LL–LA are formed from these electrodes. The average of the readings from each limb electrode is used to create the virtual electrode Wilson's Central Terminal.
2. TheaVR, aVL, and aVF augmented limb leads are estimated from the limb leads are from the identical electrodes used in the limb leads. These two leads and augmented limb leads give a view as electrical activity in the frontal plane.
3. V1, V2, V3, V4, V5, and V6 are the precordial leads. The electrical activity in the transverse plane is measured by these leads. The potential difference relating an electrode implanted on the thorax and Wilson's Central Terminal is measured by each lead. Expert physicians can utilize a variety of leads to better accurately identify a variety of illnesses. The regular conduction that disrupts perpendicular to the axis of a lead may not show up at all in the ECG lead if everything predicts normal in the axis direction. However, 12 leads provide a comprehensive image of the heart, depending on the problem at hand, even a single lead may be sufficient. Furthermore, requiring the insertion of too many electrodes in a remote setting may be inconvenient and impracticable. Due to data availability, leads MLII (a modified lead II) and V5 in this chapter and accompanying practical tasks are considered. For the established beat classification algorithms, one limb and one precordial lead offer ample data. The various lead systems are depicted in Figures 18.4 and 18.5. However, having 12 leads in a while provides a comprehensive picture

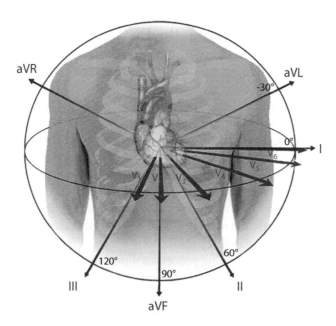

Figure 18.4 The ECG with its precordial leads (File: EKG leads.png 2016).

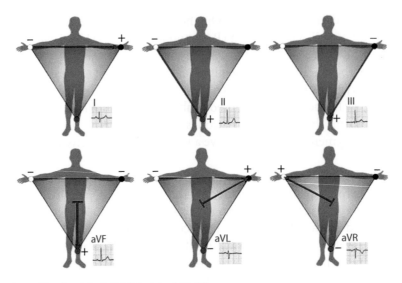

Figure 18.5 Frontal leads of the ECG (Npatchett 2020).

of the heart, depending on the problem at hand, even a single lead may be sufficient. Furthermore, requiring the insertion of too many electrodes in a remote setting may be inconvenient and impracticable. Due to data availability, we will use leads MLII (a modified lead II) and V5 in this chapter and accompanying practical tasks. For the developed beat classification algorithms, one limb and one precordial lead gives ample of information.

18.4   Artifacts/Noises Affecting the ECG

Several sounds can pollute the ECG signal, each with its own set of traits and behaviours. Some artifacts are created by fixed sources, while others are created by non-stationary and time-varying sources. The fundamental step in the ECG signal processing is noise filtering. The PLI noise, considered as key noise which to be extracted in the processing steps of first stage, is introduced by an alternating current (AC) source of power supply. The signal has a frequency of 50/60 Hz, depending on the country location. India and Europe use a 50-Hz AC supply, while the United States and a few other countries use a 60-Hz source. The effect due to stray of AC field due to loops in the electrical lines, disengaged electrodes, interference of electromagnetic due to power supply, poor earthing of ECG equipment, or large current load due to other equipment in the room are the main causes of this type of noise. During ECG recording, a low-frequency noise known as baseline wander noise arises. Its frequency range is 0.15 to 0.3 Hz. This noise is caused by the breathing process of a person, which causes the ECG signals shifting from the baseline. Other possible causes include cable movement during ECG signal recording, dirty lead electrodes/wires, and loosening of the lead electrodes/wires [9, 10].

The noise level and its relationship to the ECG signal in these artifacts are unpredictable and time-consuming. The key sources for noise in the ECG signal are as follows:

- Baseline wander
- Power line interference
- Motion artifacts
- Muscle noise

18.4.1   Baseline Wander

Power line interference is caused by capacitive and inductive coupling processes. Capacitive coupling is the transfer of energy between circuits through the use of a capacitance between them. The coupling capacitance reduces as the distance between the circuits grows. The coupling due to inductive is initiated by inductance among the conductors. A current running across a wire forms a magnetic flux, induces a current in nearby circuits. The inductance value, and the degree of inductive coupling, is determined by the structure of the conductors as well as the distance between them. Capacitive coupling often contributes high frequency noise, while inductive coupling contributes low frequency noise. In electro-cardiology, inductive coupling is a major cause of power line interference. The effect of base line wander noise is shown in Figure 18.6.

18.4.2   Power Line Interference

The power line electromagnetic field generates this noise, which peaks at 50 or 60 Hz. Its nature is fixed as regards frequencies in the affected intervals, although in the corrupted intervals, the onset, offset, length, and power of such an anomaly are unpredictable. Power line interference is caused by capacitive and inductive coupling processes. Capacitive coupling is energy transfer among circuits through the use of a capacitance between them. The coupling capacitance reduces as the distance between the circuits grows. The coupling capacitance reduces as the distance between the circuits grows. Inductive coupling, beside it, is begun by the inductance that occurs amongst the conductors. A current running across a wire produces a magnetic flux, which induces a current in nearby circuits.

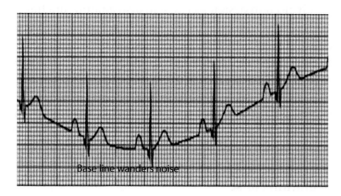

Figure 18.6 The effect of base line wanders noise.

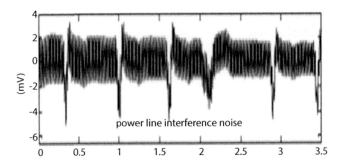

Figure 18.7 The effect of power line interference noise.

The mutual inductance value, and the degree of inductive coupling, is hence determined by the structure of the conductors as well as the distance between them. Capacitive coupling often contributes frequency noise which is, while inductive coupling contributes noise which is low frequency. The effect of power line interference noise is depicted in Figure 18.7.

18.4.3   Motion Artifacts

Motion artifacts are variations in the baseline produced by electrode movement. Motion artifacts are usually caused by the subject's tremors, movement, or breathing. The artifact's peak amplitude and duration are determined by a number of unknown variables, including electrode parameters, electrolyte values, skin impedance, and the patient's mobility. The baseline drift in an ECG signal occurs at a frequency (about 0.014 Hz) which is very low, and is most likely caused by very slow variations in the skin-electrode impedance. The huge peak closest to DC on the Fourier power spectrum also shows this noise.

18.4.4   Muscle Noise

The EMG noise is initiated by muscle contractions additional to the heart. Depolarization and repolarization waves are generated when other electrode muscles contract, and the ECG picks up those waves. The magnitude of the crosstalk is determined by the level and the quality of the probe. The stochastic (random) amplitude of the EMG signal is well known and is frequently used to design a Gaussian distribution function. The noise's mean will be considered to be almost zero, but the variance is determined by environmental variables which are based on the circumstances.

Although it should be emphasized that the precise statistical model is unknown, that muscle electric activities may produce surface potential comparable to those of the heart in contractions, drowning completely the desired signal. In subjects with uncontrollable shaking, persons with disabilities, children, and people who fear an ECG, EMG noise is common. These artifacts are caused by electrode motions distant from the skin's contact zone. Because their form and frequency are unpredictable, they are considered hard contaminations.

18.4.5   Instrumentation Noise

Noise is also produced by the electrical equipment used in ECG readings. The principal causes of this type of noise are electrode probes, cables, signal processor/amplifier, and the analog-to-digital converter (ADC). Instrumentation noise will not be completely removed, although it can be decreased with better equipment and careful circuit design. Resistor thermal noise is one sort of electrical noise (also known as Johnson noise) which is caused by electron fluctuations randomly caused by thermal agitation. k is the Boltzmann's constant, T is the temperature, and R is the resistance, and we get the power spectrum. According to this equation, resistor thermal noise at all frequencies is white; frequencies greater than 100 Hz, the power spectrum begins for fade. Because of its low frequency, another type of noise known as flicker noise is significant in ECG readings. Although the exact mechanism causing this type of noise is unknown, whose explanation is widely created by energy traps that form at the edges of two materials. The charge carriers are thought to be sporadically trapped/released, resulting in flicker noise. Because the amplitude of the measured signal is on the order of mils, flicker noise the most noticeable contributions at the electrodes.

18.4.6   Other Interferences

Other noise sources, such as instrumentation noise created by the recording section's equipment, have an impact on the ECG signal (probes, cables, ADC, etc.). Obviously, by carefully selecting high-quality devices, these forms of interferences might be considerably eliminated. Unfortunately, this noise cannot be removed, but it can be significantly diminished with high-quality hardware and a precise circuit design. The connection of electrodes, wiring, signal processor/amplifier, and ADC are the key factors [11, 12]. Attention is not paid by nurses and doctors in hospitals toward electrode placement. As a result, common mode noise is produced, necessitating the usage of 50-Hz filtering.

However, there are a number of ways to evade all of the aforementioned noises earlier filtering, including the following:

1. The original electrodes are used to trace ECG signals rather than old ones.
2. Proper electrode placement reduces contact impedances and improves the effectiveness of common mode rejection systems.
3. Using the drive.n right leg (DRL) circuit correctly (Winter and Webster 1983)
4. While recording avoid electrode movement.
5. Electromyogram is caused by the patient's movement (the placement of electrodes near the collar bone and patient's waist in place of arms and legs can be avoided).
6. Long wires should not be utilized since they distort the ECG signal (the cable with length which are shortest must be closed to body using Velcro straps or by wearing fitted clothes).
7. The patients are keep away from high-voltage sources could cause PLI.

When capturing the ECG signals from patients, such safeguards must be used. Even if the safeguards taken are not up to par, some noise will be generated. As a result, multiple strategies are needed to reduce such noise, and the following sections will go over some of the literature on the subject.

18.5   The ECG Waveform

The 10 electrodes are put on the patient's extremities and on the surface of chest in a traditional 12-lead ECG. The overall magnitude of the heart's electrical potential is then measured and recorded over time from twelve different angles ("leads") (usually 10 seconds). Throughout the cardiac cycle, the total amount and direction of the heart's electrical depolarization are captured in this way the depolarization of the atria is shown by the P wave, the QRS complex shown by the depolarization of the ventricles; and the T waves is indicated by the repolarization of the ventricles, are the three primary components of an ECG. The healthy heart develops all over the atrium, across the AV node and through the bundle of His and the Purkinje fibres, diffusing down and down through the ventricles, and into the whole bundle, in an orderly development of depolarization during each layer of the heart. The distinctive ECG trace is created by this organized pattern of depolarization [13]. An ECG provides a wealth of information of the structure of the heart and the processing of its electrical conduction system to a qualified doctor. It can be determined rate and rhythm of heartbeats, as well as the physical structure of the heart (Figure 18.8).

1. P wave: A wave with a normal duration of 0.11 seconds or less. The shape is mostly smooth, with no notches or peaks.
2. PR interval: 0.12 to 0.20 seconds is typical.

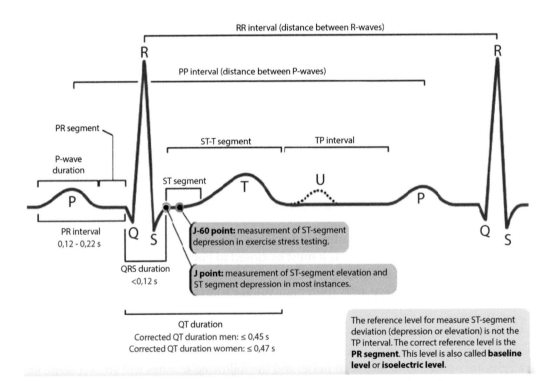

Figure 18.8 The typical ECG waveform.

3. QRS complex: amplitude more than 0.5 mV in one standard lead and larger than 1.0 mV in at the most one precordial lead, with a duration of less than or equal to 0.12 seconds. The typical amplitude is between 2.5 and 3.0 mV.

4. ST segment: In a normal ECG, the isoelectric, slanting upward to the T wave, can be slowly raised (up to 2.0 mm in some precordial leads), but never more than 0.5 mm in any lead.

5. T wave: In at least five of the six limb leads, in the direction as the QRS complex, the T wave deflection should be in the aligned generally rounded and asymmetrical, with a more steady climb than fall. In an asymptomatic adult, an isolated T wave inversion is a common form.

6. Males have a QT interval of less than or equal to 0.40 seconds, whereas females have a QT interval of 0.44 seconds.

18.5.1 Normal Sinus Rhythm

Heart arrhythmias are classified as tachycardia (heart beats too fast, more than 90 beats per minute) and bradycardia (heart beats too slow, less than 60 beats per minute), as well as supraventricular (irregularly in atria contraction) and ventricular (ventricles contract in an irregular pattern) arrhythmias.

The pacemaker is the sinus node, which fires at a consistent rate of 60 to 100 beats per minute. Every heartbeat is carried averagely to the ventricles. The usual sinus rhythm is depicted in Figure 18.7. 60–100 beats per minute (bpm) P wave: identical shape, with one P wave for each QRS, PRI: 0.12–0.20 seconds and constant, QRS: 0.04–0.1 seconds.

18.6 Cardiac Arrhythmias

Arrhythmia is defined as any value other than NSR. Cardiac arrhythmias occur when electrical impulses fail to properly coordinate heartbeats, causing the heart to beat excessively quickly, too slowly, or irregularly. The normal sinus rhythm is depicted in Figure 18.9. It is also the most prevalent cause of failure of heart [14]. Its analysis includes the following conditions for most heart disease patients.

18.6.1 Sinus Bradycardia

The pacemaker is the sinus node, which fires at less than 60 times per minute. Every impulse passes normally through the ventricles. The R-R intervals are always the same. The rhythm

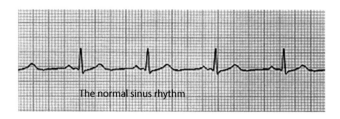

The normal sinus rhythm

Figure 18.9 The normal sinus rhythm.

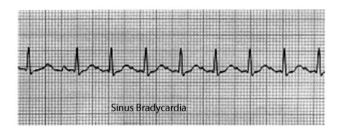

Figure 18.10 Sinus bradycardia.

is regular, and the rates of the atrium and ventricles are equal. Less than 60 beats per minute, P Wave: Uniform P wave in front of each QRS, PRI: PRI is consistent and between 0.12 and 0.20, QRS: QRS is less than 0.12. Figure 18.10 depicts it.

18.6.2   Sinus Tachycardia

The pacemaker is the sinus node, which fires at more than 100 times per minute. In a typical manner, each impulse is sent to the ventricles. The R-R intervals are constant, the rhythm is regular, the atrial and ventricular rates are equal, the heart rate is larger than 100, and the R-R intervals are constant. P Wave: Uniform P wave in front of each QRS, PRI: PRI is constant and between 0.12 and 0.20, QRS: QRS is greater than 0.12, as illustrated in Figure 18.11.

18.6.3   Atrial Flutter

A single irritated focus in the atria provides a quick, repeated momentum. The AV node prevents part of the impulses from reaching the ventricles in order to prevent the ventricles from receiving too many impulses. There is a consistent atrial beat. The ventricular rhythm is uniform if the AV node carries pulse in a predicted way. The ventricular rate will be erratic if the pattern changes. Rate: The atrial rate ranges from 250 to 350 beats per minute. The rate of ventricular is determined by the pulse ratio sent to the ventricles. When the atrial fibrillation occurs, a succession of precise P waves is produced. These "Flutter" waves have a saw tooth effect when viewed combined. QRS is defined as a time interval of less than 0.12 seconds; however, measurement can be problematic if one or more flutter waves are hidden inside the QRS complex. Atrial flutter (AFL) is a type of peculiar heart rhythm related to atrial fibrillation. Supraventricular tachycardia is a condition that affects both

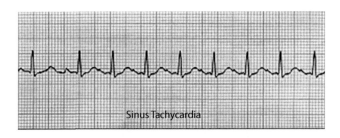

Figure 18.11 Sinus tachycardia.

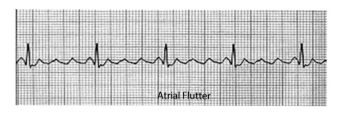

Figure 18.12 Atrial flutter.

men and women. Because the electrical signal in AFL flows in a circular pattern, atrial muscle contractions are faster than those in the lower chambers and out of rhythm (ventricles).

The heart beats quickly, but in a regular manner, similar to A-Fib. Atrial flutter is not life-threatening in and of itself, but the side effects of the slowed blood pumping it causes may cause health concerns. Atrial flutter can be detected using an ECG. Figure 18.12 depicts it.

18.6.4   Atrial Fibrillation

Because the atria are so exasperated a large number of originate impulses foci, causing depolarize atria fibrillary. The AV node stops the majority of impulses, letting only a few to reach the ventricles. All atrial activity is chaotic, and atrial rhythm is unmeasurable. The ventricular beat is wildly erratic, with no discernible pattern. The heart rate is over 350 beats per minute. Because the AV node stops the majority of impulses, the ventricular rate is substantially slower. The rhythm is said to be "controlled" if the ventricular rate is less than 100 beats per minute; if it is more than 100 bpm, known as "rapid ventricular response." In Europe and North America, it is the most prevalent dangerous aberrant cardiac rhythm, affecting about 2%–3% of the population. Furthermore, the percentage of patients affected with AF rises with age, with 0.14% under 50 years old, 4% between 60 and 70 years old, and 14% beyond 80 years old. Atrial fibrillation is typically identified on an ECG by the absence of a P wave and an erratic heartbeat pattern, as seen in Figure 18.13.

18.6.5   Ventricular Tachycardia

To override higher sites for heart control, a prominent focuses fires at a rate of 150–250 beats per minute on a regular basis. The QRS complexes will be long and strange, with duration of at least 0.12 seconds. It is not always easy to tell the difference between the QRS and the T wave, as seen in Figure 18.14.

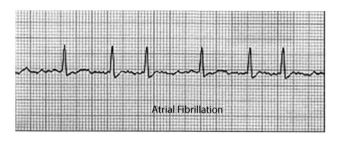

Figure 18.13 Atrial fibrillation.

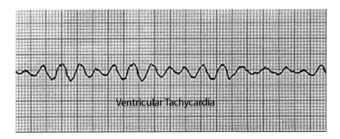

Figure 18.14 Ventricular tachycardia.

18.6.6   AV Block 2 First Degree

The AV node is in charge of some beats, while others are inhibited. Those who are not impeded move through the node and into the ventricles with a short delay. The conduction restarts properly in the ventricles. If the ratio of conduction is constant, then the R-R interval is fixed and the beat will be regular. If the conduction ratio changes, then the R-R will be uneven, as shown in Figure 18.15.

18.6.7   Asystole

The electrical activity of the heart has stopped. There is no electrical pacemaker to start the flow of electricity [15–17]. There is not any electrical activity. P Waves: not detectable; electrical activity is not visible in Figure 18.16.

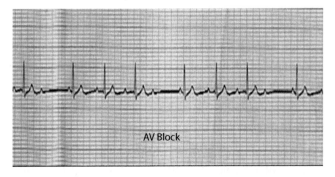

Figure 18.15 AV block.

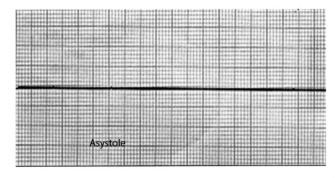

Figure 18.16 Asystole.

18.7   Electrocardiogram Databases

The arrhythmia database of the Massachusetts Institute of Technology–Beth Israel Hospital (MIT-BIH), the Physikalisch-Technische Bundesanstalt diagnostic ECG database (PTB), the American Heart Association (AHA) database, and the St.-Petersburg Institute of Cardiological Technics Database (ICT) are just a few of the ECG standard online databases available for evaluating computational algorithms in ECG signal analysis. MIT-BIH databases include subsets including the ST Change database, atrial fibrillation database, arrhythmia, long-term database, and supraventricular arrhythmia database. This arrhythmia is known for mostly used by the investigators. It was compiled from 47 subjects at a sampling rate of 360 samples per second and a resolution of 11 bits and held for half an hour. These databases use various methods for collecting ECG data (e.g., sampling frequency, sample number, and leads). However, the scarcity of public ECG datasets remains the most significant restriction in ECG analysis. It is critical for the diocese to establish the publicly available in standard databases containing a patients in large numbers with labels obtained according to the medical guidelines latest for the improvement of ECG-based computer algorithms.

Each cardiac cycle, the ECG captures the electrical signals of myocardial cells, which offers a wealth of information about the heart. As a result, it is employed widely in the arena of medical sector such as heart disease diagnostics, CVD prediction, stress and sleep monitoring, and health monitoring online via wearable devices.

18.8   Computer-Aided Interpretation (CAD)

The results of the electroencephalography (ECG) are hard to interpret because even minor waveform variations can be indicative of significant heart problems. In addition, these shifts in waveform may not always be present. As consequence, training takes years of for a medical expert to be an ECG-based CVD expert. It is a major investment in a specific skill during training. Signal interpretation takes time, even with professional skill. Interoperator and intraoperator variability is also caused by human interpretation of ECG readings. Computer-aided diagnosis (CAD) has potential to improve diagnosis accuracy while also lowering costs. Regardless of time or location, the identical signal will result in the same support of diagnosis. The approaches for implementing CAD functionality and the methods for evaluating the existing functionality are included in it. By providing both a conceptual overview of the system and the appropriate assessment methodologies, this study attempts to maintain reliability in the CAD of cardiovascular illnesses using ECG signals. Removal of noise QRS detection, P and T wave detection, and other ground operations are all part of automated electrocardiography (ECG) analysis. Noise reduction techniques include band pass filters, analysis based on Fourier Transform, and wavelet transformations.

With detection rates of above 99%, the Pan Tompkins method, several transforms such as Wavelet, Hilbert, and Empirical Mode Decomposition, and few decision logic may detect QRS complexes. Because P and T waves have tiny amplitudes, they are more susceptible to noise. However, the physical structures of the waves are critical aspects of ECG analysis. The detection accuracy for such waves was over 90% using the most modern methodologies based on enhanced Kalman filters and wavelet transforms. ECG classification solutions in general, use class testing, which involves comparing a specific record to an aberrant rhythm pattern. This occurs as a result of the wide range of ECG shape variations are handed hardly by a single algorithm. In the last decade, there has been a strong trend toward moving away from threshold-based analysis (which suffers from the introduction of new ECG recordings from patients which are new or recorded with new devices to the validation dataset) and toward data-driven approaches, includes traditional supervised machine-learning models and neural networks. Complex categorization or pre-processing algorithms are not suited for online computations and need a significant amount of computing power. To diagnosis, cardiologists largely rely on the raw ECG. Extracting sampled points from an ECG signal curve is the simplest and fastest way of feature extraction. However, one must remember that the number of features found may be a burden to the classification algorithm because of the amount of features extracted used to characterize heartbeat. As a consequence, most works that use the raw signal sample the waveform or perform certain characteristics to reduce the calculation time. Machine learning approaches are used to categorize arrhythmias in order to avoid this problem. The training of a classifier and the construction of a feature vector to represent the ECG beat are required for most machine learning classification algorithms. Each heartbeat is made up of several waves that describe distinct aspects of the cardiac cycle (P wave, QRS complex, T wave, etc.). The shape of ECG waveforms is described by morphological features such as slopes, summits and amplitude. You may be able to detect cardiac rhythm changes, like sinus versus fibrillation, in which complexes have different forms. Some studies are focused on time interval characteristics, which define ECG phenomena as the number of beatings per unit of time, such as QRS duration. The coefficients of transforming the Ermit, transforming the wavelet or the subtle cosine are morphological elements which attempt to shape the ECG-beat, instead of extracting raw data features. A combination of these characteristics was found to be effective in most research. One issue is that the ratio of training data available to detect features is too small, which might lead to overfitting. For optimal generalization and performance, the amount of features must be minimized, and two primary strategies are typically used: dimensionality reduction and feature selection. By generating a smaller number of dimensions which include the majority of the data in the dataset, the reduction in dimensions tries to reduce the space where the data is represented. Because of the many features that can be recovered from ECG data, algorithms for dimensional reductions are used often before the classifier runs. Dimensionality reducing approaches are PCA (linear or nonlinear) and linear discriminate analyses are the two examples. The quality of characteristics resulting from low quality markers is poor, filters or approximations can lead to poor performance and generalization qualities, although sophisticated algorithms of classification are used.

i) **Computerized interpretation as a stand-alone replacement for human reading:** it was not possible for interpretations by computer is to be placed immediately in the patient's chart with the warning that the result was uncertain, followed by a (corrected and) accurate results certified by a cardiologist. The ECG being captured and its clinician interpretation are critical. Some diagnostic categories were flagged as urgent and pragmatically developed. As a consequence, hospitals with an ECG system can read their emergency ECGs immediately and the rest can be read in 24 hours. Urgent ECGs are read immediately at facilities with computerized ECG carts or telephonic services; the others are read in almost 5 days. This time period is usually insufficient to have a substantial impact on the hospitalized patient's care, although it does meet record-keeping requirements in hospital.

ii) **Technologic variables:** The single ECG lead transmitted via the telephone line to a super computer system was the first step in ECG capture for computer processing. The ECG data acquisition became standard with the introduction of automatic three-channel ECG recorders. Later, bidirectional transmission technology enabled the ECG technician to get vocal feedback or automatic notice. New approaches for obtaining ECG recordings have been created as a result of technological advancements.

iii) **Computerized electrocardiographic service management:** Other advantage of the ECG processing by computer not expected from early plans for biological signal from the heart is that the ECG facility improves working patterns. To appreciate the chances for change, one needs simply to remember the traditional flow of work. When a bedside ECG is transported automatically to the facility by call-up services in every ECG cart, the Heart Station is transformed. The ECG is saved on hard discs and printed on paper as it arrives at the facility. Electrocardiographers assess and reread at least twice a shift all the acquired data.

iv) **Convenient remote interpretation:** The creation of a remote ECG interpretation workstation is another part of automated ECG processing. The physical requirement present in the facility in order to see, handle, and write the results of over reading the tracings on paper worksheets has been a significant disadvantage of ECG over reading. The computer instructions of right set would allow the ECGs to be reconstructed and read on a screen or on paper wherever the over reader happened to be with a suitable terminal. High-resolution screens have been developed, with visuals as sharp as ECG tracings in high-quality original paper which can be used to take ECG readings in the comfort of one's own home or to record emergency ECGs after hours. This remote workstation approach, which was first offered by Marquette Electronics and later by Burdick, efficient use of a cardiologist's time that rival the novel concept of computerized interpretation.

v) **Prediction of cardiac disease:** Disease prediction based on ECG is critical for the diagnosis of cardiac abnormalities and for preventing sudden cardiac death as CVDs develop abruptly. The heart's electrical signals are linked to its physiological function. The aberrant relaxation of myocardium, which can lead to cardiovascular disorders, is thought to be linked to minor alterations in myocardial electrical. These alterations are so modest that they are difficult to detect on an ECG. As a result, many cardiovascular disorders miss out on early detection. For tiny changes to be extracted as characteristics for CVDs scanning, advanced signal processing skills are required. Rapid and accurate analysis of heart-related disorders is now possible thanks to advances in cloud computing and biomedical devices that provide huge data storage and computing power [18].

18.9   Computational Techniques

Computational procedures, often known as "Numerical Methods," make use of lab computers to answer issues in a step-by-step, repeating, and iterative manner. Computational approaches have the following advantages:

(i)   They are extremely powerful problem-solving tools.
(ii)   Software and packaging for commercial use.
(iii) Can add to our understanding of a variety of engineering issues.

There are several problems in the actual world with which we must deal on a daily basis and which we have attempted to answer logically and conceptually but have failed to do so owing to their high resource requirements and processing time.

When these problems are solved organically, they function quite systematically and coherently; in most real cases, a near-optimal solution is sometimes enough. As a result, biologically inspired technologies such as soft computing could be used to deal with these types of circumstances. The basic goal of soft computing is to emulate or match the reasoning and thinking behaviour of the human mind as closely as possible. Soft computing uses many methodologies to generate hybrid technology, which inherits all of the benefits and features of individual soft computing components [19–21]. Various techniques are used to discuss some of the approaches below.

i) **Fuzzy Logic (FL):** It is a strategy for dealing with imprecise data, which are referred to as fuzzy sets. Lotfi Zadeh, a professor at the University of California at Berkeley, created the term "fuzzy logic." Instead of allowing non-membership, fuzzy logic handles data by allowing partial set membership. Fuzzy logic uses a fuzzy controller to simulate the human mind and provide approximate yet effective processes. A superset of standard Boolean logic is fuzzy logic (BL). When all fuzzy memberships are constrained to 0 and 1, fuzzy logic is similar to Boolean logic. Fuzzy logic differs from blackbox logic in that it is more likely to be based on human reasoning. Because there is no standard way for developing a knowledge base for making rules, a mapping function, or membership function, is presented that minimises the output error. Fuzzy logic is commonly used in expert systems. Pattern recognition, data analysis, operations research, linear and non-linear control, and many other domains employ them. ECG is commonly utilized in the diagnosis of cardiac problems, and fuzzy inference systems can help with system analysis. The study on fuzzy-based methodologies has progressed thanks to the neural networks for incorporation such as fuzzy inference networks, which combine the benefits of neural networks for better learning with the benefits of fuzzy sets for better prediction for human understanding network algorithm for classification in ECG analysis [24, 25].

ii) **Evolutionary Computing:** The evolutionary behaviour of living beings is known as evolutionary computing, often known as genetic algorithm (GA). It is a search and optimization methodology that employs computational models of evolutionary processes including natural selection, reproduction, and survival of the fittest. This strategy is particularly useful for determining the best answer to a wide range of situations. It simply refers to a generate-and-test method for detecting and exploiting regularities in the environment. The GA may optimize both discrete and continuous variables without the need for derivative information. The GA may optimize both discrete and continuous variables without the need for derivative information. Iteratively, GAs are applied to a set of coded solutions using three general operators: reproduction, crossover, and mutation. They employ goal function and probabilities transition rules for each iteration. GAs have been frequently used in ECG analysis to provide higher computational capabilities with less time consumption [26]. This strategy, however, is combined with others in order to maximize the benefits.ANN, SVM, and other algorithms have been applied by a number of researchers. On the other hand, there are not many approaches for using GA alone in ECG analysis. Priyadharshini and Kumar did research to improve arrhythmia classification using ECG data. The MIT-BIH Arrhythmia Database is used for this purpose. The research employs an improvised GA, as well as the C4.5 and Naive Bayes classification algorithms. In comparison to C4.5 and Naive Bayes, the GA has the highest consistent accuracy, according to the study. The study's scope could be expanded to include other machine learning algorithms, such as SVM, in order to present the best efficient way [27, 28].

iii) **Artificial Neural Network (ANN):** ANNs are a type of non-algorithmic processing system inspired by biological neurons. An ANN is made up of a large number of interconnected processing elements called neurons that work together to solve a problem. ANN is developed for a specific purpose, such as pattern recognition, using a learning process similar to how people learn by doing. Nodes are node-like components of neuron processing elements that are associated with a weight that governs the behaviour of trained ANN. The ability of neural networks to infer meaning from imprecise data could be used to uncover patterns and predict trends that are too difficult for people to do. TheLayers of neural networks are made up of a number of interconnected nodes that carry "activation functions." The majority of ANNs use a learning rule to adjust the weights in response to input patterns. At first, the connection weights are given at random and then gradually changed to lower the total system error. Starting with the output layer, weight updates make their way backward. The weight update is in the direction of "negative descent" to improve the speed of mistake elimination. Weight updates begin with the output layer and work their way backward. To enhance the speed of error reduction, the weight update is in the direction of "negative descent". The training data set should be evenly distributed throughout the class domains for optimal training. Neural networks, according to Anuradha and Reddy (2008), can be utilized to improve the classification of ECG signals [22]. The authors created an ANN-based cardiac arrhythmia classifier. ECG analysis, according to Gupta and Chaturvedi (2012), is quite useful for diagnosing heart problems. For ECG classification, the researchers used supervised ANNs and data mining approaches [23].

iv) **Support Vector Machines (SVMs):** Because of their outstanding classification and generalization features, SVMs are a particularly popular class of machine learning algorithms. It is a learning method of supervised, defines the ideal hyperplane separation to optimize the margin among both classes. This boundary of decision is then used to classify the unknown test data. There has been a lot of focus on applying SVM to ECG beat classification and its optimization. Ubeyli used, for example, SVM in four categories (normal, congestive, ventricular and tachyarrhythmia, and atrial fibrillations) with error output correction code to categorize heart beats from the Physionet database (AF). The analysis was carried out using the discrete wavelet change. They achieved 98 accuracy with a test set of 360 beats. To enhance the features choices and parameters, over fitting reduction, and classification, SVM optimization strategies have been developed.

v) **Hybrid Algorithms:** In order to increase performance, hybrid approaches for analyzing ECG signals have been intensively researched. Principal component analysis (PCA) and neuro-fuzzy classifiers are used to create a hybrid classifier. Different cardiac activities are recognized using a hybrid approach that makes use of the MIT-BIH database. The PCA method is utilized to get the relevant data from the database, and the extracted data is then analyzed and processed using an ANN and a fuzzy logic based classifier [29, 30]. Heart rate, ischemia, and STEMI extraction were all detected using hybrid detection approaches. For feature extraction, the K-means clustering technique is used and Bacterial Foraging Optimization Algorithm (BFOA) is used for identifying STEMI from ECG signals.

18.10   Conclusion

The accuracy, consistency, and reliability of the interpretation in CAD are all influenced by mathematical signal reproduction, the standards used in the programme for classifications into both normal and abnormal groups, precision in numerical method, removal of noise, and the separation of different sections within the ECG signal. CVDs are the primary factor of death in whole world which includes asymptomatic myocardial ischemia, angina, myocardial infarction, and ischemic heart failure. The primarily detection and treatment of CVDs can decrease significantly or delay risk of cardiovascular death. It records the electrical impulses of the cardiac muscles that show the regular or irregular activity (ECG). A highly successful computer-assisted approach in recent years provides fast and precise tools for identifying CVDs with the ECG output of a patient. The ECG analysis and interpretation is often carried out by professionals who depend mainly on the training, certifications, expertise, and understanding of the physician. However, even professionals cannot collect sufficient information from ECG readings. Automated diagnostic tools are becoming ever more important when diagnosing heart disease with the improvement of algorithms and physical hardware technologies, moving from doctors selecting potentially useful lesion aspects for decision-making independently. The features are unique data from ECG signals that represent the heart state. The morphological characteristics, in addition, can be observed, and wavelet characteristics and statistical properties have proved beneficial in diagnosis. The rapid development of machine learning algorithms has opened up new ways of analyzing health signals. The analyses of the ECG have become more intelligent and efficient. ECG signals collected in resting situations with clinical equipment are trained by most successful models and should be adjusted for the purpose of learning about ECG signals recorded on a daily basis. Challenges need to be overcome, however, before wearable products for online and long-term health monitoring can be used for these algorithms. It is an important challenge to detect and eliminate motion elements in the dynamic ECG data obtained by a wearable device. The most common techniques and algorithms were ANNs, SVMs, fluctuating logic, decisional trees, raw set theory, genes, and hybrid algorithms. This field requires more in-depth analysis in terms of the practical use of classification systems in spite of the abundance of previous research.

References

1. Velic, M., Padavic, I., Car, S., *Computer Aided ECG Analysis - State of the Artand Upcoming Challenges*, 21 Jun 2013, ArXiv: 1306.5096v1 [cs.CV].
2. Ubeyli, E.D., Implementing wavelet transform/mixture of experts'network for analysis of electrocardiogram beats. *Expert Syst.*, 25, 2, 150–162, 2008.
3. Ghaffari, A., Golbayani, H., Ghasemi, M., A new mathematical based QRS detector using continuous wavelet transform. *Comput. Electr. Eng.*, 34, 2, 81–91, Mar. 2008.
4. Kabir, M.A. and Shahnaz, C., Denoising of ecg signals based on noise reduction algorithms in EMD and wavelet domains. *Biomed. Signal Process. Control*, 7, 5, 481–489, 2012.
5. Clifford, G.D., Azuaje, F., McSharry, P., *Advanced Methods And Tools for ECG Data Analysis*, Norwood, MA, USA, Artech House,Inc, 2006.
6. Camm, A.. Luscher, T., Serruys, P. *The ESC Textbook of Cardiovascular Medicine*, OUP Oxford, 2009.
7. de Luna, A. *Basic Electrocardiography, Normal and Abnormal ECG Patterns*, John Wiley & Sons, 2008.
8. Purvis, G.M., Weiss, S.J., Gaffney, F.A., Prehospital ECG monitoring of chest pain patients. *Am. J. Emerg. Med.*, 17, 6, 604–607, 1999.
9. Han, G. and Xu, Z., Electrocardiogram signal denoising based on a new improved wavelet thresholding. *Rev. Sci. Instrum.*, 87, 084303, 2016.
10. Canto, J.G., Rogers, W.J., Bowlby, L.J., French, W.J., Pearce, D.J., Weaver, W., The prehospital electrocardiogram in acute myocardial infarction: Is its full potential being realized. *J. Am. Coll. Cardiol.*, 29, 3, 498–505, 1997.
11. Enemark, B., The importance of ECG monitoring in antidepressant treatment. *Nord. J. Psychiatry*, 47, s30, 57–65, 1993.
12. Ebrahimzadeh, A., Shakiba, B., Khazaee, A., Detection of electrocardiogram signals using an eefficient method. *Appl. Soft Comput.*, 22, 108–117, 2014.

13. Lyon, A., Mincholé, A., Martínez, J.P., Laguna, P., Rodriguez, B., Computational techniques for ECG analysis and interpretation in light of their contribution to medical advances. *J. R. Soc. Interface*, 15, 20170821, 2018.

14. Friesen, G.M., Jannett, T.C., Jadallah, M.A., Yates, S.L., Quint, S.R., Nagle, H.T., A comparison of the noise sensitivity of nine QRS detection algorithms. *IEEE Trans. Biomed. Eng.*, 37, 85–98, 1990.

15. Oster, J., Behar, J., Sayadi, O., Nemati, S., Johnson, A.E.W., Cliord, G.D, Semi supervised ECG Ventricular Beat Classification with Novelty Detection Based on Switching Kalman Filters. *IEEE Trans. Biomed. Eng.*, 62, 2125–2134, 2015.

16. Singh, P., Pradhan, G., Shahnawazuddin, S., Denoising of ECG signal by non-local estimation of approximation coefficients in DWT. *Biocybern. Biomed. Eng.*, 37, 599–610, 2017.

17. DeChazal, P., ODwyer, M., Reilly, R.B., Automatic Classification of Heartbeats Using ECG Morphology and Heartbeat Interval Features. *IEEE Trans. Biomed. Eng.*, 51, 1196–1206, 2004.

18. Gothwal, H., Kedawat, S., Kumar, R., Cardiac arrhythmias detection in an ECG beat signal using fast fourier transform and artificial neural network. *J. Biomed. Sci. Eng.*, 4, 289–296, 2011.

19. Manikandan, M.S. and Dandapat, S., Wavelet-based electrocardiogram signal compression methods and their performances: A prospective review. *Biomed. Signal Process. Control*, 14, 73–107, 2014.

20. Lee, J., McManus, D.D., Merchant, S., Chon, K.H., Automatic motion and noise artifact detection in Holter ECG data using empirical mode decomposition and statistical approaches. *IEEE Trans. Biomed. Eng.*, 59, 1499–1506, 2012.

21. De Chazal, P. and Reilly, R.B., A Patient-Adapting Heartbeat Classifier Using ECG Morphology and Heartbeat Interval Features. *IEEE Trans. Biomed. Eng.*, 53, 2535–2543, 2006.

22. Anuradha, B. and Reddy, V., ANN classification of cardiac arrhythmias. *ARPN J. Eng. Appl. Sci.*, 3, 3, 1–6, 2008.

23. Gupta, K.O. and Chaturvedi, P.N., ECG Signal Analysis and Classification using Data Mining and Artificial Neural Networks. *Int. J. Emerg. Technol. Adv. Eng.*, 2, 1, 56–60, 2012.

24. Goel, S., Tomar, P., Kaur, G., A Fuzzy Based Approach for denoising of ECG Signal using Wavelet Transform. *Int. J. Bio-Sci. Bio-Technol.*, 8, 2, 143–156, 2016.

25. Lei, W.K., Li, B.N., Dong, M.C., Vai, M., II, AFC-ECG: An Intelligent Fuzzy ECG Classifier, in: *Soft Computing in Industrial Applications*, vol. 39, pp. 189–199, 2006.

26. Omran, S.S., Taha, S.M.R., Awadh, N.A., ECG Rhythm Analysis by Using Neuro-Genetic Algorithms. *MASAUM J. Basic Appl. Sci.*, 1, 3, 522–530, 2009.

27. Priyadharshini, V. and Kumar, S.S., An Enhanced Approach on ECG Data Analysis using Improvised Genetic Algorithm. *Int. Res. J. Eng. Technol. (IRJET)*, 2, 5, 1248–1256, 2015.

28. Guler, I. and Ubeyli, E.D., Multiclass support vector machines for EEG signals classification. *IEEE Trans. Inf. Technol. Biomed.*, 11, 2, 117–126, 2007.

29. Dalal, S. and Birok, R., Analysis of ECG Signals using Hybrid Classifier. *Int. Adv. Res. J. Sci. Eng. Technol.*, 3, 7, 89–95, 2016.

30. Pan, S.-T., Hong, T.-P., Chen, H.-C., Ecg signal analysis by using hidden Markov model, in: *2012 International Conference on Fuzzy Theory and its Applications (iFUZZY)*, pp. 288–293, 2012.

Index

Also of Interest

Check out these published and forthcoming titles in the "Next-Generation Computing and Communication Engineering" series from Scrivener Publishing

Data Science Handbook
A Practical Approach
By Kolla Bhanu Prakash
Forthcoming 2022. ISBN 978-1-119-85732-7

Medical Imaging and Health Informatics
Edited by Tushar H Jaware, K Sarat Kumar, Svetlin Antonov, and Ravindra D Badgujar
Published 2022. ISBN 978-1-119-81913-4

Advanced Analytics and Deep Learning Models
Edited by Archana Mire, Shaveta Malik and Amit Kumar Tyagi
Published 2022. ISBN 978-1-119-79175-1

Integration of Renewable Energy Sources with Smart Grids
Edited by A. Mahaboob Subahani, M. Kathiresh and G. R. Kanagachidambaresan
Published 2021. ISBN 978-1-119-75042-0

Cognitive Engineering for Next Generation Computing
A Practical Analytical Approach
Edited by Kolla Bhanu Prakash, G.R. Kanagachidambaresan, V. Srikanth and E. Vamsidhar
Published 2021. ISBN 978-1-119-71108-7

Role of Edge Analytics on Sustainable Smart City Development
Edited by G.R. Kanagachidambaresan
Published 2020. ISBN 9781119681281

www.scrivenerpublishing.com

Printed and bound by CPI Group (UK) Ltd, Croydon, CR0 4YY

27/10/2024

14580136-0001